POLITICAL THOUGHT IN THE FRENCH WARS OF RELIGION

Through its close, critical reading of the political treatises and polemical literature produced in France in the sixteenth century, this book offers a valuable new contribution to the intellectual history of the Early Modern era. Sophie Nicholls analyses the political thought of the theologians and jurists in the Holy League as they pursued their crusade against heresy in the French kingdom, during the wars of religion (1562–1629). Contemporaries portrayed the Leaguers as rebellious anarchists, who harboured dangerously democratic ideas. In contrast, Nicholls demonstrates that the intellectuals in the movement were devoted royalists, who had more in common with their moderate counterparts, the 'politiques'. In paying close attention to the conceptual language of politics in this era, this book shows how members of the League presented visions of sovereignty that subtly replenished medieval ideas of kingship and priesthood, and endeavoured to replace them with a new synthesis of intellectual tradition and political power. In a period when 'the state' was still emerging as an idea, analysing League thought in the context of Jesuit and Second Scholastic sources positions the Leaguers in relation to innovative attempts in European Catholic circles to re-think the nature of belonging to a political community.

SOPHIE NICHOLLS is a College Lecturer in Early Modern History at the University of Oxford. She specialises in the French wars of religion and her interests range from the intersection between theological and juridical conceptions of politics, to developing conceptions of citizenship and rights in the Early Modern era.

T0385010

IDEAS IN CONTEXT

Edited by David Armitage, Richard Bourke and Jennifer Pitts

The books in this series will discuss the emergence of intellectual traditions and of related new disciplines. The procedures, aims and vocabularies that were generated will be set in the context of the alternatives available within the contemporary frameworks of ideas and institutions. Through detailed studies of the evolution of such traditions, and their modification by different audiences, it is hoped that a new picture will form of the development of ideas in their concrete contexts. By this means, artificial distinctions between the history of philosophy, of the various sciences, of society and politics, and of literature may be seen to dissolve.

The series is published with the support of the Exxon Foundation.

A full list of titles in the series can be found at:
www.cambridge.org/IdeasContext

POLITICAL THOUGHT IN THE FRENCH WARS OF RELIGION

SOPHIE NICHOLLS

University of Oxford

CAMBRIDGE
UNIVERSITY PRESS

Shaftesbury Road, Cambridge CB2 8EA, United Kingdom

One Liberty Plaza, 20th Floor, New York, NY 10006, USA

477 Williamstown Road, Port Melbourne, VIC 3207, Australia

314–321, 3rd Floor, Plot 3, Splendor Forum, Jasola District Centre, New Delhi – 110025, India

103 Penang Road, #05–06/07, Visioncrest Commercial, Singapore 238467

Cambridge University Press is part of Cambridge University Press & Assessment,
a department of the University of Cambridge.

We share the University's mission to contribute to society through the pursuit of
education, learning and research at the highest international levels of excellence.

www.cambridge.org
Information on this title: www.cambridge.org/9781108743938

DOI: 10.1017/9781108887786

First published 2021
First paperback edition 2024

A catalogue record for this publication is available from the British Library

ISBN   978-1-108-84078-1   Hardback
ISBN   978-1-108-74393-8   Paperback

This book is dedicated to the memory of my father

Contents

Acknowledgements

It is a pleasure to record my gratitude here to the various institutions and individuals whose help and support enabled me to write this book. The Arts and Humanities Research Council funded my graduate research, for which I am very grateful. Subsequently, it was a great privilege to be able to develop my ideas as Carlyle-Clayman Junior Research Fellow in the History of Political Thought at St Anne's College, Oxford, and to work in such a stimulating and convivial intellectual environment. My sincere thanks go to the Carlyle electors and Michelle Clayman for supporting this research.

My greatest intellectual debt is to Annabel Brett, who supervised my PhD thesis on the League. It is a pleasure to be able to thank her here for her learned insight and acuity, and to acknowledge the profound influence of her scholarship on my own work. I am also very much indebted to George Garnett, who first introduced me to William Barclay, George Buchanan and J.N. Figgis. I could not have asked for a better teacher.

Whilst writing this book, I have been very fortunate to be employed as a college lecturer at more than a few Oxford colleges, which not only kept the wolf from the door but also provided me with a coterie of sagacious colleagues, whose advice and support provided much-needed encouragement at various junctures. In this capacity, I would especially like to thank Peter Ghosh, for his companionship during my spells at St Anne's, as well as Gareth Davies, Howard Hotson, Grant Tapsell, Mike Broers, Jon Parkin and Adrian Gregory. I'm particularly grateful as well to Sarah Mortimer who commented on various drafts and to John Robertson for his advice as I prepared the manuscript for publication. My further thanks go to the anonymous readers at Cambridge University Press for their constructive suggestions. I would also like to thank the examiners of my PhD thesis, Mark Greengrass and Magnus Ryan, for their comments which helped to shape the direction of this book. All remaining flaws are my responsibility alone.

ix

I was very lucky to be in Oxford when Tom Hamilton and Emma Claussen were also working on the French wars of religion and to find such a genial community of Early Modern French enthusiasts. I am particularly indebted to Emma for her wisdom on the *politiques,* as well as for reading and commenting on early drafts of the manuscript. And even though our writing group never quite took off, I remain very grateful to Anna Becker and Tom Hopkins for their friendship, advice and general bonhomie.

I am enormously grateful as well to all my family and friends for their goodwill, common sense, and wit which sustained me through this project, especially to Keith and Cynthia, Steph, Mags and Matt, Ruth, Harry and Victoria, Camilla, Antonia, Squiff, the Chelts, the stumpers, as well as the Garnett and Leach families, and not forgetting Jonesy. My greatest thanks are due to my brother, Chris, and to my mother, Deirdre, for all her loving support, as well as to Alex, whose unwavering encouragement, insight and love helped to bring the book into existence under the best possible, laughter-filled conditions.

This book is dedicated to the memory of my father, David, who preferred mountains to libraries and whose sense of humour, courage and resilience remain a constant source of inspiration.

Abbreviations

Barclay, *De Regno*	William Barclay, *De Regno et Regali Potestate adversus Buchananum, Brutum, Boucherium et reliquos monarchomachos, libri sex* (Paris, 1600).
Belloy, *Apologie Catholique*	Pierre de Belloy, *Apologie catholique contre les libelles, declarations, advis et consultations . . . publiees par les liguez perturbateurs du repos du royaume de France* (n.p., 1585)
Belloy, *Apologia Catholica*	Pierre de Belloy, *Apologia catholica ad famosos et seditiosos libellos conjuratorum qui ab Alenconii regii fratris unici obitu, ad turbandam publicam regni francici tranquillitatem* (n.p., 1584)
BN	Bibliothèque Nationale
Bodin, *République*	Jean Bodin, *Les Six Livres de la République* (Paris, 1576)
Bodin, *De Republica*	Jean Bodin, *De Republica Libri Sex* (Lyon/Paris, 1586)
Boucher, *De Justa Abdicatione*	Jean Boucher, *De Justa Abdicatione Henrici Tertii e Francorum regno, libri quatuor* (Paris, 1589)
Cayet, *Chronologie Novenaire*	Palma Cayet, *Chronologie Novenaire contenant l'histoire de la guerre sous le règne du tres-chrestien roy de France et de Navarre Henry IIII*, 3 vols (Paris, 1608)

xi

Choppin, *De Domanio Franciae*

René Choppin, *De Domanio Franciae libri III* (Paris, 1574)

De Thou, *Histoire Universelle*

Jacques-Auguste de Thou, *Histoire Universelle*, 16 vols (London, 1734)

Dorléans, *Banquet*

Louis Dorléans, *Le banquet et aprèsdisnée du conte d'Arete, où il se traicte de la dissimulation du Roi de Navarre, & des moeurs de ses partisans* (Paris, 1594)

Goulart, *Mémoires de la Ligue*

Simon Goulart, *Mémoires de la Ligue. Contenant les évenements les plus remarquables depuis 1576, jusqu'à la paix accordée entre le Roi de France et le Roi d'Espagne en 1598*, 6 vols (Amsterdam, 1758)

Goulart, *l'Estat de France*

Simon Goulart, *Memoires de l'estat de France, sous Charles IX. Seconde edition, reveuë, corrigee & augmentee*, 3 vols (Geneva, 1578)

Hotman, *Francogallia*

François Hotman, *Francogallia Editio tertia locupletior* (Cologne, 1576) and (*Francogallia* 1586) François Hotman, *Francogallia* (Frankfurt, 1586) and (*Francogallia* ed. Salmon and Giesey) François Hotman, *Francogallia*, ed. and trans. R. E. Giesey, J. H. M Salmon (Cambridge: Cambridge University Press, 1972)

Rossaeus, *De Justa Reipublicae Christianae Authoritate*

'Guilielmus Rossaeus', *De Justa Reipublicae Christianae in Reges Impios et Haereticos Authoritate: justissimaque catholicorum ad Henricum Navarraeum & quemcunque haereticum a regno Galliae repellendum confoederatione liber* (Paris, 1590)

L'Estoile, M-J

Pierre de L'Estoile, *Mémoires-Journaux de Pierre de l'Estoile. Édition pour la première fois complète et entièrement conforme aux manuscrits*

	originaux, ed. M. M. G. Brunet, A. Champollion, E. Halphen, P. Lacroix, C. Read, T. de Larroque, E. Tricotel, 12 vols (Paris, 1875–83)
Montaigne, *Essais*	Michel de Montaigne, *Les Essais*, ed. J. Balsamo et al. (Paris: Gallimard, 2007)
Vindiciae	*Vindiciae, contra tyrannos* (Edinburgh [Basle], 1579) and (ed. Garnett) *Vindiciae, contra tyrannos*, ed. and trans. G. Garnett (Cambridge: Cambridge University Press, 1994)

Introduction

The Scottish jurist William Barclay invented the term 'monarchomach' in his treatise on kingship, *De Regno et Regali Potestate* (1600). He used it to describe a genre of seditious texts written in France and Scotland from the 1570s through to the 1590s, which form the spine of the material considered in this book. Broadly speaking, these works defended the notion that a contract existed between the people, their ruler and God. They argued that if the terms of that contract were broken, power would revert to the people who could, as a whole, legitimately depose, or even authorise the assassination of a monarch. 'Monarchomach' was interpreted to mean 'king-killer', and it continues to be used to describe the genre to this day.

As an advocate of royal power, particularly that of Henri IV, to whom *De Regno* was dedicated, Barclay considered the treatises of these 'monarchomachs' to be dangerously seditious and heretical. In his view, they offered a set of arguments that threatened the order of society and the wellbeing of commonwealths that needed to be comprehensively disproved. In many ways, particularly in arguing that this type of resistance theory rested overwhelmingly on unskilled readings of Roman law, he succeeded in his goal. Barclay's *De Regno* is established in the literature as one of the most authoritative Early Modern responses to arguments for tyrannicide, and his condemnation of these writers in question remains the conventional reference point in modern analyses of resistance theory.[1] Notwithstanding this familiarity with Barclay in the literature, there is good reason to revisit his characterisation of these apparently incendiary texts. Barclay's authoritative verdict is both suggestive and, at crucial junctures, limited.

---

[1] See the ubiquitous use of the term 'monarchomach' in studies of the subject (these are just a few examples): Giesey, 'The Monarchomach Triumvirs: Hotman, Beza and Mornay'; Mellet, *Les Traités Monarchomaques*; Mellet (ed.), *Les Monarchomaques au xvie siècle*; Bouvignies, 'Monarchomaquie: tyrannicide ou droit de résistance?' in *Tolérance et réforme*; Zwierlein, *The Political Thought of the League*, uses the problems with Barclay's treatment to frame his recent analysis.

Barclay included both Protestant and Catholic treatises in his description and made no distinctions between their works. A Catholic himself, he took this approach because he considered the Catholic writers to have borrowed directly from the Protestants. Partly, this was an argument of convenience: when Barclay had first started to write *De Regno* in the 1570s, he had only the Protestant treatises in mind. It was that framework, therefore, which continued to define his perspective on the later, Catholic works. Originally, Barclay had identified François Hotman's *Francogallia* (1573), the *Vindiciae, Contra Tyrannos* (1579) and George Buchanan's *De Jure Regni apud Scotos* (1579) as three notorious works which owed their origins to 'Luther's kitchen'. These writers were a few amongst many who had 'vomited' their treatises upon the princes of Europe, in Barclay's view.[2] However, two other Catholic Scots published their own responses to these ideas before Barclay. They were William Ninzet and Adam Blackwood, whose replies to Buchanan Barclay purported to deem so effective as to render his own intervention obsolete.[3] It was only in the 1590s that he saw fit to revisit his manuscript.

The years after the deposition of Mary Stuart in Scotland (1567) and the St Bartholomew's Day Massacre (1572) in France – two decisive moments for Protestants worrying about the tyrannical propensities of Catholic rule – had seen the rise of the French Holy League which threatened their very existence. The defining and unifying feature of League political thought was that it explicitly excluded Protestants, seen as heretics, from the political community which was governed ultimately by Christ, and that it correspondingly conferred a duty on the king of France to act to eradicate heresy, framed in terms of holy war. Confessional difference was, therefore, embedded in the very rationale of the League.

First established in 1576 in opposition to Henri III's attempts to pacify the kingdom by extending measures of religious toleration to the French Huguenots, the League re-emerged in 1584–5 to develop into a formidable militant force positioned against the succession of the Protestant Henri de Navarre to the French throne. After the deposition and assassination of Henri III, two significant League texts were produced justifying these actions: *De Justa Abdicatione Henrici Tertii* (1589), widely attributed to Jean Boucher, and the *De Justa Reipublicae Christianae Authoritate* (1590),

---

[2] Barclay, *De Regno*, fol. 1r.
[3] These were Blackwood, *Adversus Georgi Buchanani Dialogum*; Winzet, *Velitatio in Georgium Buchananum circa dialogum*.

written under the pseudonym of 'Guilielmus Rossaeus'.[4] Barclay appended his response to these treatises to his *De Regno*.

In his dedication to Henri IV, Barclay argued that all of the authors he discussed had sought to introduce anarchy to France and to tear the kingdom up by its roots. The dedication was probably part of an effort to assure the king of his own loyalty in the context of the ongoing controversy between the law faculty and the Jesuit leadership at Pont-à-Mousson, in which he and his colleague, Pierre Grégoire, were involved.[5] However, further on in the first book, he established a clearer reason for incorporating the two Catholic treatises into *De Regno*. Boucher's work in particular he saw as having a dangerous influence amongst Catholics:

> Has the most mighty and most perfect God reserved me to such a corrupt age that I should behold a Catholic man and preacher nurture the inventions of heretics, imitate their false word, bring on deadly seditions to realms and states, and re-forge, embellish and amplify every error about monarchy and the power of kings?[6]

Barclay took the view that Boucher had plagiarised the arguments of the Huguenot writers of the 1570s, and that his and Rossaeus' treatises were just as subversive and heretical as those of Hotman, Buchanan and the author of the *Vindiciae*.[7] In creating the terminology of 'monarchomach', and condemning political resistance on the principle that to resist the rule of a monarch was to resist the will of God, Barclay successfully, but questionably, bound the fate of these Huguenot and Catholic treatises together.[8]

---

[4] As Zwierlein notes, the assumption that Boucher wrote *De Justa Abdicatione Henrici Tertii* has remained influential, despite an absence of evidence. Nevertheless, as his analysis in *League Political Thought* demonstrates, there is no strong case to suggest that Boucher did not have a major hand in its creation, and Boucher will, therefore, be treated as the author in this current study. The authorship of *De Justa Reipublicae Christianae Authoritate* is considered in Chapter Six.

[5] Salmon, 'Catholic Resistance Theory' in *The Cambridge History of Political Thought*, 235. On Barclay's biography see Dubois, *Guillaume Barclay*; Collot, *Pierre Grégoire et Guillaume Barclay*; Baird Smith, 'William Barclay'.

[6] Barclay, *De Regno*, fol. 2r: '*Mene Deus Opt. Max. in tam corruptum seculum reservavit, ut virum Catholicum et concionatorem excolere inventa haereticorum, imitari ψευδολογιας, inducere seditiones regnis et civitatibus exitiales, atque omnem de Monarchia et Regum imperio errorem recudere, ornare, et amplificare videam*'. My translations of Barclay's De Regno are indebted to George A. Moore's 1954 translation.

[7] On the question of authorship, I follow *Vindiciae*, ed. Garnett. Hugues Daussy has more recently re-examined and restated the case for identifying the text exclusively with Philippe Duplessis Mornay: *Les huguenots et le roi*.

[8] A problem recently revisited in Zwierlein, *The Political Thought of the League* and raised by Baumgartner, *Radical Reactionaries*, 19. For treatments of League political thought as a replica of Calvinist resistance theory, see Murray, *The Political Consequences of the Reformation*, 213–14; Mousnier, *L'assassinat d'Henri IV*; Weill, *Les théories sur le pouvoir royal*; Pierre Mesnard, *l'Essor de la philosophie politique*; Mellet, *Les Traités Monarchomaques*; Lee, *Popular Sovereignty*; Turchetti,

Barclay was in some ways correct in his judgement that the Leaguers had adopted certain ideas from the Calvinist texts, showing that Boucher in particular was indebted to the *Vindiciae*, lifting sections of the text into the published version to strengthen his case against Henri III. *Francogallia* met a similar fate in the hands of League polemicists, and Hotman was startled to find it exploited in this way.[9] Such manipulation was made easier by the fact that French political thinkers were drawing from a common well of intellectual resources. In focussing, for example, on the relationship between the king and the French domain, Leaguers and non-Leaguers were often dealing with sets of political problems which were not directly connected to the problem of confessional difference and had their roots deep in the history of French political thinking and the interplay between Roman and customary law.

However, there are limitations to Barclay's approach. Not every League writer was indebted to the Huguenot texts, and the intellectual relationship is often complex. Many Leaguers were explicitly hostile to what they saw as the dangerously republican aspects of Huguenot arguments. It is even the case that Huguenot writers made thorough use of the ideas of those who would become Leaguers themselves: Hotman, along with the author of the *Vindiciae*, for example, made significant use of René Choppin's *De Domanio Franciae* (1574). Choppin would go on to join the League, probably after the assassination of the Guise brothers by Henri III in 1588, and become a member of its *chambre ardente*, a court designated to the trying of heretics, in 1591.[10] In an ironical reversal of expectations, then, in this case, the Huguenots could be said to be dependent on 'League' political thought.

A further problem with Barclay's now-notorious association of Leaguer ideas with those of the Huguenots is that it obfuscates the fact that Boucher's apparent plagiarism of the *Vindiciae* was a textual convention of the day. To cut up and splice parts of a work written in one context, and incorporate them into another, new work was part of the practice of writing, and particularly of writing polemical works in the Early Modern era.[11] The original text could thus be transposed entirely out of its original context and be used against and beyond the author's

Tyrannie et tyrannicide. Salmon, 'Catholic Resistance Theory' takes a more nuanced view, and others have placed greater emphasis on the difference between Catholic and Protestant political thought in this context: Bouvignies, 'Monarchomaquie: tyrannicide ou droit de résistance?'; Cottret, 'La justification catholique du tyrannicide'; Crouzet, *Les Guerriers de Dieu*; Van Kley, *Les Origines religieuses de la Révolution française*; Mellet, ed., *Et de sa bouche sortait un glaive*.
[9] Cayet, *Chronologie Novenaire*, 1. fol. 5v; Anquetil, *L'Esprit de la Ligue*, 2, 165–6; Kelley, *Francois Hotman*, 265–9; Hotman, *Francogallia*, ed. Giesey, Salmon, 91 n. 3.
[10] Explored in Nicholls, 'Ideas of Royal Power'.   [11] Baranova, *À Coups de Libelles*.

original intentions. *De La Servitude Volontaire*, for example, written by the Catholic jurist Étienne de La Boétie, was incorporated into the Huguenot 'alarm bell' treatise produced after St Bartholomew's Day, the *Reveille-Matin* (1573), and subsequently into Simon Goulart's *Mémoires* (1578) where it became a component of Protestant anti-tyrannical writing. The text, if we accept Michel de Montaigne's account, was thereby taken out of the hands of 'men of understanding' and transformed from a piece of delicate rhetorical performance to a highly politicised attack on tyrannical rule.[12] The textual environment in which these treatises circulated, and were repurposed, meant that such intellectual appropriation and cross-fertilisation of ideas was a feature of French political thought in this era, and a significant aspect of any intellectual history of the League.[13]

Where Barclay has made an important contribution to our understanding of League political thought, is in his verdict that the Huguenots and the Leaguers were manipulating Roman-legal principles. Modern scholars agree on this significance, and particularly the importance of interpretations of *lex regia* wherein the power transferred from people to ruler was perceived as revocable, on the basis of a contractual agreement between ruler and ruled.[14] Common legal education, and common source materials in Roman and canon law, Christian theology and classical political thought provide a strong basis for comparison between Huguenot and Catholic political theory. On the theoretical level, the intellectual foundations of League political thought are, therefore, identifiable in the scholastic theology of the theologians at the Sorbonne, and the legal-historical resources of the lawyers in the Paris *parlement*, local *parlements* and of the magistrates in the Estates General.[15] Use of these sources led to differing conceptions of the relationship between ecclesiastical and civil powers in the French commonwealth which caused civil and religious obligations to clash. These differences were a defining feature of the

---

[12] Montaigne, *Les Essais*, I.XVII, 190. As John O'Brien has recently demonstrated, *De La Servitude Volontaire* continued to be carved up and scattered around significant polemical works published in the later wars of religion, in the 1580s and '90s: O'Brien, 'Sovereign Power, Freedom and La Boétie's *Servitude volontaire* in the 1580s', *Early Modern French Studies* (forthcoming, 2021).

[13] In taking this approach, I have been influenced by the work of Warren Boutcher in his *The School of Montaigne* and 'Unoriginal Authors: How to Do Things with Texts' in *Rethinking the Foundations*, 73–92. Cf. Quentin Skinner's response, 'Surveying the Foundations', 236–61.

[14] On the significance of *lex regia*, see Skinner, *Foundations*, 2, 130–4, 331–2, 341–3; Ryan, 'Political Thought' in *The Cambridge Companion to Roman Law*, 423–51.

[15] Recent scholarship has demonstrated the significance of the Sorbonne debates in the League context, particularly the work of Amalou: 'Une Sorbonne regicide?' in *Les universités en Europe*, 77–116; Zwierlein, *The Political Thought of the League*.

frictions within the League and beyond it, reflective of the wider conflicts that characterised the intellectual debates of the Wars of Religion.[16]

Any such comparison between Huguenots and Leaguer political theorists is misleading, however, if it does not acknowledge that polemicists in the League were able to exploit the Huguenot texts so easily precisely because medieval scholasticism was foundational in Protestant resistance theory.[17] Recent studies of League political thought overlook the fact that Quentin Skinner, in *The Foundations of Modern Political Thought* (1978), argued that the Huguenot treatises of the 1570s had not developed a new approach to politics but instead embellished views that had already been expressed by medieval jurists and theologians, which were themselves dependent on scholastic analyses of sovereignty.[18] This implicitly challenges the view that the Leaguers were simply co-opting Huguenot ideas, and it is a point I wish to draw out and analyse further in this current study.[19]

Notwithstanding the significance of Robert Descimon's seminal work to uncover the nature of the 'moderate' voices in the League, which demonstrated the social and intellectual range of the membership of the movement in the 1980s, scholarship on the political thought of the League remains committed to describing it in terms of 'radicalism'.[20] The approach of Frederic J. Baumgartner's *Radical Reactionaries* (1976), was to argue that the Leaguers were indebted, on the one hand, to hackneyed medieval arguments about royal power, but were 'radical' in the extent to which they challenged that power, on the other.[21] Naturally, there are elements of intellectual change and continuity to be evaluated in the case of the League, and, in this sense, Baumgartner's framework appears sustainable: many of the theorists in the League remained thoroughly indebted to medieval ideas regarding the relationship between *regnum* (kingdom) and *sacerdotium* (priesthood); some went beyond these ideas to endeavour to produce a new synthesis of intellectual tradition and political power. However, a problem remains

---

[16] As analysed, for example, in Greengrass, *Governing Passions*.
[17] Skinner, *Foundations,* 2, 322–4; *Vindiciae,* ed. Garnett, xix–lxxvi.
[18] Skinner, *Foundations*, 2, 322–3. As Mark Goldie observed, 'Skinner recovered the Catholic political tradition in order to dispose of Protestant theories of liberal modernity', in his 'The Context of *The Foundations*', *Rethinking the Foundations*, 16. Zwierlein, *Political Thought of the League*, 128–30 does not acknowledge this fact when developing his own argument on the relationship between Calvinist and Leaguer resistance theory, or in reference to the significance of establishing the scholastic foundations of League political thought.
[19] The League receives very brief attention in Skinner, *Foundations*, 2, 345.
[20] Descimon, *Qui etaient les Seize ?*; Descimon, 'La Ligue à Paris (1585–1594): une révision'.
[21] Baumgartner, *Radical Reactionaries*.

with the imprecise nature of the category of 'radicalism', and the somewhat unreflective treatment of scholasticism it engenders.

More recent studies establish 'radical' scholasticism, or Thomism, as the defining feature of the political thought of the League, without clarification of what it means to be a 'radical' scholastic beyond a very broad framework of thinking in terms of holy war and legitimate tyrannicide.[22] Here some reflection needs to be introduced on the possible distinctions between the languages of medieval scholastic theories of sovereign power, and their uptake and synthesis by the theologians in the Salamanca school in the sixteenth century.[23] Conceptually speaking, the term 'radical' lacks precision in encapsulating such complex intellectual developments or the nature of their development and reception in France. Furthermore, if, by 'radical', scholars mean doctrines of legitimate tyrannicide, then the intellectual heritage of these arguments from antiquity through to the Early Modern period suggests that the Leaguers were not especially radical in their radicalism, nor that their uptake of such ideas was exclusively scholastic or Thomist in nature.[24] If 'radical' is taken to mean proto-democratic or revolutionary, an approach to League political thought which is now outmoded in its anachronism, then the terminology is again redundant.[25] Finally, if 'radical' is taken to mean 'constitutionalist', than we find ourselves back in a context of established, perhaps exhausted, scholarly debate in which the transferral of conciliar ideas to the political sphere is taken to be the bedrock of modern constitutionalism when, in fact, such an apparently straightforward intellectual manoeuvre is riddled with complexity.[26] To move forward, abandoning radicalism as a category of analysis should enable a more precise, less teleological reckoning of the intellectual contribution of the League to the political thought of this era.

As Barclay demonstrated, the Leaguers were at their least original in the case they made for tyrannicide and elective monarchy. With this in mind, and in contrast to the emphasis on the theologian Jean Boucher and his

[22] Renoux-Zagamé, *De Droit de Dieu*, 270–93; Zwierlein, *Political Thought of the League*.
[23] As considered by Brett, *Liberty, Right and Nature*.
[24] Turchetti, *Tyrannie et Tyrannicide de l'Antiquité à nos jours*.
[25] On democracy as a 'radical' feature of League ideas, see Mousnier, *Les hiérarchies sociales*; Barnavi, *Le parti de Dieu*; Constant, *La Ligue*; Armstrong, *The French Wars of Religion*; Allen, *A History of Political Thought*. On revolution, see Barnavi, 'La Ligue Parisienne (1585–1594): Ancetre des parties totalitaires modernes?'
[26] Zwierlein, *Political Thought of the League*, 109, hints at, but does not engage with this bigger question in the history of political thought. On this, see Skinner, *Foundations*; Nederman, 'Conciliarism and Constitutionalism'; Oakley, 'Nederman, Gerson, Conciliar Theory and Constitutionalism'; Nederman, 'Constitutionalism – Medieval and Modern'; Brett, 'Scholastic Political Thought', 130–48.

infamous text on tyrannicide that continues to dominate scholarly
accounts of League political thought, the central aim of this book is to
consider this thought collectively in its breadth and depth.[27] In this
context, the scholasticism of the sixteenth century is particularly significant. Rather than seeing it through the lens of 'radical Thomism', here the
writings of theologians including Jacques Almain, Cardinal Cajetan, Juan
de Maldonado, Domingo de Soto, Alfonso de Castro and Luis de Molina
are treated in terms of their analysis of the dynamic features of legitimate
political power and the moral theology they produced.[28] As Brett has
argued, the distinctive features of scholastic thought in the sixteenth
century are conditioned by its analysis of power within the church, and
correspondingly by an understanding that the church was a political
community, rather than in terms of two competing visions of political
power.[29] The use of such sources by the Leaguers in their campaign against
heresy in France is indicative of the extent to which they were not working
on the 'radical' fringes of political thinking, but within these existing
scholarly frameworks devoted to analysing the status of Christian commonwealths in the context of ongoing church reform and the roles of
dominium, liberty and justice within, and beyond, the limits of those
commonwealths.[30]

Until recently, the concept of 'the state', rather than the commonwealth
(as a translation of *respublica/république*), has remained the dominant
framework for thinking about political thought in the Early Modern
period, which has important implications for the League. In his
Foundations, Skinner demonstrated that medieval scholasticism was central to Protestant resistance theory and – correspondingly – to the development of a secular conception of the modern nation state; instead, this
book examines these sources in the hands of League theologians as they
analysed the purpose and nature of the Christian commonwealth, and the
increasing significance of the *patrie/patria*. Debates amongst Catholics
regarding the rights of the papacy, and foreign Catholic powers, to intervene in France played out within a juristic arena in which the definition of
the '*leges patriae*', the laws of the nation, was at stake. Correspondingly, the
political thought of the Leaguers focussed intensively on the relationship

---

[27] Boucher's *De Justa Abdicatione* recently had its status as the archetype of League political thought
confirmed by Zwierlein. The focus on Boucher is a problem that was noted by Baumgartner, *Radical
Reactionaries*, 18.
[28] Brett, 'Scholastic Political Thought', 139; Brett, *Liberty, Right and Nature*, 123.
[29] Brett, 'Scholastic Political Thought', 140.
[30] Brett, *Changes of State*; Renoux-Zagamé, *De Droit de Dieu*, 270–93.

between the *respublica* and the *ecclesia*, and between *politeia* (*la police*) and *religio* (*la religion*), within the existing frameworks of the Gallican liberties and the ancient constitution.

In approaching League political thought in this way, this book does not seek to replace the idea of a Protestant nation state, well established in scholarship, with a Catholic one; instead it argues that French Catholic theologians and lawyers, writing in the wars of religion, reinforced an existing notion that the universal Catholic community was a *patrie* or *patria* in its own right.[31] In doing so, it draws on recent scholarship on the *patria* in Early Modern Protestant writings, and on analyses of the role of scholastic thought in shaping ideas about the political community and 'the state'.[32] The emphasis on *patrie/patria* here furthers the argument that the abstract concept of 'the state' had yet to be fully formulated, and that instead we find thinkers drawing their resources from medieval, Augustinian ideas in which the *patria* referred to the heavenly city. They were also thinking about ways in which the native, earthly *patria* could be the location of a particular civic identity in classical and medieval terms, adapted (or not) to the new environment of divided Christianity. The framework of the *respublica* and the *patria* remain the focal points for analyses of the common good, conceived both in a civic and a spiritual sense. In their analysis of these concepts, theologians in the League were contributing to a European and Jesuit debate about the status of Christian commonwealths and the ongoing question of church reform in an age of confessional division.[33] The notion that Leaguer political thought had only a 'negative' influence beyond the end of the movement in the 1590s is, therefore, strongly contested in this book.[34]

---

[31] On the role of these thinkers in forming a conception of the state, see Skinner, *Foundations*, II, 349–53.

[32] Brett, *Changes of State*; Robert von Friedeburg, 'In Defense of Patria'.

[33] This is emerging as a field in the scholarship. Relations between the League and Spain are currently the most thoroughly examined in the works of Serge Brunet, especially his *'De l'Espagnol dedans le ventre!'* See also le Goff, *La Ligue en Bretagne*. Recent treatments of relations between the League, Rome and Jesuit political thought include Penzi, 'La Ligue et la Papauté' in Brunet (ed.), *La Sainte Union*; Zwierlein, *Political Thought of the League*; Renoux-Zagamé, *De Droit de Dieu*. José Javier Ruiz Ibàñez has recently thought about these issues from a global perspective: 'la Monarchie Espagnole et les Ligues' in Brunet (ed.), *La Sainte Union*.

[34] Baumgartner, *Radical Reactionaries*, 241; Holt, *The French Wars of Religion*, 221. Baumgartner considers the influence of the political thought of the League, such as it was, to have manifested itself only in a 'negative fashion', in its contribution to seventeenth-century absolutism. Scholarship has long since contended with the problem of 'absolutism' versus 'constitutionalism', and more recent analyses, for example, the collection of essays in Forrestal, Nelson, eds., *Politics and Religion in Early Bourbon France*, suggest a more fruitful path of analysis of League ideas in the context of Catholic activism and ongoing church reform. On the limits of 'absolutism' as a framework for

Part of the reason for the absence of a clearly established narrative of continuity for League political thought is due to the fact that the history of French political thought, as it stands in existing scholarship, is shown to develop in the religious wars through, on the one hand, the resistance theory of the Huguenot writers and, on the other, the scepticism of the *politiques*, adopted by those same Huguenots in the 1580s and '90s.[35] Problematically, in this kind of formulation, the *politiques* are still seen as a political party. In such discussions, theories of popular sovereignty produced by the Huguenots are seen to have been outgrown and over-taken by the rational scepticism of the *politiques* which, in the end, props up absolutist theories of Catholic monarchy as the best way to preserve the order of the commonwealth. In this way, the French wars of religion play a determining role in early seventeenth-century French political thinking. The important theoretical groundwork for that role is conventionally located in the stoic ideas of thinkers like Pierre Charron, Jean Bodin, Michel de Montaigne and Guillaume Du Vair, under the influence of Justus Lipsius, as well as in the anti-Machiavellism of theorists such as Innocent Gentillet. Within such a framework, so-called *politique* Catholics like Du Vair and Bodin, have been associated with 'rational' thinking, which precludes an analysis of their connections to the League. League political thought has been utterly eclipsed by such an understanding, consigned to the category of radical, populist reaction as an explosive, regressive, 'anti-Renaissance' moment in the history of French ideas, a 'mere bonfire of rubbish'.[36] Instead, this current study offers a revised analysis of the place of the League in the history of ideas.

analysing Early Modern political thought, see Brett, 'Scholastic Political Thought'. The use of the term 'absolute' in reference to the French monarchy was thoroughly and powerfully condemned for its oversimplification of the complex workings of the French state by Collins, *The State in Early Modern France*, considered along with other significant works by Mack Holt, Yves-Marie Bercé and Geoffrey Treasure in Knecht, 'Absolutism in Early Modern France'. Cosandey and Descimon discuss the concept and its limitations in *l'Absolutisme en France*. The question has recently been taken up again in Jouanna, *Le Pouvoir Absolu*, 24–34.

[35] Skinner, *Foundations*, 2, 249–54; Church, *Constitutional Thought*, 126–7; Keohane, *Philosophy and State*, 48–9; Allen, *Political Thought in the Sixteenth Century*, 370–7; Figgis, 'The Politiques and Religious Toleration', *From Gerson to Grotius*; Baumgartner, *Radical Reactionaries*, 18, 177. I discuss the more recent scholarship on the *politique* in Chapter Two.

[36] Wilkinson, *History of the League*, 170. The notion of 'anti-Renaissance' is originally from Hayden, *The Counter-Renaissance*, and considered in Denis Crouzet's analysis of the League in *Les guerriers de Dieu*, 374–9. See also Denis Crouzet, 'Henri IV, King of Reason?' in Cameron (ed.), *From Valois to Bourbon*, which uses this framework to explore what he identifies as the 'new political ideology' inherent in the 'rationalisation of the concept of monarchy' under Henri IV in opposition to the irrationality of the League. This 'rationalisation' thesis is also taken up in leading studies on French institutions in the period of the League: Ramsay discusses the opposition between Palma Cayet's 'Politique Rationality' and Leaguer zeal in her *Liturgy, Politics and Salvation*, 57–84. Cf. Hanley, *The*

In 1929, Maurice Wilkinson saw in the League 'a great clash of theories of government and even of contending ideals', and I aim to revive the spirit of that approach in this book.[37] Whilst Barclay and others associated the Leaguers with anarchy, identifying, in particular, the assassination of Henri III, the disruption of the commonwealth in the final decades of the religious wars, arguments for Spanish intervention and the overwhelming spiritual and temporal authority of the papacy as their *raison d'être*, it has equally been long recognised that there was a strong core of royalism at the heart of League political thought. Leaguer views on the sovereign power of the people did not detract from a fundamental loyalty to the institution of the French monarchy. As John Dryden put it, in his translation of Louis Maimbourg's *Histoire de la Ligue* (1683), 'those leaguing Catholics . . . were always for the king, and yet more, the major part of them would have him of royal stem'.[38] Dryden used the fact of League royalism to distinguish it from the republican ideas of those 'men of commonwealth principles' responsible for the exclusion crisis of his own day.[39] His views are suggestive of the fact that overemphasising the significance of popular sovereignty in League political thought, and the role of the Paris Sixteen, has the effect of rendering the League a democratic if not revolutionary movement, but that this is not in fact an idea widely reflected in the texts, most of which describe the aristocratic, even oligarchic politics of an intellectual elite that in some cases was explicitly anti-republican.[40]

The Leaguers' political thought shifted over time and in accordance with circumstance: it was contingent and diverse, often splintered. Correspondingly, on the basis of these divisions of opinion, contemporaries made a distinction between a *ligueur* and an *'archi-ligueur'*, or *'ligueur zélé'*, referring to those who ended up supporting the duc de Mayenne, and the uncompromising theologians, clergy and lawyers who formed the core of the Paris Sixteen.[41] This important distinction became somewhat lost in the historiography of the seventeenth century, which characterised the

---

Lit de Justice; Roelker, *One King, One Faith;* Wells, *Law and Citizenship;* Daubresse, *Le parlement de Paris.*

[37] Wilkinson, *History of the League,* 170.   [38] Maimbourg, *History of the League,* preface, n.p.

[39] Dryden's portrayal of the League naturally served his own purposes: he continuously and provocatively made reference to the League and the Leaguers as in some way superior to the Whigs he opposed, commenting on their 'valour and subtlety', and suggesting that even the assassination of Henri III was less 'impudent' than the trial of Charles I. Maimbourg, *History of the League,* postscript, 30, 33.

[40] Salmon, 'The Paris Sixteen', 235–66.

[41] Pierre de l'Estoile, MJ, V, 180 – for example. He uses the phrase regularly.

movement wholly as '*la Ligue des Faux-zéléz* [*sic*]'.[42] Recovering the intellectual contribution of those 'Mayenniste' Leaguers who are often overlooked in studies which emphasise the 'radical', proto-republican,
democratic nature of League political thought is, therefore, long overdue,
particularly in the context of a consideration of the relationship between
Leaguer and *politique*. Recent historical and literary scholarship on the
French wars of religion has recognised the extent to which the Leaguers
were an integral, rather than peripheral, part of the complex makeup of the
Counter Reformation in France; the purpose of this study is to incorporate
this scholarship into the history of political thought in this era and thereby
bring together historiographies that are otherwise disparate.[43]

   In order to create space for a deeper analysis of the varieties of political
thinking in this period to include the League, it is constructive to turn
back to the work of the influential French intellectual historian Pierre
Mesnard. Mesnard observed, in his comprehensive 1936 examination of
European political thought in the sixteenth century, that the history of
ideas in this period progressed through a series of dialectical oppositions.
In concluding his magisterial work, he argued that the best way to
comprehend the culmination of ideas at the end of the century was
through the decisive restauration of spiritual values in an idealist sense,
on the basis of an integral realism.[44] This important claim has been
somewhat lost in the midst of robust critiques of Mesnard's overall
approach, but it provides an important path to understanding the complexity of ideas in the late sixteenth century.[45] If Mesnard's 'idealist' sense
is taken to refer to the relationship of the rational soul to grace, and a life
of virtue, and if his 'realist' sense is taken to mean, as it would to medieval
theologians and lawyers, the good of the political community anchored
in peace and security, then a picture emerges of League political thought
as an under-examined example of this ongoing intellectual process of
reconciling the ideals of Christian living with political realism, framed
within a providential order.

   The fusion of idealism and realism further helps to explain the position
of certain liminal figures in relationship to the League. In many ways, this
approach necessarily stretches the current understanding of what it meant
to be a 'Leaguer' in political thought terms, particularly when it comes to

---

[42] Maimbourg, *The History of the League*, fol. 4r.
[43] For two important recent collection of essays in this area, see Daubresse, Haan (eds.), *La Ligue et ses frontières*; Brunet (ed.), *La Sainte Union des Catholiques de France*. See also Racaut, 'The Sacrifice of the Mass'.
[44] Mesnard, *l'Essor de la philosophie*, 674–7.   [45] Skinner, *Foundations*, I, ix–xi.

considering examples such as that of René Choppin, who produced his most significant legal analyses of the church and the kingdom before he joined the movement, and whose influence has been almost entirely neglected.[46] The affiliation of royalists like Choppin, and his friend Jean Bodin, to the League should not necessarily be seen as a rupture with their broader thinking on political authority. Instead their membership of the League is the result of reflection on the complex question of the 'common good' that does not contradict the views on political authority they had already laid out in other contexts. Analysing the connections between moderate Leaguers and those who were labelled *politiques,* demonstrates the extent to which there was a fruitful intellectual exchange to be had even amidst these apparent divisions in the Catholic community, right at the heart of the chaos of the religious wars.

The first chapter of this book puts League political thought into its immediate historical and publishing context, by way of an extended introduction to the material considered in the rest of this book. My approach to this material is to analyse the languages of political thought used by the Leaguers, by reading their published texts in their historical context.[47] The interest of the published material produced by the Leaguers lies in the fact that it formed part of a public debate on the reform and future of the French commonwealth, and that these texts were often written with an international, as well as domestic, readership in mind. Through a consideration of the ways in which medieval and classical sources were being read by theologians and lawyers in the movement, a distinctive language of political thought in the wars of religion can be interpreted through the vocabulary used by contemporaries in their published works.[48] For the purposes of this study, a working distinction is established between demotic, polemical pamphleteering of the League and the scholarly, juridical and theological treatises produced in professional and academic circles, as well as the genres in between, in order to analyse the political thought of the movement in all its registers. I have endeavoured not to exclude one category of text in preference for another, but to move between these registers. I have also

---

[46] See Nicholls, 'Ideas on Royal Power'.

[47] The implications and challenges of this methodology have been very thoroughly considered in the wider scholarship on this subject. My approach owes a particular debt to Brett, 'What Is Intellectual History Now'.

[48] Pocock, *Politics, Language and Time.* I take focussing on the languages of political thought to be a distinctive historical approach to that of an analysis of 'propaganda' and identity in the League pamphlet literature, thoroughly covered in recent scholarship, notably by Luc Racaut, with a view to examining the social phenomenon of religious violence in this era. Racaut, *Hatred in Print.*

preserved the original orthography when quoting directly from the texts, unless a modern edition is cited.

Chapter Two examines the status of political science, or prudence, in the League years, seen both through the lens of the polemical figure of the *politique*, a monstrous figment of Leaguer imagination, and from the perspective of *la science politique*, referring to the particular skills and form of reasoning required to find a solution to the crisis of the religious wars. It argues, first and foremost, that there is good reason to revisit the problem of the *politique* in the context of the history of political thought. I make this case to establish two central points, the first of which is the fact that the status of political science was at stake in these debates, in its power to approach and achieve a common good (*bien public*). The second, connected aim, is to demonstrate that, whilst it is more straightforward to see the controversies of these years in terms of 'Leaguer versus *politique*', there are significant connections here that have been overlooked. Intellectually speaking, we can, therefore, discuss the notion of the '*politique* Leaguer', and identify the common ground of understanding that united lawyers in the Paris *parlement* and the provinces.

Chapter Three considers dominant questions in the French political thought of this era regarding the status of the 'ancient' constitution, the power of election and deposition, and the divisive nature of debates about succession laws. It demonstrates the complex nature and range of responses to Hotman's *Francogallia* in these contexts, as well as exploring the role of both the Estates General and the often-overlooked Paris *parlement* in conserving the constitution. It also considers the problem of 'popular sovereignty' and its implications for League political thought, establishing that the Leaguers were only interested in the elective, and deposing powers of the 'prudent multitude' and not the wider populace. The double incorporation of the people, as a whole, into the commonwealth and the church is identified as centrally important in these debates.

Chapters Four and Five analyse the intractability of the issues raised regarding the relationship between the church and the commonwealth for the Gallican liberties, which would continue into the seventeenth century. This chapter does so through the works of three important lawyers: René Choppin, whose neglected *De Sacra Politia* is a crucial text for understanding the shape of League debates in the 1580s, Pierre de Belloy and Louis Dorléans. These works demonstrate the extent to which late medieval controversies about ecclesiastical power were resurrected in the sixteenth century, and the ways in which caricatured ideas of medieval controversialists like William of Ockham and Marsilius of Padua were used to score significant polemical points. Rather than an innovative, particularly 'humanist' Gallicanism emerging in this period, we see that the debates about the relationship between church and commonwealth remained very much embedded in medieval scholasticism.

Chapter Five focusses specifically on the issue of papal power, and particularly the heightening of tensions brought about by the question of receiving the Tridentine decrees in France. It aims both to contextualise the League debates, and to position them in relation to the ongoing question of the precise content of the Gallican liberties. The Leaguers were not defined by 'ultramontanism'; the divisions in their movement mapped onto the wider disagreements amongst French lawyers and theologians as to the scope and nature of the Gallican liberties. They were, therefore, very much part of the mainstream debates. In particular, this chapter establishes that in the work of lawyers such as Antoine Hotman and Louis Dorléans, and theologians such as Gilbert Génébrard, Jean Porthaise and Jean Boucher, the deliberations over the Tridentine decrees were anchored in the context of a revival of late medieval conciliarism. From the problem of Sixtus V's power of excommunication, to the troubled issue of Henri IV's abjuration of Protestantism, this chapter further indicates that these debates, transformed and adapted from the medieval era, would go on to define Henri IV's reign after 1594 and last well beyond the lifespan of the League itself.

Chapter Six analyses the *De Justa Reipublicae Christianae Authoritate* (1590) of the pseudonymous 'Guiliemus Rossaeus' to demonstrate how a deep analysis of the relationship between natural and divine law, in scholastic terms, was used to justify the deposition and assassination of Henri III. The author's rich engagement with Jesuit and Dominican casuistry, and the Thomist commentary tradition, made his rejection of heretic tyranny a question of individual conscience as well as of French heresy laws. This demonstrates that Leaguer analyses of papal power at this academic level were not simply a recapitulation of medieval ecclesiological debates but offered a fresh synthesis of the Thomist sources. Such theories were as much a contribution to European Catholic political-theological debate as they were an immediate polemical response to Henri III's perceived tyranny.

Chapter Seven situates Jean Bodin's political thought in his *Six Livres de la République* (1576) in the League context. It builds on the concept of the *politique* Leaguer considered in earlier chapters, to draw out further implications of a close textual consideration of the concept of the *république/respublica* in the political theory of the 1570s. This establishes a basis on

which to analysis the relationship between Bodin's political thought and
that produced by members of the League. The problem of Bodin's membership of the League is considered, as is his friendship with René
Choppin, and the League reception of his *République*. Finally, the chapter
considers the concept of sovereignty itself, and particularly the question of
whether or not a king could be said to own his kingdom. Rather than
providing the basis of an argument for territorial sovereignty, this analysis
demonstrates the extent to which the concept of sovereignty was patrimonial, and in this way distinct from the rights of subjects, who retained
a right of self-defence and private property ownership. The relationship
between the commonwealth and the king's regalian rights is thereby
positioned as a key consideration in arguments for legitimate resistance
to tyranny, that were framed in terms of obedience to the higher authorities
of natural and divine law.

The final chapter of the book examines the concept of the *patria*. The
unifying feature of the *Sainte Union* was its commitment to the eradication
of heresy for the sake of the preservation of the French commonwealth. It
was, therefore, very literally conceived of as a holy, or sacred fraternity,
committed to the crusading principles of holy war. This chapter shifts the
conceptual framework of analysis in order to evaluate the way in which the
well-being of the political community corresponded to the well-being of
the universal *patria* of the Catholic church. Here the language of loyalty to
the *patrie/patria* is seen as a fusion of patriotic ideals of citizenship with
sacred devotion to the church. The slippage between the particularity of
the French case and the universalising framework of Christian theology
thereby renders the crisis of obedience an eschatological as well as
a constitutional one. The question of whether or not there is a nascent
'nationalism' in these disputes has been thoroughly considered in scholarship, but the concept of the *patrie* or *patria* needs further thought. Whether
located in Paris, as the *communis patria*, or in France as a new Jerusalem,
the concept of commonwealth, the common good and the collective
salvation of the people is identified through the language of *patrie/patria*
in these polemics. This is particularly the case when thinkers fused
Augustinian conceptions of government with those of classical political
thought. This chapter looks at these ideas from two perspectives: the
problem of reconciling Spanish support for the League with the claim to
be defending the French *patria*, and the intellectual connections between
the ideas of the English Jesuit exiles and League political thought.

The conclusion to the book suggests ways in which a 'Leaguer Catholicism'
survived into the seventeenth century. Contrary to the commands of Henri IV

that his subjects forget the troubled era of the religious wars, former Leaguers and their progeny continued to defend their established views of the role of the church in the commonwealth: as *dévots*, or as members of the Oratory and renewed Carmelite order. Those who chose exile rather than accept the 'false' abjuration of Henri, like Jean Boucher, continued to campaign against Protestant 'heresy', and engaged actively in some of the major controversies of the early seventeenth century.

CHAPTER I

Contextualising the League

The League was a deeply ideological movement: it was a militant confraternity that determined the 'ancient' Catholic religion of France to be the strongest bond of the commonwealth, binding subject to monarch in a contractual relationship of mutual obligation.[1] The Leaguers made regular reference to the thirteenth-century Albigensian crusade, and frequently compared the Huguenots to the Cathars, in order to identify their assault on Protestantism with a just and holy war.[2] Arnaud Sorbin, one of the theologians who defended the St Bartholomew's Day Massacre, translated Pierre des Vaux de Cernay's history of the crusade in 1569; in 1585, it was republished by one the printers who was by then committed to the League, Guillaume Chaudière.[3] The Leaguers presented themselves as crusaders, members of a *Sainte Union* committed to the eradication of Protestant heresy in France and thus to the preservation of centuries of tradition in which France was seen as a new Jerusalem and its kings *Rois très Chrétiens*.[4] The appeal of the League

---

[1] *Declaration des causes*. There were two productions of the speech delivered by Bourbon – the first dated 31 March 1585 in Péronne, penned by the Jesuit Claude Matthieu, and the second 20 April 1585.

[2] Crouzet, *Les Guerriers de Dieu*, 381–2; Vicaire, 'les albigeois ancêtres des protestants'; Racaut, 'The Polemical use of the Albigensian Crusade'; Zwierlein, *Political Thought of the League*. The Huguenot author of the *Vindiciae* had made reference to crusading encyclicals as part of his bid to draw a comparison between the French monarchy and Ottoman rule, and appeal to both a Catholic and Protestant readership. With heavy irony, he claimed that waging war against French tyranny was therefore more 'meritorious' than a traditional crusade: *Vindiciae*, ed. Garnett, 178.

[3] Sorbin, *Histoire de la ligue saincte*. Sorbin had also used the Albigensian theme in his response to the *Reveill-Matin*.

[4] On the role of confraternities in the wars of religion, and the League as a crusading movement, see Crouzet, *Les Guerriers de Dieu*; Gould, *Catholic activism in South-West France*; Brunet '"Confréries ligueuses, confréries dangereuses"'; Essays by Barnes, Ramsay, and Stocker in *Confraternities and Catholic reform in Italy, France and Spain*; Barnes, 'The Wars of Religion'; Barnes, 'Religious Anxiety and Devotional Change'. Scholars have also pointed out that the League had its roots in the party of 'Malcontent' Catholic noblemen who formed an alliance in the 1560s: Joseph Lecler, 'Aux origines de la Ligue. Premier Projets et Premiers Essais' in *Études. Revue Catholique d'Intérêt Géneral*, 227 (April 1936): 188–208; Jouanna, *Le Devoir de Révolte*, 180, 188–9; Salmon, *Society in Crisis*, 201.

therefore lay largely in its crusading identity and the commitment to the eradication of heresy in France.[5]

Sources agree that the beginnings of the League are to be found in growing Catholic hostility towards Protestantism in France.[6] The movement started in the town of Péronne, when their governor Jacques d'Humières refused to surrender to the Protestant Prince de Condé or to abide by the terms of the Peace of Monsieur which had brought the fifth war of religion to a close. The ensuing Edict of Beaulieu, promulgated in May 1576, permitted the Huguenots to worship openly outside of the capital. It also posthumously pardoned the Admiral de Coligny whose assassination precipitated the 1572 Massacre, gave the Prince de Condé the governance of Picardy and recognised the rights of Huguenots to several 'safe' towns.[7] In response to this Edict, Pierre de L'Estoile described rumours in June of 1576 of the formulation of a League that included Phillip II of Spain, Pope Gregory XIII and several other French *seigneurs*. By August of 1576, he recorded that the ducs de Guise, Maine and Nemours were suspected to be its leaders.[8] In December of that year, at the meeting of the Estates General at Blois, Henri III capitulated to the demands of the League and declared himself its head.[9]

This first Catholic League was an aristocratic movement born out of frustration with the inconsistent religious policy of the monarchy, and open hostility to its attempt to bring peace to the kingdom by offering the Huguenots a measure of religious freedom and try to make amends for the atrocities of 1572. Palma Cayet's memoirs led the characterisation of the religious wars as wars of the aristocracy, rather than wars of religion, in which he persuasively presented the League as a vehicle for Guise ambition.[10]

It is clearly the case that the Guise were seen by contemporaries as contenders for the throne: the Huguenots had once, albeit ironically, even considered Henri de Guise as a respectable ruler, notably in the widely read *Reveille-Matin des François et leur voisins*.[11] François des Rosières' *Stemmatum*

---

[5] Zwierlein, *Political Thought of the League*, 104–11 has recently examined two texts in particular which contribute to this concept of 'holy war' in League political thought.

[6] L'Estoile, MJ, I, 134, 150, 165; Cayet, *Chronologie Novenaire*, 1, *avant-propos*, 1r–4r. Cf. *Conspiration faicte en Picardie*.

[7] *Édict du Roy*, 1576.   [8] L'Estoile, M-J, I, 134, 150, 165. Cf. *Conspiration faicte en Picardie*.

[9] L'Estoile, M-J, I, 134, 150, 165. There is, of course, much more to the story of Henri's volte-face regarding the League. See Greengrass, 'A Day in the Life of the Third Estate', and his *Governing Passions*, 66–122, for a close discussion of the meeting, including the limited role played by the League.

[10] A line of analysis which would be taken up authoritatively by Jacques Auguste de Thou in his *Historia sui Temporis* (first published in its entirety in 1620).

[11] As observed by Salmon, *Society in Crisis*, 200.

Lotharingiae, which described Henri de Guise's descent from Charlemagne and circulated in unpublished form from 1574, further contributed to the growing popularity of Guise in the face of Henri III's widely acknowledged failings. Rosières was a protégé of the Cardinal de Guise, and certainly wrote to flatter his patron. However, the evidence that the Guise family emerged as leaders of the first League more than any other Catholic noble who resisted the Edict is slim.[12] What we see instead, is a 'slow building up' of the Guise position in the years between 1576 and 1584, whilst the focus of French and international attention shifted to the Low Countries.[13]

The aims and ambitions of the 'first' League were laid out in the *Articles de la Ligue de Péronne*, which are recorded in Palma Cayet's *Chronologie Novenaire* (1608).[14] These *Articles* formed the basis of a twelve-point oath binding those who took it to defend the Catholic Church and eradicate heresy. The oath was premised on the notion that joining the movement would be a meritorious act. It was directed explicitly at the Catholic aristocracy and its key elements were the upholding of divine law and re-establishing service to the Roman Catholic Church; a promise to conserve Henri III's status and that of his successors as the 'Very Christian Kings'; and an aim to reinstate the provinces and the Estates of France to the rights, pre-eminences, franchises and ancient liberties which they had held under the first Christian king, Clovis. Other articles included the implicit threat of violence that, if resisted, any methods necessary could be used; that all leagues in the provinces were to conform to these articles; and that all Catholics were strongly advised to join. The *Articles* made it clear that those who did not take the oath would be considered enemies. There are therefore three key themes here which characterise the first League: the eradication of Protestant 'heresy' in the kingdom; the preservation of the Catholicity of the monarchy; the establishment of the Estates General as a mechanism through which to reform the kingdom and, if needs be, oppose royal policy.

Cayet and L'Estoile presented the 'second' League of 1584–5 as a straightforward continuation of the first, under the same Guise leadership, but these

---

[12] Henri de Guise, it seems, played no more significant a role in the first League than Humières and the ducs de Thouars, Ruffec and La Châtre who all refused to abandon their governments to Huguenot rule in 1576. Constant, *La Ligue*, 75–6; Penzi, 'Les pamphlets Ligueurs', 138–9; Amalou, *Une Concorde Urbaine*, 325 n.8, all make the case that Guise at most played a secondary role in the League of 1576. The precise nature of the Guise relationship to the League is explored in Caroll, 'The Guise affinity'.

[13] L'Estoile, M-J, I, 244; Poupé, *La Ligue en Provence*.

[14] Cayet's account of the first League largely matches L'Estoile's, except Cayet places a greater emphasis on Guise as its 'secret' leader: Cayet, *Chronologie Novenaire*, I, *avant-propos*, n.p; the *Articles* are reproduced at fol. 1r–4r.

accounts do not give due consideration to the precise problem of Protestant rule that faced the Catholic community after the death of Henri's immediate heir, Anjou, in 1584. The death of Anjou placed the Protestant Henri de Navarre in line to the throne, and his candidacy was strongly opposed.[15] Almost immediately, Navarre's uncle, the Cardinal Charles de Bourbon, suggested to the king that he succeed instead – a proposition met with some mockery if L'Estoile's account is to be believed.[16] By this time, the movement was also much more clearly under the authority of the Guise family, whose fortunes had shifted to place them once more as contenders for power. Rosières' *Stemmatum Lotharingiae* was published in 1580, and became a further source of ridicule amongst Huguenots and those Catholics who were becoming increasingly hostile to these Guise ambitions.[17] Rosières was immediately imprisoned by the king (although pardoned in 1583) and his work produced a flurry of responses, of which the *Discours sur le droit pretend part ceux de Guise* of 1580 is notable. Probably written by Philippe Duplessis Mornay, it targeted the perceived threat of the Guise family and their ambitions for the crown, demonstrating that the anti-Guise narrative, already established by *l'affaire David,* was gaining momentum.[18] In this affair, recorded by Palma Cayet, an emissary of the Guise family, Jean David, was caught in Lyon and killed by Huguenots supposedly returning from a secret meeting with the pope in Rome, organised by leading members of the Guise family. The papers found on his person purported to be written in support of Henri de Guise's claim to the throne, describing him as a new Charlemagne.[19]

During Henri III's reign (1574–89), complaints against his extravagance and erratic policies, the problematic and enduring presence of his court

---

[15] Maillard, *Advertissement au roy de Navarre* is a discussion of the fundamental laws of France, arguing that heretics are excluded from the succession. The earliest of the second League's publications is *Protestation des liguez faicte en l'assemblee de Mildebourg,* claiming that Navarre and Condé were of English descent. Philippe Duplessis Mornay was probably the author of a dialogue discussing the possibility of Navarre's conversion circulating at this time: *Double d'une letter envoiée à un certain personnage.* The publication of this pamphlet in Germany is significant in its response to the upheaval in Cologne.

[16] L'Estoile, M-J, III, 166–7.

[17] Rosières was thoroughly mocked in the *Satyre Menippée,* as will be discussed. *Satyre Menippee,* ed. Martin, 84–5.

[18] 'Discours sur le droit pretend part ceux de Guise' in Goulart, *Mémoires,* I, 7–20. Cf. Viguier, *Traicté de l'estat et origine des anciens François.* Mornay picked up the attack on Rosières once more in his 'Lettre d'un Gentilhomme Catholique François' in Goulart, *Mémoires,* I, 419. This work was written in response to Louis Dorléans'*Advertissement, des Catholiques anglois* in which he adopted the guise of an English Catholic warning the French against the dangers of Protestant monarchy.

[19] Cayet, *Chronologie Novenaire,* 1. fol. 5v. Cf. Anquetil, *L'Esprit de la Ligue* 2, 165–6. The pamphlet was entitled *Summa legationis Guysianicae ad Pontificem Max. deprehensa nuper inter chartas Davidis Parisiensis Advocati,* Darmstadt, Hessisches Staatsarchiv, A.IV, konv.50, Fast.3, and translated as 'Extraict d'un conseil secret' in Goulart, *Mémoires de la Ligue,* 1, 1–7.

favourites (*les mignons*), venality of office and excessive burdens of taxation folded easily into broader charges regarding the protection of the religion of the realm.[20] By 1585, the League was a force to be reckoned with and it spread with rapidity through the provinces, largely through the formulation of councils responsible for organising the swearing of the League oath.[21] In March of that year, L'Estoile recorded the collusion of the houses of Guise and Lorraine with the duc de Savoie, the Spanish and the pope along with other Italian potentates; 'as many Frenchmen as foreigners', he observed. The execution of Mary Stuart in England in 1587 further boosted their support.[22] The attraction of the League was no longer restricted to a noble, male elite.[23] In the provinces and the capital, the appeal of a composite, polycentric League to specific civic agendas in French cities, combined with widespread dissatisfaction with royal policy and loyal Catholicism made it a formidable force.[24]

Although there was no direct reference in League pamphlets back to the movement of 1576, established themes in the literature were revived and remodelled in 1584–5 as the Leaguers adapted their arguments to the new circumstances. The *Declaration* in 1585 justified the organisation of a League in favour of the Cardinal's succession to the throne and stated that the 'ancient' religion of France was the strongest bond of the commonwealth and that it bound subject to monarch in mutual obligation.[25] It also sought resolution through the Estates General, requiring that it meet every three years 'in complete liberty'.

[20] For example, see *Declaration des causes*. Henri's *mignons,* or *chère bande,* were young men of the provincial nobility, including Louis de Maugiron, François d'O, Jacques de Lévy, Henri de Saint-Sulpice, François d'Espinay de Saint-Luc and of which the duc d'Épernon and Anne de Joyeuse were the closest to the king (the '*archimignons*'). They were relentlessly satirised and abused in contemporary literature, of which Agrippa d'Aubigné's *Confessions de Sancy, Aventures de la baron de Foeneste* and *Les Tragiques* are a fine example.
[21] Harding, *The Anatomy of a Power Elite*, 89–96. On the federal structure of the League, see Greengrass, *France in the Age of Henri IV*, 54–5.
[22] Salmon, *Society in Crisis*, 234–75.
[23] Salmon, 'The Paris Sixteen', 235–66; Descimon, *Qui etaient les Seize?*; Descimon, 'La Ligue à Paris'; Barnavi, *Le parti de Dieu*. On women in the League, see Viennot, 'Des femmes d'État' au XVIe siècle in *Femmes et pouvoirs sur l'ancien regime*; Diefendorf, 'An Age of Gold?' in Wolfe (ed.), *Changing Identities*.
[24] Most recently, Michel Cassan, Nicolas Le Roux, Olivia Carpi, Philippe Hamon and Mark Greengrass have analysed the structure of the League in the provinces in Brunet (ed.), *La Sainte Union des catholiques*. Earlier important studies include Amalou, *Le Lys et la Mitre*; Amalou, *Une Concorde Urbaine*; Bernstein, *between Crown and Community*; Carpi, *Une République Imaginaire*; Brunet, *'De l'Espagnol dedans le ventre!'*; Marcilloux (ed.), *Laon, 1594*; Konnert, *Civic Agendas*; Ascoli, 'French Provincial Cities'; Benedict, *Rouen during the Wars of Religion*; Greengrass, 'The Sainte Union in the provinces'; Harding, 'Revolution and Reform in the Holy League'; Barnavi, 'Centralisation ou fédéralisme?'; Drouot, *Mayenne et la Bourgogne*; Wilkinson, 'A Provincial Assembly during the League'.
[25] *Declaration des causes*.

However, there are a few noticeable differences between the two Leagues. The agenda for reform is much more evident from 1584, when the prominence of the Guise family in the leadership of the second League was established. The social base of the League of 1584–5 was also broader, notwithstanding its aristocratic leadership, which spoke to an inherent populism in the movement that would eventually lead to the splintering of the League after 1588.[26] The mobilisation of the printing press from 1584 is also a striking difference from 1576, as will be discussed. Finally, as L'Estoile noted, Gregory XIII's death was significant. The pope had not thrown his support behind the League and was deeply reluctant to promote their use of arms. Although his name had been associated with the League of 1576, and in 1577 the movement was referred to in a Huguenot pamphlet as 'the papist league', in fact the pope remained a remote presence.[27] Sixtus V, in contrast, would become a muscular arm of the League and his direct interventions in French affairs – most obviously the excommunication of Henri III in 1588 for the assassination of the Guise brothers – would provoke outrage amongst opponents of the League. His interventions and those of Gregory XIV were also considered excessive, as we shall see, by certain Gallican Leaguers.

The strength of its appeal in the provinces contributed to the success of the second League in attracting a more widespread set of followers. The League's apparent lack of piety towards the *patrie* was a common theme in anti-League memoirs, chronicles and polemics, but it had a widespread and popular appeal in France. Anjou, Brittany, Provence and Touraine are amongst those that turned easily to the League, Cayet similarly noted the importance of the towns of Chalons, Dijon and Soissons.[28] The balance to be struck between loyalty to the nation, or *patrie*, as a whole, and conformity to a highly developed '*culture de ville*' in French towns is an essential aspect the League.[29] That this *culture de ville* was expressed foremost as a defence of the ancient franchises and structures of these individual towns in theory complemented the promise, made by the League, to protect the ancient franchises of *l'état*.[30]

---

[26] Barnavi, *Le Parti de Dieu;* Descimon, *Qui etaient les Seize;* Descimon, Barnavi, *La Sainte Ligue;* Salmon, 'The Paris Sixteen', 235–66.

[27] *Declaration des justes causes.*

[28] L'Estoile, M-J, III, 183–90; Cayet, *Chronologie Novenaire,* fol. 7r.

[29] As illuminated by Amalou, *Une Concorde Urbaine,* 328; Carpi, *Une République Imaginaire,* 230; Drouot, *Mayenne et la Bourgogne,* I, 131.

[30] For an example of which, see Rubis' *Discours sur la contagion de peste.*

The appeals made in League polemics to the authority of customary laws had implications for the devolved nature of the League as much as for the kingdom as a whole. Importantly, these cities continued to consider themselves as supporters of the French monarchy.[31] Although the relationship was by no means straightforward, these provinces saw no contradiction in declaring themselves 'Leaguer' and simultaneously supporting the crown, if not the individual holding the office. It is also notable that several important provincial towns were less immediately willing to give up their independence, for example, Lyon, Senlis and Amiens.[32] Senlis and Amiens only joined after the assassination of the Guise brothers in 1588, when the affairs of the kingdom began to look increasingly desperate. Nor did the people of Lyon immediately take the League oath once the Sorbonne had declared France absolved from its oath to Henri III in January 1589. They waited for a month, until the articles of the oath were read out to the local assembly of nobles and *échevins* (councillors) and first accepted by them, before the new oath was signed.[33]

Notwithstanding the importance of the provinces, the emergence of the Paris Sixteen indicates the significance of the capital for the League as a whole, as well as the divisions within the movement. By 1588, this previously clandestine wing of the League increasingly adopted a position of open revolt against the policies of the king, under leadership from the duc de Guise. In the spring of that year, the Sixteen erected barricades in the city, forcing the king to flee. Resorting to increasingly desperate measures, Henri III ordered the assassination of the duc de Guise and his cardinal brother and arrested other leading members of the League, thereby unknowingly signing his own death warrant. Excommunicated, and considered by many of his people to be a tyrant, Henri's death was widely anticipated in Paris: in the words of the League theologian Jean Guincestre 'everyone ... had in conscience thought of killing the king.'[34] The Dominican monk who took it upon himself to be the vehicle of providence, Jacques Clément, had fantasised about the act for months, and eventually – after fasting for twelve days – assassinated the king in July 1589. Clément was said to have been nursed in the 'cradle' of the League: the Parisian apartments of Jean Boucher at the College de Fortèt.[35] Boucher quickly wrote a defence of Clément's 'meritorious' action which he added to his *De Justa Abdicatione*.[36]

---

[31] Amalou, *Senlis*, 326; Carpi, 'Les Villes', 96; Greengrass, 'Toulouse', 477–8.
[32] Amalou, *Senlis*, 327; Carpi, 'Les Villes et la Ligue en Picardie' in Marcilloux, *Laon*, 36.
[33] Reure, *La Presse Politique à Lyon*, 12–13.   [34] Greengrass, *France in the Age of Henri IV*, 60.
[35] l'Estoile, MJ, III, 6.
[36] On the composition of the text and its publication history, see Zwierlein, *Political Thought of the League*.

As well as thinking of themselves as crusaders, the Leaguers drew regular comparison to the Israelites, and aligned Paris with Jerusalem.[37] League writers used the Hebrew model to present the French as God's chosen people, the 'new' Israelites who had a duty to uphold the true, Catholic faith. In the *Articles de la Saincte Union* (1588) the author argued that the promise God made to Moses to protect the Israelites in Egypt was the same as he made to Charlemagne regarding the French people.[38] In the *Dialogue d'entre le Maheustre et le Manent* (1593), the Leaguers are also compared to the Israelites, and the leading Leaguer Charles Hotman celebrated as a new Moses.[39] Furthermore, the author drew a direct comparison between the Sanhedrin and the Estates General, arguing that the latter had a similar power to the former in judging a heretic ruler.[40] The author of *l'Arpocratie* (1589), a pamphlet written in defence of Henri III's assassination, argued that it was equivalent to the delivery of the Israelites from the tyranny of the Pharoah.[41] The League lawyer Louis Dorléans also compared the League to the ancient leagues of Israel.[42] He further argued that the blood running in the bones of French kings had been mixed with that of the kings of Jerusalem, and that this ancient heritage had been corrupted when Henri III ordered the assassination of the Guise brothers in 1588.[43]

Such comparisons were widespread, not least because there were several Hebraist scholars in the League. Jean Porthaise was one of these, and part of a cohort of French Franciscan preachers who joined the movement.[44] He had also compared the League to the Israelites in his sermons of 1593 in order to justify resistance, citing the specific case of their withdrawal from loyalty to king Jereboam in the name of their faith.[45] He even used the Hebrew comparison to argue that the pope had the authority to protect the faith of a commonwealth, arguing that as the Hebrew prophet Jeremiah

---

[37] McCuaig, 'Paris/Jerusalem in Pierre de l'Estoile'.   [38] *Articles de la Saincte Union,* fol. 12r–v.

[39] *Dialogue d'entre le Maheustre et le Manent,* 94–5.   [40] Ibid., 55

[41] 'l'Arpocratie' in (ed.) Goulart, *Mémoires,* I, 99.

[42] Dorléans, *Second Avertissement,* fol. 37r. Louis Dorléans (1542–1629) was an *avocat* in the Paris *parlement* and committed member of the *Sainte Union;* one of its most prolific writers. He was also a member of the Paris *Seize* until the murder of Brisson, at which point he became a supporter of the duc de Mayenne. There is surprisingly little scholarship on this important and influential lawyer. On his background, and influence in the League years, see Gould, 'The Life and Political Writings of Louis Dorléans'. For a recent discussion of his *Advertissment des Catholiques Anglois,* see Marco Penzi, 'Loys Dorléans and the "Catholiques Anglois"';.

[43] Ibid., fol. 43r–44v (mispag.).

[44] Labitte, *De la démocratie,* 280–2, describes him, somewhat unfairly, as a 'bilious and bitter scholastic'. Other brief discussions of Porthaise include Baumgartner, *Radical Reactionaries,* 207–8; Salmon, 'Catholic Resistance theory', 230; Tallon, *Conscience Nationale,* 141. On Franciscans and the League, see Armstrong, *The Politics of Piety.*

[45] Porthaise, *Cinq Sermons* (Paris, 1594), 55.

could send a king into exile, so could a pope.[46] Reclaiming the resources of the Old Testament and the crusades from the French Huguenots, the Leaguers sought to widen their appeal and justify their increasingly contentious position regarding the authority of the papacy, and the assassination of Henri III.[47]

Presenting the League as an intellectual, genuinely ideological movement goes against the grain of the perspective of hostile contemporaries, who overwhelmingly saw the movement to have been led by a self-serving and rebellious nobility who used zealotry to disguise their ambition. In December of 1584, L'Estoile described the League in formidable terms as a storm which would wreak havoc in France, writing of the great strength of its 'winds' that knocked down church towers, ruined houses and tore ancient oak trees out of the ground.[48] By 'winds' L'Estoile meant rhetoric and also, implicitly, vanity: the power of the League lay in the conviction of its members and in the strength of their message, but this persuasive power was precisely where the danger lay.[49] L'Estoile saw it as his duty to reveal the false mask of zealotry behind which Leaguers hid their ambition, and to record their deeds as a warning to posterity.

This thread runs through anti-League writing of the era, where the movement is described in theatrical and evocative terms of tragedy and destruction, tearing at the fabric of the *patrie* itself. Étienne Pasquier wrote to a friend in 1585 on the subject saying that he saw 'a strange and horrible tragedy represented in the theatre of France.'[50] One of Henri IV's lawyers, Pierre de Belloy, warned in his *Apologie Catholique* of the same year, that the League would lead to the 'utter ruin, loss and subversion of this poor kingdom'. In the anti-League *Satyre Ménippée* (1593), the complaint was directed against the foreign supporters of the League as the ruin of France: 'Oh Paris, that is no longer Paris', mourned the character of Monseiur de l'Aubray in a *Harengue* 'but a cavern of savage beasts, a citadel of the Spanish, Wallons [Belgians] and Neopolitans, a refuge for thieves, murderers and

---

[46] Ibid., 65–8 (mispag.). Porthaise goes on to argue that it is an indirect power which the church has over civil jurisdiction, and that it cannot interfere in matters of election and succession, only in questions of faith. Further examples of Hebrew priests deposing their kings are seen in the cases of Samuel and Saul and Ahias and Jeroboam.

[47] In contrast to the claim made by Eric Nelson that there is a 'disproportionately Protestant story' of Christian Hebraism in the sixteenth and seventeenth centuries, clearly there is more to be said about the Catholic Hebraism as it responded to Protestant. Nelson, *The Hebrew Republic*.

[48] L'Estoile, MJ, III, 176. Cf. Mackenzie, *The Poetry of Place.*

[49] My thanks to Emma Claussen for pointing out the implications of L'Estoile's observation.

[50] Belloy, *Apologia Catholica*, preface, n.p.; Pasquier, *Lettres historiques*, 223. The theatricality of the League is discussed by Crouzet, 'La représentation du temps'.

assassins'.[51] The League was presented as betraying the *patrie* to foreign invaders, siding with Spain and papal authority over the 'natural' French men who sought to defend and preserve France.

Contemporary records of the history of the League, from the diaries of Pierre de l'Estoile to the published accounts of Agrippa d'Aubigné, Jacques-Auguste de Thou and Palma Cayet sought to warn future generations of the dangers of zealotry in their records of the atrocities of the wars of religion, using the League as a menacing example.[52] The 'turbulent and fanatic' nature of the League remained tenacious in Protestant and Catholic memory for centuries.[53] Prior to the twentieth century, these chronicles, collections, diaries and records of the wars of religion thoroughly affected the history of the League.[54]

It is significant, however, that contemporaries made a distinction between a *ligueur* and an *'archi-ligueur'*, or *'ligueur zélé'*, referring to those who ended up supporting the duc de Mayenne, and the uncompromising theologians, clergy and lawyers who formed the core of the Sixteen.[55] In his *Second Avertissement [sic]*, Dorléans argued that the League, like the Israelites, ought to have 'clean hands' when it came to questions of faith, and made it clear that 'brigandage' and religion did not complement each other. He compares the 'zealots' in the League to Achan from the Book of Joshua, quoting the prophets Amos and Hosea to the effect that life without rulers is a punishment.[56] This important distinction between Leaguer 'brigands' and self-styled royalists like Dorléans is significant, precisely because it suggests that the Leaguers themselves ought to be differentiated and not all considered solely through the lens of *'la Ligue des Faux-zéléz'*.[57]

---

[51] *Satyre Menippee*, 75. '*O Paris qui n'es plus Paris, mais une spelunque de bestes farouches, une citadelle d'Espagnols, Ouallons, et Napolitains: un asyle et seure retraicte de voleurs, meurtriers, et assacinateurs.*' According to Hauser, the basis of d'Aubray's lament in the *Satyre Menippee* was provided by *Advis d'un François à la noblesse catholique de France*. Hauser, *Les Sources de l'Histoire de France*, IV, 141.

[52] d'Aubigné, *Histoire Universelle*; *Tragiques*; de Thou, *Historiarum sui temporis*; Cayet, *Chronologie novenaire*. On the legacy of the wars of religion, see Berthold, Fragonard, *La Mémoire des Guerres de Religion*; Benedict, 'Shaping the Memory of the French Wars of Religion' in *Memory before Modernity*; Benedict et al., *L'Identité huguenote*; Frisch, *Forgetting Differences*; Greengrass, 'Europe's 'Wars of Religion' and their legacies'.

[53] The reference to a 'turbulent and fanatic' League is to Goulart, *Mémoires de la Ligue*, I, xii.

[54] As noted in the Introduction, Robert Descimon was instrumental in bringing about this change of approach: Descimon, *Qui etaient les Seize?*; Descimon, 'La Ligue à Paris (1585–1594)'. See also, Barnavi, *Le parti de Dieu*. A very effective recent treatment of the problem of negative perception of the League in the source materials is Marco Penzi, 'Les pamphlets Ligueurs et la polémique antiligueuse' in Berthold and Fragonard, *La Mémoire des Guerres de Religion*.

[55] For example, see Pierre de l'Estoile, MJ, V, 180.

[56] Dorléans, *Second Avertissement*, fol. 14r–v.   [57] Maimbourg, *Histoire de la Ligue*, 4r.

The task of analysing the political thought of the League requires reading their ideas in context: but this in itself is not a straightforward methodology. As indicated in the Introduction, texts did not necessarily circulate in their complete forms, or in their original contexts. Instead, they were frequently hijacked, gutted, repurposed and polemicised. In some instances, the original meaning of a text was entirely subverted. For example, in 1593, the *Dialogue d'entre le maheustre et le manant* was published anonymously, as an attempt by a member of the *Seize* to persuade a wavering Catholic of the justice of the cause. But, in the following year, Navarre's supporters published a doctored edition to convert the *Dialogue* into an unequivocally royalist work that bamboozled contemporaries and befuddled scholars.[58] Misdirection and disinformation were an essential component of the dissemination of partisan news in the period that was designed to entertain as well as move and instruct.[59] The instability of the context of such texts gives good reason to be critical of the endeavour to recover a particular, demonstrable authorial 'speech-act' from any given publication, not least because so much of the literature produced in the wars of religion was anonymous.[60]

France was stuffed with libellous pamphlets in the wars of religion, and recent scholarship has done much to excavate the publication history of these pamphlet wars.[61] One of the reasons we have access to so many (but still only a portion) of the pamphlets and images produced during the League years is that opponents of the League took it upon themselves to preserve the literature as a warning to future generations. Most of these texts have, therefore, been transmitted by hostile hands. The printing and sale of League pamphlets was forbidden from 1594, and Henri IV ordered that the remaining productions be gathered up and destroyed.[62] In April of that year, L'Estoile reported the works of Jean Boucher, Louis Dorléans and other League writers being burnt publicly in the Place Maubert in Paris.[63] And yet L'Estoile took it upon himself to run the risk of preserving

[58] [Attrib.,] François Cromé, *Dialogue d'entre le Maheustre et le Manant*, ed. Ascoli. Ascoli discusses the authorship in his introduction, 23–7; Salmon, 'Appendix: a note on the Dialogue d'entre le Maheustre et le Manant', 264–6.
[59] Themes explored in Martin, 'Rumeur, propagande et désinformation'; Kenz, 'La propagande et le problème de sa réception'.
[60] Boutcher, 'How to Do Things with Texts'.
[61] I have in mind particularly Baranova, *À Coups de Libelles*. Pallier's *Recherches sur l'imprimerie à Paris* remains an invaluable resource. See also Racaut, *Hatred in Print*.
[62] Arch Nat X1a 8641; Arch Nat X1a 1730, 30 mars 1594. See also the first article of the Édit de Nantes: http://elec.enc.sorbonne.fr/editsdepacification/edit_12#art_12_01.
[63] L'Estoile, M-J, VI, 201.

as much of this incendiary production as he could. He described his curiosity about the production of the League as being so great that he acquired

> about 300 different pieces, all published in Paris and peddled in the streets ... besides a great folio of pictures and placards ... which I should have thrown in the fire, as they deserved, except that they may serve in some way to show and expose the abuses, impostures, vanities and furies of this great monster of the League.[64]

In his *Les Belles Figures et Drolleries de la Ligue*, L'Estoile achieved his wish, presenting the 'monstrous' League through a managed, often satirical lens for future readers that magnified the follies and furies of the movement.[65]

The Genevan Calvinist, Simon Goulart, similarly sought to preserve the memory of the League in order to condemn it, though he enlivened his rhetoric even more than L'Estoile when he associated the League with the work of Satan and the forces of the Antichrist.[66] His multi-volume *Mémoires* proved invaluable for Agrippa d'Aubigné in particular, in the composition of his narrative history of the wars. In collecting the pamphlet literature of the League, Goulart hoped that people in the future would avoid the failures and errors of their predecessors.[67] The implicit distrust of ill-educated readers informs his approach to the collection of texts he had compiled, and his concern about the credulity of some led him to condemn the 'turbulent and fanatic League' in violent terms. His editorial presence is, correspondingly, heavy-handed and the entire collection designed to present the League at its most unreasonable.[68]

These collections of text present a body of largely un-authored pamphlets, detached from their original contexts and accompanied – in the case of Goulart – by para-text directing the manner in which they are to be read and understood. Given that consideration, and that most of the printed material of the League is either anonymous or the authorship contested,

---

[64] L'Estoile, M-J, III, 177–80, also quoted in Roelker, *One King, One Faith*.

[65] Lenient, *La Satire en France*. The *Drolleries* have recently been edited by Gustave Schrenck. On the history of L'Estoile's compilation, see the introduction to Schrenk's edition of *Les Belles figures*; Hamilton, *Pierre de L'Estoile*. I am grateful to Tom Hamilton for many discussions on L'Estoile and the League which have helped me to frame some of my own thoughts on the subject.

[66] Goulart, *Mémoires de la Ligue*, I, xi: '*Ami lecteur, si jamais Satan se transfigura en Ange de lumiere pour nuire à l'Eglise de Dieu, & la ruiner, s'il étoit possible, c'est de notre temps, auquel il a fait liguer ensemble les plus grands de l'Europe avec l'Antechrist.*'

[67] Goulart, *Mémoires de l'estat de France*, fol. 2r. Goulart also oversaw the printing of d'Aubigné's *Histoire* in Geneva in 1626. Cf. Huchard, *Simon Goulart et la Saint-Barthélemy*.

[68] Goulart, *Mémoires de la Ligue*, I, xii. The anti-populism of Goulart's text is matched by L'Estoile's, explored by Kenz, 'La propaganda et le problème de sa réception'.

the current book is not intensively biographical in its analysis. Rather, the texts analysed here are placed in the historical context of the religious wars, and – where possible – in the context of the texts to which a particular pamphlet or poem might be responding.

Beyond the collected editions of pamphlets and placards, many (but not all) of the printed publications produced in these years survived. After the St Bartholomew's Day Massacre, Arnaud Sorbin complained that the kingdom was overrun with *libelles* and that the 'true and natural Frenchman' was suffering from an onslaught of blasphemy against God and the king, Charles IX.[69] These *libelles* which defamed, scandalised and defended, conformed to François Bauduin's 1562 definition of the libellous text as an anonymous publication that made a public accusation against an individual or a group, outside of an ordinary institutional (in this case juridical) context.[70] They were often multi-authored under pseudonyms, or anonymous, and in the year of peak crisis in 1589, around six hundred items were printed, mostly pamphlets.[71] These *'apologies', 'lettres', 'remonstrances', 'harangues'* and *'advertissements'* were vernacular *livres de circonstances,* distinct from more academic considerations of Catholic monarchy produced by lawyers and theologians, and created an entire political culture of their own.

Writing these texts and printing them was a highly dangerous business: this was not an era of free speech in that sense. In 1586, François le Breton's presentation of his radical proposal for reform, the *Remonstrances aux trois Etats,* to the king resulted in his public execution in November of that year. The printer, Jean du Carroy, was banned.[72] The king's attempts to supress the printing of League publications were in vain, however, and only resulted in Le Breton's martyrdom, but they do indicate the immediacy and efficacy of these publications to stir up opinion against Henri III. A substantial amount of anonymous League works, visual and textual, were devoted to attacking the king directly.[73] Anonymity within the relatively closed circles of the Parisian magistracy and noble elite that L'Estoile's diaries describe was not always easy to guarantee. In 1576, a satirical pamphlet lampooning the leading houses of the kingdom was the subject of an intensive inquiry by the Du Tillet family, who were a particular

---

[69] Sorbin, *Le vray resveille-matin,* avant-propos, n.p.
[70] Bauduin, *Ad leges de famosis libellis et de calumniatoribus, commentarius,* quoted in Baranova, *Libelles,* 35.
[71] Pallier, *Recherches sur l'imprimerie,* 5–57.
[72] L'Estoile, M-J, II, 359; Pallier, *Recherches,* 64; Baumgartner, *Radical Reactionaries,* 76–8.
[73] Cameron, *A Maligned or Malignant King.*

target. Those treatises that did remain anonymous were subject to multiple interpretations, which could be both advantageous and disadvantageous for polemicists.[74]

Corresponding to the flood of news and libellous literature was a combative satirical genre which characterised this age.[75] A whole series of Huguenot and *politique* productions ruthlessly targeted the weak spots of the League: the *Bibliothèque de Madame de Montpensier* (1587), the *Prosa Cleri Parisiensis* (1589), Pierre de Lostal's *Anti-Guisart* (1586), Philippe Duplessis Mornay's *Lettre d'un gentilhomme catholique français* (1586), François Hotman's *Brutum Fulmen* (1585), his son Jean Hotman's *Anti-Chopinus* (1592), the *Masque de la Ligue découvert* (1590) and the *Lettre d'un gentilhomme François, à dame Jacquette Clement, Princesse boiteuse de la Ligue* (1590) offer rich examples of the genre. Written in Latin or the vernacular, these satires were largely produced within the circles of a privileged, largely Parisian, literary elite who moved between the court and the palace on the Île de la Cité. The library and dinner table of theologian and jurist Jacques Gillot attracted these types to gather and share their views on contemporary affairs. He, along with Pierre le Roy, Nicolas Rapin, Jean Passerat, Pierre Pithou and Florent Chrestien collaborated on the *Satyre Ménippée*. It was extraordinarily popular – running through twenty editions between 1593 and 1594, and in many ways the peak of satirical achievement in these years of anti-League polemic.[76] Influenced by Justus Lipsius' *Somnium Satyricum* (1581), the *Satyre* attacked the Leaguers at their most vulnerable points: their demagoguery and manipulation of the Estates General; their dependence on Spanish financial and military aid; their treasonous attitude to the monarchy; and finally, their false piety thinly disguising ambition and thirst for power.[77]

In response to these attacks, the printed production of the League was conceived as a weapon, defending French Catholicism against fellow Catholics and Huguenots alike. In the preface to *De Justa Reipublicae Christianae Authoritate* (1590), the author invoked the weapons of Minerva rather than Mars, arguing for the force of ink rather than blood. He saw his treatise as a form of combat in its appeal to opinion; he wrote of

---

[74] As discussed in Kenz, 'La propaganda et le problème de sa réception'.

[75] Lenient, *Satire en France*, vol. I, 1–8; Salmon, 'French Satire in the Late Sixteenth Century', 73–97; Christopher M. Flood, 'La France satirisée, satyrisée et fragmentée' in Stefanovska, Paschoud,' *Littérature et politique*. On visual satire, see Blum, *l'Estampe satirique*.

[76] Barbier-Mueller, 'Pour une chronologie des premières éditions de la Satyre Ménippée.'

[77] The second edition of the text changed its title from *Abbrégé et l'ame des Etats convoquez en l'an 1593* to *Satyre Ménippée*, in explicit reference to Lipsius' *Somnium Satyricum*. Cf. I de Smet, *Menippean satire*.

its force to provoke, weaken and destroy enemies as well as to sway the passions.[78] However, the Leaguers had been slow to recognise the power of the printing press, and such tactics have conventionally (and rightly) been more associated with French Huguenots responding to the St Bartholomew's Day Massacre, harnessing the press so effectively as to inundate Europe with pamphlets from their presses in La Rochelle, Nîmes, Montauban and Geneva.[79] By contrast, the League of 1576 churned out very little in the way of textual production: the mobilisation of the printing press from 1584 is therefore a clear difference to the movement of 1576, and the production of a manifesto in 1585 is indicative of the more cogent, more coherent and more deadly nature of the new League.[80] Fifteen editions of the defence of the Cardinal de Bourbon's claim to the throne in the place of Navarre, the *Declaration*, were produced in 1585, offering a noticeable contrast to the *Articles de Péronne* which now only exist in reproductions by Palma Cayet and Goulart.[81]

Who read these works?[82] Members of the educated, noble elite, along with lawyers, theologians, clergy, *maîtres des métiers,* the '*bourgeois moyenne*', including some merchants, largely made up the reading public of the cities. But the libraries of Parisian professionals indicate a priority of legal and religious literature, as well as an interest in classical and historical writings, and not necessarily in *libelles*.[83] On this social and cultural level, the spiritual revival and surge in circulation of ideas in and around the Sorbonne in the reign of Henri III is more significant than the popular literature being produced largely for a different readership. This *sorboniste* theological renewal was spearheaded particularly by Gilbert Génébrard and François Feuardent, leading figures in the League.[84] Claude de Sainctes, Arnaud Sorbin and Thomas Beauxamis also became ardent defenders of the Catholic church against heresy, and their literature was dispersed by Paris printers including Guillaume Chaudière, Pierre Drouart and Jean

---

[78] *De Justa Reipublicae Christianae Authoritate*, preface, n.p. On the 'power' of polemical writing in this period, see Martin, *Livre, Pouvoirs et Société*.

[79] Discussed in Kingdon, *Myths about the St. Bartholomew's Day Massacres, 1572–1576*.

[80] Pallier, *Recherches sur l'imprimerie à Paris*; Boucher, 'Culture des notables et mentalité populaire'; Wolfe, 'Henri IV and the Press' in Pettegree et al., *The Sixteenth-Century French Religious Book*; John, 'Publishing in Paris'; Racaut, 'Nicolas Chesneau; Pettegree et al., *French Vernacular Books*.

[81] This has led Marco Penzi to argue persuasively that the *Declaration* is the most authoritative statement of intent produced by the League: Penzi, 'Les pamphlets Ligueurs', 150–1.

[82] A question importantly considered by Doucet, *Les bibliothèques parisiennes*; Martin, 'Ce qu'on lisait à Paris au XVIe siècle'; Martin, *Livre, pouvoirs et société*; Chartier, *The Cultural Uses of Print*.

[83] Doucet, *Les bibliothèques parisiennes*. Cf. Pettegree, *The Sixteenth-Century French Religious Book*.

[84] Martin, *Livre, pouvoirs et société*, I, 9–14.

Jamet Mettayer.[85] The so-called new humanism of late sixteenth-century Paris was dominated overwhelmingly by the church and an important reason for the success of the League in this particular intellectual context.

Yet there is more to the appeal of the League than a resurgent spiritualism that appealed to a pious, Catholic elite. Whilst literacy rates remained low in France, the sheer number of fairly cheap pamphlets printed and sold in place, along with the growth of vernacular printing, suggests an appetite for their reception and a lucrative gain for publishers, even though the urban poor had no access to such a literature.[86] The sources tell us that the circulation of texts like the *Dialogue d'entre le Maheustre et le Manent* was wide, and that riots often broke out when booksellers disseminated these works, sometimes ending in full-scale street battles.[87] Polemical information was spread by word of mouth and through public lectures and sermons: Jean Boucher would read League publications aloud to his congregation. The appetite for news was also strong and the printing presses of France were well engineered to deal with this demand, both in France and in Europe.[88] The publication of Sixtus V's bull enforcing Henri IV's excommunication in 1591, for example, was said to have sold extremely well.[89] It was posted in the streets of Paris, Lyon, Rouen, Bourges, Orléans, Nantes, Poitiers and Toulouse in its original form, and quickly translated into French.[90] Beyond France, Pallier calculated that books announcing French news could reach Geneva in days; Madrid in a matter of weeks; Rome and London in roughly a month; parts of Germany within six months.

Paris became the hub of Leaguer textual production, where Protestant works had already been supressed, and it is estimated that around a thousand texts were produced by League printers between 1585 and 1594. The presence and support of the University played a crucial role, and most printers operated near the Sorbonne in the Rue Saint-Jacques as well as around Nôtre-Dame, the Palais de Justice and the Hôtel de Ville.[91] When control of the Parisian *parlement* came fully into the hands of the League in 1588, the production of printed material promoting their cause was further eased.[92] Of the publishing centres outside Paris, Troyes,

---

[85] Ibid., I, 22. Cf. Pallier, *Recherches sur l'imprimerie*, 44. For a full list of League printers and booksellers, see Pallier, *Recherches sur l'imprimerie*, 490–548.

[86] Pettegree et al., *French Vernacular Books*.

[87] Pallier, *Recherches*, 187, based on evidence from L'Estoile.

[88] Pettegree, 'Centre and Periphery'. Cf. Walsby, 'Printer Mobility'.   [89] Pallier, *Recherches*, 191.

[90] Ibid., 187–8.   [91] Wolfe, 'Henri IV and the Press', 177–96.

[92] Pallier, *Recherches*; Amalou, 'Entre Réforme et Enjeux Dynastiques'.

Toulouse, Rouen, Montauban and Lyon were the most significant and of these Lyon produced the most.[93] The contacts between Lyon and Paris were close, however scholarship demonstrates that Lyon had a measure of independence when it came to Paris and the League.[94] That 280 League works were produced in Lyon between 1589 and 1594 far outshines that of any other city outside Paris. Of the three lead printers in Lyon, Jean Pillehotte, Louis Tantillon and Jean Patrasson, Pillehotte received a special mandate from the duc de Mayenne in 1589 to print anything he deemed to concern the public affairs of state.[95] Whilst the mandate itself could be understood as indicative of a high level of control by the head of the League, the freedom it implies suggests an absence of regulation by the League heads.

The manifestos of the Leaguers were disseminated effectively to the wider French public, as well as abroad, and appealed both to a literary elite and a popular audience. Even though the development of a large-scale urban readership for political pamphlets would not occur in France until the end of the seventeenth century, historians can see in this era a powerful attempt to use the printing press to support the message of the League, disseminated in a variety of ways and reaching their audience on different levels, to different degrees and through different genres of text. The approach of this book is, correspondingly, to analyse the League polemic as it operated in these different registers, and to account for diversity as well as coherence of message.

---

[93] Pallier, *Recherches*, 14.   [94] Estier, '1589–1594'; Reure, *La Presse Politique*.
[95] Pallier, *Recherches*, 32.

CHAPTER 2

The Politique *Leaguer*

When Michel de l'Hôpital suggested in 1562 that religious difference and the well-being of the commonwealth (*salus populi*) were two separate questions, the idea of the *politique* took form.[1] He had articulated the view held amongst other influential magistrates and scholars including Étienne Pasquier, and which would be taken up by prominent thinkers such as Michel de Montaigne and Guillaume Du Vair, who saw toleration as the remedy for a diseased body politic, rather than a good in itself.[2] Such a position was soon supported and promoted by Huguenots as the prospect of converting Catholic France faded and their position weakened after the St Bartholomew Day Massacre, as a text like François de la Noue's *Discours Politique et Militaire* (1587) demonstrates.

The issue of the place of the *politique* in the wars of religion has, in many ways been resolved.[3] It would be entirely outmoded now, for example, to write about the *politiques* in terms of a political party in the manner outlined in the Introduction. But this does not mean the subject is closed. As the recent research of Emma Claussen demonstrates, there is much more to be said about the role of the *politique* beyond the now stale debate about their status as a party.[4] Whilst the historians of the French wars of

---

[1] Duféy (ed.), *Oeuvres complètes*, 1, 441–53, esp. 452. Skinner points out that this speech to the Estates General at St Germain was delivered in January of 1562, not August 1561 as Duféy has it: Skinner, *Foundations*, II, 250.

[2] Pasquier, *Écrits Politiques*, 48, 51, 65–6; Du Vair, *De la constance*; Montaigne, *Essais*, II.xix, 706–10.

[3] Greengrass, 'Epilogue', *Politics and Religion*, 247.

[4] Claussen, *Politics and Politiques*. I'm very grateful to Emma for allowing me to read the manuscript, from which I have benefitted enormously. On the *politiques*, see also Daubresse, Haan, *La Ligue et ses frontiers*; Greengrass, *Governing Passions*; Descimon, 'La Ligue à Paris (1585–1594)'. Further scholarship on the *politiques* includes Beame, 'The *Politiques* and the Historians'; Turchetti, 'Une question mal posée' in Wanegfellen (ed.), *De Michel de l'Hospital à l'Edit de Nantes*. On the *politique* as a polemical creation, see Greengrass, *France in the Age of Henri IV*, 46; Jouanna, 'Les ambiguïtés des *Politiques* face à la Sainte Ligue', in *Michel de l'Hospital*, 475–93; Papin, 'Duplicité et traîtrise'. Renoux-Zagamé, *De Droit de Dieu*, 271, notes the 'parallel' nature of these two discourses which she otherwise situates in opposition to one another.

35

religion have, therefore, in the large part, moved on from the problem of the *politique*, from the perspective of intellectual history and political thought, the implications of the binary division between the ideas of the *politique* and Leaguer have remained embedded in the scholarly treatment of these questions.[5] There are, therefore, important distinctions and questions that remain to be addressed when the subject matter is seen from this particular historiographical standpoint.

The purpose of this chapter is to break down the divisions between the philosophies of the League and those of the *politiques* that are produced by positing the apparent Erastian rationalism of thinkers like Montaigne, Barclay and Du Vair against the epicureanism of the Leaguers. It does this in order to go beneath the surface of what has been characterised as the turbulence and fanaticism of much of the League polemic, in order to think about the dilemma facing French Catholics in this period on the intellectual level: how to reconcile centuries of tradition with the crisis of confessional division; how to reconcile the need to obey royal authority, as it came from God, with the problem of Protestant rule; how to find the answer to these questions within political science. The intertwining narratives of the Leaguer and so-called *politique* on how to resolve the problems of the French monarchy in this period require a new evaluation, and a fresh understanding of this relationship between Leaguer and *politique* which considers the sources, and arguments that they had in common as much as those which divided them.

In the course of the religious wars, the *politique* quickly became associated with confessional neutrality: a position seen as that of having 'no religion'.[6] In polemical writing, this figure took on a strongly negative character. The difference between those who could see the 'true' good of the community, and those who sought only an appearance of that good came to be expressed in terms of the division between the *politiques*, said to lack true religion, and their opponents. For members of the League, a separation between religion and the constitution was intolerable, and correspondingly much of the Leaguer polemic is devoted to grappling with their own nightmarish vision of a France overrun with this kind of *politique* thinking. The divisions between Leaguers and *politiques* were thus exaggerated and overstated in polemical literature, to an extent that has deeply coloured current scholarship on that relationship. Contemporaries

---

[5] For example, see Crouzet, 'Henri IV', 80–1.

[6] Jouanna, *Le Pouvoir Absolu*, 177, citing the speech of the president of the *parlement* of Rouen in 1573: '*Nous n'entendons pas parler comme on a nouvellement introduit et interprété ce mot politique quasi : n'estant aucune religion . . .*'

recognised, however, the problem of artificial constructions when it came to this division between French Catholics.[7]

For certain members of the League, the definition of the kind of political prudence used to distinguish 'good' from 'bad' *politiques* was binary: there was the temporal prudence of men and the divine prudence of God. The wisdom of the former was that of darkness and death; of the latter, peace and life.[8] There was a close connection drawn between the correct, divinely infused reasoning which was defined by the relinquishing of every earthly goal for the preservation of religion, and the preservation of the French constitution. Most Leaguers argued that their movement was a *Sainte Union* precisely because it was an expression of God's will to preserve Catholicism in France by the eradication of heresy. True reasoning, from the perspective of the League, interlocked Catholic doctrine with civil well-being; false reasoning divorced the 'true', Catholic religion from the civil sphere and allowed for the possibility of Protestant rule. Its worst sin was trumpeting the values of the state over those of piety, as the sonnet at the start of the League treatise *De la puissance des roys* (1589) put it.[9]

What might be seen as the opposite argument, expressed influentially by Du Vair in his *Traité de la constance* (1594), was that religious heterodoxy might, in the end, be an evil that had to be endured, not because it was right in theory, but because the present state of affairs in France must be an unchangeable part of providential history. Persecution of heretics was not outlawed, in this perspective, only seen as an excessively costly measure, detrimental to the common good. Religious unity was still considered the ideal, but was not essential for the functioning of a body politic.[10] In this context, the distinction between Leaguer and *'politique'* views is not so much about the principles of religious unity, built on the foundations of natural and divine law, but instead about the ability of Catholics to interpret and act on God's will to conserve the political constitution in its Catholic form. Given Du Vair's own alignment with the League *parlement* from 1589, the notion of providential order giving form to the political community is a point of common ground and provided the basis for disagreement within and outside of the movement.[11] Du Vair was further opposed to the temptation of resolving complex political and theological questions through deductive political principles, and in this

[7] Pasquier, ' A Monsieur de Saincte Marthe', L. XII, IV, 286.   [8] Dorléans, *Le Banquet*, 15–17.
[9] *De la puissance des roys*, n.p.: '*Sonner l'estat et non la pieté*'.
[10] Figgis, *From Gerson to Grotius*, 130–1.
[11] Tarrête, 'Un gallican sous la Ligue'; Radouant, *Guillaume Du Vair*; Petey-Girard, Tarrête, *Guillaume du Vair*.

sense was an interesting example of a '*politique*' thinker.[12] In this context, and particularly when considering the position of lawyers in the *parlement* who joined the League like Du Vair, Barnabé Brisson, Choppin and Achille de Harlay, it is possible to conceive of a *politique* Leaguer.

As it stands, the figure of the *politique* in the polemics and beyond them, was a composite creation, and its position in these debates is indicative of a crisis of government as much as a crisis of faith. The art, or science, of politics itself was coming under scrutiny in this period of instability.[13] There is a constructive distinction, therefore, to be drawn between the *politique* of the polemics, a terrible figment of Leaguer imagination, and the *politique* theorist who reasoned about *la science politique* at an academic level. In *De la puissance des roys*, for example, the *politique* is described as one who appeared to be a devout Catholic, but in truth was nothing more than a hypocrite: someone who demanded peace where none was to be had, armed himself only for the cause of heresy and took Machiavelli for his gospel.[14] But for other Leaguers, there was a 'true' *politique* who could be rescued from the maw of depravity. As Louis Dorléans put it, 'This name of *Politique* was a name of honour/It was the just name of a just governor/Of a prudent magistrate who, through civil reason/Knew well how to govern the members of a town ... Now it is a name sullied with vice'.[15]

Even as the Leaguers condemned the monster of the *politique*, many of them sought to resurrect the 'just governors' and 'prudent magistrates' of the pre-Reformation era as a distinctly *politique* Leaguer solution to the religious wars in which the eradication of heresy, guided by the strong arm of the Roman church, remained the central priority and one which explicitly embraced the correct deployment of civil reasoning.

Scrutinising the role of the *politique* within and outside of the League polemics demonstrates the importance of not enforcing a strict division between Leaguer and *politique*, not least because such a binary approach contributes to further obfuscation in the broader context of the political thought of this era. In the clash between the League and the *politiques,* for example, it has been argued that the former held to a reactionary medieval concept of government, and the latter represented the 'new', prudent art of

---

[12] As discussed briefly in Salmon, 'Cicero and Tacitus', 49–50.

[13] A point importantly established and developed by Claussen, *Politics and Politiques.*

[14] 'Autre sonet touchant la nature du Politique' in *De la puissance des roys*, preface, n.p.

[15] Dorléans, *Banquet*, 21–2. '*Ce nom de Politique estoit un nom d'honneur, C'estoit le juste nom d'un juste Gouverner, D'un prudent magistrat, qui par raison civile Scavoit bien policer les membres d'un ville ... Aujourd'huy ce beau nom souillé de mille vices/N'est plus qu'un nom d'horreur qui destruit les Polices ...* '. Cf. *Description*, 3.

government: with figures like Étienne Pasquier and Philippe Duplessis Mornay considering religious toleration as a way of reconciling differences in the body politic; lawyers such as Jean Bodin (who is not treated as a Leaguer in such a context) and Pierre de Belloy seeing the solution of preserving the state as resting in the absolute power of the monarch; Gallican theorists like Pierre Pithou and Michel de l'Hôpital considering the possibility of separating temporal from spiritual affairs, church from state, as the resolution to the crisis of the wars of religion.[16] In these often stoic-inspired responses to the idea of political resistance, the League was presented as swayed by its own passions to violence and excess, an expression of epicureanism that delighted in vice.[17] There was no prudence in the League, only passion. Presenting the League through the lens of 'eschatalogical anxiety' supports this kind of reading of the League, which draws on the Leaguers' own presentation of their movement as the active intervention of divine providence to save France.[18]

Such an analysis has its flaws, however, in drawing sharp divisions on the basis of polemical creations. There are further implications too, for our understanding of how the political thought of this era develops in response to the crisis of the religious wars. In emphasising the 'modern' aspect of the Early Modern, for example, it has been suggested that a new 'art' of government, understood in Foucauldian terms, emerged in this era.[19] Here a distinctive break is established between the medieval era and the Early Modern: a difference between the medieval concept of *regimen*, meaning government as a primarily moral instrument of the church, directing men towards their spiritual end through political institutions, and a new, 'pragmatic', art of government involving the reconciliation of diverse interests in society and conserving the constitution.[20] In such a formulation, the conventional view of the '*politique*' figure, confessionally neutral and politically astute, acting in the name of the well-being of the commonwealth can be seen to represent what has been characterised as the Machiavellian 'pragmatism' of the late sixteenth century. Here, Machiavelli is ascribed the role of a primary 'agent of change in this genealogy of the state' in which the spheres and limitations to sovereign power are analysed without any necessary reference to the role of salvation in political life.[21] On the one hand, there is good reason for this: Machiavelli abandoned conventional

---

[16] Crouzet, 'Henri IV, King of Reason?' 73–106.
[17] *Lettre missive aux Parisians d'un Gentilhomme servituer du Roy* (n.p., 1591); *Le Labyrinthe de la Ligue et les moyens de s'en retirer* (n.p., 1590). Cf. Crouzet, 'Henri IV', 80–1.
[18] Crouzet, *Guerriers de Dieu*; Crouzet, 'La représentation du temps à l'époque de la Ligue'.
[19] Senellart, *Les arts du gouverner*.   [20] Ibid.   [21] Senellart, *Les arts du gouverner*, 15, cf. 211–41.

scholastic ideas when he removed natural and divine law from his analysis, and in doing so shifted the emphasis onto the prince's ownership of his state.[22] There is no question that Machiavelli's ideas did have an enormous impact on intellectual life in Europe in this era. However, that influence can be overestimated and easily generalised. It is just as important to acknowledge the caricatured role of 'bogey-man' that Machiavelli played in polemical writings, where he is treated as an architect of political atheism.[23]

There are two deeper issues here. The first is the problem of carving off the Early Modern from the medieval too sharply. The lines between the medieval and the Early Modern are not deep in intellectual terms, especially considering how many of the same sources and techniques of argument remain in place and when the dominant intellectual traditions were constructed on the foundations of classical antiquity, medieval jurisprudence and theology.[24] Scholars have clarified that humanism and scholasticism should not be treated uncritically, or in terms of one replacing the other.[25] The frameworks of analysis and modes of understanding associated with the medieval university system, and those associated with the *studia humanitatis* worked in parallel, often overlapping with one another. In the writings of the Leaguers and their hostile contemporaries we see this overlapping very clearly in action.

The second issue with identifying a 'new' art of government in this era is the equation of 'modern' with the notion of the secular state. A state-centric approach to the political thought of this period tends to embrace Machiavelli's ideas as a form of secularism that contributes to a modern concept of the state.[26] This was, until relatively recently, especially manifest in 'reason of state' discourse, the theory of politics which promoted the primacy of political life and as such is often associated with a detachment from moral and legal considerations. Christian morality in particular has been seen to be absent from discussions of reason of state, having 'no place' in politics.[27] As a way of calculating the best ways to preserve 'the state' this

---

[22] Skinner, *Foundations*, I, 180–6; cf. Skinner, 'From the state of princes to the person of the state', *Visions*, II.

[23] As noted in Kelley, 'Murd'rous Machiavel in France'. See also Anglo, *Machiavelli: The First Century*; Beame, 'The Use and Abuse of Machiavelli'; Cardascia, 'Machiavel et Jean Bodin'; Chérel, *La Pensée de Machiavel en France*; Battista, 'Direzioni di ricerca per una storia di Machiavelli in Francia'. Cf. Birely, *The Counter-Reformation Prince*.

[24] Skinner, *Foundations*.

[25] Skinner, *Foundations*, 49–68; Brett, 'Scholastic Political Thought' in *Rethinking the Foundations*; Garnett, 'Scholastic Thought in Humanist Guise'; Burns, 'Scholasticism: Survival and Revival' in *The Cambridge History of Political Thought*, 132–58.

[26] Senellart, *Les arts du gouverner*; 'La technisation de la Politique au début des Temps Modernes'; 'Machiavel à l'épreuve de la "gouvernamentalité"'.

[27] Viroli, *From Politics to Reason of State*, 287–88.

kind of reasoning and its fusion of scepticism and stoicism might look to be at odds with a Catholic worldview. This particular scholarly narrative of the transition from republics to states excludes forms of reasoning that endeavour to reconcile grace and nature. More recently, however, the extent of Catholic engagement with reason-of-state thinking has been very thoroughly established, particularly in the Jesuit and French contexts.[28] In the Jesuit case, the resources of Machiavelli and, increasingly, of Tacitus have been shown to be foundational in the society's response to the secularising challenge of reason of state.[29] In this context, the field of heresy becomes the ground of action, and the secular ruler charged with the responsibility of eradicating heresy.[30] It has also been argued that Catholic reason of state goes on to play a foundational role in the 'absolutist' discourse of the seventeenth century.[31] A gap remains, however, which this chapter seeks to address.

Attempts to define the role of the *politique,* visually and textually, in this period are demonstrative of an attempt to bring clarity to the 'correct' relationship between the art of government and religion, in which politics and civil reasoning were conceived as an activity promoting the Christian common good. The language and imagery of the *politique* played a central role in the circular debates about who was on the 'right' side of the civil wars, and who truly embodied the spirit of France. The new language of the *politique* that emerges in this era can lead to an expectation that the political debates such figures involved themselves in were also 'new'. However, close examination proves that the important point identified by Baumgartner in the 1970s in relationship to the League also applies to the *politiques*, that is, that the questions that had dogged the medieval era about the correct relationship between the temporal and spiritual spheres remained very much in place in the religious wars.

The artificial antithesis between Leaguer and *politique* dissolves when considering the extent to which they were on common ground, and using common resources, to come to their different points of view as to the relationship between temporal and spiritual ends. Such an approach demonstrates the extent to which the League polemics were embedded within sixteenth-century intellectual discussions of the art of government, and not simply reacting against them. The difference between the two positions depends not so much on their respective attitudes to good government, but

---

[28] As discussed in Racaut, 'Reason of State'.   [29] Höpfl, *Jesuit Political Thought.*   [30] Ibid.
[31] A path explored in Keohane, *Philosophy and the State in France.* See also Church, *Constitutional Thought*, and Richard Tuck, *Philosophy and Government.*

on the principles underpinning that understanding. From these stem the Leaguers' commitments to resistance as a form of obedience to God, and the *politique* commitment to obedience to Henri IV, framed in similar terms.

The frameworks of the state, and of 'reason of state' are too restrictive to frame the analysis of this chapter: the source material under consideration here requires an analysis of the relationship between the church and the commonwealth, considering bonds of association which are either unrelated to, or transcend, the state.[32] Whilst religion has been firmly 'put back into' the wars of religion in the context of wider scholarship, in the framework of political thought and intellectual history, this kind of approach remains a very current concern.[33] The recognition that religious conflicts of this era, and accompanying theological debates and sermonising, are the formational forces in the development of the concept of the Christian commonwealth and shifting concepts of the state is now emerging as a focus of scholarship.[34] Here the Leaguers were making important inroads in so far as they focussed on the Roman concept of *salus populi* in a dual sense: as referring to civil and spiritual well-being. They also resurrected and sustained debates as to the nature of the common good and the notion of communal fraternity, questions they held in common with their Calvinist foes.[35] In doing so, they sought to reconcile political realism with the political idealism that was a product of their Catholicism.

'In the Midst of the Dance': The Problem of Politics

In Pierre de L'Estoile's *Les Belles Figures et Drolleries de la Ligue*, the collection of pamphlets and images he saved from the Parisian bonfires in 1594, there is an image and description of the archetypal '*politique*' produced anonymously on the part of the League.[36] The image was designed to slander the figure of the *politique,* associated with someone who placed the importance of temporal, political, public affairs over the needs of spiritual life, corrupted by ambition, embodying vice. The 'portrait and description of a contemporary *politique*' (*Le Pourtraict et description d'un Politique de ce temps*) preserved in L'Estoile's *Belles Figures* offers one of the most striking condemnations of that figure in the polemics of

---

[32] Cf. Figgis, *From Gerson to Grotius*, 189.
[33] See Holt, 'Putting Religion Back into the Wars of Religion' and Heller, 'A Reply to Mack P. Holt'.
[34] Brett, *Changes of State.*   [35] Mesnard, *Philosophie Politique*, 666–7.
[36] l'Estoile, 'Le Pourtraict et description d'un Politique de ce temps' in *Les Belles Figures et Drolleries de la Ligue*.

the era. It is an image filled with curious symbolism, accompanied by some poetry, and – like many of the *placards* that L'Estoile had chosen to preserve – it is anonymous and undated.[37]

The central figure is a pagan image of a siren with the hair of Medusa, a double reference to feminine fatality, surrounded by scenes laden with symbolism. There is a poem underneath the image, which explains some of its curiosities: the presence of the turbans in the foreground, and the 'small and great gods' in the background, the foreboding cloud above the siren-Medusa, all represent the vanity of the *politique* and its imminent downfall and judgement in the eyes of God. The trumpet in the siren's hand represents the voice of sovereignty being held in contempt; the full amphora symbolising excess; on her bloody hands the blood of the people; the golden belt tying her to the tree a sign of her greed. The image itself tells the viewer even more than the poem: The siren-Medusa is bound to a tree in an inversion of Odysseus' attempt to avoid the terrible draw of the siren voices by lashing himself to the mast of his ship. The tree itself is destroyed, possibly by lightning from the cloud, and as such is a sign of infertility, perhaps matched by her twisted tails. And then there are the arresting scenes around her: A boar investigating another's dung; the forlorn figure of an impotent, beaten king with his hands bound, surrounded by toads, the symbols of Clovis; the naked children playing with bubbles – symbols of mortality, a reference compounded by the presence of their apparently dead companion. Violence, lust, death, infertility, vanity are the themes of this dark image. And there is even more violence embedded in the message to the viewer: as Perseus decapitated Medusa, the League must decapitate the *politique*.

This uncompromising representation of the *politique* is reinforced in other League texts. The *Description du Politique de nostre temps* (1588, repr. 1591) distinguished between the origin of the '*politique*' as a name of honour and its current deviated form, urging the king to 'send the Huguenots to mass', and the *Exhortation aux vrays et entiers Catholicques* (1588) emphasised the distinction between 'true' and 'false' Catholics. The *Discours sur les calomnies imposees, aux Princes & Seigneurs Catholiques, par les Politiques de nostre temps* (1588) reiterated the same theme. In *Les cruautez execrables commises par les Heretiques, contre les Catholiques de la ville de Nyort en Poictou* (1589), the author decried the 'gangrenous' effects of heresy in France and likened the '*politique*' Catholics who supported the Huguenots to chameleons: untrustworthy

---

[37] On the 'baroque' nature of this image, see Papin, 'Duplicité et traîtrise', 7–8.

and changeable.[38] Likewise the *Coppie d'une lettre escripte par un Catholique à un Politique* (1591), in the course of defending Gregory XIII's excommunication of Henri de Navarre, delivered a categorical verdict on those who referred to themselves 'simply' as *politiques*, as in fact nothing more than heretics and schismatics, hostile to the Gallican church.[39] Jean Pigenat pursued a similar line of argument in his *l'Aveuglement et grande inconsideration des Politiques* (1592). Others, as in *L'Arpocratie, ou Rabais du caquet des Politiques & Jebusiens de notre âge* (1589), took the view that *politiques* were either self-serving and only loyal to kings insofar as they received financial or other temporal rewards, or heretics.

At one level, therefore, the language of the *politique* played a significant polemical role in slandering the other side. However, it is also indicative of a deeper, more theoretical and Augustinian problem at the heart of French politics: if politics was corruptive, how could it provide a solution to the civil wars? The fact that nearly everyone seemed to agree that ambition, corruption and falsehood was the plague of French politics, did not preclude the broad consensus that the resolution to these problems could be found in political science itself, a discipline that needed to be established as having a uniquely important intellectual status. As Louis Le Roy had remarked in his edition of *Les Politiques d'Aristote* (1568), of all the disciplines politics was the most important, necessary and beneficial to everyone, yet for some reason it had 'fallen behind' the others.[40] There was a widespread recognition that the science of politics and government needed to be re-evaluated in this era, when France was simultaneously being condemned by contemporaries as a lost country, and intellectual coherence had been sacrificed to civil disorder.[41] In this context, Louis Le Roy defined the 'dignity and utility' of politics (*la politique*) as residing in its ability to instruct on how to govern humans according to the nature of countries and peoples, as well as according to the times.[42]

Discussions as to the nature of the common good, or *bien public*, of the political community as a whole in this period of French history were central to this question of identifying the correct form of political

---

[38] *Les cruautez execrables*, 5. A pamphlet written in response to Henri de Navarre's forces capturing Niort on 28 December 1588, a siege described in Cayet, *Chronologie Novenaire*, 114–16; De Thou, *Histoire Universelle*, 10, 493–6; d'Aubigné, *Histoire Universelle*, 3, 154–8.

[39] *Coppie d'une lettres escripte par un Catholique à un Politique*.

[40] Le Roy, *Les Politiques d'Aristote*, aiii^r-aiv^v.

[41] On the notion of France as a 'lost' country, see Du Bellay's *Les Regrets*. Cf. Mackenzie, *The Poetry of Place*.

[42] Le Roy, *De l'origine, antiquité, progrès, excellence et utilité de l'art politique*, fol. 8r.

knowledge. This question remained largely defined by the Aristotelian tradition, and Aristotle's observation in Book One of *Politics* that every community is constituted for a good purpose.[43] In his commentary on Aristotle's *Politics*, first published in 1568, Louis Le Roy made note of the significance of the notion that communities, or societies, were defined by their collective consent as to the nature of the common good.[44] He further identified a distinction between those communities which aimed only at the 'appearance' of good, and those which aimed at a 'true' good. The former were defined by mercantile ambitions: the amassing of wealth and a life of pleasure. The latter were defined by honesty, and so they were communities of the wise and the knowledgeable. In such communities, law and order were found. But amongst those which only pretended to aim for the common good, the values of robbers and ruffians were transcendent, in which resistance to princes and the state – in short, total civil disorder – could be justified in the name of a false good.[45] There is no small hint of Augustinianism here in Le Roy's royalist treatment of the Aristotelian texts: kingdoms without justice being nothing more than the domain of robbers.[46]

In the League context, this Aristotelian–Augustinian construction of the *bien public*, directed against both Huguenots and those they labelled *politiques*, is very well expressed in *De la puissance des roys*. Published after the assassination of Henri III, the work opposed Henri de Navarre's right to rule – his 'usurpation' of the 'title and quality of the kings of France' – on the grounds of his heresy. In its preamble are included a number of poems and a sonnet, noted previously, which described the nature of the *politique* as Machiavellian.[47] Along with this sonnet, the author included poetry by Joachim du Bellay and Pierre de Ronsard which praised the Guise family, 'born to save the Catholic religion', and condemned the heresy of Henri de Navarre. In this treatise, the author modified the analysis of the origins of politics in force and violence, associating this doctrine with the ideas of Machiavelli and Jean Bodin, and instead located the beginnings of society

---

[43] Aristotle, *Politics*, 1252a1.
[44] Le Roy, *Les Politiques d'Aristote*, 4. For a recent analysis of the reception of Aristotle's *Politics* in France, see Ingrid De Smet, 'Philosophy for Princes'. On the medieval tradition, see Dunbabin, 'Aristotle's Politics: Reception and Interpretation', 723–37.
[45] Ibid. On the *bien public* in the French context, see Collins, 'La guerre de la ligue et le bien public'; Collins, *The State in Early Modern France*, 2nd ed., xxii–xxiii; Collins, *La monarchie republicaine*, 34–8; Greengrass, *Governing Passions*, 66–122. For a history of the medieval background to the concept of the common good, see Kempshall, *The Common Good in Late Medieval Political Thought*.
[46] Augustine, *De Civitate Dei*, IV.iv.
[47] 'Autre sonet touchant la nature du Politique' in *De la puissance des roys*, preface, n.p.

in the Christian values of charity, friendship, justice and virtue. These values, the author argued, were natural, and drove men to seek the best kind of order for their society embodied in the three 'best' constitutions described in Aristotle's *Politics*. At the end of all these types of constitution lies public well-being and utility, in other words, the common good.[48] The clear implication here, as in Le Roy's works, is that there is a distinction to be drawn between communities which pursue what is considered useful (*bonum utile*) to the community to the expense of the good of the community, and those which pursue the good of the community (*bonum commune/bien public*) in the context of Christian values, as well as the goals of peace and security which can define the *bonum utile*.[49]

Working within an Aristotelian framework, the author of *De la puissance des roys* commented closely on Bodin's *Six Livres de la République* (1576). In particular, the author took issue with Bodin's concept of seigneurial monarchy, to argue in contrast to Bodin that the source of sovereign power in the French monarchy was the people, and so tyranny could and must be resisted. Locating the cohesion of human society in religious faith, conserved by the Estates General, the author argued that a prince who desecrated a legitimate assembly of the Estates, attacked society itself.[50] Further to this, he violated the law of peoples (*ius gentium*) by imposing servitude on his people. In short: 'he who desecrates the Estates, desecrates the establishment of the Kingdom and its power, which is from God'.[51] At the heart of *De la puissance des roys* lies the notion of natural, human society bound together by faith. The political life of this community is expressed in the sovereign power of the people, given from God and embodied in the Estates General, and a conception of kingship as a guardianship: a duty to protect and preserve the people and their laws in a state of liberty.

Men, the author argued, are by nature equal, and so it is impossible to persuade them to obey anyone, unless royal power is fortified by a higher

---

[48] *De la puissance des roys*, 8–9: 'Et la fin de toutes ces trois sortes d'estats, estoit le bien et l'utilité du public'.

[49] Tierney, 'Aristotle, Aquinas and the Ideal Constitution' examines the ways in which Aquinas manipulated Aristotle's ideal, mixed, constitutional framework to fit into that of monarchy, thereby establishing the scholastic foundations of an argument that would continue to frame Early Modern thinking.

[50] *De la puissance des roys*, 49–50: 'Puis que la foy est le lien qui estreint la societé humaine, les Etats, le moyen pour la conserver: le Prince qui viole la foy aux Estats, rompt non seulement ce lien, mais encore la societé mesme'.

[51] Ibid., 52: 'doncques celuy qui viole les Estats, viole l'establissement du Royaume et la puissance qui est de Dieu'.

authority, which is that of God.[52] From this perspective, the author then distinguished the significance of the 'true' religion: all religion is necessary for the establishment of a state, but 'true' religion even more so. Herein lies the prince's duty: to protect the souls of his subjects through the true knowledge and fear of God, and the bond of humans: the laws.[53] To this end, all true opinions regarding the sacred, the beautiful, the just, the good, the honest tend: a life lived in peace, friendship and concord. From this, the author concludes, the prince's duty is to exterminate evil, injustice, impiety and any ill-feeling towards religion. Any change of religion therefore cannot be contemplated. And since the King is created for the well-being of his people, it is possible to suggest that he is predominantly created for the protection of their eternal well-being rather than for their temporal, perishable, well-being.[54] The office of a Christian and Catholic king is to protect the Catholic faith, and doctrine of the Trinity, from heresy.[55]

What follows from this is a condemnation of the idea of liberty of conscience: the kings of France do not emulate Julian the Apostate, but the path of Constantine.[56] Liberty of conscience would, the author argues, transform the liberty of the true religion into impiety and atheism, and so lead to servitude and vice, of which the German principalities and the Ottoman empire are provided as examples.[57] A heretic prince, the author argues, cannot possibly defend the true religion, and so the rule of Henri de Navarre is an intolerable proposal. *De la puissance des roys* demonstrates the nature of the common good as it was perceived by scholars in the League: a protection of the spiritual and civil well-being of the people of France.

De la puissance des roys moves almost seamlessly from the civil duties of a ruler to the spiritual, but this was, in fact, a very complex relationship which will be explored in more detail in the next chapters: to argue that a political society was natural – built on the Aristotelian notion that man was 'by nature' a political animal, and through his rationality would seek to aim at the common good. However, as any French intellectual knew, ever

---

[52] *De la puissance des roys*, 60–1: '*Les hommes estans par la nature egaux, il est impossible que vous persuadiez a l'un d'obeir à l'autre, si vous ne fortifiez la puissance Royale d'une authorité plus qu'humaine, qui est celle de Dieu*'. The author's reference here is Plato, on the idea that fear of the divine is the basis of all law.

[53] Ibid., 61. He continues to use Plato as a reference here: '*C'est ce que disoit Platon, que le Prince est tenu de procurer que la partie immortelle et divine de ses subiects, qui est l'ame, soit arrestée des liens divins, c'est à scavoir de la vraye cognoissance et crainte de Dieu : et la partie animale des liens humains, c'est-à-dire des lois*'.

[54] Ibid., 62: '*Aussi s'il est veritable ce que nous avons cy devant prouvé, que le Roy est crée pour le bien du peuple, il faut estimer qu'il est plustost crée pour le bien eternel d'iceluy, que pour le temporal et perissable.*'

[55] *De la puissance des roys*, 63.   [56] Cf. Montaigne, *Essais*, II.XIX.

[57] *De la puissance des roys*, 64–6.

since the reception of Aristotle's texts in the West in the thirteenth century, this notion of natural politics had failed to sit easily with the doctrines of the church fathers on original sin. This is especially the case within the Thomist tradition, which grappled intensively with the relationship between natural and divine law to resolve the question of how political life could be a good in the context of a fallen world.[58] The figure of the Christian king in the French context – the *Roi Très Chrétien* – was key to resolving the question of how to mediate between the civil and spiritual ends for man.[59]

The political Augustinianism of the Leaguers enabled them to bind their Catholicism to the conventions of an Aristotelian framework. Government could be rooted in sin, as the French theologian Jean Gerson had argued in his *De Ecclesiastica Potestate* (1417), but this did not preclude an acceptance of such Aristotelian premises as the idea of the mixed community as the best form of constitution.[60] In the context of the wars of religion, such an approach is evident in the desire to resolve the question of the relationship between the temporal and spiritual spheres: for the Leaguers, this meant that the priesthood played a significant role in enabling the civil community to achieve the best kind of good possible in a fallen world, whilst simultaneously defending the Gallican liberties against encroachment from royal and papal powers. Correspondingly, we see in their writing a dependence on Augustinian thinking that was an important feature of their response to the so-called *politiques*.[61]

In *De la puissance des roys*, the author quoted Augustine to the effect that if a prince commanded anything against the society of the city, no one was bound to obey him; princes had no authority from God to ruin and destroy their people.[62] In the *Remontrance du clergé de France* (1585) the Leaguer bishop of Saint-Brieuc, Nicolas Langelier, used Augustine to argue that Christian kings were happier than infidel rulers, and an 'instrument' of God, precisely because they participated in the heavenly city.[63] As Louis Dorléans argued, religion was not a Scylla or Charybdis to be avoided by the ship of state, but a harbour in which to shelter.[64] Elsewhere, he quoted Augustine to support the view that 'true' Frenchmen defend their faith.[65] Even more revealing, are the views of René Choppin in his *De Sacra Politia*

---

[58] There is a substantial scholarship on this question, and I am especially indebted to Brett, 'Scholastic Political Thought'; Markus, *Saeculum*, 211–30.

[59] Krynen, *L'empire du roi*.   [60] Cf. Salmon, 'France', 458–97.

[61] On 'political Augustinianism', see Arquillière, *l'augustinisme politique*.

[62] *De la puissances des roys*, 24. Notably, he also refers here to Huguenot writings, saying they have been making that point for the last thirty years.

[63] Langelier, 'Remontrance du clergé de France', Goulart, *Mémoires*, I, 247–70.

[64] Dorléans, *Banquet*, 15.   [65] Dorléans, *Plaidoyé des gens du roy faict en parlement*, 44.

(first published in 1577), written before he joined the League, on the relationship between royal and ecclesiastical power:

> Thus, as in the City of God, the magistracy is constituted of the Royal and Ecclesiastical [powers], which associate and conjoin with one another in concert and harmony, just as if they were composed of diverse tones, with a harmony of different voices, and from which follows a temperate Commonwealth, in which the conservation and assurance of the common good of the Kingdom consists.[66]

Citing, amongst other resources, the letters of Augustine and Aristotle's *Rhetoric*, Choppin argued that ecclesiastical and royal powers related to each other like rhetoric and dialectic, both lying within the knowledge of all people, and not belonging to any separately defined science.[67]

The conventions of medieval political thought, therefore, took the Leaguers a long way in establishing their case against Henri III and Henri IV. The more immediate problem the Leaguers were grappling with was, however, the problem of politics when it was separated from the 'true' church and, further to this, separated from a clearly defined and orthodox Christian, Catholic morality. They were not alone in this. Michel de Montaigne described the political climate of this era as troubled by a 'new depravity' wherein 'men baptized public vices with new milder names to excuse them, adulterating and softening their true titles'. He argued that the Reformation was an innovation, which had so 'dislocated and dissolved' the 'unity and contexture of this monarchy' that affiliation to any one particular political movement could not evade the taint of corruption. No one escaped Montaigne's condemnation, even when he observed that those on the 'best' side of the religious wars were the ones who sought to protect the ancient religion and government (*la police ancienne*) of France. He seemed to acknowledge that this boundary between the 'best' and 'worst' in the religious wars was flimsy, if not artificial.[68] In *'De la solitude'*, Montaigne looked to be arguing that no one involved in politics, 'in the midst of the dance' as he put it, could claim to be seeking to preserve the interests of the public good:

> Let them cudgel their conscience and say whether . . . the titles, the offices, and the hustle and bustle of the world are not sought out to gain private

[66] Choppin, *De Sacra Politia*, 4–5: *'Ita ergo Magistratum utrumque constituimus in hac Civitate Dei, Pontificium ac Regium, veluti concentum quendam ex distinctis collectum sonis, et dissimilium alioqui vocum moderatione eam Republicam Moderationem retinentem, in cuius conservatione salus quoque Regni posita est'.*
[67] Aristotle, *On Rhetoric*, 1354a.
[68] Montaigne, *Essais*, II.19, 706–710. All translations are from Montaigne, *Complete Works*, unless otherwise cited.

profit from the public. The evil means men use in our day to push
themselves show clearly that the end is not worth much.[69]

In '*De la vanité*', he makes his views on the state of France even clearer:

> I perceive that in the strife that is tearing France to pieces and dividing us
> into factions, each man labours to defend his cause – but even the best of
> them resort to dissimulation and lying. Whoever would write about them
> roundly would write about them rashly and harmfully. The justest party is
> still a member of a worm-eaten and maggoty body.[70]

The problem Montaigne addressed was partly that of the dangers of
holding public office, and the corroding effect of ambition on
a magistrate's moral compass, which was a widespread concern in the
wars of religion in terms both of ecclesiastical and civil office; the demands
of necessity had eclipsed the demands of honesty.[71] The cornerstones of
conventional humanist political writing, including notions of the common
good, the importance of good advice and council, the emphasis on duty in
public life, were under threat of dissolving in the context of this wholesale
loss of virtue that Montaigne described. Montaigne's response to the
religious wars was to withdraw and reject the active political life of
a citizen in favour of the contemplative, whilst retaining a fascination
with contemporary politics.[72]

As scholars such as Montaigne sought mental refuge from the chaos of
the civil wars, the resources of stoic philosophy came to the fore. In 1588,
Louis Le Caron published his *De la tranquillité de l'esprit*, which laid out an
argument for the achievement of peace through submission to the king's
authority, using Senecan ideas to underpin a theory of political
obedience.[73] The language of consolation also started to replace the language of conversion in the writings of French Huguenots, as Calvin's, and
subsequently Théodore de Bèze's plans to convert France became compromised and weakened, and politics was increasingly seen by some as
a false, lost solution.[74] In *De la constance*, written during the siege of Paris
in 1590, Guillaume Du Vair reflected on the folly of attempting to influence the course of history and divine providence. This application of stoic
prudence to the French kingdom provided a further resource for theorists

[69] Montaigne, *Essais*, I.39, 211.   [70] Montaigne, *Essais*, III.9, 924.
[71] Montaigne, *Essais*, III.1, 726–40.
[72] Fontana, *Montaigne's Politics*. Cf. Keohane, *Philosophy and the State*, 92–118; Skinner, *Foundations*, I,
   216–21.
[73] Le Caron, *De la tranquillité de l'esprit* and cf. his *De l'obeissance deue au Prince*. Lipsius' *De
   Constantia* was particularly influential, cf. Oestreich, *Neostoicism and the Early Modern State*.
[74] See, for example, Castellion, *Conseil à la France désolée*.

of royalism: liberty consisted in conformity to a system of domination.[75] The search for the common good became increasingly associated with the restoration of order and stability through the coercive force of royal rule.

In the context of these debates, the Leaguers' answer might be seen to be less cerebral and more dynamic: their crusading doctrine of resistance was one of political action, a call to arms on the basis of obedience to natural, divine and eternal laws. Opponents of the League sought consolation in an argument for peace instead of rebellion, however most Leaguers found the opposite in stoicism. This is demonstrated in a pamphlet published in 1589 shortly before Henri III's assassination: *La Consolation de tous fidelles catholiques, qui sont affligez et persecutez par la tyrannie des ennemis de la religion catholique apostolique, et romaine.* Instead of advocating for a retirement from worldly affairs, some League thinkers used the Senecanism of the late French Renaissance in support of their justification for taking up arms, just as the Calvinists did after 1572 (notwithstanding Calvin's own scepticism towards the high value stoicism placed on human wisdom). Jean Boucher, for example, drew on Cicero's *De Officiis* to establish an authority for the idea that the political community was held together by justice, overseen by God, but it also perpetuated a connection between stoic ideas and the notion of legitimate assassination: the thought that a divinely inspired individual, or collectivity, might be able to save a political community from tyranny, by virtue of God's grace.

Leaguers did not make their argument for political action without recognition of the problem of moral corruption in the political sphere. Leaguer theologians such as Nicolas Langelier, argued that the corruption of political life in the present age could only be cured by the Roman church, in contrast to arguments such as Le Caron's which relied on a doctrine of Christian-Stoic obedience to kings.[76] In his address to the king of 1585, Langelier drew on writings of the early church fathers, and the medieval crusades, to argue for a restoration of a state wherein the clergy advised kings and had powers to intervene in political life. This view was not purely the preserve of the clergy in the *Sainte Union*; lawyers and magistrates who took up their pen in the name of the League also argued that political life could not be restored to its primitive, pristine state without the aid of the Roman church. Antoine Hotman, for example, argued that the well-being of France (*le bien de la France*), resting on the

[75] Crouzet, 'Henri IV', 82.
[76] Langelier, 'Remontrance du clergé de France'; Goulart, *Mémoires*, I, 247–70.

restoration of ancient franchises and liberties, was directly connected to the well-being of the Christian religion.[77] The irreverence and irreligion involved in the toleration of heresy had, he argued, created a public scandal.

When politics was deemed to be so thoroughly corrupted, the Leaguer answer was to restore virtue through the church, and so to rely on a substantial antique and medieval intellectual bedrock in making that claim. And yet it was not simply the case that they all thought that the civil commonwealth should be entirely absorbed by the spiritual; their Augustinianism was more complex and varied than this, as were their views on papal authority.[78] It is also clear that new answers to old problems were required. A contextual and particularly French answer was needed to the question of where and how to locate the common good: in France's ancient laws, its religion and in the nature of its people.[79] When figures like Montaigne were condemning political life and withdrawing from it, others were charging into its midst to bring about resolution. The Leaguers offered one set of solutions, but there were others who tried to find alternative paths to peace.

In the *Exhortation a la Sainte Union des Catholiques* (1589), a savage indictment of Henri III after his assassination of the Guise brothers, the anonymous League author opened the piece by identifying himself with the 'true Frenchman', the 'true Christian', and 'the true *politique*' which he distinguished from the *politique* who 'only serves God as a form of policy (*police*)'.[80] The attempts within the League to define a 'true', versus a 'false', *politique* depended on the operation of the right form of reasoning: *la prudence civile*. Here the Leaguers could draw on French history as a depository of experiences and observations acting as a guide to future political action, eloquently described in Guillaume Budé's *De l'institution du Prince* (1516) and his discussion on *la prudence civile*, and in Jean Bodin's *Methodus*, where politics is treated as subset of history. The trick, for the

---

[77] Hotman, *Traité des Libertez de l'Eglise Gallicane*, fol. 1r–1v. The first edition of this treatise was 1588, and a second published in 1594. The 1608 BNF copy has '*selon la ligue*' scrawled over the title page, and Lanier de l'Effretier may have been a co-author. The text is also known as '*Traictez des droicts Ecclesiastiques*', published in a compilation in 1612. Hotman is little known in scholarship, over-shadowed by his more famous brother, and better-known lawyers in the French *parlement*. Of all his works, his treatise 'Deux paradoxes de l'amitié et d'avarice', published in the *Opuscules francoises des Hotmans* (Paris, 1616), 113–83, has received the most attention. See particularly Keohane, *Philosophy and the State in France*, 162–3; Patterson, *Representing Avarice*.

[78] A point also observed by Renoux-Zagamé, *De Droit de Dieu*, 270–93.

[79] This does not, as will be shown, preclude appeals to the universal validity of such ideas on the basis of comparative studies of the histories of different nations, and an appeal to *ius gentium*.

[80] 'Exhortation' in Goulart, *Mémoires*, III, 511.

Leaguers, was to be able to make use of both this practical wisdom *and* the more theoretical concept of prudence drawn from natural and divine law. So, where scholars have distinguished between a 'pragmatic' art of government, grounded in history and drawn from Machiavelli, and a medieval concept of *regimen* that was highly theoretical, the Leaguers and *politiques* were in fact attempting to do both.[81]

Redefining the *Politique*

Although it is perfectly persuasive to think of the *politiques* as purely a terrible figment of Leaguer imagination, for contemporaries the form took flesh in one particular figure, that of Pierre de Belloy, a lawyer whose *Apologie Catholique* (1585) sought to undermine the League at every turn. Jean Boucher thought of him as representing all that was evil and atheistic in Machiavelli's works.[82] He was widely known to the Leaguers as Navarre's 'miserable lawyer' and was regularly a named '*politique*' target.[83]

Belloy's background was a legal one, he trained as a civil lawyer in Toulouse and in the 1570s joined the circle of Henri de Montmorency. He became an envoy to Henri III in 1574 and by the early 1580s was based in Paris, producing legal commentaries and a treatise on the law of succession in the kingdom of Portugal, dedicated to Catherine de Medici. In the 1580s, he had two narrow scrapes with the League: he was nearly executed in 1586 when he was accused by the Guise family of authoring an incendiary pamphlet against the reception of the decrees of the Council of Trent. On the assassination of the Guise brothers by Henri III in 1588, he was imprisoned in the Bastille for several years before managing an escape. Once Henri IV had regained control of his kingdom, he rewarded Belloy for his loyalty with the position of *avocat général* of the Toulouse *parlement* after 1594, a position he kept until 1609, dying three years later.[84]

Belloy's argumentative techniques were particularly effective in their characterisation of the Leaguers as 'bad' Frenchmen: seeking to sell their country to Spain, and to unleash the fullness of papal power over the Gallican church. In response, the Leaguers characterised him as a false

---

[81] See Senellart, *Les arts du gouverner.*   [82] Boucher, *De Justa Abdicatione*, fol. 184r–v.
[83] [Attrib. Le Breton], *Remonstrance*; 'l'Arpocratie' in Goulart, *Mémoires*, IV, 97–115. *Description du Politique de nostre temps.* Scholarship on Belloy remains limited. His *De l'authorité du roy* is briefly discussed in Jouanna, *Le pouvoir absolu*, 291–5, which she usefully suggests being read in conjunction with Budé's *De l'Institution du Prince.* Zwierlein, *Political Thought of the League* explores the Bellarmine–Belloy controversy. Another recent discussion of Belloy's work is Egio, 'Pierre de Belloy'. Cf. Gagne, 'Pierre de Belloy'; Martin, 'Pierre de Beloy'.
[84] For Belloy's biography see *Mémoires de l'Académie Impériale de Sciences*, 5, 59–106.

politique. In the *Description du Politique de nostre temps* (1588), which
purported to be written by a 'French gentleman', Belloy is singled out as
a supporter of heretics and one who embodied the fox-like, Machiavellian
spirit.[85] Louis Dorléans, who hated Belloy, was certainly the author of this
text; he was one of Belloy's most outspoken critics, and the body of the text
of the *Description* reappears in Dorléans' dialogue, the *Banquet et
Apresdinee* (1594), as poetry in the mouths of his characters as they
denounce the *politiques* and the false conversion of Henri de Navarre.[86]
In the confrontation between Dorléans and Belloy, it is the spirit of the
true and 'natural' Frenchman that is at stake as much as the identification
of a true *politique.*

In the course of wrangling with Belloy's arguments, Dorléans honed his
own perspective on the problem presented by the Catholic and Huguenot
politiques. In a speech he delivered before the Paris *parlement* in 1592,
Dorléans accused them of

> having nothing of the values and the primitive virtue of the ancient and truly
> natural Frenchmen, those who audaciously usurp the name of Catholic,
> adorned with the name Christian, who claim to be good Frenchmen, and
> [yet] are those who wage open war against the Catholic Church and the
> Christian Religion, and the true piety of the French? Certainly when we
> read their books, when we hear their speeches, when we see their declar-
> ations, when we uncover their ideas, we are reminded of impudent, brazen
> trash from the brothel, adorned in all the finery of prostitutes.[87]

Apart from the evident strength of feeling, what is striking in this description of the *politique,* is the emphasis on the 'primitive' virtues of the
'ancient and truly natural Frenchmen', which underpinned the efforts of
Dorléans to distinguish between 'true' and 'false' *politiques.* Dorléans made
a bold attempt in his *Banquet* to align the nature of the 'true' *politique* with
that of the League: devoted to the connection between Catholicism and the
constitution, and obedient to kings only insofar as they did not break

---

[85] *Description,* 12.
[86] As far as I know, the connection between the *Description du Politique de nostre temps* (Paris, 1588) and
Dorléans's *Banquet* has not been drawn before. It demonstrates the 'cut and paste' nature of much of
the polemic.
[87] Dorléans, *Plaidoyé,* 14: '*n'ayant rien des mœurs et de la vertu ancienne des anciens et vrayement naturelz
François, si est-ce-qu'audacieusement ilz usurpent le nom de Catholicque, se parent de ce nom de
Chrestien, se proclament bons François, eux qui sont la guerre ouverte à l'Eglise Catholicque, et à la
Religion Chrestienne, et à le vraye pieté des François? Certainement quand nous lisons leurs livres, que
nous oyons leurs discours, que nous voyons leur declarations, que nous descouvrons leurs conceptions, il
nous souvient de ces ordures de bordel effrontées et impudentes, qui se parent des atours des femmes de
bien . . .*'

divine and natural laws. In this calculation, the Leaguers were the defenders of the ancient constitution (*l'ancienne police*). Dorléans explained the
link between the *politique* and *la police* in his dialogue, when the character
of the abbot describes the idea of a *politique* Leaguer:

> If we take *police* to mean the constitution of a state, according to which each
> person should live, I conclude that the Leaguer who would live or die in the
> maintenance of this *Police* established in France by our forefathers, and
> preserved by our Kings for over eleven hundred years, is not only a true
> *Politique*, but an honourable and recommendable *Politique*.[88]

The abbot goes on to argue that those who actually go by the name of
politique in contemporary France have corrupted the use of *la police* by
'giving everything to man and nothing to God'.[89] This concern with
temporal goods demonstrated in the *Banquet* indicates that the idea of
government, or *la police,* was a natural extension of the debate about the
politique and the right kind of political prudence required to rescue France
from its current state. The true *politique* from the League perspective was
therefore a defender of the French constitution (i.e. a Catholic monarchy
under the law). This corresponded to Claude de Seyssel's definition of the
French constitution as 'so *politique* that she has entirely alienated from
tyranny'; *politique* could here be synonymous with political liberty as well
as Catholicism, and this is the connection Dorléans was trying to forge.

The attempt to redefine the *politique* as a Leaguer was one line of defence
against the condemnation the movement faced from their opponents. Yet
however much Leaguers like Dorléans would seek to label the 'false' *politique*
as non-French (often describing them as Turkish or Jewish), their opponents
had a far stronger claim to make that they were the ones who were anti-
French, not least because of their dependence on Spanish military support and
the powers of papal excommunication. The definition of the *politique* as the
best kind of citizen, or the educated statesman, in Huguenot and anti-League
texts worked against the League in the same manner: the Leaguers were
presented as attacking their *patrie,* as 'denaturalised' Frenchmen seeking to

---

[88] Dorléans, *Le Banquet*, 20: '*Car si police est la constitution d'un estat, selon laquelle chacun doibt vivre, je
concludes que le Ligueur qui veut vivre & mourir en la manutention de ceste Police establie en France par
nos majeurs, & continuee par nos Roys unze cents ans & plus, est non seulement un vray Politique, mais
un honorable & recommendable Politique*'.

[89] Ibid., 21: '*Car ils se ventent avec cest instrument de Police descavoir bien virer & gouverner les Estats, &
ny entendent rien, pours qu'ils donnent tout aux hommes & rien a Dieu, tout a la terre & rien au Ciel. Ils
nous font des Monarchies composees d'irreligion, d'impieté, de vices & mauvaises mœurs, & bref des
Monarchies de pure terre, des estats qui ne sentent que la terre, fresles compots de terre, & que Dieu
indigné brise en un instant comme ouvrages de terre*'.

sell their country to Spain, and of disguising their ambition with false zealotry.[90] The 'true' *politique* on this account was one who understood the interests of the *patrie* and served the king loyally, and who 'dissected' the questions of government on the basis of divine law *and* political reasoning (*la raison politique*) which established the basis for conserving human society.[91]

The Leaguers were well aware of the nature of this challenge. In his *Apologie pour Jehan Chastel*, published in 1595 after the Jesuit's attempt on Henri IV's life, the now-exiled Jean Boucher wrote a defence of Chastel. He argued that under ordinary circumstances, such an act would rightly be categorised as treasonous. However, in his sacrifice, Chastel had become a true martyr. When judged 'dispassionately', as Boucher put it, from the perspective of the church, the state, all divine and human law, and the fundamental laws of the kingdom, it was clear that Henri IV was an excommunicate, a heretic, a public enemy and a tyrant. Furthermore, true justice was not being exercised in France under such a rule, but instead, Boucher wrote that 'English' (Protestant) justice reigned, and so had established a 'Babylonian brothel' in the heart of French civil institutions.[92] What is noteworthy about Boucher's account in this text, one of the last truly 'Leaguer' publications after the abjuration of Navarre, is his frustration with the way in which the League had been characterised. '*Rassemblence*' was the enemy, he argued: a ruse of the devil which had brought good people to punishment. By this, Boucher was referring to a problem of misinterpretation:

> That which is termed rebellion, is in fact religion; that which is termed treason, is in fact a defence of royal majesty; that which is termed infraction of the law, is in fact the conservation of the law; that which is termed novelty, is in fact that which preserves antiquity; that which is termed sedition, is protection against future harm.[93]

Boucher's presentation of his position encapsulates the problem of the polemic, on all sides, in its distortion of the perceived truth.[94] Polemical language in this era therefore took on an important significance in itself,

---

[90] *Satyre Ménippée*, ed. Martin, 115, 149. That author also referred to the Leaguers as '*François Espagnols*', 62. Cf. Belloy, *Apologie Catholique* for a thoroughgoing attack on the Leaguers 'false' reasoning.

[91] Belloy, *Apologie Catholique*, 2.22, fol. 63r (mis pag.)

[92] Boucher, *Apologie pour Jehan Chastel*, 21–4.

[93] Boucher, *Apologie*, 11: '*Pour le general, en ce qu'on appelle rebellion, ce qui est religion, crime de leze maieste, ce qui est conserver la maieste : infraction de loix, ce qui est conserver les loix : nouvelleté, ce qui est garder l'antiquité : sedition, ce qui est protection, et obviation au mal avenir*'.

[94] Racaut has considered this from the perspective of sincerity versus hypocrisy in Boucher's writings: 'La boutique de malédiction'.

insofar as it helped to frame the ways in which contemporaries perceived the challenges of their own time. At the heart of this challenge sat the figure of Machiavelli: to engage profoundly with the problem of the *politique*, the Leaguers had to work their way around the problems posed by his carica-ture as they clarified their own vision of a Christian commonwealth.

Machiavellism

Jean Boucher argued in *De Justa Abdicatione* that there could be 'no fellowship' with tyrants in a political community; Rossaeus made the same point about heretics.[95] The ideal for these Leaguers was to live in a free political community of Catholics. The classical concept of commu-nity is key here, as a translation of *civitas,* or *koinonia*, referring to notions of fellowship, partnership and communion: the multitude gathering in agreement as to the common good of all.[96] To live a political life required this fellowship, and for a theologian like Boucher that meant fellowship in a Catholic sense. Furthermore, rationality was crucial to this notion of societal bonding. As Rossaeus argued, in what would develop in his text as a strongly Aristotelian vein, the formation of a political community was both a natural and a rational exercise. The idea of a natural community, formed of a fellowship of Catholics, was also a rational political community.[97] Therefore, a distinction between rational and irrational; medieval and 'pragmatic' approaches to the art of government doesn't quite work in distinguishing Leaguers from other Catholic thinkers. Instead, we need to investigate more fundamental questions in their political thought: notably the role of divine law, the concept of *regimen* and the idea of political community. The Leaguer concept of community, built on natural and divine law, was in these respects consciously opposed to Machiavelli's vision of a society in which those laws were absent, and in which religion featured primarily as a prop to political power and to instil loyalty to the *patria*. Machiavelli himself condemned the French for failing to understand statecraft, by giving 'too much power to the church'.[98]

---

[95] Boucher, *De Justa Abdicatione*, 144r, 145r. Cf. Cicero, *De Officiis* III.32.
[96] Aristotle, *Politics*, 1252a1.s
[97] *De Justa Reipublicae Christianae Authoritate*, fol. 1r–v: '*Neminem arbitror aliquando considerasse paulo diligentius hominis originem & conditionem qui non statim adverterit eum a natura ad civilem societatem fuisse factum & ordinatum. Neque hoc viderunt solum excellentes illi Philosophi, Platones, Aristoteles, Theophrasti, Cicerones, qui ingeniorum acumine & altitudine potuerunt in abdita naturae mysteria penetrare, sed alii etiam omnes quicunque; mediocri intelligentia praediti res obvias & communi vitae consuetudine tritas voluerunt attendere'.*
[98] Machiavelli, *The Prince*, 13.

The fortunes of Machiavelli's ideas in France ebbed and flowed: The *Discourses* were deeply influential, even as *The Prince* was rejected for its perceived atheism and doctrine of tyranny.[99] After the events of the summer of 1572, *The Prince* became firmly associated with tyranny. Huguenots blamed Machiavelli for influencing Catherine de Medici in her role in the assassination of the Huguenot leader, Gaspard de Coligny, that precipitated the massacres. The whole process of government was said to have been infected by Machiavellian influence.[100] Huguenots charged Medici with treating *The Prince* like her bible, and using it to instruct her children.[101] Innocent Gentillet wrote an authoritative rejection of Machiavellian principles in his treatise that became known as the *Anti-Machiavel* (1576); it was so influential that in his *Discours Politique et Militaire*, François de la Noue argued that he had once enjoyed reading *The Prince*, but on the wise advice of Gentillet he had come to see the countless errors beneath the façade.[102] What is striking about these Protestant rejections of Machiavelli is that they used him as a tool to appeal to *both* Catholic and Protestant readers, and so to gloss over the effect of confessional division on French political life. The intended effect of treatises which took this approach, such as the *Vindiciae*, or Théodore de Bèze's *De Jure Magistratuum* (1574), was to focus attention on the problem of tyranny instead of the presence of the reformed religion and to construct an argument for popular sovereignty centred on the role of the Estates General. However, the urgency of these anti-Machiavellian wake-up calls did not manage to persuade all Catholic readers sceptical of toleration.

The Leaguer response to Machiavelli, on the other hand, remained focussed on religion, specifically the problem of the absence of religion in political affairs manifest in the figure of the 'false' *politique* who separated religion from the art of governing. The Leaguer theologian and Hebraist Gilbert Génébrard dedicated his translation of the *Histories* of Josephus to Henri III precisely because he considered its central lessons to be a defence against this particular polemical brand which connected Machiavelli to atheism.[103] A pamphlet of 1589,

---

[99] On the fortunes of Machiavelli's texts and their reception, see Anglo, *Machiavelli: The First Century*, particularly Part Two, 'The Rhetoric of Hate', 229–416. See also, Kelley, 'Murd'rous Machiavel in France'; Beame, 'The Use and Abuse of Machiavelli; Chérel, *La Pensée de Machiavel en France*; Battista, 'Direzioni di ricerca per una storia di Machiavelli in Francia'.

[100] *Le Reveille-Matin*, 'Dialogue I', 21, 37, 107.   [101] *Le Tocsain*.

[102] Gentillet, *Discours sur les moyens de bien gouverner*; de la Noue, *Discours Politiques*, 133.

[103] Génébrard, *Histoire de Fl. Josèphe mise en françois*, preface, n.p.

tellingly entitled *l'Atheisme de Henry de Valois*, likewise argued that Henri III drew his lessons on how to rule as well as his atheism from Machiavelli. In a manuscript of 1589 on the deposition of Henri III, Machiavelli is similarly invoked in a conventionally negative sense.[104] Jean Boucher, in typically direct fashion, claimed that Henri III carried around a copy of *The Prince* with him to consult on how best to be evil. Boucher further argued that Henri IV's conversion was nothing but a Machiavellian ruse.[105] In his *Sermons* against Navarre's conversion, he also attacked *The Prince* for promoting the use of dissimulation in matters of religion, and equated Calvinism with Machiavellianism, and the *politiques* with heresy.[106] A further problem presented by Machiavelli, for Boucher, was his response to tyranny. He 'failed to blush' at the tyranny of Cesare Borgia and sought to reduce monarchy to a 'Turkish' tyranny wherein the sovereign was above the laws.[107]

Other Leaguers took a more reflective approach to Machiavelli, focussing their reactions on the origins of political community and the notion of the common good, usually on the basis of a reading of the *Discourses*, rather than *The Prince*, which generally fared better in its French reception. In *De la puissance des roys*, the author's response to Machiavelli further indicates the complexity of League perspectives on the *politique* and the question of prudence in this context. Whilst he rejected the notion that political society was born of violence, the author referred to the *Discourses* as he made the argument that even 'false' *politiques* recognised the historic status of the French people as one of liberty.[108] He followed Machiavelli's fundamentally Ciceronian discussion of the French constitution in the *Discourses* closely here, where he had argued that the French had established an essential principle of political life which was to live according to the laws and institutional arrangements.[109] 'Even' Machiavelli recognised that the French were so attached to their liberty that they could only live in peace and security as long as their kings were faithful guardians of their laws.[110]

[104] *De Justa Populi Gallici Ab Henrico Tertio Defectione*, as observed in Zwierlein, *Political Thought of the League*, 120–1.
[105] Boucher, *De Justa Abdicatione*, preface.   [106] Boucher, *Sermons*, 16–17; 43–4; 102.
[107] Boucher, *De Justa Abdicatione* fol. 122v, 143v.   [108] *De la puissance des roys*, 24–5.
[109] Machiavelli, *Discourses*, 1.58. On Ciceronianism in Machiavelli, see Skinner, *Machiavelli*; on his republicanism, see Bock et al., *Machiavelli and Republicanism*.
[110] Ibid., 24–5. His reference is to Machiavelli, *Discourses on Livy*, 1.16: 'An example of this is the Kingdom of France, which lives in security for no other reason than the fact that its kings are

The author pursued this strategy further into his argument for the defence of religion. The duty of the prince, according to the author, is to protect the religion of his subjects as Machiavelli had recognised.[111] Here, the author drew on the straightforward lessons of the *Discourses*: religion is necessary for the establishment and preservation of the commonwealth, and 'true' religion even more so.[112] Machiavelli's ideas reveal the Roman, Ciceronian vision underpinning this particular analysis of French kingship by a Leaguer which is extended to account for a more substantial role for the king in protecting the true doctrines of the church: since the king is created for the well-being of his people, it is possible to suggest that he is predominantly created for the protection of their eternal well-being.[113] The office of a Christian, and Catholic king, is therefore to protect the Catholic faith, and doctrine of the Trinity, from heresy.[114]

The Machiavellism of the late sixteenth century in France maps on to the polemical role of the figure of the *politique*. Yet, despite the regularity with which the diabolical epithet of 'Machiavellian' was hurled at particular *politiques*, like Belloy, by Leaguers, an investigation into Machiavelli's role only proves what most French thinkers had in common post-1572: a hostility to the rules of politics which stripped out divine and natural law, but an admiration for the way in which Machiavelli had mined classical history to consider the nature and needs of the 'best' constitution, and a recognition that Machiavelli's Ciceronianism could be repurposed. *Prudence civile* was deemed to play an acceptable role in a context conditioned by a less provocative, and more explicitly Christian framework than that of Machiavelli. There is, therefore, a paradox at the heart of the late sixteenth-century French response to Machiavelli, and an important observation to be made that Leaguers had this in common with so-called *politiques*. They all took the view that natural law was the basis of political life, and that its principles – of ensuring the rule of justice and checking that of expediency and force – were derived from custom. They all agreed that divine law provided Christians with ordered society and rulers, obedience to the latter conditional on the keeping of that law. For that matter,

---

constrained by countless laws which also provide for the security of its people'. The author adds the word '*sainctement*' when describing this royal role, to distance himself from the perceived atheism of Machiavelli's text. His other reference is to *Discourses* 1.58, where Machiavelli argued that the multitude was wiser and more constant than the prince, comparing the voice of the people to the voice of God.

[111] *De la puissance des roys*, 60.   [112] Ibid.

[113] Ibid., 62: '*Aussi s'il est veritable ce que nous avons cy devant prouvé, que le Roy est crée pour le bien du peuple, il faut estimer qu'il est plustost crée pour le bien eternel d'iceluy, que pour le temporel et perissable*'.

[114] Ibid., 63.

these were also the principles of the *Vindiciae* designed, after all, to appeal to Protestants and Catholics in its rejection of Machiavellian principles.[115] In this context, then, it is clear that the Leaguers were not working at the 'radical' fringes of French political thought, but at its core. In this sense, it is plausible to conceive of a *politique* Leaguer.

---

[115] *Vindiciae*, ed. Garnett, 8–13. Cf. editor's introduction on this tactic, xxi–xxii.

CHAPTER 3

Frank and Free

The authors of the *Satyre Ménippée* argued that the Leaguers were trying to sell their country to Spain and create an 'artificial' monarchy. 'We demand a natural King and leader', they stated, and 'not an artificial one: a King already made; not still to make'.[1] Compromised by their Spanish ties, and seen to be eroding the French laws of succession, the Leaguers needed to demonstrate continuity with historic traditions:

> We don't intend any change or innovation to the ancient institution and foundation of this Kingdom, on the contrary we recognise the power of the sovereign King ... our aim only concerns the handling and care of service to God, and obedience to the King, and the preservation of his state ... we push and incite for this sacred resolution to obviate the sinister designs of rebels and plotting enemies of God and the Crown.[2]

So stated the *Articles de la Sainte Union*. But the case for continuity was hard to make.

The accusation that the Leaguers were dangerous innovators had only grown in strength when the suggestion that the Cardinal de Bourbon could succeed – or be elected to – the throne dominated League discussions about the problem of Protestant monarchy under Henri de Navarre after 1584.[3] After Bourbon's death, the notion that the French throne could be

---

[1] *Satyre Ménippée*, 119: '*Nous demandons un Roy et chef naturel, non artificial: un Roy déjà faict, et non à faire ...*'. This was another way of expressing the notion that a king 'never dies', and that on the moment of one king's death, sovereign power transferred to his rightful heir – according to the Salic law in the French tradition. Cf. Belloy, *Apologie Catholique*, 109. On the medieval origins of this argument, see Kantorowicz, *The King's Two Bodies*, 314–450.

[2] *Articles de la Sainte Union*, fol. 10r: '*Nous ne tendons a aucun changement ou innovation de l'ancienne institution et establissement de ce Royaume, au contraire, nous recongnoissons la puissance du Roy souveraine ... nostre intention ne regard que la seule manutention et entretenement du service de Dieu et l'obeissance du Roy et sureté de son estat ... nous poussent et excitent de prendre ceste saincte resolution pour obvier aux sinistres desseins des rebelles et coniurez ennemis de Dieu et de la Couronne*'.

[3] *Declaration des causes*.

handed to Spain was entertained by members of the Sixteen, such as Jean Boucher, and although it was not a widely held view amongst the Leaguers, it provided good polemical fodder for the writers of the *Satyre Ménippée*.

In the intellectual context, these debates focussed on the concept of the ancient constitution. The idea of *l'ancienne police* was built on historical and juridical principles of immemorial custom that demonstrated the origins of royal power, and the 'fundamental' laws which no king could ever break.[4] It was often presented as a weapon against the hegemony of Roman law in France, and its association with the kind of fullness of sovereign power that could render a king emperor in his own realm.[5] The notion of being 'Frank and free' was central to this framework as an expression of freedom, located in Frankish antiquity, from Roman imperial hegemony: to be 'Frank' had originally simply meant to be free from imperial jurisdiction. The phrase could also be expanded to refer to *'franchises et libertés'* to refer to inviolable liberties, such as fundamental law, and the claim to freedom from Rome was most tangibly expressed in the shaking free from the shackles of Roman law in the name of the primacy of local, customary laws.[6] In the writings of scholars including Louis Le Roy, Girard Du Haillan and Étienne Pasquier, Frankish antiquity demonstrated that location of France's liberty was in the 'spirit' of her laws, expressed in a well-ordered monarchy, in which excessive power was limited by the authority of customary and 'fundamental' law.[7]

The Leaguers harnessed the idea of the ancient constitution as they made their case for Catholic monarchy: there was no separation between *la police* and *la religion* in their concept of the original, mythical foundations of France, within the framework of *'une foi, une loi, un roi'*. In some ways, this is reminiscent of Claude de Seyssel's identification of the greatness of the French commonwealth with three restraints on royal power, now very well known in the history of political thought of this era: *la religion, la police* and *la justice*.[8] Seyssel's framework of 'restraint' can be applied to the

---

[4] Pocock, *The Ancient Constitution and the Feudal Law*, 1–29. The idea of the ancient constitution has recently been revisited by Goldie, 'The Ancient constitution'.
[5] Cf. Krynen, *L'empire du roi*; Ullmann, 'The Development of the Medieval idea of Sovereignty'; Ullmann, 'This realm of England is an Empire'.
[6] Le Caron, *Pandectes du droit François*, f. IIv; Hotman's *Antitribonian*, circulated in manuscript form in 1567 but not published until 1603, is exemplary of this methodology. Cf. Filhol, 'The Codification of Customary Law', 265–83; Kelley, 'Second Nature'.
[7] Pasquier, *Recherches de la France*, I, 323–5, 493; du Haillan, *De l'estat et succez des affaires de France*; Le Roy, *De l'excellence du gouvernement royale*. Cf. Dubois, C-G. *Celtes et Gaulois au XVIe Siècle*.
[8] Useful discussions of Seyssel's political thought include Skinner, *Foundations*, II, 260–75; Church, *Constitutional Thought*; Nadeau, 'Les constitutionnalistes Français'.

League years, in the broad sense that the question of restraint on royal power by the French clergy and the papacy was certainly an important and contested feature of League political thought. However, there are limitations to applying the Seysselian model in broad terms to the latter half of the sixteenth century, not least because the context in which these ideas were being analysed had changed. The Seysselian formulation only remained pertinent to the discussion on a very general and basic level. The historian Girard du Haillan, for example, agreed with Seyssel on this level, confirming that the establishment of good government, of justice, of *la police* set France apart from other Christian countries. He suggested, however, that in the context of the religious wars, those institutions had fractured, and that order described by Seyssel no longer existed.[9] Seyssel's framework did not always provide a satisfactory model, therefore, for late-sixteenth century thinkers, because Seyssel's 'great monarchy' was by the 1570s in a deeply precarious situation that would culminate in the assassination of Henri III in 1589.

The Leaguers used the notion of *l'ancienne police* to embellish their crusading argument that there could be no society with heretics. They declared the law of Catholicity a 'fundamental' law at the meetings of the Estates General in 1576, 1588 and 1593, exploiting the indeterminacy of the fundamental laws to argue that since Clovis, the kings of France had always been Catholic and that their religion was prescriptive on their heirs. Louis Dorléans, in particular, doubled down on the connection between Catholicism and the ancient constitution. In his *Advertissment des Catholiques Anglois*, he identified the role of the French monarch as the inheritor of Clovis, and therefore of a model for the active combating of heresy by a French king, as a central feature of the constitution.[10] In making these arguments, Dorléans was perpetuating a myth common in Gallican thought that France had always acted to expel heresy, and building on the crusading theme of the polemics, as well as the definition of the 'true' *politique*.[11] For Dorléans, France was, in his words, '*le chateau de la religion Catholique*', and the king of France was *Très Chretien*, taking an oath to defend the church at his coronation.[12] Dorléans made the claim that '*François*' meant 'Christian' in the Catholic sense, implying a religious as well as civil freedom.

According to the Leaguers, France was exclusively Catholic, and Henri de Navarre could never inherit the French crown without violating the very

[9] Du Haillan, *De l'estat et succez des affaires de France*, 82.   [10] Dorléans, *Avertissement*, 22, 23.
[11] Tallon, *Conscience Nationale*, 46.   [12] Dorléans, *Avertissement*, 47; 94–6.

essence of what it was to be French. As the author of the *Declaration* argued, the people of France would 'never submit' to the rule of a heretic.[13] In this context, Dorléans identified the true *politique* with the defence of *l'ancienne police* in his *Banquet*.[14] Jean Porthaise argued that Leaguers were not fighting for Spain, or for the duc de Mayenne, but for their religion and freedom: their '*ancienne franchise*'.[15] The author of *De la puissance des roys* identified the aim of his treatise as a defence of the ancient liberty and customs of the people: he defined true kingship as 'just rule over a frank and free people'.[16] On this understanding, the Huguenots and their supporters were the enemies of France; the Leaguers were loyal to the 'true' definition of the French constitution.

The notion of being 'Frank and free' naturally suggests a connection to Hotman's *Francogallia*, however Hotman was not the only French theorist to draw the link with antiquity, nor was his provocative book warmly received by all Leaguers. It has been observed in scholarship that the Leaguers relied less on these resources, specifically *Francogallia*, than is conventionally thought.[17] Indeed, many Leaguers expressed anger at being associated with the 'popular' arguments of the Protestant 'heretics' who aimed at turning France into an '*estat populaire*' on the model of the Swiss cantons.[18] The Leaguers predominantly saw themselves as supporters of *l'estat royale*.[19] Whilst the Leaguer dependence on Huguenot sources has been tempered in recent scholarship, there remains substantial space for opening up the implications of all of these arguments about the nature of the ancient constitution further to consider the concept and role of '*l'ancienne police*' in shaping views on popular sovereignty and elective monarchy.

The concept of *la police*, the vernacular translation of the Greek '*politeia*', and the complex mark it left on the intellectual landscape of the later sixteenth century in its reference both to a way of life, and to a particular constitutional organisation, is central to an understanding of French

[13] *Declaration des Causes*. As Ralph Giesey has pointed out, this work actually recognised the legal hereditary right of Navarre to inherit the throne, but claimed that since he had abjured the Catholic faith he had forfeited that right and therefore the Cardinal de Bourbon was the rightful successor. Giesey, *Le rôle méconnu de la loi salique*, 203–4.
[14] Dorléans, *Le Banquet*, 20. [15] Porthaise, *Cinq Sermons*, 6 [mis pag].
[16] *De la puissance des roys*, 16–17; 10–12. Cf. Bodin, *République*, 2.2, 35–8. The author was reacting to Bodin's definition of seigneurial monarchy, which he interpreted as a form of tyranny.
[17] Baumgartner, *Radical Reactionaries*, 72.
[18] Dorléans, *Avertissement des Catholiques Anglois*, 18; *Premier et second advertissements des catholiques anglois*, 105–7. For alternative accounts on popular sovereignty in the League, see Salmon, 'Catholic resistance theory'; Baumgartner, *Radical Reactionaries*; Labitte, *De la Démocratie*.
[19] *Justification des actions des Catholiques*, 3–4.

political thought in this era.[20] *La police* is still conventionally associated with Seyssel's use of the concept as a restraint on royal power. However, it was a more ambiguous and fluid term than the reception of Seyssel's ideas in modern scholarship suggests, and therefore bears closer consideration. *La police* could be used to describe restraints on royal power; the precise type of prudent policy required to run a well-ordered political community engineered towards protecting the common good (rather than a particular set of laws); or the constitution itself, conceived as the embodiment of political order.[21] In this chapter, the emphasis will be on the latter, as it was constructed on the basis of customary laws, and on the guardians of those laws: the institutions of the Estates General and the Paris *parlement*. It builds on an understanding that the French Thomist–Aristotelian commentary tradition had succeeded in converting Aristotle's *Politics* into a thesis on monarchy, and that the third correct constitution, polity (translated as *la police*), was analysed within a royalist framework. The upshot of this approach is a shift of emphasis from 'constitutionalism' and popular sovereignty, to the nature of the commonwealth itself, the definition of *respublica/république* and its implications for the meaning of the *bien public*. In this conception, the interests of the *république* were represented by the Estates General and protected by the Paris *parlement*: the Aristotelian 'multitude' converted into a largely aristocratic body.[22]

The concentration of powers into the hands of sovereign monarchs by the end of the Middle Ages had meant that sovereigns could not let *la police* escape their sphere of influence. But this power was difficult to impose in practical terms; the elaboration and application of norms of government testified to a diffused, rather than centralised, monarchy.[23] France was a fragmented network of localities and powers asserting independent jurisdiction, divided into *pays d'election* and *pays d'état*. From the king's council, to the *parlement* of Paris and out into the localities, governors, seneschals, bailiffs and provosts undertook the activities of government in the king's name. Jurists had also begun to claim, from the twelfth century onwards, that magistrates could make and enforce statutes in their own cities. The definition of *l'ancienne police* therefore involved agreement on

---

[20] Aspects of this discussion of *la police* are reproduced, with kind permission of the press, from Nicholls, 'Sovereignty and Government'.

[21] For these distinct uses of the term, see, for example, Gentillet, *Anti-Machiavel*, 269 [251]; Montaigne, *Essaies*, II.19, 615; Seyssel, *The Monarchy of France*, 1.11, 56–7.

[22] See, for example, Aristotle's discussion of the possibility of the many being wiser than the few: *Politics*, III. 1281a40–b7.

[23] See Delamare, *Traité de la Police*, vol. 4, 170; Napoli, "Police"; Rigaudière, 'Les ordonnances de police'.

the relationship between royal powers and the requirements of local government which allowed for a measure of legislative independence from sovereign authority that was hard to find.[24] Henri II's request of the two presidents of the Paris *parlement*, in 1555, to assemble 'all the laws concerning *la police*' in concern at their lack of regulation, is symptomatic of the potential for a loss of control over the realities of government in France's diffused monarchy, and a lack of clarity as to the extent of the powers of *police*.[25]

The definition of *la police*, seen from this perspective, raised the question of how to reform and rule over France's 'decentralised, patrimonial and collegiate' governmental system.[26] In the context of the League years, the relationship between a decentralised governmental system to that of sovereign power was of tantamount importance. As discussed in Chapter 1, the League became increasingly a league of the towns rather than a movement dominated by the leadership of a fractious nobility (particularly after 1585); it was therefore a movement that became increasingly defined by the independence of the provincial *parlements* and the active role played by local magistrates and clergy in support of the cause.[27] The work of the Lyonnais Leaguer Claude Rubis is expressive of this relationship, particularly his *Discours* of 1577, which referred in the title to '*l'ordre, moyen & police tenue pour en purger, nettoyer & delivrer la ville*', and to the twelve councillors who had joined the League as the '*pères de leur patrie*'. It was a point raised in *De la puissance des roys* as well, in reference to the ability of local *échevins* to represent their city in defence against a destructive ruler.[28]

This discussion of *la police* highlights the tension between the sovereign and the body politic understood in both its juridical and Aristotelian modes (accepting that these are by no means mutually exclusive), predicated on the relationship between head and body. What that suggests, is that the location of sovereign power is the key to understanding this concept of *la police* as it featured in League political thought. The great rallying cry of the League was the defence of Catholicism, but it was also that of order: without the order provided by a Catholic monarch ruling

---

[24] Explored in Rigaudière, *Penser et construire l'état*; Leyte, *Domaine et domainalité*.
[25] Rigaudière, 'Les ordonnances de police', 132–3; Olivier-Martin, *La police économique*, 47–8.
[26] Lloyd, *The State, France and the Sixteenth Century*, 48–83. Cf. Collins, *The State in Early Modern France*.
[27] See the collection of articles in Brunet (ed.), *La Sainte Union des catholiques de France*, 23–156. Cf. Allen, *Political Thought in the Sixteenth Century*, 346.
[28] *De la puissance des roys*, 24.

justly over the French commonwealth, there was anarchy, and correspondingly there could be no commonwealth. In the *Articles de la Sainte Union*,
the author closed the manifesto with a discourse on the relationship
between the 'sun' of justice and Catholicity.[29] The question, therefore,
was how to preserve order through *la police*, without sacrificing liberty,
both religious and civil.

Locating Sovereign Power

When Jean Boucher declared Henri deposed, he had worked from the
argument that the source of political authority in the French kingdom
resided in the body of the people and the church. Crucially, the people, in
Boucher's account, made up both the church and the *respublica*; they were
doubly incorporated. As a body, they constituted kings and retained sovereign power within that body.[30] As they had elected Henri, Boucher argued,
so they could depose him.[31] He considered Henri's assassination to have been
an act of God, and the people; Henri III had committed a double crime,
against the people and against the church. His tyranny by practice meant
that he could be assassinated by any individual in the *respublica*.[32]

Jean Boucher's *De Justa Abdicatione* presented the case for the legitimate
assassination of a tyrant based on the existence of a Roman-legal contractual relationship between king and people. Taken, as Barclay had spotted,
from the *Vindiciae*, and indirectly indebted, therefore, to the medieval
postglossators, Boucher drew on the concept of the *universitas* as a fictive,
legal person acting through its representatives. In this way, the people as
a whole could be said to elect and depose kings in a way that could never
apply to people as individuals; the individual assassin in Boucher's treatise
is an exceptional individual inspired to action directly by God, but who can
only act once the tyrant is declared deposed by a representative body.[33] The
contractual arrangement at the heart of Boucher's argument was, therefore,
built on the medieval concept of corporations.[34] The history of the political
thought of the League has conventionally extrapolated from these arguments a theory of popular sovereignty, but in fact this only accurately

---

[29] *Articles de la Sainte Ligue*, fol. 30v, 34v. I also have in mind here Annabel Brett's discussion in
Changes of State, about the notion that order is a key concept for Aristotle in thinking about the
formal nature of the city, not unity: Brett, *Changes of State*, 123.

[30] Cf. Barclay's views on this process: Barclay, *De Regno*, III, iv, 125–7 on Stephanus, *Princeps Monitrix Musa*, song xxxiv.

[31] Boucher, *De Justa Abdicatione*, 1.2, fol. 13r; 1.17, fol. 17v–19r.   [32] Ibid., 4.19, fol. 281r–285r.

[33] Ibid., fol. 167r–170v.

[34] Discussed in *Vindiciae*, ed. Garnett, xxii–liv and see Ryan, 'Corporation Theory', I, 236–40.

describes the principles of thinkers like Boucher if the notion is understood as a purely representative concept of popular sovereignty, from which the ordinary people of France are entirely excluded, and is not conflated with an *état populaire* understood in a democratic sense.[35] Whilst the League certainly advocated a substantial role for the Estates General, the third estate did not represent the popular classes, but the judicial elites, *parlementaires* and royal officers.[36] Anti-democratic sentiment remained the norm for the lawyers and theologians in the League who shared the general contemporary antipathy towards a constitution associated with disorder and injustice.

Contemporary characterisations of the League certainly tended to portray it as an appalling image of democratic anarchy, for this was an effective polemical move in an era when democracy was to be feared and condemned. The Horatian image of the 'beast of many heads' was frequently associated with the League, as the images in '*l'histoire de la ligue*' demonstrate, showing the birth of the League as a monster produced in hell.[37] But whilst the League was a 'popular' movement insofar as its appeal amongst townsmen was substantial, arguments for the ability of the wider population to participate in politics were extremely rare.[38] An *avocat* of the *parlement* of Paris, François le Breton, was one such unusual Leaguer notable for his apparently political commitment to improving the conditions of the poor in his *Remonstrances aux trois Estats* (1585), where he argued that the nobility should be excluded from the next meeting of the Estates General. Instead, the magistrates and bourgeois of Catholic cities should organise the meeting, and, in the absence of sufficiently moral representatives, the '*manans*' – townsmen – and '*gens de biens*' – artisans – would take charge.[39] Le Breton's execution by the king's command in 1586

---

[35] On popular sovereignty in the League, and democratic ideas, see Baumgartner, *Radical Reactionaries*, 215; Labitte, *De la Démocratie*, treats this question with some care. Recent scholarship has shifted the terms of the debate: Zwierlein, *Political Thought of the League*, rightly emphasises questions of papal and clerical power; Jouanna, *Le Pouvoir Absolu*, argues that the Leaguers reinforce the power of absolute monarchy, 272–81. The broader implications of this question for the history of political thought, however, remain significant, and are particularly pertinent in the context of French ideas from the 1570s onwards: Bourke, 'Introduction', in *Popular Sovereignty in Historical Perspective*, 3. It is useful, furthermore, to think in terms suggested by Melissa Lane and connect popular sovereignty to office-holding: Melissa Lane, 'Popular Sovereignty as Control of Office-Holders: Aristotle on Greek democracy', in *Popular Sovereignty in Historical Perspective*.

[36] My thanks to one of the anonymous readers of the manuscript for suggesting this point.

[37] *Histoire de la Ligue*, 1594. BN, Cbt des Estampes, M 88285–88287.

[38] On the problem of poverty and excessive taxation, see *Articles de la Saincte Union* and the *Serment de la Saincte Union* (1588).

[39] François Le Breton, *Remonstrances aux trois Estats*. Cf. L'Estoile, M-J, II, 359; Pallier, *Recherches*, p. 64; Baumgartner, *Radical Reactionaries*, 76–8.

indicates the extent to which this *avocat* had moved beyond the boundaries of even the most provocative ideas in his own era.

In this context it is worth, therefore, revisiting Boucher's argument in *De Justa Abdicatione* from this anti-democratic perspective.[40] Three questions form the axis of the *De Justa Abdicatione*, which is dedicated to 'all Christians everywhere'. First, Boucher asked whether it was just for the people of France to depose a king; second, whether there was legitimate cause for deposing Henri III; third, whether the people could take up arms against the king without waiting for a formal deposition.[41] The answers to these questions were all positive, but Boucher did not linger over the question of the origins of political authority and the establishment of political institutions in *De Justa Abdicatione* (his treatment is distinct in this and in many other respects from Rossaeus' *De Justa Reipublicae Christianae Authoritate*). He suggested, though did not explore, the idea that men were by nature free and from this he established that the formation of government was a process that arose from necessity. The people had established their kings because they, as a whole, agreed that 'the political power which belonged immediately to them should be transferred to one person for the benefit of the people'.[42]

Boucher had argued that a war against Henri would be a '*bellum sacrum*', a sacred war in defence of the whole church and people, and he even tried to claim that the church would support the assassination of a tyrant.[43] In this sense, the familiar Ciceronian maxim of 'the safety of the people is the supreme law' assumes both secular and spiritual connotations.[44] Henri III had failed to protect the Catholic faith against Protestantism, and by this 'heresy', as Boucher understood it, had therefore failed to protect the commonwealth. Importantly, Boucher only considered a political community to be 'good' (i.e. a *communitas perfecta*) if directed towards a spiritual end: reconciliation with God.[45] This explains his idiosyncratic description of the power of the Estates General in his sermons as that of

---

[40] Elements of what follows are reproduced, with kind permission from the press, from Nicholls 'Catholic Resistance Theory'. As Zwierlein, *The Political Thought of the League*, has noted (18, n.4), Boucher's text is more cited than read. This current treatment is meant to address that issue.

[41] Boucher, *De Justa Abdicatione*, 1.1, fol. 4r.

[42] Boucher, *De Justa Abdicatione*, 1.12, fol. 13v: '*Porro ut e re populi fuerit Reges sibi constituere . . . ex eo patet, quod cum natura liberi omnes essent, neque vero bonum esset agere quenque quod liberet, sed communi iure opus esset, cui se omnes conformarent . . . .multi in id consenserunt, ut quae penes eos immediate politica potestas erat, ad unum aliquem publici commodi causa transferretur*'.

[43] Boucher, *De Justa Abdicatione*, 1.20, fol. 23v–24v; 2.15–2.16, fol. 65v–79r; 3.26, fol. 201v; 4.15, fol. 273v–274r.

[44] Ibid., 1.21, fol. 24v; Cf. Boucher, *Sermons*, 70.

[45] Also explored in Boucher, *La Couronne Mystique*.

'loosing and binding' in the kingdom in an echo of the Petrine commission (Matthew 16.18–19). He conceived of the Estates as the 'eternal guardians' of the sovereignty of which they are the origin and the source.[46] Using a traditional Thomist formulation, Boucher argued that the church does not diminish the Estates' direct jurisdiction in temporal affairs but instead guides this 'natural power' and sovereign authority by affirming and strengthening it.[47] Because the clergy was the first order in the Estates General, this suggested an enhanced role for the Gallican church in civil affairs which is confirmed by Boucher's claims in his sermons regarding the duty of French priests to protect the French kingdom and church.

The crux of Boucher's argument consisted in the theory that the people were doubly incorporated in such a way as to bind the *respublica* and the universal *ecclesia* together:

> The right [of deposition] is double, one of the Church, which is peculiar to Christians, and the other of the People or the Commonwealth, which is common to all nations, peoples and religions (although these two go together among Christians in such a way that one does not destroy the other, and each relies on and is strengthened by the help of the other).[48]

This strategy enabled him to go on to make a case for the ability of the pope to depose French kings, but it also had important implications for the role of the French clergy in the *respublica*. Boucher used Old Testament examples, underpinned by Roman legal principles of contractual obligation, to support his argument that a king is constituted by the *respublica*.[49] But it is less widely recognised that in describing the contracts between God, king and people, Boucher established a clear role for the priesthood: 'the priest is superior to the people, the king to the individual, and the people or kingdom to the king'.[50] In the *Vindiciae*, the author emphasised that the king and people contracted together to protect the church and uphold divine law and went so far as to suggest that when the priest Jehoiada made a covenant between God, king and people (II Kings 11 and II Chronicles 23:16) he had civil jurisdiction when he oversaw the

---

[46] Boucher, *Sermons*, 250.   [47] Ibid., 263–5.
[48] Boucher, *De Justa Abdicatione*, fol. 7r: '*Ius porro illud cum duplex sit, Ecclesiae unum, quod peculiare est Christianorum, Populi seu Reipublicae alterum, quod est commune omnium gentium, populorum ac religionum (quamquam ea apud Christianos sic concurrunt, ut unum alterum non destruat, & alterum alterius auxilio nitatur ac iuvetur*'.
[49] Boucher, *De Justa Abdicatione*, 1.18, fol. 19r–20r; cf. *Vindiciae*, 21. Cf. Garnett. 'Law in the Vindiciae, Contra Tyrannos'; Giesey, 'The Monarchomach Triumvirs'.
[50] Boucher, *De Justa Abdicatione*, 1.18, fol. 19v: '*Ex quo constat ut populo sacerdotem et private principem, sic principe populum seu regnum priore loco esse*'.

contract, but nowhere does he suggest that this civil jurisdiction was retained in modern times. His treatment of the priesthood is as a mouthpiece of God.[51] The covenants in the *Vindiciae* are thus designed to protect both the *respublica* and the church against any failings by the person of the king. This is also the case in Boucher's *De Justa Abdicatione*, but with the important modification that the priesthood is superior to both the people and the king.[52] The church had a duty to uphold the sacred contract made with God. Any violation of either contract, made with God or the people alone, was vindication for Boucher of the church's right to intervene in temporal affairs.[53] Boucher contended that although the people could exist without a king, they could not exist without the priesthood because of their double incorporation; salvation could only be achieved through the church.[54] The consequence of this argument was that the king held his office on the condition that he protect the church, and any failure to do so would result in a breach of contract and his deposition – either by the people or the church.

Barclay referred sarcastically to 'pope' Boucher, accusing him of taking for himself the powers of popes and princes and 'holding in his hand divine and human sanctions like a second Moses'.[55] Yet Boucher's position on papal temporal power was fairly balanced. He argued that whilst the right of deposing kings was 'in' the Church, this did not mean that the pope or even 'those below him' could overthrow rulers at their whim or exercise full jurisdiction over them. Boucher claimed instead that when the salvation of the people and kingdom, or the king himself, was at stake, then the pope could release the people from their duty of obedience and find another 'more suitable' ruler.[56] Towards the end of the *De Justa Abdicatione*, Boucher then undermined any power he had attributed to the pope in the temporal sphere. He argued that the people (including the Gallican church) could pre-empt any formal deposition by the pope in the case of an emergency and overthrow a tyrannical ruler, as in the case of Henri III.[57] Boucher's argument that the priesthood was superior to the people underpinned his belief that the *Sorbonistes'* decision to depose Henri III was legitimate; it is also why Boucher placed a significant amount of emphasis on the role of the universal church in his political theory in *De Justa*

---

[51] *Vindiciae*, 38 48, 129.   [52] Compare *Vindiciae*, 129; Boucher, *Sermons* 1.16, 102–8. 1.
[53] Boucher, *De Justa Abdicatione*, 1.5–8, fol. 7v–11v.   [54] Ibid., 1.11, fol. 13r.
[55] Barclay, *De Regno*, V.v, 357: '*Atque ita Boucherius Regem spernens, Papam praeveniens, ipse sibi et Pontifex Maximus, et Princeps supremus, divinas et humanas sanctiones, tanquam alter Moyses, in manutenens, omnibus regni ordinibus multas et mortes arbitratu suo minitatur*'.
[56] Boucher, *De Justa Abdicatione*, 1.5, fol. 7v–8r.   [57] Ibid., 4.3, fol. 221r–224v.

Abdicatione, but he also demonstrated concern for the position of the Gallican church. Henri's inability to contain the problem of heresy presented a direct threat to the Gallican church and all the French faithful, as did his inclination towards religious toleration.[58] Boucher argued that the only way to guarantee the protection of the Gallican church was to accept the decrees of the Council of Trent, particularly in relation to heretics.[59] He therefore clearly subordinated the Gallican church to papal authority, conceiving it as a part of the universal *ecclesia*, but this did not preclude retaining certain powers on behalf of the French priesthood. Henri III was a dangerous schismatic who, Boucher argued, threatened the entire polity by failing to reject heresy; it was therefore incumbent upon the priesthood to take action against him. Boucher's treatment of the sovereignty of the people as a whole was predicated on the corporation theory of Roman law, but it was not purely an argument for the sovereignty of the *respublica* in the sense that it included, and negotiated with, the concept of the *ecclesia* as well.

Barclay thought that Boucher was a democrat, thinly disguising his democratic plans with flimsy royalism.[60] He took the view that Boucher's reasoning was deeply flawed, that he had used the resources of theorists of democracy to make a case for the deposition of kings. In this way, Boucher had made a ridiculous confusion of monarchy and democracy.[61] However, Boucher's limited definition of the people was reflected in the aristocratic organisation of the League; even the *Seize* was not as 'popular' as it appeared.[62] Boucher, like other League authors, argued that man was equal – but by equality here he meant in living in fear of God, and as God's creation, rather than a political concept of equality.[63] He was careful to define the people not as the 'many-headed monster', but the 'prudent multitude':

> By the term 'people' . . . is to be understood not the unstable and indistinct crowd, which is a beast of many heads . . . it should be taken for the prudent multitude, bound by right, of nobles, Senators and men with the particular authority of virtue, probity, judgement and dignity.[64]

Boucher relied here on the scholastic, canonist tradition which had long drawn connections between the Aristotelian multitude and the '*valentior*

---

[58] Ibid., 2.16, fol. 69r–79r; 3.4, fol. 144v–147v.   [59] Ibid., 2.17, fol. 80v–82r.
[60] Barclay, *De Regno*, V.xii, 383–5.   [61] Ibid., V.xiii, 383–6.
[62] Salmon, 'The Paris Sixteen', 243–4, 258.   [63] Cf. *De la puissance des roys*, 60–1.
[64] Boucher, *De Justa Abdicatione*, 1.9, fol. 11v–12r: '*intelligendum populi nomine isto loco non inconditam et confusam turbam, quae bellua multorum capitum est . . . sed procerum, Senatorum ac praecipua virtutis, probitatis, iudiciique ac dignitatis authoritate hominum prudentum ac iure coacta multitudine sumi*'.

pars': the weightier, morally upright part of the community which had the power of election ('*maior et senior pars*'). These were the people who acted in the interests of the whole, and were quantitively and qualitatively superior to the rest, and not to be automatically equated with a republican vision of political freedom.[65] To preserve the order of the constitution (*police/politeia*), the appropriate portion of prudent people needed to be in office according to Boucher, not the plebeians, whom he referred to as 'the beast of many heads'. Boucher certainly did not have a democratic framework in mind when he located this sovereign power in the Estates and argued that Henri III was guilty of treason against France for usurping their authority. The Leaguers did not see themselves as fusing two forms of constitution; in fact they could capitalise on the ambiguities of the Aristotelian translations that had produced a concept of monarchy that encapsulated both 'royal' and 'political' elements long in existence.

At the core of William Barclay's rejection of Boucher's thesis on the *respublica* was his elision of the people, the realm and the commonwealth. Barclay argued that Boucher had utterly confused these, and in so doing had failed to distinguish between species and genus in his political theory: a realm is a commonwealth, in Barclay's analysis, in the same way a man is an animal.[66] Barclay's complaint was akin to Bodin's rejection of the idea of the mixed constitution on the basis that it was illogical and that it divided sovereignty.[67] But Boucher considered what he was doing to be firmly within a monarchical framework. Where the real complexity lay, in fact, was in his attempt to doubly incorporate the people, into the *respublica* and the *ecclesia*. This feature lay at the heart of his political thinking.

Guardians of the Constitution

The focus of attention on the Estates General as a mechanism for restoring order to France by Huguenots and Catholics alike in this period is symptomatic of the widespread disenchantment with the French crown and its policies.[68] The Estates had become a largely defunct institution at the start of the century, having met only three times in the fifteenth century, but in contrast, they were summoned five times in the sixteenth

---

[65] See Marsilius, *The Defender of the Peace*, ed. Brett, D.I, 12.4, 67–8. See also Brett's definition of *valentior pars* at l-li and Garnett on the canonist origins of the *maior et sanior pars* in his *Marsilius of Padua*, 90, n.173. Garnett discusses the problems with equating these kinds of arguments with republicanism at 1–48.

[66] Barclay, *De Regno*, V.xiii, 387–90.   [67] Bodin, *République*, 2.1, 227–8; *De Republica*, 182–3.

[68] Greengrass, *Governing Passions*, 66–122.

(1560, 1561, 1576, 1588, 1593).[69] In 1561 and 1576, concerted, but ultimately unsuccessful, effort was made to enshrine the regular convocation of the Estates General in the French constitution, and after 1614 the Estates would not meet again until 1789.[70] Nevertheless, in the period of civil war the Estates seemed increasingly to offer a forum for solutions and the reform of the kingdom.

In 1560, Chancellor Michel de l'Hôpital gave a speech to the meeting of the Estates General in Orléans, claiming that the ancient kings of France had often followed the custom of convoking the Estates in order to communicate with their subjects, to take their advice and counsel over major issues concerning the kingdom, as well as to hear their grievances and complaints.[71] l'Hôpital's opinions were influential, and widely referred to in the writings of, for example, Du Haillan and Louis Le Roy.[72] The Estates General had therefore become associated with broader claims about the authority of customary law in the period, and were by no means the preserve of resistance theorists. The difference lay in the extent of the powers attributed to the institution by thinkers like Hotman and Théodore de Bèze. Hotman described the meeting place of king and council as 'the most august and holy temple of Gallic justice' in his *Francogallia*, and Bèze used the Estates General as a vehicle for the Calvinist conception of the role of inferior magistrates in a polity, employing the Genevan model influentially in his *De Jure Magistratuum*.

In the League, notwithstanding the caution with which some Leaguers approached Huguenot political thought, the Estates were similarly, and conventionally, viewed as the only way to resolve the problems of the civil wars. In the *Declaration,* written in support of Charles de Bourbon's candidacy for the throne, the Estates were presented as the 'ancient remedy for domestic complaints', thus perpetuating the connection between the ancient constitution, customary law, and the argument for continuity with tradition.[73] Others addressed the king directly: in the *Remonstrance au Roi* by the Estates General in 1588, published shortly after, the Leaguers proposed the Estates as the only possible remedy for the ills besetting

---

[69] Russell Major, *Representative Government in Early Modern France.*
[70] Thus echoing the desire expressed in the *Discours sur les estats de France* that the Estates should meet annually.
[71] *Oeuvres complètes,* I, 378. [72] Cf. Church, *Constitutional Thought, 161.*
[73] Anon., *Declaration des causes, qui ont meu Monseigneur le Cardinal de Bourbon, & les pairs, princes, seigneurs, villes & communautez catholiques, de ce royaume de France, de s'opposer à ceux qui par tous moyens s'efforcent de subuertir la religion catholique, & l'estat* (n.p., 1588), 7. Eugène Saulnier has argued plausibly that the author of this pamphlet was the Jesuit Claude Matthieu in *Le rôle Politique du Cardinal de Bourbon,* 122, n.3.

France, warning that if the king treated the institution as 'illusory' and it failed to produce concrete results, then he would lose what remained of his people's faith and love for him.[74] Louis Dorléans described the Estates as the embodied representative of the *régnicoles*, a juridical term for the inhabitants of the kingdom.[75] In its power, Dorléans included the ability to make or break 'fundamental laws', but it is significant that he did not envisage the Estates acting without the king, or the *parlement*, in the performance of this role.[76] As in Boucher's *De Justa Abdicatione*, the people, defined as the 'prudent multitude', acted through the Estates in a corporate sense: this is what it meant to refer to France as a *corpus reipublicae universum*.[77]

As members of the League started to hunt for arguments for the legitimate deposition of tyrants in the late 1580s, underpinned by a principle of royal election, they sought support from within existing conventions in French political thought. The idea that *la police* required the guardianship of prudent magistrates was usually presented within the framework of reform, rather than radical change. This role of guardianship, or tutorship, was deeply significant to the political thought of the era, in the context of both the Estates and the Paris *parlement*.[78] The fact that the role of the *parlement* was predominantly that of a judicial 'check', enacted through the registering of royal edicts and the power of remonstrance was widely accepted in French political thought at the time.[79] Lawyers in the Paris *parlement* saw themselves as the supporters of a particular, juridical conception of the French monarchy, or a 'legislative tutor'.[80] Indeed, they reinforced an existing position on the place of that institution in the constitution.

To start with the role of the Estates General, this was thoroughly explored in a treatise entitled *Des Etats de France et de leur puissance* by Matteo Zampini, one of many of François Hotman's archenemies. First published in Italian and Latin in 1578 and dedicated to Catherine de Medici, Zampini's treatise appeared in French in 1588, published by one of the League's Parisian printers, Rolin Thierry, and with a new dedication

---

[74] 'Remonstrance au Roi. Par les Etats de la France' in Goulart, *Mémoires de la Ligue*, 3, 103.
[75] Dorléans, *Response*, 158–9.
[76] Dorléans, *Response*, 149. Cf. [Anon.] *Articles pour proposer aux Estatz et faire passer en loy fondamentalle du Royaume*, 7–8.
[77] Boucher, *De Justa Abdicatione*, fol. 152v–155r.
[78] Daubresse, *Le Parlement de Paris*; Roelker, *One King, One Faith*.
[79] Church, *Constitutional Thought*, discusses this point at 143–4 in reference to Du Haillan and Étienne Pasquier.
[80] See Hanley, *The Lit de Justice*, and Shennan, *The Parlement of Paris*.

to the League chancellor, François de Montholon.[81] As the original dedi-cation implies, Zampini's treatise was intended as an advisory text on the role of the Estates General as the 'perfect body of the kingdom' and source of a sovereign's supreme power.[82]

Zampini grounded his argument in nature, and therefore reason, as the source of the perfection of the French political community.[83] Prudence governs Zampini's claims, and he declared it was by 'natural necessity' and the 'election of men governed and persuaded by prudence' that royal power was first introduced to the community; basing his principles on the notion that communities were required for defence, and so taking on board the Machiavellian point that the author of *De la puissance des roys* had rejected, that man is inclined to force and violence.[84] 'By necessity' the community in itself has the 'natural' power to do everything which is 'necessary and profitable' in a 'well-ordered assembly'. He defined that power as absolute, whether it remained with the community or was transferred to the monarch.[85]

In France, Zampini argued, power was transferred by the Estates to the king, on his election.[86] However, there were exceptions to this royal law. In times of necessity, some power was returned to the Estates, not absolutely, but with restrictions as to time, place and persons: here Zampini employed the distinction between 'ordinary' and 'extraordinary' contexts to explain how and when this power could revert to the Estates. Such cases included the understanding that the Estates could assemble to depose an ineffectual king and elect a new one in his place, and the notion that when the succession is uncertain, the Estates govern. Finally, the inalienability of the kingdom is also guaranteed in his analysis. Historically, Zampini

---

[81] Pallier, *Recherches sur l'imprimerie*. On Zampini, see Raybaud, 'La Royauté d'après les œuvres de Matteo Zampini' in Bontems et al., *Le Prince dans le France*; Allen, *History of Political Thought*, 380–3; Baumgartner, *Radical Reactionaries*, 91–2; Giesey, Salmon, 'editor's introduction' in Hotman, *Francogallia*, 94–5.

[82] Zampini, *Des Etats de France et de leur puissance*, fol. 2v–3r. [83] Ibid., fol. 13r–16r.

[84] Ibid., fol. 19r, 21r–v: '*Par la necessite doncques assez cogneu par la nature, & par l'election d'hommes conduits & persaudez par la Prudence, la preeminance Royalle a este introduire en la communauté*'.

[85] Ibid.; '*Personne ne peut douter, la puissance estant pour mesme raison necessaire entre les hommes, pour laquelle est necessaire la communauté, que la nature qui les a induicts en icelle, ne les aye nécessairement, & par mesme moyen proveu de l'autre, & de la façon que luy estoit de besoin, & sans laquelle la communauté n'eust duré, & qu'en apres la luy aient balhee, ne luy aie balhé par mesme raison faculté de la pouvoir transférer à leur prince, sans lequel en vain seroient rangez en communauté & receu la puissance. Donques par necessité, la communauté en soy-mesme a puissance de la nature, de faire tout ce au'est nécessaire ou profitable en une assemblée bien ordonnée, à puissance de la céder a son Roy, & en somme, ou qu'elle soit au peuple, ou au Roy, telle puissance pour sa conservation & bon gouvernement est en foy absoluë & à tout pouvoir*'.

[86] Ibid., fol. 24r–v.

showed, the Estates had the power to create the principal offices of the kingdom, to guard its safety, to make laws, to decide on important matters, to receive ambassadors, to conserve the church and exterminate heresy, to mete out military discipline and justice, to establish the boundaries of the kingdom, to administer justice, to judge rebels against the crown, to correct princes, and to treat the causes of divorce between kings and queens.

This balancing act between acknowledging the full sovereign power of the French monarch but also conferring fairly extensive powers onto the Estates General was taken up in other League texts but given a different treatment. *De la puissance des roys*, for example, described the relationship between the king and the Estates in some detail. The author drew heavily on the chroniclers Aimon de Fleury and Philippes de Commines, and the historian Du Haillan, to argue that anyone who prevented or diminished the power of the Estates committed a crime against God, the king and the commonwealth. Importantly, the author did not conceive of the power of the Estates General independently from the king. Strikingly, he argued that one such exceptional person did not simply arise out of a group of citizens 'as happens amongst bees': such an individual was divinely appointed, but could not rule without a council.[87] The author elaborated on the relationship between the king and his council, embodied in the Estates, and the two are seen to operate in harmony with one another:

> I say that the King is the head of the Estates, the deputies are his councillors, who are members of the aforementioned Estates ... the head cannot order anything against the advice of these members, in order that the head should not be in discord with them. And thus the power being in the King as head, the fact remains that ... the same power as that which is of the Prince and the Estates resides supremely in the Prince. The Estates have firstly had this power from God, then they transferred it to the Prince, with the result that he uses it legitimately for their defence and protection. So long as he will use that power in that way, the members will not break from their head, but when the head will not be healthy but infected and decomposed, in evident danger of corrupting the rest of the body, the body will separate; because that is not a naturally born head, but deliberately imposed by an act of will.[88]

---

[87] *De la puissance des roys*, 26–7. Here he was opposing the mythical idea of a lawgiver as the founder of a constitution, as it was discussed in Machiavelli's *Discorsi*.

[88] *De la puissance des roys*, 32–3: 'Je dy que le Roy est le chef des Estats, les deputez sont ses conseilers, qui sont les membres desdicts Estats. Tout se doit publier au nom du Roy, comme chef, et non au nom des Estats, qui ne sont que les membres. Le chef n'ordonnera toutefois rien contre l'advis d'iceux, puis que la teste ne doit discorder d'avec les membres. Et par ainsi la puissance estant au Roy comme chef, il reste que ce ne sera pas une pure Aristocratie de plusieurs seigneurs en puissance egale, comme quelque Politique à escrit, mais

In this curious organological description, the author was trying to capture the concept of a revocable transfer of power enshrined in certain interpretations of the Roman *lex regia*. In making this argument, the author engaged explicitly with Jean Bodin's case in his *République*, positing that the arrangement he described would not be a purely aristocratic or seigneurial government, but 'the same power', residing in the Prince, which he gets from the Estates.

Overwhelmingly, scholarship on the political thought of the League has focussed on their concept of elective monarchy, contractual agreements and above all, the role of the Estates General to the neglect of the Paris *parlement*. This is because emphasis on popular sovereignty requires a focus on the representative institutions of the French constitution, and as a judicial court the *parlement* of Paris cannot be read in this context: its members bought (or were given) their offices, which could then become hereditary, and they acted as guardians of the laws. Nevertheless, these lawyers did constitute a significant a check on royal power. Furthermore, a close look at League political thinking demonstrates, at the heart of the League of the 1580s, a strong commitment to the authority of the Paris *parlement* over that of the Estates. This contradicts contemporary representations of the League as the enemies of the *parlement* in the capital: Belloy wrote, for example, that the actions of the League were contrary to '*la police humaine*', in the French case, governed by the rule of law and the Paris *parlement*.[89] Yet it is quite clear that there was a strong *parlementarist* core, led by the lawyers in the League, which indicates a tension within the movement over this question of which institution protected the constitution.

It was particularly the question of whether or not the prince was 'above', or 'below' the laws that dominated the issue of the role of *parlement* in the sixteenth century. This set of debates very often introduced complexities and tensions into arguments both for the 'absolute' power of a prince, and for the submission of the prince to the laws. Guillaume Budé, for example, made an influential argument for the power of the prince as *legibus solutus*, arguing that the people had transferred their *maiestas* to the prince through the *lex regia*, but he also submitted princes to the judgement of the

---

une mesme puissance que celle du Prince et des Estats, qui reside souverainement au Prince. Les Estats ont eu premierement ceste puissance de Dieu, puis l'ont transferé au Prince, afin d'en user legitimement pour leur defense et protection. Tant qu'il en usera ainsi, les membres ne se separeront point de leur teste, mais lors qu'elle ne sera plus saine, ains infectée et pourrie, en danger evident de corrompre le reste du corps, le corps s'en separera; car ce n'est pas une teste née naturellement, mais volontairement imposée'.

[89] Belloy, *Apologie Catholique*, 3.1, fol. 89v, on *la police humaine*.

parlement, whose powers he framed in reference to the Roman senate, the Greek Areopagus and the general council of the Amphyctyonians.[90]

The influence of Budé on this question remained significant in the latter half of the sixteenth century. A notable Leaguer who was intellectually indebted to Budé and who remained deeply committed to the institution of the Paris *parlement* as a guardian of the constitution was René Choppin. In this, ironically enough, he remained consistent with the principles of the two works which had gained him the favour of Henri III in the 1570s: *De Domanio Franciae* and *De Sacra Politia*.[91] It was to Budé that Choppin referred as an expert in the preface to *De Domanio Franciae*, and in his eulogy to *parlement*. In the latter, Choppin built on this authority of Budé's to claim that the powers of the *parlement*, insofar as they preserved royal edicts and consented to new ones in the interests of the kingdom as a whole, were the greatest source of protection and well-being of the people.[92]

In *De Domanio Franciae*, René Choppin attributed an important role to the *parlement* in defending the domain against abuses, both ecclesiastical and civil. The *ad hominem* attack on Choppin, Jean Hotman's treatise entitled *Anti-Choppinus*, took advantage of this fact, subsequently accusing Choppin of betraying his own views on the role of *parlement* by refusing to join Henri IV when he left Paris, and considering his attacks on the *parlements* of Tours and Châlons to be deeply hypocritical.[93] However, Choppin was consistent in his defence of what he saw as the true power of the *parlement*. He refused to accept Henri III's attempts to circumvent the authority of the Paris *parlement* when it came to the question of alienating ecclesiastical lands, a principle consistent with his views in *De Sacra Politia*, which was republished in 1587 and 1589. For Choppin, not unlike Boucher, the civil and the ecclesiastical order worked together in a system of mutual support, whose laws were protected by the *parlement*. If the ecclesiastical polity was the 'soul' of any Christian commonwealth as Choppin argued, then the 'magistrate of the commonwealth' was the law, and minister of both God and the community. The duty of the *parlement* was therefore, to protect the soul of the commonwealth: in refusing to follow Henri IV,

---

[90] Budé, *Annotationes*, Dig. I.9., fol. 96r–97r.

[91] Aspects of the discussion that follows here, and in subsequent chapters as they encounter Choppin's ideas, are drawn from Nicholls, 'Ideas on Royal Power' and reproduced with the kind permission of the editors.

[92] René Choppin, 'Eloge de l'auctorite qua la cour de parlement', in *Les Oeuvres de Me René Choppin*, 409.

[93] According to Hauréau, *Histoire littéraire du Maine*, 39, the League *parlement* of Paris burnt the *Anti-Choppinus* publicly in support of their lawyer.

Choppin may well have considered himself as fulfilling that duty.[94] In Choppin's Gallican view, the role of the king was as the patron and protector of the 'civil polity' of the church – not its owner – and this was a position held in obedience to the holy Roman see.[95]

There is no extant text to demonstrate that Choppin ever explicitly converted his views on the role of *parlement* into resistance theory, but by joining the League it could be argued that he converted them into action instead. It is very significant however, that resistance theorists in the 1570s did perceive a use for these claims. It was on the subject of the Paris *parlement* as a guardian that the author of the *Vindiciae* found reason to mine the resources of *De Domanio Franciae*. As Jean Baricave noted, the author follows Choppin's discussion almost verbatim.[96] Instead of the Leaguers exploiting Huguenot resistance theory, in this case – as in Hotman's later edition of *Francogallia* – we see the inverse. When Louis Dorléans argued that the *parlement* was the permanent incarnation of the Estates General, his argument might appear to have been drawn from the *Vindiciae*. However, the provenance of this argument, picked up notably in the works of Budé and Choppin, demonstrates that it has far deeper roots in French political thought than the resistance theory of the late sixteenth century. In making his case, Dorléans was explicit in distancing himself from what he considered the 'republican', representative, ideas of the Huguenots represented by texts such as the *Francogallia*.[97]

In a speech to the Paris *parlement* in 1593, the duc de Mayenne conceded that the election of a king would be confirmed by a decision of the Estates General, but that only the *parlement* could render such an act legitimate.[98] De Thou, in recounting this episode, suggested that Mayenne was trying to recover '*l'ancien esprit de la Ligue*', in reference to the views of the Leaguer nobility who sought to preserve what they conceived of as the ancient role of *parlement*.[99] Mayenne's attitude to *parlement* had been fairly consistent since his consolidation of his authority in Dijon in 1588–9. In the articles that were drawn up to confirm loyalty to the League, magistrates were

<hr>

[94] Choppin, *De Sacra Politia*, preface.
[95] Ibid.: '*Scilicet huc semper Francorum Regum studia spectarunt, ut et libertatem Gallicae Ecclesiae sartam tectam custodirent (eius iura institutaque haud sinentes everti) nec propterea debitae Sanctissimo Solio obedientiae excuterent iugum; Quos Pontifex etiam quisque Reges expertus est Sacrae Sedis cultores officiosissimos, observantissimos, obsequentissimos*'.
[96] *Vindiciae*, 146–7; ed. Garnett, *Vindiciae*, 120–2; Choppin, *De Domanio Franciae*, II.xv.15. Cf. Baricave, *Défence*, 611.
[97] Dorléans, *Responses*, 149, 153, 158–60; Dorléans, *Avertissement des catholiques anglois*, 18; Dorléans, *Premier et second advertissements des catholiques anglois*, 105–7.
[98] Bernard, *Procès-verbaux des États généraux de 1593*.   [99] De Thou, *Histoire Universelle*, XII, 666.

asked to sign an agreement of obedience to Mayenne, but also to conserve the central *parlement* in its 'ancient splendour'.[100] It is notable that the *Articles de la Sainte Union* discussed reform in reference to the Estates, but their reception and interpretation in Dijon – under Mayenne's guidance – was a 'parlementarist' one.[101] Mayenne, in attributing such a crucial role to the *parlement* in 1593, confirmed its judicial role but, in doing so, highlighted a tension within the movement he led between those who sought to bolster the role of the Estates General and those who would diminish it.

Notwithstanding claims made by certain Leaguers, usually lawyers in the *parlement*, to respect and support its role in French politics – notably from Dorléans, 'Rossaeus', Antoine Hotman and René Choppin – in practice, the movement never fully gained control of that institution. The establishment of Navarre's *parlement* in Tours and then Châlons reinforced this dilemma.[102] The perceived allegiance of the League to the notion of papal indirect power clashed too fundamentally with the Gallican ideas propounded by their opponents, and this, when combined with support for Spanish intervention presented too clear a contradiction of the principles to which so many members of the *parlement* held.[103] In the end, when the League became so apparently invested with foreign powers, their battle was effectively lost. Added to this was the violence of attacks on members of the *parlement* by the League, of which the plot to assassinate the president of *parlement* Achille de Harlay in 1587 was a shocking example for contemporaries, but the execution of his replacement Barnabé Brisson in 1591 even more so.[104] These methods, and those of imprisonment, put obstacles between the League and the *parlement*, even as those who remained in Paris rather than move to Tours sought to resolve these particular troubles of the kingdom.

When Henri IV's reign began in proper terms, and after Tours and Paris reunified, the power to consent to taxation was effectively transferred to Paris, and the Estates rendered redundant until the revolution of 1789. What historians can see, therefore, in the League years, is an interesting confrontation – within the movement and without – between the argument for the primacy of the Estates General and that of *parlement*, with the

[100] A translated copy of the Articles presented to the *parlement* of Dijon is reproduced in Wilkinson, *A History of the League*, 174.
[101] *Articles de la Saincte Union*, fol. 22r–23v.
[102] Penzi, '*Tours contre Rome au début du règne d'Henri IV*'.
[103] A clash discussed in detail in Daubresse, *Le Parlement de Paris*. Cf also Parsons, *The Church in the Republic*, and Bakos, "Meddling Chaperons' in her *Politics, Ideology and Law*, 91–106.
[104] Cf. Barnavi, Descimon, *La Sainte Ligue*.

latter winning out in the end. The argument for the superiority of the Paris *parlement* became known as the preserve of the *politiques*, but nevertheless it is clear that the *politique* Leaguers in *parlement* had also seen that institution as the medicine for the French constitution, even if they failed to persuade contemporaries of the true nature of their commitment to it.

The Ancient Constitution

The antiquarian revival during the civil wars encouraged the search for the origins of that constitution in Frankish antiquity, with a particular emphasis on the recovery of superlative laws and customs to reinstate the French monarchy in its 'original' form. Sixteenth-century thinkers sought to construct what they considered to be an historical account of the origins of the ancient constitution as the product of prescriptive customary law acting as a guarantor of freedom. Such an argument was developed influentially in Hotman's *Francogallia*. Hotman used this historical basis to claim that his *Francogallia* was the 'history of a fact', and in it he aimed to 'uncover' neglected French custom and thereby reconstruct the original Frankish constitution.[105] *Francogallia* was quite sentimental in its attachment to the French *patria*: like Ulysses with Ithaca, Hotman claimed a deep connection to his homeland that had further imparted to him a sense of duty to rescue it from its current crisis. A conflagration, in the shape of civil war, had beset France, he wrote in his preface, and it was his humble ambition to throw a bucket of water over the fire.[106]

Hotman's solution was anchored in the ancient French constitution, demonstrating that the wisdom of the *Francogallian* ancestors was such that they had founded a kingdom in liberty. Hotman sought to recover that ancient constitution, and in doing so put forward a polemical argument for the elective power of the people, based on custom.[107] At the core of his pseudo-historical analysis lay the institution of the public council as representative of the corporate people as a whole. Kings, and laws, were instituted by popular consent in the ancient Frankish kingdom, and Hotman sought to make the case that this ancient constitution should be

---

[105] He wrote this in a letter to his friend Jacob Cappel in 1575: François Hotman, Jean Hotman, *Hotomanorum et clarorum virorum ad eos epistolae* (Amsterdam, 1700), 49. Cf. Garnett, 'Scholastic Thought in Humanist Guise', 799.

[106] Hotman, *Francogallia*, preface, 8. All English translations are from *Francogallia*, ed. Giesey and Salmon, unless otherwise cited.

[107] See Filhol, 'The Codification of Customary Law in France', 265–83, and Dauchy, 'French Law and Its Expansion in the Early Modern Period'.

reinstated. Since antiquity, the public council had transformed into the Estates General, and it was through this mechanism, Hotman argued, that consent was to be given, or withdrawn. *Francogallia* is a book about the power of the tacit consent of the people, expressed through customary law, and thus deeply scholastic in its foundations, despite Hotman's claims to be working within the framework of the *mos gallicus docendi*.[108]

Francogallia was widely read and immediately recognised for the political provocation that it was, despite Hotman's protestations that he was simply recounting the history of the Frankish kingdom. The text was taken both to be historically inaccurate, and a dangerous, Protestant, attack on the French monarchy.[109] As the result of both the criticisms levelled at *Francogallia*, and the changing political circumstances of the 1570s and 1580s, Hotman altered his text twice: Salmon and Giesey estimate that the first edition of *Francogallia* therefore makes up only 56 per cent of the final text.[110] What is especially noticeable about Hotman's new editions, is his attempt to temper the parts of the text he had come to regret in the intervening years.

From 1580, Hotman had been acting as an agent of Henri of Navarre and his cousin the prince of Condé. In 1584, he was instructed to make the case for Navarre's succession to the throne against that of the Cardinal de Bourbon, the candidate of the League. The changing circumstances of Navarre's prospective inheritance of the throne put Hotman in an awkward position, necessitating an entire reversal of the views he had put forward elsewhere regarding the laws of succession, specifically the rights of uncles over nephews in his *Quaestionum illustrium liber* (1573). In making the case for Navarre, he now had to demonstrate that nephews could inherit before uncles. He did this in two treatises, and these ideas were absorbed into the new edition of *Francogallia* in 1586.[111]

Even more troubling for Hotman, however, was the fact that friends had alerted him to the exploitation of the central thesis of *Francogallia* on the part of the League. From Hotman's perspective, it was alarming to read in the captured League papers during *l'affaire David* a history of Pepin's elevation to the throne after Childeric III's deposition as a justification for the replacement of Henri III with the duc de Guise.[112] After all,

---

[108] Garnett, 'Scholastic Thought in Humanist Guise', 799.
[109] See, in particular, the responses of Antione Matharel and Papire Masson to *Francogallia*: Matherel, *Ad Franco-Galliam . . . responsio*; Papire Masson, *Responsio*.
[110] Hotman, *Francogallia*, ed. Giesey and Salmon, 51–2.
[111] François Hotman, *Disputatio*; *De Jure successionis regiae*.
[112] Cayet, *Chronologie Novenaire*, 1. fol. 5v. Cf. Anquetil, *L'Esprit de la Ligue*, 2, 165–6. As suggested in the Introduction, these papers were certainly a Huguenot forgery.

Hotman had used exactly that point of reference in Frankish history to make a case for the power of the people to depose kings in his *Francogallia*.[113] Hotman's own book was being used against him, and the cause he stood for. He sent a copy, along with the *Articles de la Ligue* and the Edict of Beaulieu, to his friend Georg of Hesse, commenting on the *Articles* that it was 'aimed at the destruction of the kingdom of France and at the profit of the Roman religion'.[114]

In his 1586 edition of *Francogallia,* Hotman modified his arguments in an attempt to distance himself from any association with the League, and to reinforce Henri de Navarre's claim to the throne.[115] In a new chapter, Hotman argued that the fundamental laws of the kingdom were unchangeable, even though their source was the people's tacit consent, represented by the public council; the upshot of this argument was to restrain the power of the Estates General (public council), as much as royal power.[116] The authority of the public council is no longer invoked without reference to the Paris *parlement,* and it is time alone that brings about hereditary succession: a custom that is 'gradually received'.[117] The king remains contractually bound to his subjects in this analysis, but the role of the council has been diminished.

This change of front is further demonstrated through Hotman's changing attitude to the role of the Paris *parlement:* Where in 1573 and 1576 the public council had been the main institutional focus for restraining the power of kings, Hotman did a complete volte-face on the role of *parlement,* expanding and enlarging its role, along with that of the *chambre des comptes* to police the fundamental laws of the kingdom. Through the right to remonstrate, the Paris *parlement* could act as a bulwark against arbitrary decision making on the part of the French king, but in bolstering the authority of this institution, Hotman was undermining the principles of

---

[113] *Francogallia* 1586, XIII, 156–65. Hotman here made the case that Pope Zacharias had no temporal authority over Childeric, and only consented to the deposition rather than directly authorising it. Such a position was not necessarily diametrically opposed to that of the League. The 1576 edition of *Francogallia,* cited here, also contains some ad hominem attacks on Matharel 'a noisy, impudent and unclean fellow' and Papire Masson, 'a renegade Jesuit and hired sycophant'.

[114] To Hesse 15. Feb. 1577 (Darmstadt HSA, No.2), cited in Kelley, *François Hotman,* 266, n.4. Kelley suggests that Hotman may have been involved in the publishing and circulation of the Latin translation of the pamphlet.

[115] *Francogallia* 1586, XXV, 188–200. Cf. Hotman's spat with Matteo Zampini, Henri III's Italian counsellor, who ended up defending the Cardinal de Bourbon's right to inherit the throne: Zampini, *De Successione praerogativae*; Zampini, *De la Succession du Droict*; Hotman, *Ad Tractatum Matthaei Zampini.* Hotman could publish this text so swiftly because it is largely drawn from his 1585/88 treatises.

[116] Garnett, 'Scholastic Thought in Humanist Guise', discusses the problems of this argument, 801–2.

[117] *Francogallia* 1586, 189.

his earlier editions of *Francogallia*. Ironically enough, this feature of his work indicated Hotman's intellectual debt to the work of the League lawyer René Choppin, whom Hotman's son Jean would go on to attack for his League connections in the *Anti-Choppinus*.[118] In his subsequent versions of *Francogallia*, Hotman owed several unacknowledged debts to Choppin's *De Domanio Franciae* (1574), in a twist that subverts conventional readings of the Leaguers as plagiarists of the Huguenots.

There were legitimate reasons for comparing certain Leaguer ideas to Hotman's, but taking into account the modifications he made to *Francogallia* over the years casts further light on the complex nature of that intellectual relationship. Louis Dorléans, for example, turned the principles of *Francogallia* against the Huguenot cause, arguing that it would conflict with the ancient laws of France to accept the kingship of Henri de Navarre. In his *Advertissement, des catholiques anglois aux françois catholiques* (1586), in which Dorléans adopted the guise of an English Catholic, writing to his French peers in warning of the terrors of rule by a Protestant monarch, he singled out Hotman's *Francogallia*[119]:

> In their *Francogallia*, which is one of the most detestable books seen to this day, and which was composed to set all of France on fire, they cry that it is lawful to choose whichever King matches their appetite. You should then say to these heretics, that the King of Navarre is not to our taste, and that he can stay in his Béarn.[120]

When Dorléans said *Francogallia* was designed to 'set France on fire', he doubtless had in mind Hotman's claim in the preface to be quenching the very flames that Dorléans claimed he was stoking. Here Dorléans turned the Huguenot's own argument against him, observing that the same law of custom and preference made the case against Navarre more forcefully than it defended him. Dorléans endeavoured to present the Huguenots as constructing a conspiracy in which they would crown their own leader king and

---

[118] Hotman, *Francogallia*, XIV, 173, 176, 178–81, in reference to Choppin, *De Domanio Franciae*, II. vii.8; III.vii. 6, 10, 15–17; III.xix.12.
[119] Republished in augmented form: *Premier, et seconds [sic] advertissements des catholiques anglois aux François catholiques*, and to which Dorléans also wrote a response: *Responce des vrays catholiques françois*. Cf. Duplessis Mornay's *Lettre d'un gentilhomme catholique français* and the anonymous *Response a un ligueur masque du nom de catholique anglois*.
[120] Dorléans, *Advertissement des Catholiques Anglois*, 77: '*En leur Françoise-Gaule, qui est l'un des plus detestables livres qui ait veu le jour, et que l'on a composé pour mettre toute la France en combustion, ils chantent qu'il est loisible de choisir un Roy à son appetit. Dites doncques aux heretiques, que le Roy de Navarre d'est à vostre appetit, et partant qu'il se tienne en son Bearn*'.

thereby introduce heresy to a country that had for twelve hundred years remained Catholic.[121]

This second point is especially noteworthy. Hotman had always claimed to have adopted the strategies of the *mos gallicum docendi* in contrast to the *mos italicum*, eschewing Roman law for native French customs. It has been shown that the *Francogallia* did not live up to these standards and remained indebted to medieval Roman jurisprudence in more ways than Hotman would care to admit.[122] He was forced to adopt this position more openly, however, when he threw his legal weight behind Navarre's claim to the throne. In attacking *Francogallia*, Dorléans used Hotman's original strategy against him: he argued that the Roman law of representation which underpinned Navarre's claim to the throne had no authority in France, and instead the customary law of 'proximity of blood' had primacy.[123] In defending Navarre's right to succeed, Hotman had ended up defending the application of Roman law to the French succession, a practice he had condemned in the first edition *Francogallia*. Dorléans thereby sought to position the League in defence of the truly ancient constitution, grounded in French customary law, whereas the Huguenots, with their heresy, were the ones both shoring up imperial, Roman law and introducing unwelcome, dangerous novelties to France.

Salic Law

The argument from the ancient *politia* clearly had its limits. Precisely because it was rooted in an ancient, almost mythical, past, an ancient constitutionalist argument could easily be manipulated to support opposing claims, and arguments over the role of the various institutions of the French constitution were not easily resolved. A feature of the French constitution which was less mutable, however, was the Salic law. This referred to the first written law-code of the Salian Franks issued under Clovis.[124] In effect, it was a law of primogeniture which prevented the female line from inheriting Salian land, but in its origins contained no reference to royal succession. It had taken on a legendary status by the sixteenth century, by which time it had become known as the first law of the French people. It was said to be the

---

[121] Dorléans, *Advertissement des Catholiques Anglois*, 75–6.
[122] Garnett, 'Scholastic Thought in Humanist Guise'.
[123] Dorléans, *Advertissement des Catholiques Anglois*, 77–87.
[124] BN Lat 4628 A: the Carolingian version of the Salic law is most likely the version known to French writers until the middle of the fifteenth century. Cf. Giesey, 'The Juristic Basis of Dynastic Right to the French Throne'.

'most excellent' of all French laws, because it excluded foreigners from inheriting the throne.[125] This '*salicophilie*' reached its zenith in Guillaume Postel's 1552 work *La Loy Salicque* in which Postel described the Gauls as the first people (post-Flood), and the Salic law as the 'first temporal institution that there was in the world'.[126] In this context, the Leaguers had a harder time persuading other Catholics that they were not introducing innovations to the constitution. Charles de Bourbon's claim to the throne was not straightforward, and even though Henri III had, under League pressure, declared him officially a *prince du sang* in 1585 (and therefore, implicitly, his heir), there were plenty who did not accept this.[127]

The Leaguer argument that the law of Catholicity was a fundamental law was presented as running counter to the dictates of Salic law which determined Navarre's succession to the throne in 1584. Anti-League polemicists accused the League of violating Salic law, and thereby attacking France. Pamphlets like the *Anti-Guisart* (1586) and the *Discours sur le droit pretendu par ceux de Guise* (1580) argued that Salic law 'saved' France from 'gynaecocracy' and quoted Seyssel in praising it for rescuing France from foreign rule.[128] The emphasis on foreign rule was particularly potent in an anti-League context, given the potential threat of a Spanish monarch on the French throne. Duplessis Mornay argued in 1589 that under Salic law, Navarre's inheritance had been confirmed for many years in the minds of Frenchmen.[129] In Belloy's *Apologie Catholique*, the refutation of League arguments on the subject of the Cardinal de Bourbon's candidacy for the monarchy is categorical. Bourbon's inheritance is forbidden by Salic law, which gave the crown to the next male heir '*factus dominus*' by the death of his predecessor. Belloy argued that even the king could not alter this law.[130]

[125] Seyssel, *The Monarchy of France*, 1.7. *Pour ce que plusieurs*, a work first written in 1464, made Salic law central to the French succession and was enormously influential in the sixteenth century. It was published twice alongside Seyssel's work as *La Loy Salique, premiere loy des Francois*.
[126] Giesey, *Le rôle méconnu*, 157, and more broadly 187–8. For Hotman on Salic law, see Hotman, *Francogallia*, 269–75.
[127] As Giesey has shown, Baldus de Ubaldis (the medieval Italian lawyer), had made it canonical in French succession by the beginning of the fifteenth century that a *prince du sang*, regardless of his distance from the direct line, would have the same claim to the throne as a son of the existing king would, unless that king already had a son, in which case he took priority. This prediction came true when it became clear that the Bourbon family would succeed to the Valois family as the next *princes du sang*. Giesey, *la loi Salique*, 192–6. Giesey describes fully the arguments for and against Navarre's succession, 199–256.
[128] 'l'Antiguisart' and 'Discours sur le droit pretendu par ceux de Guise' in Goulart, *Mémoires*, I, 19; 386–7.
[129] Attrib. Duplessis Mornay, *Lettre d'un gentilhomme Catholique françois*, 19.
[130] Belloy, *Apologie Catholique*, 2.18, 136. Cf. Innes, 'Robert Persons's *Conference* and the Salic Law Debate'.

League writers had several options on their hands in countering these attacks, and in their rejoinders further evidence emerges of the variety of reactions in the League to the thesis of elective monarchy in Hotman's *Francogallia*. The *Dialogue d'entre le Maheustre et le Manant* took what might be termed the 'conventional' approach, in making apparently straightforward use of the *Francogallia* when it came to the question of succession.[131] The *Maheustre* (the nobleman) in the dialogue represented the position of the Catholic anti-Leaguers: they recognised, the character argues, that the king was the legitimate and natural ruler of France, they resisted 'popular violence' and democracy, and they wished to expel the Spanish from France.[132] By denying the succession to Navarre, the *Maheustre* argued that the League were guilty of treason. The *Manant* (the character of the townsman) replied with a familiar argument: the general laws of Christianity and the particular laws of France prevented a heretic from succeeding to the throne. He justified the doctrine of election in a passage which was excluded from the anti-League version of the text published in 1594. He argued that the French crown was, originally, not hereditary but elective since its very inception, and that the Estates General made kings and established them by a solemn election. If the children of those kings inherited the throne, this was not because the crown was hereditary, but because of the 'affection' of the French people for the memory of their king.[133] The *Manant* argued that the election took the form of a reciprocal oath between the people and the king, using examples from French history which were most likely lifted from *Francogallia*, to show the power of the people, acting through the Estates, to elect their king since Pharamond's reign. The *Manant* embellished this *Francogallian*, ancient-constitutional argument with a League twist: the king's promise to conserve and protect the Catholic faith was a fundamental law of France

---

[131] According to Ascoli: *Dialogue d'entre le Maheustre et le Manent*, 52–3. Cf. Ascoli, 'A Radical Pamphlet of Late Sixteenth Century France'; Baumgartner, *Radical Reactionaries*, 210–21; Salmon, 'Appendix: A Note on the *Dialogue d'entre le Maheustre et le Manant*', 264–6.

[132] *Maheustre*, 51: '*Je vous diray ce sur quoy nous nous fondons à suivre le Roy; et vous faire la guerre; il y a trois principaux poincts. Le premier, que nous soustenons le Roy legitime et naturel de la France, auquel appartient la domination de l'Estat. Le second, que nous sommes catholiques François, qui résistons à une violence populaire, qui se veut introduire au préjudice des privilèges de la noblesse et pour l'esteindre et former une démocratie. Le troisiesme poinct est, pour chasser l'Espagnol qu'avez appelle en France, et nous maintenir contre vous et eux*'.

[133] Ibid., 70: '*Je vous ai cy devant prouvé suffisamment que les royaumes ne sont de succession mais d'election à l'exemple de la première institution, estant certain que le peuple dont sont composez les Estats font les Roys et les establissent sur eux par une élection solomnelle, et si en la France ou autres royaumes l'on a souffert que les enfans et frères des Roys, ou parens, ayent succedé à la couronne, ce n'a este par le droict de succession, ains seulement par l'affection que les François portoient à la mémoire de leurs Roys ...*'

which could not be abrogated.[134] Here it is the coronation oath that binds the king and people, as a symbol of the former's election.

Other Leaguers, however, directly contradicted the *Francogallia* and attacked it openly, in keeping with the broader Catholic response to the controversial text since its first publication in 1573. In his *Discours par lequel il appareistra que le royaume de France est electif et non hereditaire*, the lawyer and historian Pierre de Saint-Julien took the notion of being 'Frank and free' to refer to the Catholicity of the French commonwealth. He took as his principle the notion that the French were a free people since their first liberation from the Romans. The decision to introduce a political government, ruled by a monarch, was taken by general agreement once the French stopped being vagabonds and became possessors of land (i.e. once they exercised *dominium*).[135] Saint-Julien then argued that Pharamond, the first king of the Franks cited frequently in the medieval period as the originator of Salic law, was a foreigner who did not have true dominion over the Gauls.[136] Quoting Du Haillan verbatim, who had made a strong case that Pharamond did not create Salic law, the author shows that it had never applied to France.[137] Through restoring the authority of the Estates General, Saint-Julien sought to demonstrate that the kingdom of France would return to its ancient 'flourishing' state and be brought back to the 'cradle' of the Roman Catholic church.[138] The author of the *Discours* offered his Catholic readership an historical account of why the French kingdom was unequivocally elective without relying on Hotman's arguments to make his case.

Contributing further to the ruptures within the Hotman family, Antoine Hotman joined the anti-Francogallian movement when he argued for the Cardinal de Bourbon's legitimate right to inherit the throne. In his treatise *Sur la Declaration du Roy pour les droits de prerogative de Monseigneur le*

---

[134] Ibid., 70–1.

[135] *Discours par lequel il appareistra que le royaume de France est electif et non hereditaire*, 8. On St-Julien as the author of this text, see Labitte, *De la Démocratie chez les prédicateurs de la Ligue*, 154–5. St-Julien made the same argument in his *De l'origine des bourgognons, et antiquité des estats de Bourgogne* (Paris, 1581): my thanks to one of the anonymous readers for pointing this out.

[136] Cf. des Ursins, *Les écrits politiques* I, 156, 159; II, 20,41.

[137] *Discours*, 11–16; Du Haillan, *De l'Estat et Succez des Affaires de France*, fol. 9v; 101v–104r. In the preface to his work, Du Haillan testified to his admiration for the lawyer and historian Jean du Tillet and his work *Receuil des Roys* which circulated in manuscript form before being published posthumously by his nephew in 1577. It is possible, as Craig Taylor has argued, that du Haillan took his argument from du Tillet. However, Ralph Giesey has suggested that du Haillan was familiar with du Tillet's sources before the publication of the *Receuil des Roys* in his *Le rôle méconnu de la loi Salique*, 175. For more on du Tillet, see Kelley, 'Jean du Tillet'.

[138] *Discours*, 25–8.

Cardinal de Bourbon (1588), Hotman argued that the Cardinal's right was based on the 'simple law of proximity', also known as collateral succession.[139] By this, he meant the law of consanguinity, originally a Roman law, by which Bourbon was closer in blood to Henri III than Navarre (as Antoine de Bourbon's brother), and therefore had a stronger claim to the throne.[140] This law overrode the law of primogeniture. In arguing in this fashion, Antoine Hotman explicitly attacked François' thesis that the line of succession should change in Navarre's favour.[141] In doing so, Antoine also explicitly challenged Pierre de Belloy's argument that Navarre's inheritance was based on primogeniture. Antoine ruled out Belloy's perfectly legitimate argument by claiming that the law of primogeniture did not apply in cases of collateral succession.[142] Antoine also had to counteract the argument that on the basis of the 'law of representation', Navarre was the rightful heir. Another Roman law on property inheritance, this law argued that in the case of there being no direct descendent, an heir could be traced back to the lineal, ancestral line to find one living individual. In this case, a nephew had a greater claim than an uncle, so Bourbon's right was non-existent. Antoine argued that this law too did not apply in collateral succession, thus building his case against both François Hotman and Pierre de Belloy.[143]

Antoine Hotman's argument did not rely solely on a Roman-legal case to defend Bourbon's succession. He also constructed an argument on the basis of a feudal analogy of the relationship between God and king, a point he expanded on more thoroughly in another work of that year, *Advertissement sur les lettres octroyees a M. le Cardinal de Bourbon*. God, he writes, is the '*seigneur*' of the French king. Here Antoine argued that the king held his title by the grace of God and therefore owed him faith and homage; and feudal law made a provision that if a lord became a heretic, he no longer ought to be obeyed. He pursued the comparison, arguing that at the time of the coronation ceremony a pact is made between God, king and subject. Antoine argued that this pact was not indicative of an election, but

---

[139] The discussion which follows owes a much to Giesey's *la loi Salique*, particularly 224–34.

[140] Giesey shows that in making this argument, Hotman had to circumvent the problem that collateral succession only permitted ten degrees of separation. To do this, he turned to Baldus who provided the example of François I, who declared Charles, duc d'Alençon, as his heir – despite the fact that he was separated by thirteen degrees. Bourbon was separated by twenty-one degrees, so without Baldus' example, Hotman would have been unable to construct his argument. Giesey, *la loi Salique*, 227.

[141] On François Hotman's argument, see Giesey, *la loi Salique*, 226–7.

[142] Ibid., 228. For a table showing Bourbon's right to inherit the throne, see Antoine Hotman, *Advertissement sur les lettres octroyees a M. le Cardinal de Bourbon*, 27 [mispag.].

[143] Giesey, *la loi Salique*, 227; Hotman, *Declaration*, 100–1.

an investiture. In feudal terms, this meant the transfer of the fief from lord
to vassal in return for obedience. The terms '*foedus*' and '*pactum*' apply,
referring to the mutual promises in the coronation ceremony.[144] Hotman
argued that such a pact did not prevent the monarchical authority from
being passed on via hereditary succession, but in fact perpetuated it in that
state so long as the original pact was observed.

Antoine and François Hotman employed their legal training to an
extensive degree in their battles over the succession laws. Where they
agreed, however, was in dismissing the arguments of Matteo Zampini in
his *De la Succession du Droict* (1589), which argued that Navarre could not
inherit the throne because his father was not declared the next in line to the
throne before his death in 1562 (when there were three other princes alive
closer in line than him).[145] Navarre was not able to 'represent' his father
and succeed. However, Zampini's thesis could not prevent Navarre from
inheriting after the death of the ageing cardinal. Zampini's work provoked
a fiery response from François Hotman accusing the Italian 'foreigner' of
ignorance of the French monarchical system, and ignoring the rules of
ordinary succession.[146] Antoine Hotman followed suit in attacking
Zampini's argument as weak and incorrect in his *Advertissement sur les
lettres octroyees à Monsieur le Cardinal de Bourbon*, restating his own thesis
on why Bourbon should inherit. He did so anonymously, but this clearly
indicates the extent of fracture within the League polemic itself, and it has
contributed to uncertainty in scholarly analyses of Zampini's work.[147]

The Leaguers did not present a unified front on the central questions of
the nature of the French constitution and its various institutions. Neither,
however, did their opponents. Ideas changed over time and according to
circumstances, and texts like the *Francogallia* were modified accordingly.
French political thought in this era follows a series of complex and

---

[144] Hotman, *Declaration*, 35–6. It is possible that Hotman borrowed this idea from the *Vindiciae*,
which described the relationship between God and king in feudal terms: 'Kings are the vassals of the
King of kings ... the king receives the kingdom from God in order to judge His people and guard it
against enemies. A vassal accepts law and conditions from the superior lord; the king from God,
ordering that he should always observe His law and keep it before his eyes. If he does so, then both
he and his descendants will possess the kingdom for a long time; if he does not, they will suffer the
opposite'. *Vindiciae*, ed. Garnett, 20.

[145] Zampini, *De la Succession du Droict et Prerogative de Premier Prince du sang de France*.

[146] Hotman, *Ad Tractatum Matthaei Zampini responsio*.

[147] John Allen argued that Zampini's theory of sovereignty in this work was essentially Bodinian, and
therefore 'absolutist'. Baumgartner made the case that whilst Zampini's analysis of the power of the
Estates might have been acceptable to 'radical' Parisian leaguers, his concept of absolute sovereign
power would not have been. Alternatively, Salmon and Giesey have noted similarities between
Zampini's work and Hotman's *Francogallia*. Allen, *A History of Political Thought*, 380–3;
Baumgartner, *Radical Reactionaries*, 91–2; Hotman, *Francogallia*, ed. Salmon, Giesey, 94–5.

entangled paths of scholarly conventions, common intellectual influences and disputes, notably that of the succession law and the question of elective monarchy. Out of this, the Leaguers do not emerge as especially dependent on Huguenot thinking, nor devoted to a concept of popular political power or republican thinking, but as theorists of royal power working within the framework of intellectual conventions of the day. The most significant feature of their political thought was the inclusion of the church in their concept of the ancient constitution. The notion that the people were doubly incorporated, as Boucher had argued, has important implications for debates about Gallican liberty, and the ways in which the church was considered to be 'in' the commonwealth.

CHAPTER 4

The Church 'in' the Commonwealth

For the Leaguers, the ancient French constitution was inconceivable without the church; the freedom of the Franks dovetailing with the Christianity of King Clovis, who was baptised at the dawn of the sixth century. The heritage of antiquity was wrapped in the ideology of political Augustinianism, and medieval ideas thereby permeated the political thought of the sixteenth century. The views of William of Ockham, Marsilius of Padua, John of Paris and Giles of Rome were evoked to dispute once more the concept of papal-temporal power and the rights of kings in their kingdoms. This chapter examines these debates from the perspectives of two League lawyers, René Choppin and Louis Dorléans, and one of the most hostile Catholic opponents of the League, Pierre de Belloy.

The Ancient Constitution of the Gallican Church

If France really was, as Dorléans had put it, 'le chateau de la religion Catholique', then the structure, and identity, of its commonwealth depended on a functioning relationship between la religion and la police.[1] The wars of religion had thrown an already tense relationship into chaos, and part of the stated purpose of the League was to restore a 'correct' balance between the two, a balance which was dependent on the eradication of Protestantism.

Demands for reform of the French church in 1576–7, particularly from the clergy, demonstrated the ongoing significance of pressure points in the argument for Gallican liberty.[2] Within the broader problem of religious unity, highlighted at the meeting of the Estates General at Blois in 1576, such demands emphasised the necessity of the reception of the Tridentine decrees, and the problem of the alienation of benefices, dealing in particular with the

---

[1] Dorléans, *Avertissement*, 47.   [2] See Greengrass, *Governing Passions*.

problematic legacies of the Pragmatic Sanction of Bourges (1438), the Concordat of Bologna (1516) and the definition of the Gallican liberties.[3] The Sanction had been drawn up by a national assembly of the French church and issued by Charles VII; significantly, it confirmed the decree of the Council of Basel (1431–5), that a General Council of the church should be held every ten years.[4] The *avocat général* to François I, Jacques Cappel, subsequently argued that it was the first legislation to define the Gallican liberties.[5] However, the unresolved tensions between the supporters of the Pragmatic Sanction, and the defenders of the more royalist Concordat, continued to make trouble into the sixteenth century when debates over episcopal election and church property raged alongside the crisis of the Reformation.[6] These tensions prevented what is now known as 'Gallicanism' from becoming a coherent doctrine before the Four Articles of 1682. Pierre Pithou did create an effective synthesis of the Gallican liberties in 1594, in his rejection of the power of popes to command anything which pertained to France in favour of the laws and canons of the Gallican church.[7] However, as the work of historians of the seventeenth century has shown, these definitions of Gallican liberty remained most contentious and divisive in their details.[8]

Such questions continued to frame the debates of the 1580s and 1590s, and both spoke to the indeterminacy of the relationship between the temporal and the spiritual in French law. The meeting of the Estates in 1576 had offered an opportunity to persuade the king of the need for unity and conformity of religion in France as a path to peace. This was the attitude taken by the Archbishop of Lyon, Pierre d'Epinac, who became a central figure in the League of the 1580s. Epinac's discourse on the necessity of contiguity between the faith of the chief magistrate and his people expressed a key aspect of the League's campaign to avoid the perceived disaster of confessional division they observed in England and Germany. In his published *Harengue* of 1577, he made clear the need to clarify the relationship between *la religion* and *la police*, the twin pillars of the French community. Epinac identified religion as the principal foundation of political community (*communauté politique*), arguing that the need

---

[3] *Protestation de l'ordre du clergé; Extraict des registres des Estats tenus à Blois en 1576.*
[4] Cf. Parsons, *The Church in the Republic*, 14–51.
[5] Salmon, 'Gallicanism and Anglicanism', 158; Baumgartner, 'Louis XII's Gallican Crisis of 1510–1513', in Bakos, *Politics, Ideology and the Law*, 55–72.
[6] Protestation de l'ordre du clergé; Extraict des registres des Estats tenus à Blois en 1576.
[7] Pithou, *Les Libertez de l'Eglise Gallicane.*
[8] Bergin, *The Politics of Religion in Early Modern France*; Franceschi, *La Crise Théologico-Politique.*

for a place of worship was the peculiar rationality guiding this decision, and religion was the bond of men in civil society.[9] Correspondingly, religion provided order and unity; a well-founded commonwealth was one based on unity of faith (rather than justice, as in the Aristotelian account).[10] Epinac defined the 'natural' French citizen as a Catholic, and argued that the kingdom had been Catholic since Clovis' baptism. France was 'glorious' when united under one faith, here associating Catholicism with the increase of territory and successful government.

Epinac's concerns were echoed by the lawyer René Choppin, in his *De Sacra Politia* (1577), in which he used the *cahiers de doléances* from the meeting of the Estates General in 1576 to frame his analysis of the reforming program he laid out. Choppin was later seen to be the lackey of the clerical Leaguers, and this was how he was portrayed in the *Anti-Choppinus*. He had spoken out in 1586 in the name of the right of the Paris *parlement* to decide on matters of alienation of ecclesiastical property: opposing Henri III's attempts to gain papal authority to do so without the consent of the *parlement*. His plea, in 1580, on behalf of the clergy over the rights of the church to feudal lands was published in French as *Oraison pour la clergé de France* in 1590, when the League was at the height of its power. Most provocatively, however, Choppin wrote in support of Gregory XIV's excommunication of Henri IV in 1591, the *De pontifice gregorii ad gallos diplomate congratulatoria oratio*.[11] These writings, and his membership of the *chambre ardente*, established by the Sixteen from 1591 to persecute heretics, confirmed his status as an *archi-ligueur* in the eyes of contemporaries, and it was only through his contacts with the de Thou family that he escaped exile once Henri IV gained control of the kingdom.[12]

Choppin's *De Sacra Politia*, republished in Paris during the crucial years of League dominance in 1587 and 1589, was less widely referenced than his *De Domanio Franciae* at the time, but his frequent cross references between the texts indicates that he intended them to be read as complementary works. In taking this approach, Choppin appears to have recognised, in the ubiquity of claims such as those of Pierre d'Epinac, the deep-rooted problem of defining the relationship between *la religion* and *la police* within

---

[9] Epinac, *Harengue*, 11–12. For a detailed examination of Epinac's role in the League see Richard, *La papauté et la Ligue française*.

[10] Epinac, *Harengue*, 13.

[11] He may also have written other works which are no longer extant, including *De mutuis regis populique officiis*, dedicated to the League 'king' Charles X, which was never published. Robinet, *Dictionnaire universel*, 11, 678–9; Ménage, *Vitae Petri Aerodii*, 210.

[12] de Thou, *Histoire universelle*, T. 14, 669, referring to T. 12, 558. My thanks to Mark Greengrass for this reference.

the commonwealth. An analysis of *De Sacra Politia* demonstrates the ways in which the reforming agenda of the clergy in the 1570s was taken up by lawyers and became aggravated in the League years. It also clarifies the way in which lawyers read the complaints of the clergy through the lens of the problem of *dominium,* and thereby contributed to the ongoing debates about the liberties of the Gallican church.

De Sacra Politia was designed to encourage the king to take immediate action to reform the church; Choppin cites the advice of Nicephorus Gregoras, the Byzantine theologian, to the emperor Andronicus on reforming the church and reinforces this with his own comments on the sagacity of publishing edicts and hurrying deputies to reform the church, in order to give hope to those who were suffering for their religion. Writing in Latin, Choppin was also explicitly writing for a European audience: he expressed hope that the Scottish and English would see the error of their ways and return to the 'true' church. He dedicated *De Sacra Politia* to the king, but his preface addressed the clergy, asking for their forbearance in reading his work which – he observed – might cause them some concern that their rights were being curtailed in his analysis. He requested that they accept the need for some compromise in order to restore peace and unity to the church, emphasising the role of the clergy and confraternities in praying for the wellbeing of the civil polity in particular. In doing so he clarified his position on the mutually reinforcing duties of kings to the 'external' discipline of the church, and of the clergy to the 'external' discipline of the civil polity.[13]

Choppin's central argument built on the idea of an affinity between *la religion/religio* and *la police/politeia*, which Epinac had also drawn on in his *Harengue*, to argue that the kings of France were the patrons and protectors of the civil polity, and the 'exterior' of the church. In the preface, he explained the relationship of mutual support between the civil and ecclesiastical polities:

> Amongst all the good regulations that Christian Princes have divinely established to maintain and conserve the state of civil society, it seems to me that there is none so excellent and laudable, than to place and put in the same degree of honour and respect these two things: religion and political justice, which are bound by the same cord, and deal with each other as though through a kind of kinship that they have maintained. Because not only do prelates and leading clergymen teach and instruct in religion, and magistrates in that of justice, [but] each on their side and through their

---

[13] *De Sacra Politia*, preface, n.p.

different functions affirms and conserves the state of public affairs, and they
have no difficulty in reciprocal aid, or in supporting one another in the
management and administration of affairs.[14]

For Choppin, the church was 'the soul of the Christian Republic, having
the same force within, as prudence does in the human body'. In its
external government, this ecclesiastical polity, the embodiment of wisdom in the political community, was also an elective community. In
keeping with medieval theological argument that invites comparison
with John of Paris', *De Potestate Regia et Papali* (c.1302, published in six
editions in France between 1506 and 1683), Choppin ended up arguing
that the church was governed like a political community: it was incorporated, and elective.[15] Strikingly, Choppin's reference here was to
Romulus, quoting him on the election of priests through the voice and
suffrages of the people: establishing that the ecclesiastical and civil were
interlocked from the foundation of Rome, and thereby creating
a connection between this idea and that of the ancient liberties enshrined
in the French constitution.

If the ecclesiastical polity was the 'soul' of any Christian commonwealth
as Choppin argued, then the 'magistrate of the commonwealth' was the law
and minister of both God and the community. Choppin limited the duties
of this magistrate to the external discipline of the church. In support of
this, he used patristic sources, quoting Eusebius on Constantine to establish that bishops have charge of the internal workings of the church, the
emperor of the external. For Choppin, resorting to the origins of the
relationship between church and empire clarified that the French king's
role regarding the church in his kingdom was that of a guardian and
protector:

> The intention and end at which the Kings of France aim all their pursuits is
> to conserve the liberty of the Gallican church entirely and protect [it]
> without diminishing its rights [or] shaking off the submission and obedi-
> ence which they owe to the holy see. Popes recognise the kings of France to

---

[14] Ibid., '*Cum multa divinitus ad Civilem Societatem tuendam instituta sunt a Principibus Christianis: tum nihil praeclarius, quam quod has duas res paribus invicem studiis coli voluerunt, et Dei immortalis Religione, et Iustitiam Politicam : que habent commune aliquod vinculum, et quasi cognatione quadam inter se continentur. Non solum enim distinctis operis officiisque Pontifices Religionem interpretando, Magistratus iura dicendo Rempublicam conservarunt: verum mutua quoque alter ab altero subsidia rerum gerendarum petere consuevit*'.

[15] Choppin, *De Sacra Politia*, preface, n.p. This was an issue raised in 1561 at Orléans and again at the assembly of the clergy at Blois in 1579. Choppin also refers to a similar legal case he took on in January of 1577. On John of Paris, see Leclercq, *Jean de Paris*. More recently, see Jones, ed., *John of Paris*.

be very obedient, officious, devoted, affectionate in the honour and respect they devote to the *saint siege*.[16]

In Choppin's view, the role of the king was as the patron and protector of the 'civil polity' of the church, not its owner. This formulation of the royal role corresponded to his analysis in his *De Domanio Franciae*, where he had also written of the French kings as guardians and protectors of their public domain. Likewise, the rights of sovereignty and feudal bonds of loyalty could not be alienated or sold. The French king was the 'spouse' of the kingdom and the public domain a dowry (discussed further in Chapter 7).[17] Significantly, Choppin went onto argue that the temporal goods of the church could also be said to be incorporated into the domain, a discussion he cross-references in *De Sacra Politia*.[18] The issue of property ownership was, therefore, key to deciphering the relationship between church and civil government: Choppin chose to resolve this issue by arguing that the king had charge of the 'external' goods of the church, referring to its property, but no direct role in the internal workings of the church. Choppin concluded that the king did not have fullness of royal power over the ecclesiastical. *De Sacra Politia* called for a recognition that most ecclesiastical offices were elective, even when taking the regalian rights into account. If a king restored election in the church, Choppin hinted, it would increase his majesty.

Choppin went to some lengths to make the case that the controversial Concordat of Bologna actually supported this point and gave the king oversight of elective benefices, making him a patron rather than a lord.[19] This argument became harder to sustain when it came to the regalian rights, however, and here Choppin argued that bishops were not the vassals of kings and should not be obliged to take oaths of loyalty as required by the Concordat.[20] On the sensitive subject of investiture, Choppin argued that the bishops of France had always performed this ceremony for the kings of their country, but that, conversely, kings customarily kept the offices in question elective and allowed the clergy freedom of action (here he refers to Constantine and the Arian controversy).[21] This last claim was untrue, but Choppin wanted to make a case in this work for the claims of customary over written law. By arguing from customary law, Choppin

---

[16] Choppin, *De Sacra Politia*, preface, n.p. '*Scilicet huc semper Francorum Regum studia spectarunt, ut et libertatem Gallicae Ecclesiae sartam tectam custodirent (eius iura institutaque haud sinentes everti) nec propterea debitae Sanctissimo Solio obedientiae excuterent iugum: Quos Pontifex etiam quisque Reges expertus est Sacrae Sedis cultores officiosissimos, observantissimos, obsequentissimos*'.

[17] Choppin, *De Domanio Franciae*, II.1.2, 175.   [18] Ibid., I.13.6, 141–2.

[19] Choppin, *De Sacra Politia*, I.1.16   [20] Ibid., 1.7.   [21] Ibid., 1.7.26

could still claim to be preserving the powers of kings and clergy, but evidently he privileged the latter over the former.[22] On the subject of the interventions from the Roman church in France, Choppin therefore supported the reception of the Tridentine decrees, without contradicting his argument about royal power over the church. He argued that for the sake of reforms to the French church, and particularly concerning the quality of person taking up positions in the church, they should be received.

De Sacra Politia was a comment on Gallican liberties as much as an argument for ecclesiastical reform. Choppin established parameters for the Gallican liberties, citing in particular the ordinance of 1369 under Charles V and Urban V which prevented popes from excommunicating any town in the kingdom of France, and identifying the Pragmatic Sanction as the primary source of Gallican liberties, wherein the principle of episcopal election was enshrined.[23] The trouble with the Pragmatic Sanction, however, was that it failed to resolve the question of the relationship between a benefice and a piece of property, and thus it failed to clarify the perennial problem of defining the limits of spiritual and temporal *dominium* within France.[24] This was where Choppin sought to bring some clarity.

Choppin established that when it came to the royal right to nominate benefices, the pope could not contradict the will of the 'lay patron' or this would lead to an *appel comme d'abus* (here he refers to the meeting at Orléans in 1560). Finally, he made the observation that popes did not deliver public judgements simply for ceremonial purposes but for the 'pleasure of the will and command of the people'. He cited classical Roman sources to support this and argued that the pontiffs would not proceed with anything that went against the wishes of the Roman people. Without allowing for the possibility of papal involvement, Choppin maintained that discipline could not be guaranteed in the church. His reference to Deuteronomy 17 as the basis of a case that it was a royal and political law of the kingdom to execute the commandments of God is

---

[22] The subject of customary law was a long-standing professional interest of Choppin's, influenced no doubt by his mentor Christophe de Thou. Choppin was financially rewarded by Henri III for his collection of customary laws, *De Legibus Andium municipalibus* (Paris, 1581), and was made a perpetual *échevin* of Angers as a result. On his withdrawal from public life after the League years, he produced another collection of the customs of Paris: *De Civilibus Parisiorum moribus* (Paris, 1596).

[23] Choppin, *De Sacra Politia*, preface.

[24] As indicated in Guymier, *Caroli septimi Pragmatica sanctio a Cosma Guymier glossata*, which was published again in 1504, 1532, 1556 and 1666. Guymier's treatise is usefully discussed in Lange, 'Gallicanisme et Réforme'.

especially significant, not least because Deuteronomy 17 came to underpin arguments for the election of a Catholic king in the League of the 1580s; it is also a reminder of Choppin's conventional claims in *De Domanio Franciae* that the French kings were subject to the restraints of natural, divine and fundamental law.

In *De Sacra Politia*, Choppin sought to restore the French church to a position of moral integrity in the kingdom, and so his text was also a critique of the failings of the sixteenth-century church which – importantly – allowed for some intervention of the monarch in ecclesiastical affairs, even whilst constructing a case for the responsibilities and rights of the clergy over their own institution. Choppin did so on the basis of the ancient laws and customs of the Roman church, in which the bishops had care of the internal workings of the institution, and the emperor the external (his references here are to Eusebius, and St Paul's letter to Timothy).[25] He extended this desire to restore the church to its original condition to the Gallican church, and here Choppin sought to balance out the juridical demands of recent laws (particularly the Concordat of Bologna), with that aim.[26] He cited the system of the *appel comme d'abus* as a customary method of protecting the church against both papal and royal abuses; and the regalian rights, as an ancient method of protecting church discipline (and not, he clarifies, designed to be used for a king's own sordid profit).[27] This system of mutual obligations and restraints was the key to church reform according to Choppin, but it rested on the precarious requirement that a king recognise the customs that are in place.[28]

In making his argument in *De Sacra Politia*, Choppin argued that the rights of the clergy need not conflict with the regalian rights of the king, or the liberties of the French people. The argument was dependent on the differentiation of types of power: absolute, or 'full', versus administrative power. It was also a question of differentiating between *dominium* understood as government, and *dominium* understood as ownership of property. As in so much of Choppin's work, his emphasis was on the customary laws which had underpinned the liberties of the Gallican church and the rights of the king.

[25] Choppin, *De Sacra Politia*, I.1   [26] Ibid., I.4   [27] Ibid., VII.15.
[28] Cf. Bodin's argument in the *République*, that rulers ought to recognise the validity of customary law, but that they could not be coerced into doing so: Bodin, *République*, 1.9, 136–7: '*Mais quant aux coustumes generals et particulieres, qui ne concernent point l'etablissement du Royaume, on n'a pas accoustumé d'y rien changer, sinon apres avoir bien et deuement assemblé les trois estats de France en general, ou de chacun Bailliage en particulier, non pas qu'il soit necessaire de s'arrester à leur advis, ou que le Roy ne puisse faire le contraire de ce qu'on demandera, si la raison naturelle, et la justice de son vouloir lui assiste*'.

Pierre de Belloy's Challenge to the League

Pierre de Belloy's response to the re-formed League of the 1580s demonstrates the extent to which the relationship between *la police* and *la religion* came under pressure as the question of succession came to the fore. It was a question intensely debated amongst royalist Catholics as they considered their obligations to the church and to the commonwealth. Belloy's *Apologie Catholique* is a central text in these polemics, provoking controversy in the League by challenging its legitimacy from a series of reasoned legal positions. According to Louis Dorléans, Belloy was one of the most troublesome heretics ever to have plagued the Roman church since the Donatist and Arian controversies.[29] Belloy drew on René Choppin's work openly and his text therefore offers an especially significant insight into the problem facing the Leaguers of demonstrating how their position on the succession could fail to clash with Gallican liberties.

Belloy's *Apologie Catholique* was primarily a response to the succession crisis of 1584, and correspondingly it made a robust case for Navarre's right to inherit the throne. Within its range of fire were particularly the clerical Leaguers, whom Belloy accused of preaching 'war, rebellion and disobedience', to the 'subversion of Christian government'.[30] Belloy first wrote the treatise in Latin, after which it was swiftly translated into French and published in 1585, and again in 1586. It was also translated and published in English in 1585 as *A Catholicke Apologie against the libels, declarations, advices, and consultations made, written, and published by those of the League, perturbers of the quiet Estate of the Realme of France. Who are risen since the decease of the late Monsieur, the Kings onely brother.* This work, along with his *Examen du discours publié par ceux de la Ligue contre la Maison royalle de France* (1587), and *De l'authorité du Roy* (1587), prompted a volley of exchanges, including *Responce a un livre de Belloy plein de faulsetez et calomnies, deguisé souz cet excellent, & beau titre de l'authorité du Roy* (1588); *Sommaire résponse à l'examen d'un hérétique, sur un discours de la loy Salique, faussement prétendu contre la Maison de France & le Branche de Bourbon* (1587). Either Belloy or his colleagues penned a response to these League attacks as the *Replique fait à cette response* (n.p., 1587), and the debates continued into 1588 with the *Réponse aux Calomnies proposées contre les Catholiques* (n.p., 1588) and Antoine Hotman's *Advertissement sur les letters octroyées a M. le Cardinal de Bourbon* (n.p.,1588).

[29] Dorléans, *Plaidoyé des gens du roy*, 12. Cf. Boucher, *Sermons*, 25, which also compares the current state of France to the Donatist crisis.

[30] Belloy, *Apologie Catholique*, 2.21, fol. 65v.

Belloy's work was sufficiently influential to reach his intended international readership, and Cardinal Bellarmine waded into the debates around the *Apologie Catholique* under the name of 'Franciscus Romulus'. His treatise was published in Latin as *Responsio ad Praecipua Capita Apologiae. Quae Falso Catholica inscribitur, pro successione Henrici Navarreni, in Francorum Regnum*, and translated into French in 1588. The English Jesuit Robert Persons also identified Belloy as an opponent in his *Conference about the Next Succession* of 1594 (discussed in Chapter 8), and, in a reply to Persons' *Conference*, Sir John Hayward conversely defended Belloy's position in 1603.[31] All of this suggests that the *Apologie Catholique* should, therefore, be considered as playing a dominant role in the polemics of these fraught years, and that along with Belloy's wider oeuvre, particularly *De l'authorité du Roy*, and his *Examen du discours*, his ideas are worthy of far closer scholarly attention than they have hitherto received.

The foundation of Belloy's argument in the *Apologie Catholique* was the succession law of France, and it was specifically written as a response to the case made for the Cardinal de Bourbon's succession to the throne.[32] In this context, Belloy characterised the Leaguer's argument as follows:

> The disturbers of the peace and the laws of the Kingdom argue in particular against the King of Navarre, so that he shall never be King of France unless he is first consecrated, anointed and crowned according to the ancient custom upheld in their opinion since Clovis the first Christian King: and that nature alone cannot create kings, without the traditional ceremonies observed at the succession of a new Prince.[33]

Belloy's reference to 'ancient custom' is particularly telling; in the *Apologie Catholique* he sought to erode arguments for the election of kings based on custom, and the notion that the Catholicity of the French crown was a fundamental law. Belloy considered the Leaguer ancient constitution to be flawed in this context because of its emphasis on the power of ceremony, rather than the question of the Catholicity of the monarchy. He thus shifted the frame of the debate in a subtle, but effective, manner.

---

[31] Hayward, *An answer to the first part of a certain conference*.
[32] It was very likely written as a response to the *Declaration* of 1585, circulating in manuscript form.
[33] Belloy, *Apologie Catholique*, 2.12, fol. 43v: 'Les perturbateurs du repos & des loix de ce Royaume respondent particulierement contre le Roy de Navarre, qu'il ne sera jamais Roy de France, qu'il ne soit premierement sacré, oinct, & couronné selon l'ancienne coustume, gardée à leur advis, depuis Clovis le premier Roy Chrestien: & que la seule nature ne le peut faire Roys, sans les cérémonies ordinaires, à l'advenement d'un nouveau Prince'.

The *Apologie Catholique* is divided into three parts: the first, dealing explicitly with the 'troubles of the kingdom', is a defence of the laws of hereditary succession, particularly the Salic law, with a detailed examination of the house of Bourbon's claim to the throne. The second, more extensive part continues with the issue of Navarre's succession, but then broadens out into some of the wider political questions facing France: the issue of heretic rule; the king's rights over the French church; the issue of freedom of conscience; the power of excommunication; and the reception of the Tridentine decrees. The third part of the treatise takes up the issue of treason and returns to the question of the succession laws of the *princes du sang*, strengthening Navarre's case, and drawing on the genealogies of the Capetians, Carolingians and Merovingians to do so. In this final part, Belloy reiterates his emphasis on the 'treasonous' and rebellious nature of the League.

The second part of the *Apologie Catholique* takes up the question of ecclesiastical jurisdiction in order to attack the clerical Leaguers. Belloy explicitly sought to prevent these clerics from making 'another monarchy' in France by challenging the succession on hierocratic principles. In Belloy's analysis, the church in France was under the jurisdiction of the crown, and so there could be no threat of theocracy. In this context, Belloy argued that 'the commonwealth is not in the church, the church is in the commonwealth'.[34] In taking this quotation from the fourth-century bishop Optatus of Milevis, Belloy wrote in accordance with convention. He used this authoritative reference as part of his attempt to clarify the relationship between the temporal and the spiritual spheres, arguing (from a strongly juridical perspective), that the key issue in debate was the king's legal rights over the church in his kingdom. Belloy cited Optatus' observation on the relationship between the church and the commonwealth in the course of his address to the clergy in the *Apologie Catholique* (2.11), in order to make the case that since princes had first encountered and authorised the Catholic religion, they were the dispensers and treasurers of ecclesiastical property.[35] The language is significant here, particularly the notion that

---

[34] Optatus, 'De Schismate Donatistarum Adversus Parmenium' in Migne, *Patrologia Latina*, 2, col. 999: '*non enim respublica est in Ecclesia, sed Ecclesia in respublica est, id est, in imperio Romano*'. Cf. François Bauduin's preface to the Latin edition of Optatus' *De schismate Donatistarum* (Paris, 1563), translated in French in 1564, and his commentary on the Latin: *Delibatio africanæ historiæ ecclesiasticæ, sive Optati Milevitani libri VII. ad Parmenianum de schismate donatistarum. Victoris Uticensis libri III. de persecutione vandalica in Africa. Cum annotationibus ex Fr. Balduini j. c. commentariis rerum ecclesiasticarum* (Paris, 1569). Parsons, *The Church in the Republic*, uses Optatus' famous phrase in its title, but nevertheless does not attribute much significance to the interest in Optatus in the period.

[35] Belloy, *Apologie Catholique*, 2.11, fol. 39v. Cf. 2.19, fol. 62r on the Donatists.

princes 'authorised' Catholicism, and Belloy went on to make reference to the first Christian emperor Constantine's position as the guardian and distributor of the goods of the church, in the manner of the ancient kings of Judah.[36] Belloy took the view that the king was a possessor of his kingdom entire (with the exception of the private property of individuals) that included the property of the church.[37]

In the course of making these arguments, Belloy depended on the authority of Choppin, whom he cited as one of the principle authors referred to in the *Apologie Catholique*. Belloy built his case for the regalian rights on aspects of the *De Domanio Franciae*; *De Sacra Politia*, however, was evidently less suited to his position. The key difference between the two lawyers lay in their approach to the role of the clergy in the Gallican church: Belloy subordinated the clergy to the authority of the king without allowing, as Choppin had, for elective office. Instead, Belloy argued, drawing heavily on canon law to do so, that the bishops of the primitive church had recognised the rights of the French king over the national church (2.25). Belloy exploited the ambiguities of the Pragmatic Sanction of Bourges (2.11) to argue a case for the king's fullness of power over both church reform and persons and property. His argument amounted to a defence of the absolute royal power over church and state, claiming that the French monarchy 'has always had, thanks to God, complete sovereign power, institution, jurisdiction over and government of the clergy'.[38]

As well as establishing, with great clarity, the extent of the king's regalian rights, Belloy commented extensively on ecclesiastical jurisdiction in the *Apologie Catholique*. In this, he revived some significant medieval debates to construct an attack on papal temporal authority. Louis Dorléans compared Belloy to the Donatists and Arians, but he also drew comparisons between Belloy and the fourteenth-century Franciscan theologian William of Ockham.[39] This was a perceptive observation. The influence of Ockham's ideas in France in this era is an interesting question, as Ockham contributed an authoritative voice on the question of papal dominion.[40] Belloy, as we

---

[36] His sources here make a comprehensive list, from Augustine's letters to the Old Testament (particularly the well-trodden path provided by 2 Kings 13 and Deuteronomy 17), as well as Baldus de Ubaldis on canon law, and further references to Roman law.

[37] Dist.20.23: 5.

[38] Ibid. 2.11, fol. 40v: '*laquelle a eu tousiours graces à Dieu toute puissance souveraine, institution, iurisdiction, & polices sur les Ecclesiastiques . . .*'.

[39] Dorléans, *Second Avertissement* , fol. 68v. Jean Boucher also compared Belloy to Ockham, and to Marsilius of Padua, arguing that he had used these authors to argue for the submission of the church and the Estates General to the power of the king: Boucher, *Sermons*, 252–3 [mis-pag].

[40] Note Almain's commentary: Almain, *Ockam, super potestate summi pontificis*.

might expect, appeared to approve of Ockham, quoting his views on Zachary's advisory role in the deposition of King Childeric (2.19). Even more revealingly, Belloy attacked the ideas of Augustinus Triumphus of Ancona (1243–1328) in the *Apologie Catholique*, who had become embroiled in the same controversy with Nicholas III as Ockham, over papal dominion, and whose views were diametrically opposed to Ockham's. Augustinus Triumphus' texts had been revived in the sixteenth century in the name of reasserting papal hegemony in Europe: his *Summa de Potestate Ecclesiastica* was published twice in Rome, in 1582 and 1584, and Belloy appeared to know the text well.[41] In many ways, then, Belloy can indeed be seen to have adopted the persona of a medieval controversialist and defender of the powers of temporal rulers. He also explicitly used conciliar arguments to erode papal influence in France and undermine the authority of the Council of Trent.

Belloy revealed his Ockhamist persona in his attack on '*les Papicoles*' in his chapter on papal power (2.19). Here he treated the *Sainte Union* as adopting, wholeheartedly, the views of Augustinus Triumphus on papal authority. In order to summarise the Leaguer position, Belloy synthesised discussions in Augustinus' *Summa*, including the power of popes to revoke conciliar decrees (an idea condemned at Constance and Basel); the power of popes over emperors; the (forged) Donation of Constantine; the Petrine commission; and the power of the keys to loose and bind. Belloy drew this section to a close by connecting these claims to the clash between Boniface VIII and Philip IV. He claimed that Augustinus' arguments led to Boniface VIII's excommunication of Philip IV and the declaration of that 'extravagant' decree *Unam Sanctam* in which Boniface claimed fullness of paper power over royal authority.[42] Belloy used this intellectual heritage to effective polemical purpose: depicting the *Sainte Union* as representative of a particular set of hierocratic views on papal power to which they by no means all subscribed.

Belloy's critique of papal dominion came further to the fore in his undermining of the Council of Trent. His case against the council was based on the argument that Trent was an illegitimate convocation, in which the pope played the role of judge and jury, and the views of the reformers were not heard (2.24). Belloy made an explicitly Gallican case, appealing to the authority of the Councils of Constance and Basle as the

---

[41] Noticeably, Bellarmine had declared it 'egregious' and sought to moderate the views of papal power put forward in the *Summa*.

[42] Belloy, *Apologie Catholique*, fol. 57v [mis-pag].

foundations of the liberties, rights and franchises of the Gallican church. These, he explained, were then further clarified in the Pragmatic Sanction of Bourges (2.25). Belloy was dependent here on the analysis of Charles Du Moulin's treatise against Trent: *Conseil sur le fait du Concile de Trente* (1564), describing the author as 'the greatest lawyer of his age' (2.20).

Du Moulin's major objections to the council began with the conciliar observation that the council itself was illegitimate, having been convened under the sole authority of the pope. Furthermore, the council was only interested in the private profit of the pope and his lackeys, not the 'public health and wellbeing' of the church. The council was, Du Moulin argued, contrary to the conciliar decrees of Constance and Basle, against the majesty and authority of the king, the rights of the crown and above all against the rights, liberties and immunities of the Gallican church. It effectively abolished the Pragmatic Sanction, he further argued, thus removing the French crown and people's right to elect their own bishops.[43] It also undermined the rights of provincial councils, and it attributed more power to the pope than he had ever had before.[44] In short, by Du Moulin's reckoning, the Council of Trent went against every key principle of Gallican liberty.

Belloy followed Du Moulin in challenging the legitimacy of Trent and in claiming that the council attacked Gallican principles by establishing that trials of clergy members should be undertaken on papal authority, not by provincial councils. The inability of the councillors to clarify the question of episcopal election and residence was probably one of the greatest failures of Trent. The consequences of this absence of clarification, and the appearance of papal hegemony over the proceedings, allowed Belloy, in tune with Du Moulin's ideas, to declare Trent a presumption of papal fullness of power.

Belloy was not, however, a slavish intellectual follower of Du Moulin. The latter had presented Trent as an invasion of French legal rights – especially the right to elect bishops, and the rights of provincial councils – but Belloy was not prepared to go to the lengths of suggesting that canon law had no authority in France. In fact, his argument depended on making use of the contradictions inherent in canon law regarding the status of provincial churches and the powers of kings. Innocent III's declaration that French kings had no temporal superiors in their kingdom (*Per Venerabilem*, 1202) was a foundational claim for any Gallican writer, and Belloy duly took it into

---

[43] But note the existing problem of the Concordat, overlooked by Du Moulin in this passage.
[44] Du Moulin, *Conseil sur le Faict du Concile de Trente*. For more on Du Moulin and Gallicanism, see Kingdon, 'Some French Reactions to the Council of Trent'; Kelley, 'Fides Historiae', and Thireau, *Charles Dumoulin*.

account.[45] However Belloy did note (on the basis of the authority of the thirteenth-century canon lawyer Hostiensis, whom he describes as a 'good historian'), that Innocent contradicted his constitution (*Novit*, 1204) which endeavoured to prevent King Phillip Augustus from asserting a feudal claim to Normandy.[46] Hostiensis had observed that the effect of Innocent III's pronunciation contradicted this claim. Belloy correspondingly found the decrees of Clement V of 1306 and 1311 (revoking those of Boniface VIII), a stronger foundation for the independence of French royal power than Innocent's declarations (2.19).

Belloy's views on Hostiensis' historical analysis, and his admiration of Charles Du Moulin is demonstrative of his legal training in the *mos gallicus docendi*. Whilst Belloy did not reject the authority of canon law in France entirely, he implied strongly that French law was superior to the claims of canon law, within the French territories. He argued from the basis of French law, by which he meant the decrees of parlement, but also what he referred to as 'inviolable custom' enshrined in the *appels comme d'abus*, the system by which the French *parlement* could appeal papal decisions of French law (2.21).[47] Like the Hotmans, Bodin, Choppin and Dorléans, Belloy was as interested as they in the authority of customary law, and equally as careful to exploit the current intellectual trend for the purposes of his own argument.

In Choppin's *De Sacra Politia*, the *appels comme d'abus* were treated as a mechanism for the clergy to address problems with the king's management of the church, but in Belloy's case (emulating Du Moulin again), they are turned into an anti-papal weapon. In this way, Belloy could sidestep the issue of whether or not a king had to acknowledge the authority of customary law in his realm or could override it (as Jean Bodin had argued). Belloy argued that, since the time of Louis XI the French, *parlement* had followed an inviolable custom (*usage inviolable*) of appealing against abuses by the pope *and* clergy. Without this 'remedy', he argued, 'the priests would make another Monarchy in France, and more powerful than the Royal monarchy, for the support and dignity of which all good Frenchmen should rather die, than endure the fact that it should be diminished'.[48] Belloy assembled a powerful collection of arguments

---

[45] D. 4.17.13 [46] D. 2.1.13.

[47] Custom since parlement had rejected Louis XI's attempts to abrogate the Sanction in 1467. Génestal, *Les Origines*; Kelley, *Foundations*, 180–1. Kelley notes Charles Dumoulin's appeal to the appel 'which he regarded as a kind of general antidote for curialist encroachments'.

[48] Belloy, *Apologie Catholique*, 2.21, fol. 57v [mis-pag]: '*les Prestres seroient en France une Monarchie autre, & plus puissante que la Royale, pour le soustien & dignité de laquelle tous les bons François doivent plustost mourir que d'endurer qu'elle soit diminuée*'.

here. He made the appeal to ancient custom into a patriotic call to Frenchmen to defend their monarchy. Creating a picture of a priestly monarchy in France was a potent image of the perceived attempt by the ecclesiastical community to destroy the ancient customs and structures of the French monarchy.

Belloy drew on a substantial arsenal of arguments to portray the League as treasonous in its relation to royal authority, and destructive of Gallican liberty in its relation to papal authority. In its juridical approach, Belloy built a case against the League that relied on portraying it as a movement that corresponded to the vigorous reassertion of papal power in the Tridentine years. In the *Apologie Catholique*, the League was presented as an extension of papal authority into France, disregarding the boundaries between royal and papal power established since the reign of Phillip IV, and thus threatening the stability of the kingdom as a whole. What remains to be seen, is how the Leaguers responded to Belloy's attacks, particularly when it came to the important questions of relationships between command and obedience within the French polity.

Command and Obedience

At its most fundamental, Belloy made an argument for unequivocal submission to the authority of kings, and on this bedrock of obedience he was able to construct an image of the League as treasonous in its rejection of Navarre's claim to the throne. Belloy would not even permit the possibility of resisting a king who had committed any sins, and he argued that papal excommunication had no impact on temporal power.[49] Here he weakened one of the central arguments made by theologians in the *Sainte Union*: that excommunication prevented an individual from taking up the French crown, and could – *de facto* – lead to a king's deposition.

The principle with which the Leaguers grappled was the question of whether a papal excommunication had any authority in the civil sphere. Whilst it was straightforward to argue that an excommunication removed the king from the community of the church, it was not as straightforward to argue that he was also removed from the office of king. Members of the *Sainte Union* adopted various strategies to deal with this issue. In an anonymous *Advertissement* of 1589, the League writer justified the legitimacy of the civil effects of the papal excommunication of Navarre, explicitly

---

[49] Belloy, *Apologie Catholique*, 1.8, fol. 31r–v.

framing his arguing against '*politiques*' such as Belloy.[50] The author tried to
establish that both Henri III and Henri de Navarre posed a threat to the
entire body of the French commonwealth, and that – as Catholics – they
were subject to the jurisdiction of the church in spiritual matters in the
same way as any other believer. This was further reinforced by the argument that the kings of France were under the jurisdiction of canon law in
this respect:

> If any *Politique* tries to say that a King of France can't be excommunicated:
> it is easy to respond that, being the child of the Church he is subject to its
> discipline in the same manner as all other Christians, and there is not
> a single canon of the church from which he would be exempt.[51]

This was a very conventional line of argument on the power of excommunication over kings. Other Leaguers embraced the comprehensive authority of canon law, as in the *Iurisconsultus Catholicus de theologorum assertione,*
published in 1590, which justified the excommunications on an entirely
juridical basis.[52] Louis Dorléans on the other hand, rested his case on the
basis that the pope was the highest authority in the church, and that
correspondingly the excommunication of Navarre removed him from the
community of the church and from the office of king. The crown itself was
Catholic, he claimed, and the coronation ceremony a Catholic ceremony.
Heretics, he argued, as enemies of '*l'État Royal*', could not conform to any
of the defining features of the French monarchical office which he identified with the first Christian king, Clovis.[53]

Dorléans positioned almost everything he wrote for the League as
a response to Pierre de Belloy, taken to represent the position of the
'false' *politiques*. In 1586, he adopted the guise of an English Catholic,
writing to his French peers in warning of the terrors of rule by a Protestant
monarch. The *Advertissement, des catholiques anglois aux françois catholiques, du danger où ils sont de perdre leur religion* (1586) was republished in
1590 in an amplified edition (*Premiers et seconds advertisements …*), to
which Philippe Duplessis Mornay responded with his *Lettre d'un gentilhomme Catholique françois contenant breve response aux calomnies d'un
certain prétendu anglois* (n.p., 1586). Dorléans then reverted to a French
persona and wrote a response to his own treatise: *Responce des vrays*

---

[50] *Advertissement aux Catholiques sur la bulle de nostre Sainct Pere.*
[51] Ibid., 28–9: '*Que si quelque Politique s'advance de dire, qu'un Roy de France ne peut estre excommunié: il
      est facile de respondre qu'iceluy estant enfant de l'Eglise est subiet à la discipline d'icelle comme tous les
      autres Chrestiens, n'y ayant aucun canon de l'Eglise par lequel il en soit exempté*'.
[52] *Iurisconsultus Catholicus de theologorum assertione.*   [53] Dorléans, *Avertissement*, 71–3.

catholiques françois, à l'Avertissement des Catholiques Anglois, pour l'exclusion du Roy de Navarre de la couronne de France (1588). In the opening pages, he included a list of 'defamatory' works addressed in the argument which included Belloy's *Apologie Catholique.*

Dorléans' rejection of Belloy's ideas was based on three lines of thought. The first addressed the question which dominated the League polemics after 1584, of whether an excommunicated Huguenot could legitimately rule over French Catholics. This was a challenging case to build, not only from a theological perspective, but from the perspective of French succession law. In the context of the latter, Dorléans adopted the view that care for souls transcended other duties on the part of the king, and in this way he and other Leaguers sought to argue from continuity and convention rather than disruption and disorder.[54]

Second, to strengthen the theological basis of this vision of the French succession, Dorléans had recourse to the authority of Thomas Aquinas' *Summa Theologiae,* the discussion of apostasy (IIaIIae 12) and the decretal *Nos sanctorum* (C.15.6.4) which declared the subjects of excommunicated persons to be absolved from their oath of allegiance. In the *Summa,* Aquinas had argued that dominion and unbelief were not necessarily inconsistent, because dominion was a product of the *ius gentium.* However, princes who had apostatised from the faith should not be obeyed; their subjects were *ipso facto* absolved from their oath of obedience in such cases. The right to punish such rulers remained with the Church, and Aquinas suggested that 'great corruption of the faith might occur' in political communities where apostasy in the ruler goes unpunished.

This argument was, in various forms, a foundational argument in the political thought of the League, and the basis of statements of Leaguer unity: the *Articles* and the *Declaration.* The idea that Christian kings had a special commission from God to rule Christian people underpinned the argument that neither a heretic nor a tyrant could rule in France. It was combined with examples from French history, particularly the baptism of Clovis, which were then used to construct a case that France had a unique status in the eyes of God and Paris was in many ways a new Jerusalem. Dorléans is no exception to this general rule of thumb for Leaguer arguments. However, whilst his account was explicitly dependent on

---

[54] Dorléans, *Apologie ou defence des Catholiques,* 10–11: *'le Roy est trop instruit en la Foy pour ne croire point qu'il n'est pas constitué Roy que pour maintenir l'honneur de Dieu, que c'est son devoir d'avoir soing du salut de son people.';* Cf. *Les raisons pour lesquelles Henry de Bourbon soy disant Roy de Navarre ne peult et ne doit estre recue approuve Roy de France'* (1591).

the authority of Aquinas, he did make an adjustment to the Thomist case. Instead of subjects being absolved from their oath of obedience *de facto*, Dorléans made the *de iure* case.[55] This was probably a consequence of the many attacks on Sixtus V's bull of excommunication, which explicitly removed Navarre's right to succeed, but which lawyers such as Belloy and François Hotman argued had no authority in France.

The third line of argument pursued by Dorléans concerned the status of the clergy in the French kingdom. Although Dorléans accepted that the papal bull of excommunication had a coercive effect on a king's dominion, he argued that the responsibility for judging heretics within the kingdom lay with the French clergy. Their status was second only to the king, he argued.[56] In a traditional analysis, Dorléans put forward an argument for the interdependence of civil and ecclesiastical institutions in France on the basis of utility, necessity and the individual conscience. To preserve the state and protect religion and the conscience, he argued it was essential to reject Navarre's claim to the throne.[57] In an appeal to the writings of St Paul – and Plato, Aristotle and Cicero – Dorléans argued that loss of faith in a political community dissolved the bond of loyalty amongst men which was essential to the preservation of that community. He employed the established analogy of body and soul in describing the relationship between civil and ecclesiastical institutions, and further argued that religion was the foundation of monarchy and the key to preserving the ancient constitution. Dorléans did not directly cite the work of Choppin or d'Epinac, discussed previously, but it is clear that he was drawing on similar resources to make the case for the intimate connection between *la religion* and *la police*, piety and justice, in the French commonwealth, as they had.

Dorléans identified this close relationship between religion and politics with 'Gallic harmony': without religion, he argued, the political body would become a monster, lacking its natural shape.[58] He directly contradicted Belloy on the implications of this argument for the status of the clergy in the kingdom, arguing that the clergy were the first order, and that their sacramental duties were not exclusively part of the church, but also part of the civil community, thus entirely reversing Belloy's interpretation of the notion that the church was 'in' the commonwealth.[59] The clergy were a part of the French constitution, and changing that fact would

---

[55] Ibid., 240–1, 398–9.   [56] *Response des vrays Catholiques*, 240–1; 398–9; 453; 464; 468–9; 493.
[57] Ibid., 467.   [58] cf. *De Justa Reipublicae Christianae Authoritate*, fol. 3v–4r.   [59] *Response*, 468.

change and corrupt the political community as a whole.[60] Dorléans
pointed to the coronation oath, in which the kings of France swore to
take council from the clergy, and to the activities of *parlement*, in which the
clergy have a voice.[61] There were therefore two duties of the French clergy
by his reckoning, the first of which was sacramental, and the second of
which was civil. The second duty concerned the conduct of political affairs
in the kingdom (*conduite de la police*), according to the civil laws. It was this
dual role, performed by the clergy, which distinguished France from other
pagan or non-Christian communities.[62] The church, according to
Dorléans, was one of two guardians of the French constitution: the church
and the Paris *parlement* (understood as a permanent incarnation of the
Estates General).[63]

Dorléans described France as a single society in which religion and
politics operated harmoniously, and where unity could only be preserved
by Catholic monarchy. He explained that Optatus' famous phrase 'the
church is in the commonwealth', referred to the fact that the law of
the kingdom was the law of religion: this was what Dorléans called the
'necessity' of religion in the person of the king, and in all public persons
(i.e. corporations). The law of the Christian religion was the law of the
respublica, but the laws of the *respublica* were not the laws of the church –
which, Dorléans wrote, had its own government (*police*) and discipline.
The *respublica* was thereby embedded in the universal community of the
church, an argument which was the foundation of medieval political
thought and proposed notably by Belloy's least favourite author,
Augustinus Triumphus.

The Gallican debates of these years have been framed in terms of
a 'new' humanist solution to the problems that bedevilled the medieval
era in regards to defining the Gallican liberties.[64] As the debates under
consideration in this chapter indicate, however, there is not much that is
noticeably 'new' in these debates. Instead, we see the repurposing of
medieval arguments in Early Modern polemics. The challenge that
Pierre de Belloy presented to the League was, eventually, the idea that
won out: the notion that obedience to royal authority was an obligation
that triumphed over all others. It did not, however, resolve the essential
question of the relationship between the internal and the external forum,

---

[60] Ibid., 467. NB. Epinac made the same point.   [61] *Response*, 469–70.
[62] He goes on to discuss incompatibility of paganism with Christianity, but toleration of Judaism.
[63] Cf. Salmon, 'Catholic Resistance Theory', 223.   [64] Parson, *Church in the Republic*, 1–13.

which was ultimately the question of conscience. In the context of League political thought, the idea that the church was 'in' the commonwealth would go on to be evoked in the assemblies of the clergy as debates over internal French reform, and the relationship between royal and episcopal power, continued unresolved.[65]

---

[65] Salmon, 'France', 458–97; Martimort, *Le Gallicanisme de Bossuet*; Poncet, *La France et le pouvoir pontifical*; Bergin, *The Making of the French Episcopate;* Parsons, *The Church in the Republic,* 227–73; Krynen, *l'Empire du roi*; Bergin, *The Politics of Religion*; Franceschi, *La Crise Théologico-Politique;* Courtine, *Nature et empire de la loi*.

CHAPTER 5

'Brutish Thunderbolts': Papal Power and the League

The Leaguers never argued that disobedience against a legitimate, Catholic king would be permitted. Their position of resistance depended on categorising Henri III as a heretic tyrant, and Navarre as a heretic. However, in this context, the Leaguers were very easily presented as supporting papal hierocratic claims over those of the king's regalian rights. Condemning papal intervention in France was a much more commanding position to adopt than defending it. François Hotman termed Sixtus V's bull of excommunication in 1585 a '*brutum fulmen*', which his English translator rendered as a 'Brutish Thunderbolt', suggesting that Sixtus' action usurped the jurisdiction of the French monarchy.[1] The *parlement* of Paris appealed against the Bull on behalf of the liberties of the Gallican church and the rights of the French king.[2] In the course of the controversies of the 1580s, the Leaguers were portrayed as a vessel for the ambitions of Rome. Indeed, this was such an effective condemnation of the League in the polemical literature that it retained a tight grip on the scholarship of the League until very recently.[3]

The issue of the extent and scope of papal authority in France was utterly contentious, within and outside the League. Between 1585 and 1594, the papacy made several direct intrusions into French temporal jurisdiction. Sixtus V excommunicated the Prince de Condé and Henri de Navarre for heresy in 1585, removing their property and goods on the basis of the 'fullness of power' he claimed for popes over monarchs.[4] Sixtus drew his

---

[1] Hotman et al., *Brutum Fulmen Papae Sixti V*; Hotman et al., *The Brutish Thunderbolt*.
[2] 'Remontrance au Roi, par la Cour de Parlement', in Goulart, *Mémoires De La Ligue*, 1, 222–6.
[3] Aspects of what follows are published as Nicholls 'Gallican liberties and the Catholic League', reproduced here with the kind permission of the press. On ultramontane Leaguers, see Morel, *l'Idée Gallicane*, 159. Roelker restated the ultramontane threat of the League to the Gallican parlement in *One King, One Faith*, 174–5. On the other side, Baumgartner, *Radical Reactionaries*, 236, draws brief attention to the presence of Gallicanism in the League, as does Tallon, *Conscience Nationale*, 141. In contrast, Zwierlein has recently considered the position of the 'anti-papal' Leaguers in his *Political Thought of the League*.
[4] 'Declaration de nostre Saint-Pere le Pape Sixtus V', in Goulart, *Mémoires*, 1, 214–22.

authority explicitly from the Petrine commission which, he argued, conferred power on the popes which surpassed that of all the kings and princes on earth.[5] His interventions in French affairs evoked the clash between Boniface VIII and Phillip IV (1296–1303), a parallel that was widely drawn by lawyers and theologians at the time.[6] William Barclay, for example, used the argument that Phillip IV had clearly established his authority over the temporal sphere against Boniface's claims to contradict Jean Boucher's claim that the papal power of excommunication relieved subjects of their oaths of obedience.[7] The stakes for the Leaguers were, therefore, high, in justifying their resistance to Henri III and Henri IV against this backdrop of controversy.

In 1589, tensions within and beyond the League were further exacerbated by the excommunication of Henri III after the assassination of the duc de Guise and his brother, the cardinal, on the king's order in December 1588, reflected in the explosion of polemical pamphlets in 1588–9.[8] After Henri III's assassination, Sixtus V sent a legation to France, headed by Cardinal Enrico Cajetano (Cajetan) and assisted by Bellarmine, to mediate between the *Sainte Union* and the Catholic supporters of Henri de Navarre. However, the tensions between the two *parlements* – the king's at Tours and that of the League in Paris – were only aggravated by the papal intervention. It produced a flurry of responses defending the Gallican liberties, including Michel Hurault's *Antisixtus* (1590); Guy Coquille's *Discours des droits ecclesiastiques* (1590), and his *Mémoires pour la réformation de l'état ecclesiastique* (1592); Claude Fauchet, *Traicté des libertez de l'eglise gallicane* (c.1590); Charles Faye d'Espesses [attrib.], *Discours* (1591); Louis Servin, *Vindiciae secundum libertatem ecclesiae Gallicanae* (1590); Pierre Pithou, *Libertez de l'eglise gallicane* (1594).

In December of 1589, Cardinal Cajetan proceeded directly to Paris from Lyon and had Sixtus V's bulls of legation recorded and published, with reserve for the Gallican liberties, in direct opposition to Henri de Navarre's request that he present himself at Tours. In January of 1590, Pierre de L'Estoile recorded an *arrêt* by the *parlement* of Tours against Cajetan's 'treasonous' legation, forbidding communication with the Cardinal as an

---

[5] As Baumgartner points out, it is very telling that Sixtus V was responsible for placing Bellarmine's *Controversies* on the papal index, thoroughly disapproving of Bellarmine's description of papal power in the temporal sphere as 'indirect'. Baumgartner, *Radical Reactionaries*, 234.

[6] Dupuy, *Histoire du différend d'entre le Pape Boniface VIII et Philippe le Bel*; Génestal, *Les origines de l'appel comme d'abus*; Rivière, *Le problème de l'église et de l'état*; Favier, *Philippe le Bel*; Kern, *Kingship and Law*. Martin, *Les origines du gallicanisme*.

[7] Barclay, *De Regno*, 451.   [8] See Pallier, *Recherches*.

enemy of *l'état,* unless the Cardinal presented himself to the king in Tours.[9] Accusing the legation of treason, and assuming legislative legitimacy for the *parlement* in Tours, precipitated an exchange of parliamentary declarations thoroughly documented in scholarship.[10]

In March 1591, a second legation arrived under Cardinal Landriano, sent by Gregory XIV. Gregory had confirmed Sixtus V's bulls and demanded all laymen and clergy to abandon Navarre or face excommunication, as well as renewing the excommunication of Navarre and the deprivation of his succession to the French throne. These bulls were published in June 1591 and were immediately opposed in an *arrêt* by the *parlement* at Châlons. Clement VIII sent a further legation to France under Cardinal Plaisance, whose bulls were registered in October 1592 and gave the legate the authority to oversee the election of a Catholic king of France. These bulls were again condemned by Châlons, and once again this condemnation was rejected by the Leaguer *parlement* in Paris. The actions of the *parlements* of Tours and Châlons were undertaken in the name of Gallican liberties and the French laws of succession, a fact which has led scholars to emphasise the Gallican character of Navarre's supporters.[11] The resulting polemics took on European significance with the involvement of Cardinal Bellarmine, and the translation of Gallican pamphlets into English.[12]

The fact that the very definition of the Gallican liberties was obscure contributed further to the problems of papal intervention in France. As Antoine Hotman rightly observed, Gallican theorists in his own era could not agree on basic definitions.[13] Nevertheless, in his treatise on these liberties, Hotman attempted to find a reasonable path through the controversies that beset French civil and ecclesiastical law in this context, indicating that a balance was to be struck between establishing freedom for the

---

[9] In the 1776 supplement to his *Mémoires-Journaux,* quoted in Penzi, 'Tours contre Rome', 330.

[10] Boüard, 'Sixte Quint, Henri IV et la Ligue'; Daubresse et al., *Le Parlement en Exil*; Parsons, *The Church in the Republic*; Marco Penzi, 'Tours contre Rome'; and the following works by Tizon-Germe: 'Nonces et Legats en France (1589–1594)'; *Henri IV. Le roi et la réconstruction du Royaume*; 'Juridiction spirituelle et action pastorale des légats et nonces en France pendant la Ligue (1589–1594)'; 'La Réprésentation Pontificale en France au début du règne d'Henri IV (1589–1594)'; De Waele, 'De Paris à Tours'.

[11] Penzi, 'Tours contre Rome', 338–45. Penzi explores the views of Louis Servin on the legation, in Servin, *Recueil de ce qui fut dict par M. Servin. lors de la Lecture des Lettres Patentes du Roy du 5e Janvier 1590, contenants Déclarations de S.M. à la Venue d'un des Cardinals de la Cour De Rome envoyé par le Pape au Royaume de France* (n.p., n.d.).

[12] See Salmon, 'Gallicanism and Anglicanism', for a comparison of the two national churches in this period and the polemics of each, and his *The French Religious Wars in English Political Thought* for a discussion of this French polemic in the English context, and 'Appendix A', 171–80, for a list of French works published in England between 1560 and 1598.

[13] Hotman, *Traité,* fol. 1r.

clergy from the 'aspirations' of Rome, but also from the encroachment of the secular powers.[14]

Hotman, much like René Choppin, made it clear that he did not see the Gallican church as positioning itself against royal authority. He argued that the church had granted certain unique privileges to the French king because, uniquely, the French king was the patron and principal founder of the church of France and not, like the kingdom of Naples, a vassal of the pope:

> The liberties of the Gallican Church are not papal concessions; they are not rights acquired externally or against the common law. Because in order that France is wholly conserved in a [state of] liberty – more than any other Catholic nation – one cannot say that she has been freed, so much as she has always been autonomous and free since her beginnings.[15]

Hotman's argument closely associated France's ecclesiastical liberty with its political freedom. He argued that, from its beginnings, France was better preserved than other Catholic countries and so had no need to claim privileges from the Roman church, particularly because the Gallican church was in sympathy with the dignity of the holy see: 'they are not against each other, they are both legitimate: and the balance between them is conducive to the maintenance of the Church and the removal of heresy and atheism'.[16] Hotman took the view that insofar as the property of the French church was concerned, it should remain an issue for civil jurisdiction, and his position was again similar to that of Choppin in this respect.

Antoine Hotman gave the Gallican liberties a central role in the preservation of the well-,being of the French kingdom, and of Christianity itself. But he was quick to explain that this did not mean the Gallican church had either excessive licence from, or complete subjection to, Rome. These elusive liberties were instead to be found in the balance struck between recognising the priority and supremacy of the Roman church, and the

---

[14] Ibid., fol. 3r-v: '*Il est bon aussi de remarquer que en diverse façons les libertez de l'Eglise Gallicane sont maintenues. Car ce n'est pas seulement pour un affranchissement des prétentions de Rome, mais aussi des iurisdictions Royalles & laïques, ce qui se recognoist par toutes les remonstrances & disputes qui ont este faictes par les Ecclesiastiques*'.

[15] Ibid., fol. 6r: '*Mais les libertez de l'Eglise Gallicane ne sont point concession des Papes, ce ne sont point droits acquis outré & contre le droit commun: Car pour s'estre la France conservée en son entier, plus qu'autre nation qui soit Catholique, on ne peut pas dire qu'elle ait este affranchie : mais elle est franche & libre des sa premiere origine*'.

[16] Ibid., fol. 1v-2r: '*Au lieu que la liberté de l'Eglise Gallicane peut compatir avec la dignité du sainct siege: et ne sont point deux choses contraires l'un à l'autre, elles sont toutes deux legitimes: et la proportion correspondante entr'elles, sert à maintenir l'Eglise, et en retrancher l'heresie & l'atheisme*'.

honours and prerogatives owed to it, and nevertheless preserving France from excessive papal interference. In specific reference to papal prescription, Hotman argued that the papacy ought not to acquire any more rights than they had held up until that moment.[17] He explicitly blamed Boniface VIII for claiming temporal powers for himself in *Unam Sanctam*. However, he argued that it was the not the king, but the Estates of France and the clergy who were responsible for declaring the liberties and franchises of the Gallican church in this particular episode of French history in which Phillip IV so often plays a triumphal role.[18]Antoine Hotman described the French as a 'Frank and free' people, who would obey the papacy in so far as could be expected of people of such a nature, so long as the popes acted with an honest proportion of power. He sought to persuade his reader that the temporal and spiritual jurisdictions could exist in harmony, because the papacy had always been a part of French history.[19]

The extent to which even the most devoted Leaguers subscribed to the notion of papal *plenitudo potestatis* in both spiritual and temporal spheres was, therefore, for the most part, importantly circumscribed. There were some Leaguers who unequivocally supported papal hierocratic claims; for example, the priest François Pigenat, who demonstrated his approval of Boniface VIII in his *L'aveuglement et grande consideration des Politiques, dict Maheustres* (Paris, 1592). However, there were also those in the League who took a more temperate approach to this historic episode. Dorléans was careful to present his claims about ecclesiastical fullness of power as a power inherent in the church, not the individual of the pope, in a classic conciliar move. He notionally took Phillip IV's side against Boniface but shifted the emphasis of his analysis to attack the false *politiques*. He argued that the Catholic supporters of Navarre, whom he describes as 'these fantastic Frenchmen', were hypocrites to draw on the authority of Phillip's actions against Boniface, whilst simultaneously supporting the claims of the

---

[17] Ibid., fol. iv-2r: ' . . . *c'est le bien de la France, que de luy conserver cette franchise & liberté. C'est mesmes le bien de la Chrestienté, moyennant que nous ne la prenions point pour une licence effrénée, pour un desbordement de raison, ny pour la soustraire de la révérence & submission qu'elle doit au sainct siege de Rome. Ains en le recognoissant premier & supérieur de l'Eglise, & luy déférant les honneurs & prérogatives qui luy appartiennent : conserver neantmoins la France en telle façon, que les Papes n'y aquirent par usance & longue possession; plus de droits qu'ils y ont eu iusques à présent*'. My thanks to Magnus Ryan for pointing out this significant reference to papal prescription.

[18] Ibid., fol. 42v–43r.

[19] In this particular point, their ideas are not so far from those of Claude Fauchet and Etienne Pasquier, who both acknowledged the historical papal role in French affairs. See Jotham Parsons, 'Papauté, histoire et mémoire gallicane au XVIe siècle', in *Revue de l'histoire des religions*, 226 (2009), 315–28.

heretic Navarre to the throne.[20] Voicing a clerical opinion, Jean Porthaise suggested in a sermon that Phillip IV had been wrongly excommunicated by Boniface VIII, as his subsequent absolution demonstrated. The differ- ence, Porthaise argued, between then and the present situation with Navarre was that there was no threat to the stability of the kingdom: it had not been a question of heresy.[21]

Gilbert Génébrard's *De Clericis* (1589), published in French as *Excommunication des Ecclesiastiques*, made an authoritative Leaguer state- ment condemning the clergy who associated with Henri III after his excommunication.[22] A respected theologian, it was precisely this question of the power of excommunication and the duty of Catholics to obey it, which drew him into the polemics of the League. Henri III was clearly a tyrant, in Génébrard's view, for assassinating the duc de Guise and his cardinal brother. Furthermore, the papal excommunication which fol- lowed had removed all of his temporal possessions, thereby relieving his subjects from their obedience.[23] Génébrard was explicit that the League had embarked on a 'holy war', and acted 'for the management of the Gallican church, the privileges of that church, the Pragmatic Sanction, the Council of Trent, the Catholic, Apostolic, Roman Religion ... the foun- dations of our fathers, our lives, our goods, our *patrie*, our liberty and that of our parents, friends, children and posterity'.[24] Génébrard pursued these ideas further in his *De Sacrarum Electionum ad Ecclesiae Gallicanae Redintegrationem* (1593), where he argued against the Concordat of Bologna, denying the king the right to control benefices in the manner brokered in that particular deal and thus developing an argument that Choppin had also made in his *De Sacra Politia*.[25] What is notable about Génébrard's work is, as Thierry Amalou describes, the vigour with which he denounced the royal election of bishops as 'illegitimate'.[26]

---

[20] Dorléans, *Plaidoyé*, 131–2. Dorléans is explicit that the decrees of illegitimate 'antipopes' were not to be accepted.

[21] Porthaise, *Cinq Sermons*, 38.

[22] Génébrard, *De Clericis*; Génébrard, *Excommunication des Ecclesiastiques*. Génébrard submitted to Navarre's monarchy in 1593, but this did not prevent him from being banished from Aix by the local parliament in 1596, after he published his *De Sacrarum Electionum Iure* which argued that bishops should be elected by the clergy and people, not by the king. Cf. Thierry Amalou 'Le bannissement d'un chef ligueur'.

[23] Génébrard, *Excommunication*, 12–16.

[24] Ibid., 60: '*Pour la manutention de l'Eglise Gallicane, privilèges d'icelle, pragmatique Sanction, Concile de Trente, Religion Catholique, Apostolique, Romaine ... fondations de nos pères, pour nos vies, nos biens, Patrie, pour nostre liberté, & de nos parens, amis, enfans, postérité*'.

[25] Génébrard, *De Sacrarum Electionum Jure et Necessitate*.

[26] Amalou, 'le banissement', 12; Daubresse, *Le Parlement de Paris*, 240.

Both the clerical Leaguers and the lawyers finessed their positions on papal power quite carefully. They did not, however, always agree amongst themselves on this issue. Dorléans, for example, had argued that the king's role over the church was administrative and executive, but nevertheless included the authority to elect bishops. He thought of the *Roi très Chrétien* as the 'vicar of Christ', and in his *Responce des vrays Catholiques* (1588), he explored the idea that pope and king ought to work in harmony. Both, he suggested, receive their power from God (although differently: Dorléans reminds his reader that the king receives his power from God, but through the commonwealth). Like the separate arms of the human body, one attends to spiritual jurisdiction and the souls under its charge, the other temporal jurisdiction and its kingdom.[27] But whilst Dorléans and Génébrard differed on this point, both were in agreement that a fundamental duty towards the Gallican church amongst its members was to protect it from heresy.[28] Génébrard's defence of the Pragmatic Sanction is consistent with that goal, and his demand for the renewal of the Gallican church through rejecting the Concordat situates his text both within the League polemic, but also within the broader context of a particular set of Gallican demands for reform of canonical election in France in this period.

In terms of their interpretation of the history of Franco-papal relations, these Leaguers were careful not to be seen to destroy Gallican liberty. As Dorléans put it: 'What offense is it against the sacred Canons, against the laws of the Gallican church, against the laws of the Kingdom and the King, to demand that everyone leaves the heretic party and returns to the bosom of the Catholic Church?'[29] It was essential to the League that their followers and the those they sought to persuade accepted that the movement acted in defence of ancient liberties of the church and the civil polity, and that its members were only engineering change in the name of eradicating heresy: it was a defence of custom over dangerous innovation.[30] In the final analysis, this came down to the vision of political thinkers in the League for

[27] Dorléans, *Response*, 239–40. Dorléans' description of the relation of the two powers is reminiscent of Bellarmine's.
[28] Génébrard, *De Sacrarum Electionum*, 148–70.
[29] Dorléans, *Plaidoyé*, 132: '*Quel offence contres les Saincts Canons, contre les droictz de l'Eglise Gallicane, contre les droictz du Royaume et du Roy, d'exhorter un chacun de quicter le parti de l'heresie, et se retirer au giron de l'Eglise Catholique?*'
[30] There were some modifications to this resilient argument for continuity that suggested the presence of a more nuanced understanding of the need for genuine change to the laws in this era: the lawyer Pierre Grégoire put this point elegantly in his defence of the reception of the Tridentine decrees, when he argued that the Boniface–Phillip episode demonstrated the importance of understanding that circumstances and morals change with the times, and so too must the laws. Pierre Grégoire, 'Response au Conseil donné par Charles Dumoulin sur la dissuasion de la publication du Concile de

their Christian commonwealth: a France in which ecclesiastical and civil affairs were managed for the benefit of the collective salvation of the people.

Conciliar Authority and Tridentine Reform

The rejection of a medieval argument for papal fullness of power on the part of some Leaguers was clearly not persuasive for any opponents of the League. But the matter was further complicated by the question of whether or not to receive the Tridentine reforms in France. In the context of arguments like those of Pierre de Belloy, late medieval conciliar doctrine was harnessed to make the case against the League. The conciliar doctrine outlined at Constance, and confirmed at Basel, established that the council of the Roman church had its authority directly from Christ, and, as such, its commands, ordinances and statues were to be obeyed by all, including the pope. The council, representative of the whole body of the church, was superior to the individual of the pope and could depose him.[31] Two French theologians, Jean Gerson and Pierre d'Ailly, took a leading role in these debates, and their conciliar theory became embedded in the doctrines of Gallican liberty produced in the sixteenth century.[32] The challenge to papal authority presented by the conciliar case could easily be expanded and extended, both to shore up the power of kings in their civil sphere, and to make a case for the devolved government of dioceses, thereby enhancing the role of the French bishops within the French church.

At Constance, Jean Gerson presented his treatise *De Ecclesiastica Potestate* in which he explicitly rejected the theory of papal power outlined in Boniface's *Unam Sanctam*.[33] Gerson argued that the pope did not have temporal power at the same time as possessing heavenly *imperium*; the power to 'loose and bind' was a spiritual power, which did not extend to the worldly sphere. The pope's 'fullness of power' was instead constituted of the power of governance and jurisdiction over the church, conferred by the Petrine commission. Significantly, for the early modern debates,

Trente en France, par Pierre Grégoire Tholosain', in *Caroli Molinaei Franciae et Germaniae Celeberrimi Jurisconsulti*, 5, 425–6.
[31] See the decrees *Sacrosancta* (1415); *Haec Sancta* (1415); *Frequens* (1417). Tierney, *Foundations of the Conciliar Theory*.
[32] Salmon, 'France', 461; Patrick Arabeyre, 'Le spectre du conciliarisme chez les canonistes français du XVᵉ siècle et du début du XVIᵉ siècle'; and Alain Tallon, 'Le conciliarisme au risque du concile: les ecclésiologies conciliares au temps du concile de Trente', in Arabeyre, Basdevant-Gaudemet (eds.), *Les Clercs et Les Princes*, 253–70; 285–96; Tallon, *La France et le concile*, 421–547.
[33] Gerson, *De ecclesiastica potestate et de origine iuris et legum tractatus*.

Gerson defined ecclesiastical power as both of governance (*potestas ordinis*), and jurisdiction (Considerations 2–3). Governance, the priestly power, was sacramental and non-coercive; jurisdiction was the power over the internal forum: the conscience. Coercive power, such as that of excommunication, belonged to the church as a whole, given from Christ, and so could only be made manifest when the church was gathered in a council (Cons. 4). Crucially, Gerson's argument stripped the pope of the right to excommunicate kings, thus embellishing John of Paris' argument regarding the administrative nature of papal power over temporal. The connections between the conciliar theory, expressed by Gerson, and the Gallican debates of the sixteenth century, were explicit. Jacques Almain's Gersonian response to Tomasso de Vio Gaetani (Cajetan) and his statement of papal hierocratic theory in his *Auctoritas papae et concilii sive ecclesiae comparata* (1511) ensured that this association continued to be alive and active in France, as did Edmond Richer's publications.[34] Gerson's renowned sermon, '*Vivat Rex*' was translated into French and published in Paris as *Harangue faicte devant le roy Charles sixiesme et tout le conseil* (1588). The 'failed' conciliar doctrine of the fifteenth century thereby became absorbed by arguments for Gallican liberty in the sixteenth and seventeenth centuries.[35] Attachment to a conciliar resolution to the problems of corruption in the church remained profound in France.

The reconvening of the Council of Trent in 1563 focussed the French debate on the question of ecclesiastical, conciliar reform.[36] René Choppin had seen no necessary tension between accepting the king's position as head of the French church and receiving the Tridentine decrees in France in 1576. However, this was to become a defining feature of the position of the League in the 1580s, with the Edict of Union in 1588, and of the decisions of the meeting of the Estates General in 1593, both confirming the demand to accept the Tridentine decrees.[37] In this way, the movement brought itself into tension with those theorists of Gallican liberty who

---

[34] Almain's piece makes extensive use of Jean Gerson's *De Potestate Ecclesiastica* in particular. The conciliar heritage of the Almain–Cajetan debates is discussed in Olivier de La Brosse, *Le Pape et le Concile. La Comparaison de leurs Pouvoirs à la Veille de la Réforme* (Paris, 1965). Cf. Gerson, *Opera*, ed. E. Richer.

[35] See Arabeyre, 'Le spectre du conciliarisme chez les canonistes français du XVᵉ siècle et du début du XVIᵉ siècle' and Tallon, 'Le conciliarisme au risque du concile : les ecclésiologies conciliares au temps du concile de Trente', in Arabeyre, Basdevant-Gaudemet (eds.), *Les Clercs et Les Princes*, 253–70; 285–96. My reference to 'failed' conciliarism is to John Neville Figgis' idea that conciliarism was most significant in its failure: Figgis, *From Gerson to Grotius*, 41–2.

[36] Tallon, *La France et le concile de Trente*; Kingdon, 'Some French Reactions to the Council of Trent'; Martin, *Le Gallicanisme et la Réforme Catholique*; Crimando, 'Two French Views of the Council of Trent'.

[37] And cf. *Articles pour proposer aux Estatz et faire passer un loy fondamentalle du royaume* (n.p., 1588).

ardently rejected the authority of Trent in France, in the same way that they rejected papal authority as a whole.

Voices in the Paris *parlement* chorused against Trent to the extent that, despite attempts on the part of the League to clarify that the decrees would only be accepted with reserve for Gallican liberties, its demands were met with uncompromising opposition: Jacques Auguste de Thou and Jacques Faye d'Espesse in particular contributed to the certainty that the Leaguers were simply imposing the will of Sixtus V on France.[38] In 1583, Philippe Duplessis Mornay had also written a text, in the guise of a Catholic, warning against the emergence of leagues in defence of Trent: *Avertissement sur la Réception & Publication du Concile de Trente, fait sous la personne d'un Catholique Romain.*[39] Here, he explained that the two jurisdictions, the temporal and spiritual, 'fraternise together in this kingdom, and they hold one another's hand under the authority of a sovereign'.[40] This 'brotherly' relationship of the two jurisdictions had been compromised in recent years, he argued, by the pope's attempts to seize absolute authority over temporal jurisdiction. The Council of Trent, he argued, had only served to perpetuate and worsen this state of affairs. Trent, therefore, was presented as exacerbating tensions between the French monarchy and the papacy which had existed for centuries.

The sense that the Tridentine debates were an ongoing feature of French political, Gallican thinking, which were then folded into the League polemics, is compounded by the response of Pierre Grégoire, law professor and colleague of William Barclay at Pont à Mousson, to Charles Du Moulin's *Conseil sur le fait du Concile de Trente*. Pierre de Belloy, as discussed in the previous chapter, had used this to frame his own anti-Tridentine position. It was timely therefore, of Grégoire to involve himself in this controversy through his *Response au Conseil donné par Charles du Molins, sur la dissuasion de la publication du Concile de Trente en France* (1584). Grégoire's patron, Charles the Duke of Lorraine, was a supporter of the Guise brothers in their opposition to Henri III's policies towards the reformers. His treatise was published in Lyon by the League printer Jean Pillehotte, and can, therefore, be read as contributing to the subsequent League case for accepting Trent.[41]

---

[38] Martin, *Le Gallicanisme et la Réforme Catholique*, 210–302.

[39] Republished in Goulart, *Mémoires*, I, 511–38.

[40] *Avertissement sur la reception & publication du Concile de Trente*, n.p.: '*Alors les deux jurisdictions, Spirituelle & Temporelle, fraternisoient en ce Roiaume ensemble, & tenoient la main l'une à l'autre soubz l'authorité d'un souverain*'.

[41] Scholarship which has addressed this treatise has not done so in the context of the League. See Crimando, 'Two French views of the Council of Trent'. The two main works on Grégoire are

Grégoire opened his work by restating what he considered to be the purpose of a church council, which was to resolve general problems in the church. Trent, he argued, was legitimately convened in the manner of all general councils, and as such acted with God's grace. In doing so, he dismissed Du Moulin's issue with the legitimacy of a council convened by papal authority alone.[42] Henri II had no reason to reject Trent, he argued, and any disputes over the legitimacy of the council were more to do with civil disputes between the emperor and Henri II than the question of papal authority. Grégoire's argument here was that *'l'estat total de l'Eglise'*, the whole constitution of the church, was under discussion at Trent, not the Gallican privileges on which Du Moulin focussed. Grégoire's implication was that the Tridentine decrees ought not to be interpreted as a petty and covert attack on Gallican liberty under the guise of a general council, but as a movement to reform the universal church.[43]

On the question of episcopal election, a central issue highlighted by Du Moulin in the reception of the Tridentine decrees, Grégoire returned once more to some staple arguments of the French clergy when it came to royal power over the church. Du Moulin had argued that Trent declared that bishops could not be elected by lay powers, and thus overturned the French king's Gallican right to elect his bishops.[44] Referring to this point, Grégoire argued that the relevant (twenty-third) session of the council stated that lay powers *alone* could not elect bishops. The French kings' right to investiture was in fact a 'privilege', not a 'right', which emphatically did not prevent the legitimate election made by the clergy.[45] Hunting down Du Moulin's argument through its every twist and turn, Grégoire continued on to one of the principal problems of royal–papal relations in its history: the question of whether or not clergy had to submit to the authority of secular jurisdiction. Du Moulin claimed that Trent sought to

---

Collot, *l'école doctrinale de droit public de Pont à Mousson*; and Hyver, *Le doyen Pierre Grégoire de Toulouse*. On Grégoire's *De Republica*, there is also Gambino, *Il De republica di Pierre Grégoire*.

[42] Grégoire, 'Response', 404; Du Moulin, *Conseil*, fol. 6r–7r.

[43] Grégoire, 'Response au Conseil donné par Charles Dumoulin', 5, 387–8: *'Par laquelle response sera montré que s'il plaist au Roy de le faire publier & entretenir de point en point selon sa forme & teneur; se sera comme Prince Catholique, & suivant les traves & vestiges de ses Ayeulx très-Chrestiens Roys & toujours bien affectionnez à la Religion Catholique, sans s'amuser au contraire prétendu conseil, qui s'arme des privilèges de France que quelques uns disent vouloir conserver, n'estant rien moins de leur intention que de l'honneur de la France, qu'ils ont misérablement charbonnée & divisée sous pretexte de la défendre.'*

[44] Du Moulin, *Conseil*, fol. 7r–v.

[45] Grégoire, 'Reponse', 416–17: *'Et encore cela est par privilege & non de droit, & pour garder qu'il n'y ait tumulte en la province, & pour scavoir quelles gens sont esleus en son Royaume, non pas pour les eslire ny pour empescher l'election légitimement & canoniquement faite par le Clergé.'*

exempt the clergy from this authority, and that to accept this decree in France would be a crime of treason.[46] Grégoire argued that no king would deny that the two jurisdictions, civil and spiritual, were separate. He thereby came down on the side which sought to judge ecclesiastical and civil crimes in distinct courts. In an attempt to turn Du Moulin's argument on its head, Grégoire argued that it would be more of a crime of treason on Du Moulin's part to accept that the clergy could be judged by kings. On the contrary, on Grégoire's account, it was the king's duty to protect the church's liberties in such areas.[47]

In his attempt to define the relationship and distinctions between civil and ecclesiastical jurisdiction, Grégoire's text can be compared to Choppin's *De Sacra Politia*, which sought to protect the custom of the *appels comme d'abus*, and ecclesiastical dominion over church land, without contradicting the notion that the French king was head of the church and had a pastoral duty of care over it. Choppin had also placed the question of election at the centre of his treatise and endeavoured to reform a system which had come under so much abuse at the hands of French kings *and* clergy.

Subsequent to these controversies in 1583–4, the Leaguers were mostly in agreement that the decrees of Trent should be accepted. Some were dogmatic, like Pierre d'Epinac, who appended the Tridentine confession of faith to a pamphlet addressed to the clergy in his diocese as the authority on how to handle heretics.[48] Along with heresy, the issue of corruption, both within and outside of the church, added fuel to the already controversial issues raised by Trent.[49] In the *Remontrance du clergé de France* (1585), for example (probably written by Nicolas Langelier, with the support of the Cardinal de Bourbon), some central concerns of the Leaguer clergy were addressed in a searing attack on Henri III's morals, ending in a reference to the idea of kings doing public penance for their sins.[50] In the course of its historical analysis of the duties of Catholic kings which drew on authorities from Clovis and Charlemagne to Bernard of Clairvaux, the *Remontrance* demanded the acceptance of the decrees of the Council of Trent, both in the cause of clarifying doctrine, and reforming

---

[46] Du Moulin, *Conseil*, fol. 16v.   [47] Grégoire, 'Reponse', 420.   [48] d'Epinac, *Advertissement.*
[49] On the question of the League's response to the challenge of religious reform more broadly, see Ramsay, *Politics, Liturgy and Salvation*; Armstrong, *Politics of Piety.*
[50] A reference to the Council of Chalon (831), requesting Charlemagne to do public penance: '*Remontrance du clergé de France, Faite au Roi le 19 Novembre 1585, par Monsieur l'Eveque de S. Brieu, assisté de Monseigneur Illustrissime Prince & Révérendissime Cardinal de Bourbon, Archeveques, Eveques, & autres Députés*', in Goulart, *Mémoires*, I, 249.

the French church. Alongside this, the text called for the restoration of episcopal elections in France, and a ban on selling church lands. The argument of the *Remontrance* was built on the authority of ancient liberties which had established a clear role for the clergy in the French kingdom, and yet – the author argued – had fallen into disrepair as the clergy's jurisdiction in civil and criminal matters was more often than not impeded.[51] On this account, the Gallican liberties were ecclesiastical in their very nature, and so precluded much emphasis on the king's role beyond that of patron and guardian of the church.

The opinions of the French clergy were further expressed in pugnacious terms in Boucher's sermons of 1594. There he argued – in keeping with his views in the *De Justa Abdicatione* regarding the power of the clergy in the Estates General – that the Estates had already accepted the decrees, with the authority of the Duc de Mayenne and other Catholic princes. Boucher extended this argument to encompass the ancient laws of France which, he claimed, clearly demonstrated the authority of the clergy in ecclesiastical cases, and so supported the independence of the clerical courts.[52] Without concern for the niceties of persuading defenders of Gallican liberty, Boucher laid the blame for all of these problems wholesale at the feat of 'Gallicans', whom he seems to equate with false *politiques*, for obstructing the reception of the decrees.

Another pamphlet of 1588/9 went to some length to defend League members against Belloy's accusation of being 'bad Frenchmen' for not protecting Gallican liberties. The false *politiques*, the author argued, should acknowledge that the Tridentine decrees did not prejudice the liberty of the Gallican church or the rights of the king. Trent was an expression of the 'divine mind' and as it was wrong to modify or limit God, so it was wrong to modify or limit the Tridentine decrees.[53] The purpose of Trent was to provide a 'medicine' for the disease of heresy in the country, and the '*politiques* and their Belloys' ought to accept this point.[54]

Louis Dorléans similarly directed his defence of Trent against Belloy, and in doing so made the case for the monarch's administrative role in the Gallican church as well as arguing for the reception of the decrees: like Choppin, he considered there to be no necessary conflict. However, he waded into more controversial territory when he made the case for the unquestioning acceptance of Trent, comparing it to the ancient Council of Chalcedon. As the decrees of Chalcedon were accepted, even the one

---

[51] Ibid., 259–62. [52] Boucher, *Sermons*, 375, 400–2. [53] *Remonstrance aux trois estats.*
[54] Ibid., 10–14.

raising Constantinople to the same status as Rome, so should those of Trent be, he argued.[55] Trent was, therefore, authoritative because it was a legitimate council of the universal church and not – as Belloy and many other opponents of the League had claimed – an illegitimate meeting of a few papal supporters, seeking to secure their own interests.[56]

The League contained within it nearly as much variety as the doctrine of Gallican liberties itself. Hostile, polemical views of the League and its close relationship with the papacy have been seen to exaggerate the extent to which members of the movement subscribed to a thesis of papal *plenitudo potestatis*. Some, certainly, were more dogmatic than others, and there is a distinction to be made between the perspective of the clerical Leaguers and the lawyers here. Above all, however, it was Trent that divided the Leaguers from the rest of the French Gallican thinkers, and indeed it would be Trent that would destroy the meeting of the Estates General of 1614–15.[57] In this way, the national, Gallican questions that tore the French civil polity apart were deeply affected by the international impact of the Catholic Reformation. As the many references to England and Scotland in League texts demonstrate, and particularly to the 'Babylonian', 'whorish', injustice of the English Protestant court: the great fear of the Leaguers was that France would become like England, ruled by a heretic, and so would be a commonwealth without justice.[58] Accepting the Tridentine decrees in France was one clear path to conformity with the orthodox Catholic religion that would, correspondingly (and in theory only), enable a realignment of *la religion* and *la police* within the French commonwealth.

Abjuration and Resolution

In July 1593, Henri IV announced his intention to abjure Protestantism.[59] The question of whether or not Henri had genuinely converted, having had a true change of heart, was thoroughly debated, particularly in light of his short-lived conversion of 1572, and the excommunication of 1585. To many Leaguers, Henri's action was immediately seen as a false abjuration, lacking the confirmation of a papal absolution, or any formal, public catechism or penance. Instead of bringing about an immediate peace, it

---

[55] Dorléans, *Second Avertissement*, fol. 51r–v.   [56] 'Anti-Guisart', in Goulart, *Mémoires*, I, 378.
[57] Noted by Greengrass, *Governing Passions*, 97.   [58] Boucher, *Apologie pour Jehan Chastel*, 21–4.
[59] Wolfe, *The Conversion of Henri IV*; Greengrass, 'The Public Context of the Abjuration of Henri IV', in Cameron (ed.), *From Valois to Bourbon*, 107–26; Racaut 'N'estans chrestiens que de nombre & nom', in S. Daubresse et al., *La Ligue et ses frontières*.

only served to reignite the debates about heretical kingship, encouraging League theologians and lawyers to reinforce their case against him. But whilst the ink of Leaguer pens continued to flow, the authority of the Estates General had been undermined by Henri's abjuration, and the movement would crumble on the completion of Mayenne's negotiations with the king. It is further evident that, by this stage, in the eyes of hostile contemporaries, the League had become a parody of itself. The broadsheets published in these years ruthlessly demonstrate that fact, as did the publication of the *Satyre Ménippée* and the appropriation of the *Dialogue d'entre le Maheustre et le Manant* for the royalist cause in 1594.[60]

Nevertheless, most Leaguers did not lose their conviction that Henri IV was a heretic. The sermons that Jean Porthaise subsequently published were delivered in the summer of 1593, addressed the specific question of Navarre's abjuration of heresy. In these sermons, Porthaise laid out a defined political role for the clergy, in calling the people to arms against an illegitimate ruler, and determining the choice of a legitimate king.[61] In the course of defending the authority of papal excommunication in the civil sphere, Porthaise was highly critical of his contemporaries: both those who defended 'false' Gallican arguments, and those French bishops who had absolved Henri IV from his excommunication without the authority of a papal absolution.[62]

In Porthaise's first sermon, delivered in St Denis in July of 1593, he described the nature and purpose of the priesthood itself, and he did so in particular reference to the duty of the priest at war. He argued that in the case of wars against kings, the primary objective of priests ought to be the restoration of the true service of God in order to pave the way to salvation. He explicitly stated that rebelling against a king who could not be recognised as such in divine law was a duty of the French priesthood.[63] Importantly, he clarified that the church only involved itself in temporal affairs when they touched spiritual affairs, and pertained to the salvation of individuals.[64] Porthaise made direct reference to Belloy as he made these arguments, and sought to fold his response to Belloy into an attack on Huguenot polemicists as well.[65]

---

[60] Two images of particular note, produced in L'Estoile's *Drolleries*, are *La pauvreté et lamentation de la Ligue*, and *Les Entre-paroles du manant de ligué et du maheutre*, which depicts the royalist version of the treatise. These are discussed in Hamilton, *Pierre de L'Estoile*, 160–1.

[61] Cf. Armstrong, *Politics of Piety*, 163. I don't quite agree with Armstrong that Porthaise's position here is noticeably distinct from those of other Leaguers such as Boucher, but it is certainly the case that he develops an elaborate political role for the French clergy in his sermons.

[62] Porthaise, *Cinq Sermons*, 25–8. [63] Ibid., 16. [64] Ibid., 4–6.

[65] Ibid., 91–2. In the category of 'Huguenot arguments', Porthaise interestingly attributes the notion that obedience to the person of kings is governed solely by the *ius gentium*. This could well be an

Porthaise argued that it was necessary to rebel against Navarre's tyranny, because it was tyranny against *la religion*. Navarre's rule made it impossible for his subjects to attain salvation when there was a spiritual disjunction between the French people and the person of the king: '*les francois ont tombé en discord de la personne du Roy*'.[66] This was a direct challenge to Belloy's argument that the 'person' of the king was unaffected by excommunication. For Porthaise, the inverse was the case: the excommunicated king was an excommunicated person and could not therefore be obeyed by Catholic subjects. Further on in the sermon, he clarified this position by stating that the participation in mass was necessary for the exercise of all virtues, but most importantly for the conditions required to reign legitimately. A king of France who could not participate in mass could not rule France, he argued, giving the example of Childeric who was famously excommunicated by Pope Zacharias.[67]

France was subject to divine law, Porthaise argued, and not merely to the *ius gentium* which, when considered by itself (i.e. as an expression of nature), was an explicit threat to religion.[68] The *ius gentium* featured importantly in these debates about the relationship between *la religion* and *la police*, defining the parameters of the civil sphere on a universal basis. Quoting the thirteenth century decretal, *Per Venerabilem*, Porthaise went on in his next sermon to argue that papal authority was an indirect power, only to be exercised in emergencies (*casualiter*, not *regulariter*).[69] Porthaise made it clear that in the election and succession of monarchs, the church had no authority, but that nevertheless the capacity and utility of the *Royaume Très Chrestien* was a spiritual affair. He explicitly argued against Jean Bodin as well as Belloy here, in subjecting kings to popes in spiritual matters, and arguing for the right of the pope to excommunicate a king.[70]

Porthaise's third sermon demonstrated that the very identity of the French commonwealth consisted in it being Catholic in head and members. He argued that a faithful people could only have a king of the same religion, on the basis of Deuteronomy 17, which he used as evidence that

---

allusion to the *Vindiciae, contra tyrannos*, and the grounding of political arguments in natural, rather than divine law (though of course, the author endeavoured to strike a fine balance between the authority of those laws in defining the contractual nature of kingship).

[66] Porthaise, *Cinq Sermons*, 15–18.   [67] Ibid., 33–4.   [68] Ibid., 48.

[69] Ibid., 79–85. *Decretales* 4.17.13; Friedberg, II, cols 714–16. *Per Venerabilem* declared that the French king acknowledged no temporal superior in his kingdom, but also that in cases of ambiguity in civil and ecclesiastical crimes, the final authority lay with the apostolic see. In such circumstances, the apostolic see exercised the office of the secular power. Cf. Krynen, *L'empire du Roi*, 348–51, on the implications of this decretal in medieval French debates.

[70] Porthaise, *Cinq Sermons*, 91–3.

the priesthood had a role in ordaining monarchs of Christian peoples.[71] Porthaise claimed that it was an error of both *politiques* and Huguenots to claim that the pope could not remove a king's territorial dominion if he became a heretic.[72] And in order to do this, he drew on the notion of the ancient constitution: describing the origins of Gaul since the first reception of Christianity. Clovis, the first Christian king, instituted a Christian monarchy in order to defend the people and the church against heresy. Since Clovis' baptism, he claimed that a law was made to ensure that a heretical king could be not simply excommunicated, but also deposed.[73]

Louis Dorléans referred to Henri's abjuration as a 'false sun', considering it a masterpiece of dissimulation that only persuaded the false *politiques* because they could use it to protect their own atheism and conserve their own wealth.[74] In contrast, he argued, the position of the *Sainte Union* was to defend the true religion, and the relationship between religion and justice that defined the French commonwealth, by continuing its commitment to holy war. In his *Banquet*, he reiterates the position he had elaborated in his works of the 1580s, but expands the framework of the discussion to include the issue of conversion. Dorléans was particularly careful in dealing with the question of whether or not the *Sainte Union*, under Mayenne, could be considered to be responsible for the conversion in the first place.[75]

Blame, as we might expect, falls on the moral character of *le bearnois* in the *Banquet*. Navarre is portrayed as trying to corrupt the Catholic church from within, and the character of the abbot suggests that, like a fox trying hide amongst dogs, he will easily be sniffed out.[76] However, if his dissimulation is not uncovered and publicly condemned, the character of the abbot goes on to outline the dangers of the false conversion to the body politic, which can only flourish under the Catholic religion.[77] The horrors of the Saint Bartholomew's Day Massacre are even invoked as evidence for what happens to the commonwealth when it is not united as a Catholic community.[78] This is very significant: the same arguments which were being used against the League at this time, such as the need to unify the body politic once more, were employed by Dorléans here to strengthen the opposition to Navarre.[79] The *Banquet* makes a thorough case against Navarre, arguing that accepting him as Catholic will in fact be to the

[71] Ibid., 8. Deuteronomy 17, particularly 9–11. [72] Porthaise, *Cinq Sermons*, 43. [73] Ibid., 60.
[74] Dorléans, *Banquet*, 1–9. [75] Ibid., 44–5. [76] Ibid., 49–50. [77] Ibid., 52–6.
[78] Ibid., 61–2.
[79] Note Greengrass, *France in the Age of Henri IV*, 84–5, on the position of thinkers like Du Vair in this period: stoic and profoundly alert to the complexity of accepting Navarre's conversion.

ruination of the entire Catholic religion, and it will give more courage to the confederation of heretics in Germany and England who are conspiring to destroy Catholicism in France.[80] The abbot compares the Archbishop of Bourges (who declared the conversion to be genuine) to Théodore de Bèze absolving Jean Calvin from heresy.[81]

Whilst the conversion of Navarre brought many Catholics over to his side, and eventually enabled the king to quell the uprising of the *Sainte Union*, some Leaguers willingly chose exile rather than submit to what they perceived as the heretic rule of a false Catholic.[82] One of these was Jean Boucher, who delivered his sermons against the conversion in August 1593. In the preface to the published sermons, Boucher claimed to have no other mind (*esprit*) than that of the church. By this he meant to contrast his own position with the supporters of Navarre, the 'enemies of reason', whom he sought to expose to ridicule. Boucher's nine sermons thoroughly eviscerate Navarre's position from every angle: the general evil of hypocrisy and dissimulation in matters of religion; the ways in which the false conversion was orchestrated; the nullity of the absolution; Navarre's status as an excommunicate; the need for an election of a Catholic king. Boucher presents the conversion as a threat of apocalyptic proportions to the well-being of the French commonwealth, and direct evidence of the devil trying to attack the 'most Christian kingdom in the world'.[83] Boucher used the Ciceronian maxim from *De Legibus* to make the case that the '*salut du peuple*' was at stake, both in a civil and a religious sense, and presented the position of the League as the 'arm' the church, defending it from heresy.[84] Building on an established theme in the Leaguer polemics to compare France to the ancient kingdom of Israel, Boucher uses a long section of his second Sermon to compare Navarre and his followers to king Saul and the loss of his right to rule through sin.[85]

On 22 March 1594, Henri IV entered Paris and took up his place as king of France. But his kingship was by no means secure; at least twelve attempts were made on his life before Ravaillac murdered the king in 1610.[86] One such notable attempt was that of Jean Chastel in December of 1594.[87] Chastel was a young law student, educated at the Jesuit college of Clermont

[80] Ibid., 120, 200–1.   [81] Ibid., 156.
[82] The fate of these exiles is the subject of Descimon, Ibáñez, *Les Ligueurs de l'Exil*.
[83] Boucher, *Sermons*, 62–3.   [84] Ibid., 89.   [85] Ibid., 100–20.
[86] Mousnier, *l'assassinat d'Henri IV*.
[87] Examined by Robert Descimon, 'Chastel's Attempted Regicide (27 December 1594)', in Forrestal, Nelson, eds., *Politics and Religion*; Collins, 'Jacques Clément et Jean Chastel'. Cf. Mousnier, *l'Assassinat d'Henri IV*.

and evidently, as his trial record demonstrates, impressed by the sermons of the Leaguer preachers that he had heard in the city, but also convinced by Jesuit arguments for tyrannicide.[88] The source of these ideas was deemed to have come from Chastel's tutor, Jean Guéret, whose room was found to contain books on tyrannicide, and who was subsequently executed for treason. Chastel himself made no attempt to escape after wounding the king, and was immediately arrested.[89] He was quickly tried and executed, and – as the Jesuits were also implicated in the plot – they were expelled from the protection of French jurisdiction by the Paris *parlement*.[90] Boucher, true to form, wrote a defence of Chastel from his exile in Flanders. His *Apologie pour Jehan Chastel* was published in 1595, under a pseudonym, and republished in 1610. It was translated into Latin in 1611, thus contributing to the ongoing debate about legitimate tyrannicide precipitated by the actions of Ravaillac.[91]

Chastel's attempt at assassinating Henri IV, and the Leaguer response to this event and to the problem of Henri's abjuration, demonstrates the extent to which these problems remained unresolved. This issue would, as the extensive scholarship on Henri IV demonstrates, go on to define the king's reign. Although, therefore, the League eventually fell apart in the face of an overwhelming desire on the part of the king's subjects for peace, their ideas on the political role of the clergy would have a longevity that outlived the immediate context of their development.

[88] NB. The work of the Spanish Jesuit Juan de Mariana, *De Rege et Regis Institutione* (1599) was condemned by the *parlement* of Paris after Henri's death in 1610. Cf. 'Procès criminal de Jehan Chastel', in *Mémoires de Condé*, 6 vols. (1743), 6, 161. Cited in Baumgartner, *Radical Reactionaries*, 222.

[89] Pierre de L'Estoile preserved an image of the monument erected in the place of Châtel's former home, which had been burnt to the ground after his arrest, in his *Drolleries*.

[90] The *Arrest de la Cour de parlement contre Jean Chastel, escholier, estudiant au College des jesuistes, pour le parricide par luy attenté sur la personne du Roy* was published in multiple locations in 1595, including Paris, Montpellier and Tours. Cf. *Procedure faicte contre Jean Chastel Escholier*; Fouqueray, 'Le Dernier Interrogatoire et l'éxecution de Jean Chastel d'après le procès-verbaux inédits'.

[91] Constantin François de Vérone [Jean Boucher], *Apologie pour Jehan Chastel*; Constantino Francisco de Verone, [Jean Boucher] *Iesuita sicarius*.

CHAPTER 6

Scholasticism in the Political Thought of the League

In defining 'the people' as a corporation and arguing that sovereign power was underpinned by natural and divine law, we have seen that political thinkers in this period were engaging with a set of questions that had also defined medieval attempts to explain the connection between temporal and spiritual powers. The question of the relationship between natural and divine law was key: the hierarchy of laws described by Aquinas in the *Summa Theologiae* was the method of reconciling Augustinian views on dominion as a consequence of sin, with Aristotelian ideas that politics was natural to man, and an expression of virtue. But such thinkers also sought to innovate and use new methodologies to test the limits of those established debates in the context of the Reformation and Counter-Reformation. It is in this context that the flourishing of scholasticism of the Salamancan School in the sixteenth century played an important role. This chapter demonstrates the extent to which fresh readings of the Thomist, and wider scholastic canon, were employed by members of the League in their analysis of the problem of heretic tyranny: most strikingly, in the *De Justa Reipublicae Christianae Authoritate* (1590).

The *De Justa Reipublicae Christianae Authoritate,* published in 1590 under a pseudonym, is a complex treatise, both in its content and in terms of any attempt to place it in context.[1] Composed of eleven chapters in the first edition, and ten in the second, 1592 edition, it is one of the most sustained treatises on political thought produced by a Leaguer, and therefore one of the most significant. The first three chapters deal with the origins and power of commonwealths, the power of kings and the definition of tyrants. The following two then turn to the problem of the new faith, first thinking about Calvinists in the pagan context, then establishing that the French Huguenots can neither properly be called Christian, nor French. The following three chapters, and the penultimate, focus on

---

[1] A condensed version of this chapter is published as Nicholls, 'Questions of authority'.

Navarre's faults as a ruler, and his heresy in particular, as well as a more general discussion of the evils of heretic kings. They include a chapter on the question of whether or not the pope can legitimately excommunicate a heretic king. The tenth chapter, at the peak of its anti-heretical fervour, treats the subject of tyrannicide. Finally, the work concludes with a call to arms and a rallying of the faithful to join the League against Navarre.

Limited archival resources mean that the authorship is still uncertain. The author signed under the pseudonym of 'G.G.R.A. Peregrinus Romanus' in the first edition, and 'Guilielmus Rossaeus' in the second (1592). League theologians Gilbert Génébrard, Jean Boucher and the Archbishop of Senlis, Guillaume Rose, have been suggested as possible authors, but it is also plausible that it was written by either, or both, of the English Catholic exiles William Gifford and William Rainolds.[2] Rainolds has most often been cited as the author in modern scholarship, partly because the author demonstrates such a thorough knowledge of English history and affairs. However, the evidence remains inconclusive.[3] Thomas Morton was the first to identify 'Rossaeus' as William Rainolds in 1605, and Robert Persons followed his cue in their exchanges of the early seventeenth century, as did several others.[4] However, as Salmon has pointed out, Persons had also claimed that William Gifford wrote the work in his *A Manifestation of the Great Folly of Certayne Secular Priestes* (1602).[5] Given that Persons was at Douai with both Gifford and Rainolds, it is disconcerting, or perhaps a deliberate obfuscation, that he was unable to attribute authorship to either one definitively.

All we know of the author is that he was a supporter of the duc de Mayenne, and that he had 'Burgundian blood', which doesn't connect him to any of the proposed authors in particular.[6] Burgundy was certainly loyal to the League, and to Mayenne who was its governor, and it is particularly

---

[2] Labitte, *De la démocratie*, 296–7, and Allen, *A History of Political Thought*, 351, n.51, both note that the authorship of Rose is dubious.

[3] Amongst the most telling evidence that Gifford and Rainolds may have collaborated is their other collaborative work, *Caluino-turcismus*. Comparing Calvinists to Ottomans was a common theme in Catholic polemic, but it bears comparison to chapter five of *De Justa Reipublicae Christianae Authoritate*: 'Quod Calvinismus sit Paganismo, aut Turcismo longe detestabilior', fol. 152r–187v . Treatments of the question of authorship are as follows: Labitte, *De la Démocratie*, 295–9; McIlwain, 'Who Was Rossaeus?' in his *Constitutionalism and the Changing World*, 178–82; Baumgartner, *Radical Reactionaries*, 145–7; Clancy, *Papist Pamphleteers*, 59–60; Weill, *Les Théories sur le Pouvoir Royal*, 237; Allen, *A History of Political Though*, 351, n.51; Salmon, *The French Religious Wars*, 75, n.27; Salmon, 'An Alternative Theory of Popular Resistance', 138, n.9; Amalou, *Le Lys et la Mitre,* 92.

[4] McIlwain explores this evidence in 'Who Was Rossaeus?', 179–82.

[5] Salmon, *The French Religious Wars*, 75, n.27.

[6] *De Justa Reipublicae Christianae Authoritate*, fol. 475v. Baumgartner cautiously suggests Rose as the author on this basis, 146–7.

striking that 'Rossaeus' mentions his heritage at a point when he was making use of Bodin's analysis of the customs of Burgundy, and Commines' chapter on Burgundy's annexation to France (1477–82).[7] Given Rossaeus' emphasis on the significance of local privileges and customary law, we might reasonably have expected him, therefore, to make something more of his heritage. However, he is dismissive of it, and thus leaves his reader permanently in the dark, it would seem, as to his identity.

We do, at least, know that the author was a Leaguer: he dedicated the work to Mayenne, and explicitly justified the actions of the League in terms of holy war, offering his work as an intellectual contribution that instructed the faithful in their duties and listed the reasons to defend the French commonwealth from heresy.[8] However, whilst it is clear that the text was originally written in the context of the League, and should be read, in the first instance, in the French context; the second edition, published in Antwerp in 1592, suggests a broader intellectual context than that of the League, and a particularly warm English reception. Potentially, this supports the idea of an English author. William Gifford, who had been at Douai and later Rheims, edited this edition and removed its tenth chapter, thus rendering it less dangerous as a text, by emphasising Catholic authority rather than 'monarchomach' themes. In this context, it would have been a useful contribution to the campaign that Robert Persons and publisher Richard Verstegen were waging against William Cecil from Antwerp.[9] This, at the very least, suggests a broader reception history for this work than the immediate circumstances of domestic Leaguer politics after the assassination of Henri III.[10] The subject of the treatise, as its title suggests, is the authority of Christian commonwealths, rather than a justification of a particular moment in French history. In that sense, it can be read as part of pan-European discussions in this period in Catholic communities about

---

[7] Barthélemy de Chasseneuz is the great influence here, his *Commentaria . . . in Consuetudines ducatus burgundiae* gathering the customs of Burgundy together for the first time, but also making an important point about the position of customary law vis-à-vis royal authority to the effect that customs of the people, confirmed by kings, had the force of law. The author of the *Vindiciae* also drew on the Burgundian example to make the point that the kings of France promised to protect the laws of Burgundy in their accessions into Dijon. See *Vindiciae*, 136, and n.469. Cf. Garnett's useful cross-reference here to Choppin's *De Domanio Franciae*, II.i.2.

[8] *De Justa Reipublicae Christianae Authoritate*, preface (no page).

[9] Pettegree et al., *Netherlandish Books*; Houliston, *Robert Persons's Jesuit Polemic*, 47–70.

[10] There is an error in Baumgartner, *Radical Reactionaries*, 271, n.1, which suggests that there is no striking difference between the two editions: the removal of this chapter from the 1592 edition is extremely significant.

legitimate political authority. Indeed, no reading (European, English or French Leaguer) necessarily precludes the other.

The dedication of *De Justa Reipublicae Christianae Authoritate* to Mayenne is expressive of the distinction between the Mayenniste Leaguers and the '*archi-ligueurs*' of the *Seize*. Whilst it can still be considered a call to arms, the text is conventionally viewed in the scholarship as far superior to Boucher's *De Justa Abdicatione Henrici Tertii*: the former understood to be the work of a man of genuine talent, the latter that of a well-informed pedant.[11] There is some truth to this kind of observation: Boucher's accumulation of resources in *De Justa Abdicatione Henrici Tertii* shows little regard for their provenance, and instead provides an encyclopaedia of arguments in a pretty crude, repetitive scholastic framework. It was a true *livre de circonstance* that had shock value in its immediacy: it aimed to achieve a particular goal, and it was not the best example of Boucher's thinking (his sermons and later works are rather better).[12] In contrast, Rossaeus' text is more scholarly. It is also somewhat more cautious in its politics, as evident in its more restrained approach to legitimate tyrannicide. That it was Boucher's *De Justa Abdicatione Henrici Tertii* that felt the full effect of William Barclay's outrage in his *De Regno*, rather than Rossaeus' text, which came in for little more than a condemnation for using 'heretic' arguments, further suggests, along with the wider reception of Rossaeus' work, that contemporaries saw more worth in it than Boucher's.[13] It is also true that Barclay's condemnation of Boucher is a little misleading insofar as it emphasises the most provocative elements of the text. With that in mind, the reading of Rossaeus offered in this

---

[11] The difference between the subtely of Rossaeus' treatise and that of Boucher has often been noted, but Anquetil described it with particular gusto. Anquetil, *l'Esprit de la Ligue*, 1, xxix–xxx: '*Il y a entre l'ouvrage de Roze et celui de Boucher, la différence qu'on met entre un savant poli, quoique prévenu et passionné, et un pédant fougueux. Ce n'est pas que le livre de Roze ne fourmille de principes dangereux, d'erreurs, de paralogismes, de calomnies, d'imputations odieuses ; mais du moins ses expressions sont ordinairement ménagées, son style clair, et élégant ; au lieu que Boucher vomit les invectives et accumule sans choix et sans pudeur les mensonges les plus grossiers ; ses injures sont toujours directes ; son style est boursouflé, traînant, ennuyeux. De ces deux livres, également mauvais pour les principes, l'un est l'ouvrage d'un homme de génie, l'autre la production d'un pédant érudit*'. Boucher, in fact, has not done at all well with his historical reputation. Louis Maimbourg, the seventeenth-century French Jesuit academic, decided that Boucher's ferocious manner of expression was a crime against Christ himself. More recently, John Allen contended that 'very few political partisans can have lied with such verve and such audacity': Maimbourg, *Histoire de la Ligue*, 56; Allen, *A History of Political Thought*, 49.

[12] Recently, it has been suggested that it was published before the assassination, and in a different version: see Zwierlein, *The Political Thought of the French League*.

[13] It is possible, given Rossaeus' reliance on Buchanan's *De Jure Regni* for the key points of his 'monarchomach' aspects of his argument, that Barclay also felt he had already answered Rossaeus' challenge in the first two books of *De Regno*.

chapter seeks not to efface, or replace, Boucher's text, but simply to emphasise instead the broader intellectual context within which texts which included support for legitimate tyrannicide were written. Looking at a text like Rossaeus' from the perspective of justifications of legitimate Catholic royal rule helps to expand the intellectual framework within which such works are evaluated. Most significantly, it demonstrates the precise nature of the importance of scholastic sources in these debates, which, in contrast to the emphasis on 'radical Thomism' in recent scholarship, suggests a different reading.

Scholastic Arguments for Tyrannicide

Making a Bartolist distinction between usurper tyrants and legitimate rulers turned tyrants, Rossaeus divided the latter category into three types: the tyrant who took possession of his subjects' goods, the tyrant who acted contrary to the laws of the commonwealth and finally the tyrant who acted to the destruction of the Christian faith.[14] His sources here are utterly conventional. It is, however, important that he made such fruitful use of Buchanan's *De Jure Regni*, which provided him with the argument that legitimate assassination of tyrants was possible in a monarchy.[15] Rossaeus quoted the passages from *De Jure Regni* in particular where, in the dialogue, the character of Thomas Maitland took the line that those who transgressed the boundaries of human society by breaking laws were to be regarded as enemies of God and men, and classed as wolves or beasts, not human beings.[16] Rossaeus converts this into a discussion of tyranny, where Maitland (not yet persuaded by his interlocuter Buchanan on the treatment of tyrants) is only discussing robbers, adulterers and bandits. Rossaeus fuses this point with another of Buchanan's, rejecting Maitland's suggestion that all tyrants should be obeyed.[17] It is striking that Rossaeus chooses to manipulate Buchanan's text at these points, even though other

---

[14] These are defined at fol. 84v–93v. Named sources include Aristotle's *Politics* (2.5), Cicero's *De Legibus* (3.31), Suetonius' *Lives*, the constitutions of the Council of Mainz (813; the reference is possibly to Franz Behem's Mainz edition of the constitutions, published in 1549.) Rossaeus' quote is to the effect that a king who fails to rule according to justice and piety is a tyrant, at fol. 85r, and the Roman Codex 1.14.4 (*Digna vox*). This last (extremely common reference), on the obedience of rulers to the laws, also appeared on the title page of the *Vindiciae*, and is quoted in the text, ed. Garnett, at 101 and 132.

[15] *De Justa Reipublicae Christianae Authoritate*, fol. 387r.   [16] Cf. Aristotle, *Politics*, 1253a.

[17] Buchanan, *On the Law of Kingship among the Scots*, ed. Mason, 88–9, 116–17. Rossaeus also refers to book seven of the *Rerum Scoticarum Historia* where Buchanan describes tyrants as a 'mark set up for universal hatred'.

arguments of Buchanan's would have suited his purpose more exactly.[18] However, there was one crucial area where Buchanan's *De Jure Regni* could not be used to support Rossaeus' case: he did not provide a political theory in which heresy in a king equated to tyranny.

Rossaeus was at pains, in his tenth chapter on tyrannicide, to distance himself from Protestant writings even as he quoted them in support of his own argument. The title of his chapter is as follows: 'Against the mad Protestant idea that any private individual may butcher their enemies, Christian kings, whom they call tyrants; and [concerning] the manner in which true tyrants may legitimately and rightly be killed by a private individual'.[19] The precise nature of this 'mad Protestant idea' was the threat it posed to Catholic ('Christian') rulers: Rossaeus did not want his argument extended to allow for resistance to Catholic monarchy. For this reason, he made a clear distinction between 'false' Calvinist opinion, and meritorious, Catholic works: Luther, Calvin and Bèze all fall into the former category, and Jacques Clément into the latter.

Rossaeus described Clément as having acted as a citizen of Paris and France, and as a member of the universal Catholic church simultaneously, 'armed with the spirit of God' to defend the church against corruption and destruction when he murdered Henri III.[20] This description of Clément's actions importantly fuses the national community with the body of the Roman church. Nevertheless, Rossaeus does concede an intellectual debt to the Calvinists in the form of a syllogism: *Maior Calvinistarum* tyrants can be killed; *Minor Catholicorum*, heretics are tyrants. Heretic kings, who were created to defend and protect the Catholic church, can therefore be killed.[21] Indeed, it is not the case that Rossaeus rejects the ideas of Bèze, Buchanan and Mornay out of hand. Rossaeus' treatment of tyranny instead highlights two central themes of his text: that it is impossible to

---

[18] For example, Buchanan, *Dialogue*, 154–63.
[19] *De Justa Reipublicae Christianae Authoritate*, fol. 383v.
[20] Ibid., fol. 389r–v. Theodore de Bèze and the author of the *Reveille-Matin*, an anonymous pamphlet attacking the crown, produced between 1573 and 1575, are the particular targets of this section.
[21] Ibid., fol. 389v. '*Si enim per eorum civitates, & palatia, & aulas, haec Protestantium doctrina insonverit, fas esse cuique subdito regem tyrannum interfecire: quum deinceps ad hanc propositionem generalem tyrannos sine exceptione omnes comprehendentem, vera ratio, vera philosophia, verissimaque theologia hanc magis particularem adiunxerit, Reges haereticos qui reges creati ut ecclesiam Catholicam defendant, potentia sua regia deinceps ad eiusdem ecclesiae Catholicae oppressionem & Catholicorum suorum subditorum destructionem abutuntur perfectissimos esse tyrannos, id quod tam certo & pene necessitate quadam inevitibili sequitur, ut nunquam rex aliquies vere & ex animo possit esse haereticus, qui non eodem momento eademque ratione evadat tyrannus: hoc quum ita sit, quid opus est singillatim deducere quid ex his ita positis efficatur, cum cuique infanti sit manifestum & evidens*'. In the marginalia, '*Maior Calvinistarum*' and '*Minor Catholicorum*' are written.

be both Huguenot and French, and that a Huguenot cannot conceivably be king of France.

Working within William Barclay's characterisation of Rossaeus' work, his Protestant sources might seem to be most significant in his discussion of tyrannicide. However, a close reading of the text demonstrates that in fact an authoritative scholastic commentary tradition underpins his argument far more importantly. The flourishing of Thomism in French intellectual culture in the sixteenth century is, therefore, the most important intellectual context for Rossaeus' argument for tyrannicide. This refreshed emphasis on Thomist study had its beginnings in the University of Paris, with the decision of Pierre Crockaert to abandon the convention of lecturing on Peter Lombard's *Sentences* and instead comment on Aquinas' *Summa Theologiae*.[22] Crockaert's decision had profound repercussions, most clearly demonstrated by the work of his student, Francisco de Vitoria (1486–1546), who was to become one of the central figures of the movement now known as the 'second' scholastic. Vitoria never published in his lifetime and the *Relectiones* are the notes taken down by his students. Five thousand students are estimated to have attended his lectures at one point or another, and twenty-four of his pupils held university chairs at Salamanca.[23] He and his equally influential colleague Domingo de Soto (1494–1560) had both studied at Paris before returning to teach in Spain. Similarly, their students travelled to France.

By the time of the French religious wars, the mode of thinking associated with this second scholastic was firmly established. French thinkers embraced Thomism once more: Thomas Beauxamis (1524–89), the Franciscan François de Feuardent (1539–1610) and Gilbert Génébrard, Archbisop of Aix from 1591, were particularly important figures, and the latter two were loyal Leaguers.[24] Feuardent was a fierce critic of Henri III, and an *archi-ligueur* who joined with Boucher and Jean Garin in opposing Mayenne and taking an intransigent position on Navarre's conversion.[25] These theologians were working within a Thomist framework, but it is also clear that Spanish influence played a significant role in this era of French

---

[22] This revival is discussed in Skinner, *Foundations*, 2, 135–73.
[23] Hamilton, *Political Thought*, 175.
[24] Thomas Beauxamis was a theologian of the Carmelite order and positioned himself against the *archi-ligueurs*. In 1575, he published *Remonstrance au peuple françois*, which was continuously reprinted throughout the League era.
[25] Feuardent, *Sepmaine première des dialogues* (1585), published again in 1589 and in Latin in 1594. Feuardent also did an important edition of the Salamancan scholastic Alphonso de Castro's work on heresy in 1578. Feuardent is given some consideration in Armstrong, *The Politics of Piety*, but is certainly deserving of further scholarly attention.

scholarship. Figures such as the Spanish Jesuit Juan Maldonado (1533–83), who studied theology at Salamanca under Soto and Francisco de Toledo (1532–96), who would become the first Jesuit Cardinal, particularly helped the cross-pollination of Spanish and French thought in this period.

In 1563, Maldonado took up a position to teach philosophy at the Jesuit Collège de Clermont. From 1565–73 he was professor of theology, and from 1572–6 was asked to help in the conversion of Navarre and other princes of the court who had embraced the new religion. Maldonado was extremely influential in Paris, and his lectures so popular that places had to be booked in advance.[26] It was most likely through Maldonado's lectures that the controversial theology of a thinker such as Soto would have circulated in Paris. Although these professors travelled Europe and their lectures were received with success, their published works found an audience only within certain elite circles.[27] It is significant therefore, that Rossaeus referred to Soto's *De Justitia et Jure* explicitly. Soto's work was published in Lyon, which became one of the League publishing centres, in 1559, 1569 and 1582, as were Vitoria's *Relectiones* in 1586 and 1587. Whoever Rossaeus was, therefore, he certainly had access to these new and influential treatises which touched in so many important ways on the idea of the Christian commonwealth.

In *De Justa Reipublicae Christianae Authoritate*, this influence is perfectly clear in citations of Aquinas and Peter Lombard, which sit alongside references to Domingo de Soto's *De Justitia et Jure*, and commentaries on Aquinas' *Summa* by Cajetan (Tommaso de vio Gaetano), Bellarmine and Francisco Toledo. Rossaeus' references further included works of casuistry by Toledo, and the Italian Dominican Bartolommeo Fumo, as well as to Sylvester de Priero Mazzolini's popular *Summa Summarum*. Jan Vermeulen (Molanus) *De Fide Haereticis Servanda* is also quoted, as are Jean Gerson's *Considerationes*.[28] It is plausible, though not certain, that Rossaeus also drew on Vitoria's *Relectiones*.

---

[26] Prat, *Maldonat*, 187.   [27] Martin, *Livre, pouvoirs et société*, 1, 16.

[28] *De Justa Reipublicae Christianae Authoritate*, fol. 422v–424r. The Bellarmine reference is to his Louvain lectures, which he delivered from 1570 and are a commentary on Aquinas' *Summa*. The manuscript remains unpublished, but it receives some treatment in Le Bachelet, *Bellarmin avant son Cardinalat*. It is pertinent to the discussion of authorship, as discussed, that William Gifford attended those lectures. Cajetan's commentary was published in 1698. The remaining references are to the following texts: Fumo, *Summa Casuum Conscientiae*; Sylvestro Mazzolini, *Summa Summarum*; Molanus, *De Fide Haereticis Servanda*; Domingo de Soto, *De Justitia et Jure*; Toledo, *Summa Casuum Conscientiae*. Toledo's commentary on Aquinas' *Summa* was probably written in the 1560s and circulated in manuscript, but was not published until 1869: Toledo, *In Summam Theologiae S. Th. Aquinatis Enarratio*; cf. Höpfl, *Jesuit Political Thought*, 390. Regarding the references to Toledo and Bellarmine, Baumgartner incorrectly notes that Rossaeus is here referring to their commentaries on Peter Lombard's *Sentences*. Rossaeus' marginal references to '2.2.q.64.art.3'

Three points are worth making initially: first, that Rossaeus was lifting his argument, not from Protestant texts primarily, but from a well-established commentary tradition. His references to the Thomist staples of the *Summa*, the *De Regimine Principum*, and to the *Sententiae* of Peter Lombard, are embedded in the commentaries and other more contemporary texts that he quotes, which, in turn, often refer to each other: there is a colossal intellectual tradition at work here. The second point is that the sources Rossaeus uses are discussions of legitimate homicide, and of heresy, not explicitly of tyranny. Fumo, for example, makes no mention of tyranny in the passage cited by Rossaeus; he writes simply that homicide is legitimate if it is done in accordance with the law, and not arbitrarily.[29]

The final point is that Rossaeus often brings together diverse citations to make his case. For example, he combines Toledo's commentary on legitimate homicide with his commentary on the question of whether sinners could be killed. Rossaeus wanted to convince his readership that heretic tyranny was the worst form of attack on a Christian commonwealth, because it attacks the collective body and soul, even if that was not precisely the point being made in the sources he quoted. In this sense, his syllogism of '*minor Calvinistarum; maior Catholicorum*' takes on a new significance: the idea that tyrants can be killed might come from Protestant sources, but without the superior authority of the Catholic scholastic commentary tradition, it is meaningless.

The sources cited by Rossaeus operate in such a way as to blend Roman legal arguments with Thomist commentaries, in order to demonstrate that a right of self-defence could also apply to a political community as well as to an individual.[30] They support the argument that the political community had the right to resist a tyrant who threatened that community, in the same manner as an individual had the right to resist an individual attack. For example, Soto's *De Iustitia et Iure* works through the argument that although ordinarily killing a man is not per se a good thing, when it comes to the question of the common good ('*bonum commune*') then it can be. When the common good is threatened, then it is up to the person who has been entrusted as its guardian ('*custodia*') to deal with the malefactor as a doctor amputates limbs from a body. In the case of usurper tyrants, Soto confronts the problem that the decree of the Council of Constance in its

leave us in no doubt that it is to the commentaries on the *Summa* Rossaeus was referring. It is also not certain that any such commentaries on the *Sentences* were ever written by these authors. Baumgartner, *Radical Reactionaries*, 274 n.49.

29 Fumo, *Summa Casuum Conscientiae*, 88.
30 See Skinner, *Foundations*, II, 123–34, on this application.

fifteenth session had proclaimed tyrannicide to be against church doctrine, a point Jean Gerson had argued. Soto reverts, ironically, to an argument Gerson had made in a different context, when he had suggested that usurper tyrants could be rejected on the basis that (as the *Digest* states) 'it is licit to repel force with force'.[31]

It is consistent with his reference to Soto that Rossaeus should cite the *Summa Casuum Conscientiae* of Soto's pupil, Jesuit theologian Francisco de Toledo, and in particular his chapter on homicide.[32] Toledo had argued that so long as the killing of a tyrant is performed by public authority, for the common good, it is possible. He added a secondary clause to this, stating that if a tyrant rules and the citizens have been unable to expel him, then a private individual could take action and assassinate the tyrant. Referring to *De Regimine Principum* and Aquinas' commentary on the *Sentences*, Toledo followed Aquinas' dual definition of tyranny here, and stated categorically that 'it was not a sin for Brutus to kill Caesar'.[33] Rossaeus also refers to Toledo's commentary on IIaIIae 64, articles 2–3, where Aquinas considered the question of whether it is lawful to kill a sinner and whether this can legally be done either by a private or a public person.[34]

Cajetan's commentary on the *Summa*, cited by Rossaeus, refers to the same *quaestio* as Toledo, but the next article: on whether private individuals can kill sinners. Cajetan cross-references his discussion to *De Regimine Principum*, arguing that tyrants could not be killed by an individual, but by public authority. Like Soto, he also refers to the Council of Constance, which had discussed the question of when it is licit to kill tyrants.[35] Cajetan

---

[31] Soto, *De Justitia et Jure*, V.1.3 fol. 139r: '*Nocentium hominum interfectio, non est per se bona, sed quatenus in bonum publicum refertur: ergo illi praecise incumbit, cui cura commissa est & custodia communis boni: quemadmodum amputatio membri, quae proficua est corpori, medico praecise incumbit cui cura infirmi demandatur, ut iudicio secundum medicas loges id fiat*' and '*Quare si respublica superiorem habet, ille adeundus est, ut remedio succirrat: sin vero, illa potest in ipsum coarmari. Dum ante potes non est, tunc Deus est orandus, in cuius manu cor Regis existit: quique & propter peccata populi finit nonnunquam hypocrita regnare. Atque in hoc casu intelligenda est sanctio Concilii Consantiensis, sessionem 15, ubi tanqam haeresis condemnatur eorum error, qui affirmabant cuilibet licere tyrannum occidere. Si vero tyrannide invasam rempublicam obtinuit, neque unquam ipsa consensit, tunc ius habet ipsum extinguendi: nam vi repellere licet*'. Cf. Gerson, 'Considerationes Principibus et Dominis Utilissimae' in *Opera Omnia*, ed. du Pin, 4, 624.

[32] Toledo, *Summa Casuum Conscientiae*, 536–46.

[33] Molanus, *De Fide Haereticis Servanda*, 174–5, makes the same point in reference to the same part of the *Summa*. The implicit reference to Cicero's *De Officiis* is also present in Soto's *De Iustitia et Iure*.

[34] Toledo had also used this as the basis for the argument in his *Summa Casuum Conscientiae*. Toledo, *In Summam Theologiae Enarratio*, II, 328–32.

[35] Aquinas, *Summa Theologica*, ed. Cajetan, 375–6; Aquinas, *De Regimine Principum*, I.vi, 16–19. I am following a particular scholarly convention of attributing the text to Aquinas, whilst recognising the fact that Aquinas abandoned the treatise in 1267, when it was subsequently completed by Tholomeo of Lucca. See Blythe, *On the Government of Rulers*; Aquinas, *Political Writings*, ed. Dyson, xix, n.4. It

followed the Bartolist distinction between two types of tyrant: the usurper and the despot, which Rossaeus had also used. The latter, Cajetan writes, are tyrants *ipso iure* and they can be killed, but only by public authority.

Finally, Mazzolini de Priero's *Summa Summarum* takes Aquinas' *Summa* IIaIIae 42. art. 2, on sedition, as its basis for legitimate resistance: 'those who resist . . . in order to defend the common good are not to be called seditious themselves . . . Tyrannical rule is not just, because it is not directed to the common good . . . Disruption of such a government does not have the character of sedition'.[36] Mazzolini's definition of tyranny here is explicitly dependent on Aristotle's *Politics* and *Ethics* (books three and eight respectively), as a ruler ruling for his own private benefit rather than for the common good. It also depends on Aquinas' own definitions of common good and illegitimate rule. Aquinas had defined the people in Ciceronian terms as: '"an assembly of those united by agreement as to what is right and by a common interest", so, clearly, sedition is opposed to justice and the common good'.[37] The remainder of Mazzolini's passage continues to rely on Aquinas, repeating the point already discussed, namely that a tyrant could only be killed with public authority, not the private presumption of an individual. Finally, Aquinas' commentary on the *Sentences* of Peter Lombard provides Mazzolini with the argument that one who has unjustly acquired dominion (the usurping tyrant) can be killed in order to liberate the country (*patria*).[38]

A point Rossaeus does not acknowledge amongst these citations, is that although – as these sources show – a usurper tyrant can fairly easily be dismissed as an illegitimate ruler, the case of a tyrant who (originally) legitimately held the title of ruler is far more complex and less easy to circumvent regarding church doctrine, particularly in the case of an individual assassin working without explicit public authority. This is why he makes an explicit reference to Gerson arguing that it is a natural law to repel force with force in the context of his definition of a tyrant as one who rules contrary to nature *and* the laws of Christian charity in pursuing his own good.[39] Soto had already assimilated Gerson into this discussion, but it is notable that Rossaeus makes explicit reference to this French

is significant, in my view, that the authors under consideration in this analysis attributed the work to Aquinas.
[36] Mazzolini, *Summa Summarum*, 397.
[37] Augustine, *City of God* 2.21; Cicero, *De Republica* 1.25.
[38] The reference to Aquinas' commentary is II. Dist. 44.q.2.
[39] *De Justa Reipublicae Christianae Authoritate*, fol. 423v. He refers to Gerson's *Remedia contra adulatores* and his *Considerationes*.

theologian, when he could simply have gone straight to the *Digest*, or indeed to Soto. First, this slightly looser definition of tyranny suits Rossaeus' purpose better, which is to defend the assassination of Henri III but also to suggest that Navarre, whether or not one accepted the legitimacy of his claim to the throne, was equally vulnerable. Second, Gerson's theory of power inherent in the community was essential for the construction of a theory that the community had the right of self-defence, even against a ruler it had chosen.[40]

The works of these 'doctors of the scholastic' provide the author with strong support for his own point that he did not need to rely solely on what he called 'false Protestant doctrine' to construct an argument for legitimate tyrannicide. In particular, Rossaeus' use of this scholastic material provided him with a language of rights which in part emerged from the Gersonian tradition, in which the political community had the same right as an individual to defend itself. It further provided him with a clearer thesis of sovereign power. For Rossaeus, a tyrant is defined as someone who is not in receipt of the authority of the church, or the power of the common-wealth, thus making the Gelasian distinction between *auctoritas* and *potestas*. What remains to be seen, is whether or not this scholastic tradition plays an important role in the rest of the treatise. As we shall see, it is just as significant for Rossaeus' broader understanding of political community and the role of natural law, as it is for his analysis of tyrannicide.

Natural Political Community

The authority of Christian commonwealths provides the structure of Rossaeus' text, in which Christian virtues reign. It is a natural-law-based account, explicitly couched in anti-Machiavellian terms.[41] Correspondingly, its defining feature is Thomist–Aristotelian: Rossaeus writes that it is an axiom of the theologians that grace does not destroy nature, but that the gifts of nature are from God, and illuminated by the arrival of Christ.[42] The commonwealth is built upon these natural principles, and Rossaeus defines

---

[40] By referring explicitly to Gerson on this point, it would seem that Rossaeus was aware that he needed this thesis of political power which, as Brett has argued in *Liberty, Right and Nature*, 76–87, 119–22, was not available in Aquinas' original discussion. Cf. Barclay's pun in *De Regno*, 67–8, on Gerson's 'inconsiderate' role in influencing Rossaeus on this subject.

[41] *De Justa Reipublicae Christianae Authoritate*, fol. 24r. His reference is to Machiavelli's *Discourses on Livy*, 2.2.

[42] Ibid. '*Est enim ratum et fixum Theologorum axioma, gratia non tolli naturam, sed potius ea quae primo sunt nobis a summo naturae conditore naturaliter collata dona, eadem superveniente Christi divino lumine magis augeri et roborari.*'

the Christian republic, using Aristotle's language, as one in which the citizens both rule and obey. He fuses this with the Augustinian tradition when he argues that Christian kings are also bound by the laws of justice and of piety.[43] The Christian commonwealth is a 'perfect' community when it is embedded within the universal church and governed according to the laws of Christian justice.

Unlike Jean Boucher, who does not elaborate on the origins of political community, Rossaeus spends some time in his opening chapter explaining the natural genesis of political life as an instinct of man. Following convention, Aquinas' *De Regimine Principum* provided the intellectual template for this discussion. Here Aquinas, in Aristotelian terms, had argued that whilst man is directed towards his end by his own rationality, he cannot achieve this end in solitude. Man must live in a community in which there is 'some general ruling force to sustain the body and secure the common good of all its parts'.[44] The phrase 'some general ruling force' is a revealing one, as it indicates that Aquinas' thesis is not about the precise location of political power. Aquinas does not provide a full account of precisely how power reverts back to the community in the case of a tyrant. Sovereign power is found first in the community by nature, as the result of man's rational participation in the eternal law, and it is never entirely alienated from the body of the community. But Aquinas did not clarify the way in which power was transferred from God to community to ruler, or how it could revert back. This particular 'juridical dynamic', as Brett has argued, was instead provided in the sixteenth century in the context of the debate between Jacques Almain and Cajetan from 1511 to 1512 over the precise nature of the power of the pope over the body of the church.[45] To

---

[43] *De Justa Reipublicae Christianae Authoritate*, fol. 25r. '*Christianae ergo respublicae quae ita certis legibus imperandi et obediendi sunt astrictae, ut reges nisi secundum pietatem et iustitiam imperare non possint, nec subditi obedire nisi in iis quae iusta, pia & Christianae sanctitati consentanea sunt, longe superant respublicae vel paganas, vel haereticas, in quibus principi sine ullis limitibus tributa est quid libet pro arbitrarum praecipiendi authoritas. Illae enim quia ab homine reguntur ad rationis & iustitiae normam imperante, reguntur non tam ab homine quam a Deo*'. Cf. Aristotle, *Politics* III. 16; Augustine, *De Civitate Dei contra Paganos*, XIX.13–14; Aquinas, *Summa Theologiae*, IIaIIae 58. See also Arquillière, *l'Augustinisme Politique*, 117–53.

[44] *De Regimine Principum*, I.i, 3: '*Multis enim existentibus hominibus, et unoquoque, id quod est sibi congruum, providente, multitudo in diversa dispergeretur, nisi etiam esset aliquis, de eo, quod ad bonum multitudinis pertinet, curam habens, sicut et corpus hominis, et cujuslibet animalis deflueret, nisi esset aliqua vis regitiva communis in corpore, quae ad bonum commune omnium membrorum intenderet*'. 'Some general ruling force' is Robert Dyson's translation in his edition of *Aquinas, Political Writings*, 7.

[45] The texts in question are Almain, *Libellus de auctoritate ecclesiae*; *Aurea opuscula* and Gaetano, *Auctoritas papae et concilii sive ecclesiae comparata*; *Apologia de comparate auctoritate papae et concilii*. All can be found reprinted in collections of the works of Gerson: Jean Gerson, *Opera*, ed. Richer and

see what kind of use Rossaeus was making of this discussion of political power, implicit in the accounts of legitimate homicide referred to previously, we need to begin with his analysis of the origins of political community. This analysis provides us with evidence that he was using Aquinas' work as a template, but also that he was working within the same intellectual milieu as more recent scholastic thinkers, such as Soto and Vitoria.

Rossaeus argues that, unlike other animals, man does not have the natural ability to provide his own necessities for living. Whereas the bull has its horns, a boar its tusks and a lion its teeth and can rely on strength to survive, man is brought into the world weak, distressed and wholly reliant on others.[46] On this basis, everyone unites (*coalescerent*) equally into the body called the commonwealth.[47] This is a commentary on Aquinas' idea, borrowed from Aristotle, of natural necessity – the notion that it is necessary for man to live in a community in order to survive. Rossaeus

ed. Du Pin. Brett demonstrates that whilst the Cajetan–Almain discussion transferred an enduring debate of the medieval period into the sixteenth century, it made a subtle but important shift in the terms of the discussion by making it a question of the location of *potestas*. Brett argues that Almain uses Gerson to construct his analogy between the power of the individual and the power of the community, thus giving the community an inalienable right of self-preservation akin to that of an individual. It is not present in the part of the *Summa Theologiae* to which Almain refers (IIaIIae 64, art.2). Almain shows that 'it is easy to see how the power a king uses is the community's power. Hence, he is said to act by public authority . . . '. Brett, *Liberty, Right and Nature*, 119 and Brett, *Changes of State*, 124–6.

[46] *De Justa Reipublicae Christianae Authoritate*, fol. 1r–v: '*Facile enim fuit animadvertere reliquis animantibus a primo ortu naturam tam provide consuluisse ut ipsis per se suppeteret, quicquid ad vitam tuendam erat necessarium, ut non magnopere aliorum subsidiis indigerent. Alia enim rostris, alia unguibus, alia plumis instruxit. Tauri cornibus, apri dentibus, morsu leones se tuentur, quae robore non valent solertia nituntur; & pleraque; non minus fuga & occultatione se defendunt, quam velocitate & viribus: quorum tanta est & tam admirabilis varietas, ut multi Philosophi in eorum indagatione aetatem suam totam contriverint. Homo autem tanta cum miseria & imbellicitate ex matris visceribus effunditur, ut trunci instar immobilis iaceat, nec sine alterius ope vel labra maternis uberibus possit admovere*'. Cf. *De Regimine Principum*, I.i, 2: '*Est autem unicuique hominum naturaliter insitum rationis lumen, quo in suis actibus dirigatur ad finem. Et si quidem homini conveniret singulariter vivere, sicut multis animalium, nullo alio dirigente indigeret ad finem, sed ipse sibi unusquisque esset rex sub Deo summo rege, in quantum per lumen rationis divinitus datum sibi, in suis actibus se ipsum dirigeret. Naturale autem est homini ut sit animal sociale et politicum, in multitudine vivens, magis etiam quam omnia alia animalia, quod quidem naturalis necessitas declarat. Aliis enim animalibus natura praeparavit cibum, tegumenta, pilorum, defensionem, ut dentes, cornua, ungues, vel saltem velocitatem ad fugam. Homo autem institutus est nullo horum sibi a natura praeparato, sed loco omnium data est ei ratio, per quam sibi haec omnia officio manuum posset praeparare, ad quae omnia praeparanda unus homo non sufficit. Nam unus homo per se sufficienter vitam transigere non posset. Est igitur homini naturale, quod in societate multorum vivat*'. Cf. Aristotle, *Politics*, 1.2. William of Moerbeke's thirteenth-century translation of the *Politics* provides Aquinas with 'social and political animal' rather than the Aristotelian original which just has 'political animal'.

[47] *De Justa Reipublicae Christianae Authoritate*, fol. 3r: '. . . *omnes pariter in publicum quoddam corpus (quam Rempublicam vocamus) coalescerent; & mutuis auxiliis in generale corporis illius bonum & salutem intenderent*'.

further demonstrates his familiarity with Aquinas by arguing that no one can be a part of the body (of the community) who does not need the help of another in the preservation of his own self.[48] Aquinas had argued in his *Summa Theologiae* that preservation of self was the most fundamental law of nature (thus suicide is the most unnatural act, and self-defence the most natural).[49] In supplying a natural deficit, the community thereby becomes man's most natural way of life. The structure of Rossaeus' argument follows that of *De Regimine Principum* closely.[50]

Rossaeus' account has further, more contemporary, similarities to the descriptions of the natural genesis of community in the influential lecture of Francisco de Vitoria on civil power, delivered in 1528, as well as to Soto's discussion in *De Iustitia*.[51] Clearly, *De Regimine Principum* was a common source, and these kinds of descriptions of the relationship between nature and politics, with their heavy Aristotelian inflection, are a characteristic, if complex, aspect of Christian political theory up to this point. There are two reasons why it is worth considering Rossaeus' take on natural political community: the first is that it reaffirms the point made previously, that Rossaeus was indebted to sixteenth-century scholastic commentaries on Aquinas. The second is that it further distinguishes Rossaeus' text from the Huguenot writings of the 1570s. Rossaeus' extended discussion of man's natural desire for society does not find such a close equivalent in, for example, the *Vindiciae*. Indeed, the *Vindiciae* makes mention of natural law as the basis of political society, but the author was far more concerned to establish the basis of the operation of that society on Roman-law contract theory, and thus avoid having to explain the relationship between natural and divine law. The author deliberately avoided any discussion of the original formation of communities before the election of kings.[52] In contrast, Rossaeus' discussion of the natural right of the political community to defend itself derives its authority from his analysis of the reasons why man, distinct from beasts, naturally, and rationally, seeks out community, and from there goes on to establish laws, magistrats and kings. The resulting analysis of the agency of the political community is more

---

[48] Ibid., fol. 1v: '*Neque enim ulla est corporis pars, quae non alicuius opifici labore et auxilio ad sui conservationem egeat*'.

[49] Aquinas, *Summa Theologiae*, ed. Blackfriars, 38, IIaIIae 64. art.5, 33.

[50] *De Regimine Principum*, 1.i, 1–3.

[51] For their discussions of the natural genesis of political community, see Soto, *De Justitia et Jure*, 1.2. art.1, fol. 5v–6v ; Vitoria, *Relectiones Theologicae*, 1.3–5, 178–81.

[52] See *Vindiciae*, ed. Garnett, xxxiii–xxxv, xliv–xlv. Garnett restated his argument that the structure of the *Vindiciae* was provided by Roman legal sources, in response to a challenge from Anne McClaren: McLaren, 'Rethinking Republicanism'; Garnett, 'Law in the Vindiciae'.

indebted to Vitoria's lecture on civil power, and Soto's discussions of civil justice, than to the arguments of the *Vindiciae.*

Rossaeus' interest in the idea that political institutions are as much the result of nature as man's instinct to form into societies is demonstrated by his fascination with extra-European, often newly discovered lands in which natural political life could exist independently of Christianity and legitimately. This discussion also suggests an awareness of the kind of analysis undertaken by Vitoria in his *De Indis.* As the scholastics in Salamanca had done, Rossaeus allows space for legitimate natural civil association which had as its end morality and justice, as less complete than the Christian political community, which has as its end eternal life as well as those virtues.[53] Rossaeus used his knowledge of the discovery of new lands in the fifteenth and sixteenth centuries to reinforce his case that political life was a natural, universal human phenomenon. His frequent and extensive use of the *Novis Orbis Regionum ac Insularum Veteribus Incognitarum una cum tabula cosmographica* (1532), a compilation of travel literature, as a source is testimony to his fascination with recent geographical discoveries.[54] In the farthest western reaches of America, Rossaeus shows how from living by 'wild and beastly customs', the people there were compelled by rational instinct to join in the life of civil society.

Strikingly, Rossaeus chooses examples of nomadic tribes – the Numidians of Africa, the Tartars of Russia, the Germanic peoples and Sarmates – to show that, by natural inclination, people all over the world form communities. Evidently Rossaeus did not think that a settled defensive and sovereign position is required to define a community. The Tartars wandered the world nomadically without determined boundaries of sovereignty, or under any single authority.[55] However, he emphasises that they

---

[53] *De Justa Reipublicae Christianae Authoritate* fol. 82r. Cf. *De Regimine Principum*, I, xvi, 96–100; *Summa Theologiae,* ed. Blackfriars, 32, IIaIIae 10, art.8–11.

[54] *Novis Orbis Regionum* was first published in Basel in 1532, based originally on Montalboddo's *Paesi novamente ritrovati* (1507), which was republished five times in Italian, six in French and twice in German. Additions were made to the *Novis Orbis Regionum* in the subsequent editions of 1537 and 1555.

[55] *De Justa Reipublicae Christianae Authoritate,* fol. 3v: *Nostraque tempestate eadem ratio quosdam in extremo occidente Americanos, olim bestiarum fere ritu viventes, in magis civilem vitae societatem compulit. Quin etiam agrestes in ultima Septentrione Tartari qui unius imperio non continentur, neque vero civitatibus includuntur, neque certos habent ditionis terminos, sed sub papilionibus degunt, & tamdiu uno in loco cum uxoribus & gregibus agunt quoad terram circumiacentem depasti fuerint, plurimumque ab aliorum hominum civili humanitate absunt, non tamen singuli disperi, sed tanta multitudine vagantur; quanta opus est & magnam civitatem complendam, & ad mutuam omnium defensionem, & ad iniurias undiquaque depellendas: quo prorsus modo olim vixisse Numidas Africae, & Germanos, & Sarmatas, & alios universos in illo longissimo Europae atque Asiae tractu populos, fidelium historicum monumenta prodiderunt'.*

did so not as scattered individuals, but as a multitude. The gathering together of human beings into a community is therefore not identified with precise geographical boundaries, but by the simple fact of coming together by natural instinct.[56] According to Rossaeus, it is not the 'eloquence of man' (contradicting Cicero in his *De Inventione*), nor the 'authority of kings' nor any 'artificial' cause that men chose to contract into a community, but an innate natural – and also rational – sense that such a life would fulfil the needs of both body and soul.[57] He argues, once again in tune with Aquinas, that it is highly unnatural for man to live in the kind of disorder he describes as 'Babylonian' confusion; communities which maintain order and peace are fulfilling the requirements of human nature.[58] Here he refers to societies untouched by Christianity in America, Africa and Asia, and uses them to show that hierarchy, by which he means the establishment of laws, magistrates and princes, is part of this natural genesis and proper order of political society.[59] He specifically mentions the example of America before the Spanish arrived, showing that they already had civil structures of their own in place. This passage is comparable to one in *De Indis* where Vitoria argued that the 'barbarians' of the new world did have legitimate dominion over their own territory, showing that they had 'order in their affairs' and recognisable political structures already in place.[60] Marginal references are to the *Novis Orbis Regionum* and Josephus but we can speculate, particularly when it comes to the use of the American example, that Rossaeus had also read *De Indis*.

In the course of this discussion, Rossaeus does not, for obvious reasons, consider the logical possibility that allowing for legitimate non-Christian dominion could also be used to defend the idea of France being under the rule of a non-Catholic. We should distinguish, as Rossaeus does, that

---

[56] Cf. Friedeburg, 'In Defense of Patria', 358–9.

[57] *De Justa Reipublicae Christianae Authoritate*, fol. 3v–4r: '*Eos autem in hanc vitae communionem contraxit, non hominum eloquentium persuasio, a quibus erant penitus inanes, non regis alicuius authoritas, quae adhuc nulla prorsus extitit; non denique artificiosa aliqua causa, qualem homines ignari quandoque comminiscuntur, sed ipsa naturae communis indoles, a solitudine abhorrens, & ad societatem civilem propendens, ipsa ratio ostendens hoc esse aptissimum vitae & salutis tuendae medium, ipsa mentis humanae solertia & perspicacitas, ipsum dico naturae lumen, quo perceptum est hunc vivendi modum fuisse & corporibus utilem, & animis salutarem, & posteritati continuandae necessarium, & tum singulorum commodes tum universorum rationibus maxime convenientem. Natura ergo hominum coetus & communiones induxit, natura civitates fabricavit, natura rempublicam instituit*'.

[58] *De Justa Reipublicae Christianae Authoritate*, fol. 4v.

[59] It is also likely that Rossaeus was offering an alternative to Belloy's argument that even the most barbarous of people recognise the natural obligation they have to their monarch, and therefore do not oppose themselves to his or her authority. Belloy, *Apologie Catholique* 2.21, fol. 92v. Belloy regards inviolable obedience to a king as a dictate of the *ius gentium*.

[60] Vitoria, *Relectiones Theologicae*, I, 308–9. Cf. Aristotle, *Politics*, 1328b6–22.

particular question from that of heretical rule: in the eyes of the Leaguers Henri IV was a heretic, not a pagan. For Rossaeus, as with Aquinas, it is one thing to be ignorant of Catholicism entirely, and quite another to reject it explicitly.[61] Rossaeus explains, when he discusses tyranny in chapter three of the treatise, that pagan commonwealths shared a common goal with Christian commonwealths: the well-being of the people, the *salus populi* and 'common good'. By *salus populi*, Rossaeus is explicit that he means both spiritual and civil health: *salus* refers both to the soul, as well as to the well-being of the people as a whole, incorporated into a body.[62] Correspondingly, he employs an Augustinian distinction between two types of justice which exist in civil society: external and internal, during an elaboration of Aristotle's argument that it is an effect of law to make men good (*Politics* 3.6). At 3.2, Rossaeus explains the external 'good' of the civil body as a whole in terms of civil peace (an acquired virtue), and the internal 'good' of the soul of that body as moral (infused) virtue.[63] There are therefore two 'ends' of any commonwealth: civil peace and individual moral virtue, which are obtained by the presence of good legislators and magistrates who provide for these ends through law.[64] Justice, in the civil

---

[61] Cf. Aquinas, *Summa Theologiae*, vol. 32, IIaIIae 12, art.2, 101–3: ' . . . unbelief in itself is not inconsistent with dominion, since that was brought in by the *Ius Gentium*, which is human law. The distinction between believers and unbelievers, however is of Divine law, and this does not annul human law'. And also Vitoria, *Relectiones Theologicae*, I.i, 19–20.

[62] *De Justa Reipublicae Christianae Authoritate*, fol. 91r. Cf. fol. 13r. '*Omnes pariter in publicam quoddam corpus (quam Rempublicam vocamus) coelescerent; & mutuis auxiliis in generale corporis illius bonum & salutem intenderent*'. Rossaeus wrote that, although pagans (i.e. Cicero) wrote the law '*salus populi suprema lex esto*', when translated into Christian terms, this *salus* – in a Christian commonwealth – means the *salus animarum*, the salvation of the soul. The 'supreme law' is Christ's law. Rossaeus refers to this argument again at 8.6 (fol. 306r), when arguing for the excommunication of heretic kings.

[63] *De Justa Reipublicae Christianae Authoritate*, fol. 67v: '*Ergo iustitia externa, civilis pax & tranquillitas, cum quieta bonorum iuste acquirendorum possessione, primum est quod antiquissimi mortales in communionem civitatis, & reipublicem confluentes respecerunt. At quoniam haec sola consideratio manca est, & longe humilior quam pro humanae dignitatis altitudine quum & bestiolae quadam gregatim viventes, ut apes & oves, & leones etiam aliquando externam quandam iustitiam & ordinem servent: idcirco eaedem respublica eadem natura duce alium sublimiorem finem sibi proposuerunt, nimirum ut praeterea cives boni essent, mentesque suas moralium virtutum ornamentis excolerent. Quemadmodum enim videbant se duabus partibus constare animo & corpore, & illum hoc longe esse praestantiorem, quando fine illo hoc instat immobilis saxi nihil agere nec se movere posset; absurdum putabant ita externa corporis emolumenta curare, ut internum animi decorum omnino negligerent*'.

[64] Ibid. fol. 68r–69v: '*Hoc vero tam alte in omnium hominum pectoribus a Deo naturae conditore infixum inhaesit, ut nemo unquam Philosophus de republicae scripserit, nemo aliquando legislator rempublicae formaverit, nemo unquam Magistratus politicus civitatem rexerit, qui non cives suos bonos efficere conatus sit . . . Ergo certum est respublicae omnes fuis legibus atque institutis eo contendisse, ut praeter externam pacem, interius quoque virtutibus probitatis, temperantiae, continentiae, fortitudinis, civium suorum animi imbuerentur*'.

sense, takes on that architectonic quality Aquinas had described in his discussion of justice at ST IIaIIae 58 and 60.

At 3.3, Rossaeus begins to distinguish between pagan commonwealths and Christian commonwealths, by arguing that 'true' justice is only achievable in the latter. Rossaeus connects the well-being of the political community to veneration of God, arguing that 'true' justice is only meted out in a 'perfect' community, that is, one which is both self-sufficient, in Aristotelian terms, and Christian, in Augustinian terms.[65] Although nature 'leads' all men towards the achievement of external justice in the context of communal living (i.e. in a political community governed by magistrates and laws, as we saw), Rossaeus argues that knowledge of the Christian faith 'illuminates' justice more clearly. That is to say, Christianity enables the achievement of the kind of internal moral virtue required for the attainment of eternal life.[66] Rossaeus uses the model of the Hebrew commonwealth to demonstrate that God, as well as being the creator of natural law, would intervene to provide his people (through Moses), with temporal law.

This argument was of particular pertinence to France. Although Rossaeus accepts that political communities did not have to be made up of, or be governed by, Catholics in order to claim legitimacy, he argues that the rejection of Catholicity compromises the status of an already evangelised commonwealth.[67] In order to establish precisely how Rossaeus could argue that a non-Catholic could not legitimately govern France, however, we now need to turn to his analysis of the connection between natural and divine law in Christian commonwealths.

[65] Ibid., fol. 70v, cf. fol. 71v–74v: '*Quum enim iustitia quae humanam vitam omnemque societatem perfecte continet & moderatur, in eo sit posita ut suum cuique tribuatur; nisi Deo omnium conditori eum quem par est honorem impendimus iniustissimi sumus, etiamsi cuique hominium generi, & principibus, parentibus, & vicinis, & reliquis, quod iustum est concedimus*'. His references here are to Cicero's De Natura Deorum and the connection between the success of Rome and the cultus deorum, which was precisely the connection Augustine sought to disrupt in his De Civitate Dei contra Paganos.

[66] Ibid., fol. 71v–72r: '*Quod ergo homines natura duce externam iustitiam in communi vita sequebantur, hoc Christi disciplina multo magis ratum habuit & adiectis maximis aeternae vitae praemiis acribus iustitiae studium in Christianorum pectoribus accendit. Quod virtutes morales appeterent illisque; praediti ad praeclaribus de amicis, de parentibus, de civibus, de toto reipublicae statu merendum instruerentur & hoc quoque, sanctissima Christi religio confirmavit, & adiecta intrinsecus spiritus gratia mentes suorum sic illustravit; ut multo quam prius flagrantiores in harum virtutum studium incumberent. Quod etiam Deum esse, in eiusque honorem sacra quaedam agenda esse persuasum haberent, nec hoc refutavit, quod ipse nimirum creator aeterna naturae lege homines creaturas suas edocuerat, & lege temporali per Moysem lata Iudaeis olim praescripserat*'.

[67] In a manner consistent with the Leaguer polemics, he frequently holds England up as an example to the French as a warning of what happens in such cases. For comparison, the best example of this kind of approach in the polemic is Louis Dorléans, *Premier, et Second Advertissements des Catholiques Anglois aux François Catholiques*, to which Mornay responded with *Lettre d'un Gentilhomme Catholique François*.

Natural and Divine Law

In Rossaeus' analysis, as in the original Thomist account, natural law is the source of human, civil law; it is the rational and moral underpinning of human society in that it is directed, and directs, towards the common good of man. It is also man's rational participation in the eternal law. Nature, we saw, institutes commonwealths; in fact man's natural reason, 'the light of nature', causes him to join together into a community under the rule of magistrates and of laws.[68] Rossaeus has a concept of the political community as autonomous and self-sufficient, however he is not offering a doctrine of 'pure nature' as, for example, Francisco Suarez was to do when he radically displaced the relationship between natural and eternal law enshrined in the Thomist account.[69] Rossaeus fuses the Aristotelian account of politics with aspects of Augustinian ideas when he discussed the relationship between the civil polity and the church. The essence of Rossaeus' political theory is that any Christian political community is embedded in the universal community of the church, and consequently the jurisdictional sphere of a king is not impermeable, but porous. A heretic tyrant cannot serve Christian justice and breaks both the natural and divine laws which limit his power. He is therefore subject to the judgement both of civil magistrates and the priesthood.

Rossaeus accepted that kings and people were bound in a relationship of reciprocal obligation governed by human and divine law, and he argued that this was a defining characteristic of Christian kingdoms.[70] However, the limiting effects of natural and divine law on a king's dominion do not, in themselves, explain Rossaeus' political thought. Indeed, Rossaeus argued that a king could not transgress these limits in common with contemporaries such as Jean Bodin and the Huguenots.[71] In this case, there are two distinguishing features of Rossaeus' thought: the first is the distinction he draws between authority and power; the second is the role he allocates to the priesthood, particularly to the Gallican bishops, in the choosing and deposing of kings.

In Rossaeus' account, the people and the priesthood provide a king with both his power (*potestas*) and his authority (*auctoritas*) in such a way as to

---

[68] *De Justa Reipublicae Christianae Authoritate*, fol. 3v–4r quoted previously. The reference to the 'light' of natural reason is an acknowledgement of Aquinas, *Summa Theologiae*, 1a2ae. 91.2.

[69] Courtine, *Nature et Empire de la Loi*, 149–56.

[70] *De Justa Reipublicae Christianae Authoritate*, fol. 40v–41r.

[71] *Vindiciae*, ed. Garnett, 127–9, for example. Clearly, in the case of the *Vindiciae*, the relationship between natural and divine law is dependent on the (deliberately) unclear relationship between the sacred and secular parts of the contracts in this treatise.

absorb the natural political community into the sphere of Christian justice.[72] This distinction between power and authority as a way of distinguishing lay from ecclesiastical power was not a revelation in the sixteenth century, it was originally the invention of Gelasius I.[73] However, the work of Francisco de Vitoria in particular demonstrates that theorists in the sixteenth century were using this distinction as a way of defining the jurisdictional sphere of a king.[74] Rossaeus employs this distinction between power and authority in a different manner to, for example, Vitoria. Vitoria had described the transfer of authority, not power, from commonwealth to king. Authority, understood as executive power, comes from the community; power, as a capability, comes from God. Rossaeus, on the other hand, describes the transfer of power from the community as a transfer of *potestas*, indicative of both the executive power of the office and the fullness of a king's power.[75] From the choice of the people united into a community, the king receives his temporal power. The source of sovereign power is indirectly from God, mediated through the community of the people.

The source of a king's divine authority, from which he derives the ability to legislate over internal religious affairs, is the priesthood in Rossaeus' account. At the coronation ceremony, presided over by the Archbishop of Rheims, the king is anointed and swears to rule according to the Christian faith and justice.[76] Rossaeus argued that a Christian commonwealth functions best

---

[72] Cf. Arquillière, *l'Augustinisme Politique; Canning Ideas of Power.*

[73] See his famous letter to emperor Anastasius, in 494. Cf. Ullmann, *The Growth of Papal Government.*

[74] Vitoria, *Relectiones Theologicae,* I.v, 189 1.5 '*Quamuis enim a republica constituatur . . . non potestate, sed propriam authoritatem in regem transfert, nec sunt duae potestates, una regia, altera communitatis*'.

[75] *De Justa Reipublicae Christianae Authoritate,* fol. 17v. '*Verum quidem est potestatem & regimen publicum a populo ad reges esse delatum & penes reges manere, sed ita ut rex regem agat non tyrannum, non carnificem: hoc est iuste, civiliter, politiceque regat non iniuste, immaniter, tyrannice. Ergo si quidem res iuxte, si ordine, si iuxta praescriptas a natura & iure gentium conditiones, si regaliter, hoc est, si in bonum & utilitatem publicam gubernet, etiam si nonnumquam in officio delinquat, & tolerandum fatero & honore afficiendum*'. Cf. fol. 305v. '*Tamen cum Christianus homo commissum sibi a Deo regimen quodcunque accipit, primo loco Christiana fides est attendenda, & diligentissime providendum: ut omnes de pace belloque, de mercatura & quiete civili leges, cum legibus Christianis convenient*'.

[76] The *Somnium viridarii de iurisdictione regia et sacerdotali,* commissioned by Charles V in 1376 contains an influential description of the grace which this unction transmits to the French king, but probably the earliest description is that of Hincmar of Rheims in the ninth century. *De Justa Reipublicae Christianae Authoritate,* fol. 31r: '*Rex, verus est Rex priusquam coronatur, & coronatio nihil est aliud quam nota & insigne eius, qui iam antea perfectus erat rex. Quid autem ordo coronationis, hoc est generalis omnium Gallorum, imo omnium christianorum, episocoporum, procerum & populi vox? Regia (inquint ad regem) potestas tibi non est a natura a generatione sola, sed nunc tibi traditur per episcopos omnipotentis Dei authoritate*'. Broadly speaking, this is a response to the alternative argument, reiterated by Belloy in his attack on the League, that a king's authority comes directly from God at the moment the former king dies: in effect, the king 'never dies'. Cf. Giesey, *The Royal Funeral Ceremony;* Hanley, *Lit de Justice;* Kantorowicz, *The King's Two Bodies,* 314–450. Tyler Lange has recently discussed Kantorowicz' legacy and argued for a reappraisal of constitutional practice

when royal authority is given episcopal support.[77] This does not mean that a king has no measure of independence from church jurisdiction, only – as Rossaeus shows at 3.5 – that, in spiritual matters, he is subject to episcopal decision.[78] This inversion of the argument that the French monarch was the source of the bishop's regalian rights is symptomatic of Rossaeus' version of 'ecclesiastical' Gallicanism.[79]

The result of the distinction Rossaeus makes between the sources of sovereign authority and of power is that a heretic cannot rule France. Rossaeus demonstrates this, in deference to centuries of French political tradition, by reference to the idea of the *Roi Très Chrétien*. Since the baptism of Clovis, he argued, the dynastic succession had taken place in this manner; without the coronation ceremony the king could not be said to act with the consent of the people.[80] For such arguments, Rossaeus was indebted to the medieval chroniclers, especially Aimon de Fleury, but also to the work of sixteenth-century French historians such as Du Haillan and François Belleforest who are referred to consistently throughout the treatise. Rossaeus' version is distinct due to its emphasis on the transfer of legitimacy (by popular consent), as well as grace, in the ceremony. Whilst it

---

and source material in French political theory in this period: Tyler Lange, 'Constitutional Thought and Consitutional Practice', 26.

[77] *De Justa Reipublicae Christianae Authoritate*, 73r: '*Et hanc totam regis potestatem quasi ecclesiasticam sacramque functionem spiritus sancti Christique Apostolus Petrus perelegantur significavit quum appellavit statum testamenti novi, sacerdotium regale & regnum sacerdotale [1.pet.2.9; Exod.19], quia nimirum reges Christianorum ita optime regio se nomine dignos ostendunt, si sacerdotio Christi in ecclesia sustinendo & sacerdotum ecclesiasticas leges corroborando suam regalem authoritatem impendunt, in quo proprie verti cardinem & medullam regii inter Christianos splendoris omnes antiquissimi & sanctissimi episcopi docuerunt, omnes fortissimi atque optimi Imperatores crediderunt*'. Rossaeus spends a few pages discussing the submission of imperial power to ecclesiastical; Athanasius & Ambrose in particular are quoted as sources.

[78] *De Justa Reipublicae Christianae Authoritate*, 74v–78v.

[79] Salmon, 'Gallicanism and Anglicanism' in his *Renaissance and Revolt*, 157. Cf. Dupuy, *Histoire du Différend d'entre le Pape Boniface VIII et Philippe le Bel* for earlier texts like the *Rex pacificus* which argued for the French king's jurisdiction over bishops.

[80] *De Justa Reipublicae Christianae Authoritate*, fol. 252v–253r: '*Quod nisi haec omnia iureiurando sanctissime prius confirmaverit, nunquam consensu populi rex acclamari potest, nunquam ab Archiepiscopo Rhemensi oleo coelesti inungitur, nunquam ab episcopis Gallicanis diadema capiti eius imponitur, nunquam iure & ordinie gestat sceptrum & gladium regalis Maiestatis insignia ab episcopis eisdem tradita: nunquam ab eis dici potest, "hae omnia tibi tanquam legitimo haeredi authoritate omnipotentis Dei traduntur, per nos qui hic adsumus, episcopos". Ille fortasse eodem iure quo alia permulta, hoc est vi, furore militari, iure latronum & praedonum quia potentia valet, ista potest involare. At iure reipublicae Gallicanae, iure Christiano, iure Ecclesiastico, eo iure quo omnes hactenus a magno Clodovaeo Galliae reges legitime alii aliis successerunt, populi nimirum & nobilitatis & cleri libera voluntate non potest ista adipisci*'. Cf. Beaune, 'Clovis dans les grandes chroniques', 191–212; Beaune, 'Saint Clovis: Histoire, Religion et Sentiment National'; Beaune, *Naissance de la Nation France*; Guyotjeannin, *Clovis chez les Historiens*; Salmon, 'Clovis and Constantine'. On the idea of the *Roi Très Chrétien* see Krynen, *L'Empire du Roi*, 345–83.

may be tempting to draw a comparison here to the *Vindiciae* (as well as *Francogallia* and *De Jure Magistratuum*) regarding the coronation ceremony as a moment of transferral of popular sovereignty, the important difference is that Rossaeus uses the coronation and the dual transfer of power and authority from people and church to argue that a Protestant heretic cannot uphold the Catholic faith, and hence the pact between people, church and king is broken on the moment of excommunication. In this sense, Rossaeus' discussion of episcopal power is more appropriately compared to the works of fellow Leaguer, Gilbert Génébrard.[81]

Rossaeus' eighth chapter on the power of popes to excommunicate kings provides further evidence of the relationship between divine and natural law. This section of the treatise treads very lightly over some well-established ground regarding the relationship between temporal and spiritual sovereignty.[82] For example, Rossaeus explains again that the investiture of Christian kings sustains their obligation to defend the Catholic faith, and they cannot be considered legitimate rulers without first receiving unction.[83] He clarifies that the civil 'good' of the community is subordinate to the spiritual, and that Christian kings are subject to the judgement of the pope. He is explicit that this subjection of kings, baptized into the universal body of the church like any other Christian, is a matter of divine law, not of 'changeable' human law.[84] But although he spends some time discussing the translation of empire at the hands of the papacy, and the crowning of emperors by popes, Rossaeus is not an unequivocal hierocrat.[85] He did not think that popes could depose kings, and the famous example of Pope Zachary and King Childeric serves only to demonstrate that the French people would not take such an action without

---

[81] Rossaeus was certainly familiar with Génébrard's work, as demonstrated by his reference to Génébrard's edition of the *Chronologia Hebræorum* at fol. 308v–311r.

[82] Rossaeus' references in the eighth book are predominantly to patristic works and scripture. Whilst he discusses topics such as the papal deposing power and the translations of empire, which were the hunting ground of medieval canonists, his only reference to canon law (in this book) is to the decretal *per venerabilem* at 309v.

[83] *De Justa Reipublicae Christianae Authoritate*, fol. 310v.

[84] Ibid., fol. 304r, 310r, 311r–v: '*At vero ut omnes illi quocunque modo honores eos adipiscantur, so Christiani sunt, summo ecclesiae pastori ita subsint u tab eo possint corrigi, adeoque & excommunicati, & deponi, si in haeresim incidant, ver contra reipublicae Christianae generale bonum graviter delinquant, hoc adeo certum est, quam certum est eundem regem esse Christianum, esse Christiani gregis ovem, quam certum est eum esse ecclesiae Christianae filium, esse in ecclesia Christi baptizatum, esse ecclesiae Christi disciplinae subiectum, eique praeesse in ecclesia Catholica Episcoporum qui pro eius anima Christo supremo iudici rationem est redditurus. Est enim hoc non humani iuris sed divini, non mutabile sed aeternum, non in cuiusque vel regis vel populi libera voluntate positum, sed expresse a Christo & Apostolis mandatum*'.

[85] Ibid., fol. 307r–309v.

the advice of the pope.[86] Rossaeus is explicit that the famous 'power of the keys' described at Matthew 16 (the power of 'loosing and binding'), was a spiritual, not a temporal, power.[87] Most importantly, it is in this chapter that Rossaeus explains the manner in which the political community is embedded within the body of the universal church.[88]

Rossaeus attempts to maintain both a sphere of independence for the Gallican church and for the French king. As regards the authority of the king, he draws an analogy with imperial power, arguing (on the basis of Roman law), that the emperors could legislate on church matters but only, he argues, if they conformed to canon law. As he had stated in the third chapter: a ruler who orders anything against the church is not to be obeyed.[89] Rossaeus' treatment of the episcopal role in the legitimising of kings is symptomatic of the mingling of ecclesiastical and civil jurisdiction in France in this period.[90] As he demonstrates at length in the seventh chapter of the treatise, as a heretic, Navarre cannot rule France thanks to the heresy laws which are in place, both in France and in Roman and canon law.[91] Rossaeus is explicit that this is a question of human, civil law as well as divine law, a point which is further demonstrated by his use of legal and ecclesiastical sources to argue against Navarre.

After the arrival of Christ, Rossaeus explained, the political community was perfected when politics (the political 'sword') was directed towards procuring ecclesiastical peace.[92] In this way rulers and civil magistrates, who were first established by natural law, became subject

---

[86] Ibid., fol. 306v. Rossaeus makes no reference to canon law here, but it is worth noting that Gratian's *Decretum* provided the basis for either argument (a) Zachary deposed Childeric or (b) Zachary excommunicated Childeric, and thereby released his subjects from their oath of obedience.

[87] Ibid., fol. 302v.

[88] Ibid., fol. 306r: '*Quia etsi publica rerum terrenarum commoditas populari prudentia & acumine discerni poterat, eaque naturali sagacitate provideri utrum regnum vel alter principatus cuiuscunque generis tali societati futurus esset commodior; tamen quia idem Christiani sciebant regionem suam fuisse generalis corporis reipublicae Christianae membrum particulare, cuius privato bono sic erat consulendum, ut prius ad commune bonum totius attenderetur; idcirco eundem regem postulabant a generali Christianorum pontifice (quem Christus ecclesiae totius quasi in sublimi arce speculatorem posuit ut inquit D. Augustinus) quo ille simul animadverteret quemadmodum cum universalis ecclesiae bono particularis illius provinciae utilitas consisteret*'.

[89] Ibid., fol. 77v: '*Et in hoc quidem munere, quo reges suum gladium ac ecclesiasticae disciplinae defensionem conferunt, & fidem Christianam ab Episcopis traditam suis edictis corroborant, ita priore consistit vera Christianorum regum authoritas, ut quum secus faciunt, causaque ecclesiasticas ad sua tribunalia rapiunt, ordinem divinitus & a Christo & a natura constitutum perturbant . . .*'. Rossaeus' references are to Justinian's Code, Constitutions 5, 6, 42, 109, 123, 131. He also refers here to Deuteronomy 17, a centrepiece for Leaguer arguments that Catholicity was a 'fundamental law'.

[90] Monter, *Judging the French Reformation*. Tyler Lange briefly discusses this development in his 'Constitutional Thought and Constitutional Practice'.

[91] *De Justa Reipublicae Christianae Authoritate*, fol. 256r–287r.   [92] Cf. Luke 22.38.

to bishops.[93] The significant role Rossaeus allots to the bishops of the Gallican church in his political theory offers an obvious contrast to Jean Boucher who had argued for the right of the theologians at the Sorbonne to declare Henri III excommunicated prior to the papal bull.[94] Rossaeus is explicit that Sixtus V's bull deprived Navarre of any right to rule France, as it would any 'pseudo-king', but he attributes the authority to carry out the verdict of the bull to the Gallican bishops.[95] The French king has a duty to protect the Gallican church but it is the Archbishop who is its *pater*; Rossaeus is clear that Henri de Navarre cannot be said in any way to be the owner of the goods of the Gallican church.[96] Rossaeus appeals directly to the bishops of the Gallican church to perform their duty in expelling Navarre from the kingdom.

Rossaeus' treatment of civil and episcopal power in this treatise is symptomatic of a concept of political community defined in terms of political Augustinianism, in which the goals of justice and faith are intermingled.[97] Rossaeus defined a Christian commonwealth as one in which the civil and the ecclesiastical combine, in the same way as body and soul make up man.[98] But whilst he discusses Christian commonwealths in

[93] *De Justa Reipublicae Christianae Authoritate*, fol. 72v: '*Principes autem & magistratum civilem quem prius in naturae lege ordinaverat, ita iam gratiae lege reformavit, ut tum demum perfecte munere suo fungerentur, quum mistica regeneratione in ecclesiam insiti, episcopis regenerantibus, ut filii patribus, ut oves pastoribus, ut discipli magistris, quemadmodum Christus praeceperat se subiicientes, politicum suum gladium dirigerent ad eam extrinsecam ecclesiae pacem procurandam, cuius interna sacramenta diximus episcoporum fidei fuisse commissa.*'

[94] Rossaeus explores papal power at 8.5; for the Petrine commission see fol. 301v–302r. Boucher's argument was also supported in the anonymous pamphlet *Advertissement aux Catholiques sur la bulle de nostre Sainct Pere*. In further contrast, Antoine Hotman argued in his *Traité des Libertez de l'Eglise Gallicane*, that an excommunication only took full force of law once the Paris *parlement* had agreed to its legitimacy.

[95] *De Justa Reipublicae Christianae Authoritate*, fol. 323r–327v, fol. 334r: '*At quid episcopis faciendum est ad hanc tempestatem quae Galliae imminet dispellendam? Nimirum ut cum principibus quos habent Catholicos, contra pseudoregem quem habituri sunt haereticum, cum proceribus & civitatibus Christianis et Catholicis contra illos Atheos & Calvinianos, suas operas iungant, sua consilia conferant, & suis armis spiritualibus eorum arma temporalia corroborent*'. He also reminds the Gallican clergy at large of this obligation, in a manner reminiscent of Génébrard's appeal in his *De Clericis* to those members of the clergy who had continued to administer the sacraments to Henri III after his excommunication.

[96] Ibid., fol. 326r, 509r–513v. Cf. Belloy, *Apologie Catholique*, 2.11, fol. 38v–43v. The regalian rights were a divisive point amongst Gallican theorists and there was no consensus amongst the Leaguers. Antoine Hotman, for example, argued that the king did own the goods of the church: *Traité*, fol. 61v. Important French discussions of these concerns are to be found in Charles de Grassaille's *Regalium Franciae* (1538) and René Choppin's *De Domanio Franciae* (1572). Cf. Nicholls, 'Ideas of Royal Power'.

[97] *De Justa Reipublicae Christianae Authoritate*, fol. 81v: '*ad naturalem republicae cuisque finem, qui in externa iustitia & morum probitate positus est, eorum regna dirigi voluerint; supernaturalem autem finem aeternae vitae ad quam sola fides Christianae ducit*'.

[98] Ibid., fol. 82r. '*Quum enim civilis status & ecclesiasticus una efficient respublica non aliter quam corpus & anima unum hominem, homo & Deus unum Christum, elementa & corpora caelestia unum mundum . . .*'

these general terms, Rossaeus is clear that the peculiar relationship between France and the papacy means that there are some exceptions to these general rules regarding Gallican liberty. Interestingly, he turns to the letters of the eleventh century bishop and canon lawyer Yves (Ivo) of Chartres to establish his argument for Gallican independence.[99] Rossaeus argues that France has a relationship with the church which distinguishes it from other Catholic countries:

> Hence if anyone wanted to define the condition of the people of France and the kings of France after the reception of the faith of Christ ... special tribute is owed to France [regarding] the love of country and of charity which are common to all communities of people: as in the case of religious zeal and respect for public justice, these advantages have been lavished on France above other Christians.[100]

The moment of evangelisation is a defining moment of French identity, according to Rossaeus: the rejection of heresy is a characteristic of the French nation.[101] In this way, Rossaeus could argue that the Huguenots were not French, and he describes them as akin to Ottoman Muslims in their relationship to the Catholic faith. He goes on to accuse them, in chapter six, of being 'pseudo-French' and 'Gallo-Greeks'.[102] For Rossaeus, the Huguenots could not be conceived of as members of the French political community because they were deemed heretics; nor could they make a contract with a French Catholic king. For the Christian commonwealth

---

[99] Ivo of Chartres, *Iuonis episcopi Carnotensis epistolæ*. Letters 28, 49, 105 and 134 are referred to between fol. 312v and 314v.

[100] *De Justa Reipublicae Christianae Authoritate*, fol. 196v: '*Quare si quis populum Gallicanum regnique Gallicani statum post receptam Christi fidem definire & tanquam oculis intuentium repraesentare voluerit, quoad patriae amorem & charitatem ea quae sunt omnibus similiter populis communia, Gallis tribuere debet: quoad religionis vero zelum & iustitiae publicae reverentiam, magna Gallis supra alios Christianos praerogativa est largienda*'.

[101] Ibid., fol. 195r–v: '*Et hanc ego religionem Gallicanae reipublicae populique maximum ornamentum & primariam tanquam partem colloco, quae etiamsi in aliis quoque populis Christianis omnibus primas iure suo obtineat, tamen Gallicae nationi necesse est praerogativam magnam tribuere, quando afflatus spiritu sancto Apostolos videmus ad eam convertendam diligentius quam ad aliam quamuis Europae gentem incubuisse, & conversos Gallos ad eandem fidem maiori sinceritate & Constantia adhaesisse, nec unquam ut aliae nations eam vel aperta Apostasia, vel occultis haeresibus contaminasse*'; and '*Post ecclesiam autem Christi in Gallia stabilitam, & civilis quoque status illic egregie multis aetatibus floruit, non tam propter imperii amplitudinem, aut victoriarum gloriam, aut alia huiusmodi trophea, quae tamen concedo fuisse in eis rara & admiranda, quam propter optimum iustitiae temperamentum, propter aequissimas leges, Parlamentorum gravitatem, prudentissimam reipublicae distributionem, qua reges moderato cum imperio praesunt omnibus, nobiles iusta cum libertate subsunt regibus, plebei ita rebus agrariis & attibus manuariis, intenti publicis inserviunt utilitatibus, ut tamen ab aliorum populorum servitute multum absint: omnes autem, & reges & nobiles & plebei generalibus reipublicae legibus subiiciunture, & inprimis obedient religioni*'.

[102] Ibid., fol. 197v–198r.

to function according to the laws of justice and piety, in which both the internal and external lives of its citizens were cared for, it could not contain heretics. For this reason, Rossaeus describes the Huguenots as infecting the body politic, and excludes them from French society.

Blackwood's *Pro Regibus Apologia*

Rossaeus engaged with the scholastic distinction between jurisdictional authority and the ownership of property when he took issue with the problem of the inalienability of the French domain. Here he took aim at the work of Pierre de Belloy, and at the Scottish civil lawyer, Adam Blackwood, who had pipped Barclay to the post in writing a comprehensive rejection of George Buchanan's *De Jure Regni apud Scotos Dialogus* (1579).[103] Blackwood's *Pro Regibus Apologia* was first published in Paris 1581 and republished there in 1588, when the League was at its height.[104] As well as an attack on Buchanan, the text also functioned, as the title indicates, as a broad defense of royalism. It was Blackwood's definition of kingship, and more precisely his understanding of a monarch's ownership of his kingdom, to which Rossaeus took exception.

Blackwood had argued, as Belloy did, that everything in the kingdom belonged to the king, for his use and as his property. In doing so, Blackwood sought to circumvent the argument that a king was the administrator of the domain, not its owner.[105] Rossaeus referred to this same passage, amongst several others, of Blackwood's at 2.9 and 1.5, along with references to Belloy's *Apologie Catholique*. There he addressed a number of broad questions, amongst which is that concerning whether the possessions of individual

---

[103] Blackwood had been educated at the University of Paris, and later in Toulouse. After teaching philosophy at Paris in the late 1560s, he received, from Mary Stuart, to whom he remained loyal, the gift of an appointment as councillor at Poitiers which he kept until his death. His *Pro Regibus Apologia* was first published in 1581 and republished in 1588. On Blackwood, see Burns, *The True Law of Kingship*, 185–221; Lloyd, 'The Political Thought of Adam Blackwood'. Blackwood's other works include his *De Coniunctione Religiones et Imperii* and the *Martyre de la Royne d'Ecosse* published in response to Mary Stuart's execution.

[104] *Pro Regibus Apologia*. Rossaeus also had a complicated relationship with Buchanan's work. He refers to the *Dialogus* and Buchanan's *Rerum Scoticarum Historia* (1582) at various points in his treatise, demonstrating familiarity with both. Whilst willing to make use of these when they suited his argument, Rossaeus took a strong stand against the deposition of Mary Stuart and Buchanan's defence of her dethronement in book 16 of his *History* at 1.4. fol. 11v–12v. In confronting Blackwood's analysis of kingship, Rossaeus was not by extension defending Buchanan's.

[105] Blackwood, *Pro Regibus Apologia*, fol. 226r: '*Regum enim omnia sunt dominio, singulorum usu. Regum sunt omnia proprietate, singulorum possessione*'. Blackwood's reference for this is Seneca, *De Beneficiis*.

citizens belong to the king.[106] He responded generally to these at 1.6, noting in passing the benefit to a commonwealth if the citizens possess their own goods fully. Here he sought to demonstrate that the arguments of Belloy and Blackwood were against divine, natural and human law, and that the rulers they described were therefore tyrants, not kings. In the second chapter, Rossaeus deepened his analysis of Christian monarchical power and here he engaged in more detail with those arguments of Belloy and Blackwood, but with particular emphasis on the latter.

Whilst he explains how 'perverse and barbarous' he considered Blackwood's argument to be, Rossaeus did accept that it was not unreasonable to expect private goods, at some time and to a limited extent, to be put to the service of the commonwealth or even in devotion to a prince. In this he referred to the authority of Jean Gerson's *Conclusiones de diversis materiis moralibus*, where he put the case for self-sacrifice on behalf of the common good.[107] However, Rossaeus went on to argue that the king was the owner, possessor and lord of these goods is something no one of sound mind would assert.[108] Rossaeus' argument is subtle. He was not denying a hierarchy in the relationship between king and people, but instead took a clear issue with the question of whether or not the monarch has ownership of all property. In Rossaeus' view, Blackwood's argument reduced all citizens of Christian commonwealths to the status of beasts or owned slaves, who were the property of their masters and had nothing but their

---

[106] Belloy, *Apologie Catholique*, 2.8. 75–80.

[107] The reference is to no.24 of his *Conclusiones de diversis materiis moralibus*, also known as *Regulae Mandatorum*. Rossaeus was probably thinking in particular of this passage: '*Multa ex genere mortalia sunt quorum similia possunt effici nova, dum trahuntur extra rationem suam, quemadmodum dolere deliberate de bono alterius est mortale delictum; si vero hoc fiat pro zelo iustitiae et boni communis cui contrarium est tale bonum, ille dolor virtus erit*' in (ed.) Glorieux, 9, 100–1. Gerson was frequently referenced in this kind of debate. Blackwood, for example, refers to Gerson just before he makes the statement quoted above by Rossaeus. In this particular passage, Blackwood responds to Buchanan's interpretation of 1 Samuel 8 in his *Dialogus* when the Israelites ask Samuel to give them a king. Buchanan argues the description Samuel then gives of monarchical power is actually a description of tyranny. In another response to Buchanan, William Barclay's *De Regno et Regali Potestate*, Barclay's interlocutor in the dialogue – Bouthillier – comments that Buchanan's interpretation of 1 Samuel 8 is in agreement not only with Aquinas, but also Deuteronomy 17 and finally, with Gerson in his *Considerationes*. Barclay takes issue with Gerson's interpretation of 1 Samuel 8 in some detail, engaging in particular his concept of *ius*. It has often been noted that 1 Samuel 8 was a much disputed piece of scripture in treatises on monarchical power in this period, but the role of Gerson in this debate has not been considered and is perhaps worth pursuing.

[108] *De Justa Reipublicae Christianae Authoritate*, fol. 54v: '*Equidem privatorum bona omnia esse aliquo modo reipub. eiusque usibus debere inservire, ad cuius salutem singulorum hominum vitam, ipsorumque etiam principum par est impendere; hoc a ratione non abhorret. At vero regem esse omnium in suo regno proprietarium, possessorem, & dominum, nescio an quis unquam sanae mentis asseveravit*'. The reference is to Gerson, *Conclusiones de diversiis materiis moralibus*.

bodies to nourish them.[109] All they had was the right to use their master's property. By making his argument in this way, Rossaeus established that the status of Christian citizens was one of liberty, though he does not pursue that line of thought at this point. He went on to call on Roman law to ask 'who does not know that nature, the parent of all things, or certainly that the law of peoples – derived from this principle of nature – introduced ownership of things?'[110]

Although he used a Roman legal point to support his argument here, Rossaeus also established that the distribution of property was something which is accomplished naturally, by a law common to all. Natural law was the inviolable principle underpinning Rossaeus' analysis, as it was in Bodin's *République*. The illustrations Rossaeus uses, such as the scriptural passage from 3 Kings 21, where King Achab tries to take Naboth's vineyard, are used in support of his argument that the polity is governed by natural law. All this, he argued in an address to the reader, demonstrated that, in a Christian polity, the king was not the owner (*dominus*) of all things, but an administrator.[111]

Rossaeus' analysis of *dominium* further demonstrates the scholastic under-pinnings of his analysis of Christian commonwealths. Commenting on Aquinas in his lectures entitled *De Legibus,* Vitoria had discussed the kinds of powers belonging to the commonwealth and the king. He argued, against the notion that the king as *dominus* had government of everything, that the king 'is not a proprietary master; he cannot make use of public things at his pleasure, in the sense of doing whatever he likes with my horse, as I do'.[112] Nor, he continued, could a king give away any

---

[109] His reference is to *Politics* 1.3, but it seems more likely to be a combination of passages: 1252b where Aristotle describes the ox as the servant of the poor; 1253b23 where he describes a slave as a piece of property, a 'tool in charge of other tools'; and 1254b16 where he writes that the use made of slaves hardly differs at all from that of tame animals (despite the distinction he makes between them that natural slaves participate in reason so far as to recognise it, but not so as to possess it, whereas other animals obey not reason but emotions).

[110] *De Justa Reipublicae Christianae Authoritate*, fol. 54v: '*Et quis ignorat quod vel prima rerum omnium parens natura, vel certe ius gentium ex ipsis naturae principiis haustum rerum proprietatem induxit?*' The reference is explicitly to *Institutes*, I.2.

[111] *De Justa Reipublicae Christianae Authoritate*, fol. 55r–v: '*Sed vide mihi Christiane lector, quam incredibiliter politici isti in Christianorum politia aberrant, qui Christianas respublicas nec primoribus labris videntur attigisse, quas penitus invertunt, & pro certa veritate perspiciam falsitatem legentibus obtrudunt. Tantum enim abest a vero regem esse rerum omnium proprium dominum, populum autem & proceres usufructuarios ut contra potius verissimum sit, illos esse rerum suarum dominos, quum rex regalium opum tantum sit administer & dispensator, ideoque & illi multo liberius sua possunt vendere, distrahere, alienare, quam rex patrimonium & thesaurum regium, eo quod vere istius nihil sit quam oeconomus ad populi totius utilitatem*'.

[112] The central point of reference here is Aquinas' *De Regimine Principum*, though this comes after some discussion of Aquinas' commentary on Aristotle.

part of his kingdom unless it was for the benefit of the community he governs. Vitoria concluded 'this is clear also because the commonwealth has not transferred its direct right of ownership to the king, but only its beneficial right'.[113]

There is a similar argument in Soto's *De Justitia et Jure*, which drew the connection to natural law more explicitly than Vitoria. Soto's discussion of *dominium* in the fourth book addressed the question of whether any single man can be master, *dominus*, of the whole world. Within this analysis, he argued that a king was not the owner of his subjects' property, because 'by natural law, even though the community has handed over to the prince its own power, its own dominion and jurisdiction, it has not however [handed over] its own possessions; and so the prince cannot make use of them, unless it be necessary in the interests of the same community'.[114] Even though his references in the context of this particular discussion are not to these scholastic thinkers, Rossaeus – as we have seen – was indebted to them in other parts of his analysis. Soto's definition in particular expresses the type of argument Rossaeus was seeking to make, regarding the relationship between the king and community as it was underpinned by natural law.

Rossaeus' argument bears comparison and contrast to François Hotman's *Francogallia*. In his argument on patrimony, Hotman had relied heavily on the analysis of another French jurist, Jean de Terre Rouge. Terre Rouge had argued that, because of the nature of the French succession ('simple' rather than 'patrimonial'), the king of France could not alienate any part of his realm. This, he argued, was founded in customary law established by the kingdom as a whole, of which kings were only administrators.[115] Hotman made a more complex distinction in *Francogallia* between types of property than the author of the *Vindiciae* (though Hotman modified the point from earlier editions), distinguishing between the property which belonged fully to the king; the property given by the people for his maintenance, over which he had a right of use; and the fisc, which was for the safety and preservation of the kingdom. The king could not alienate any of these without the permission of the people represented in council.[116] Rossaeus' analysis is not wrought in such strict legal terms, nor with such distinctions, but he also used the

[113] Vitoria, *Relectiones Theologicae*, I, 202.
[114] Soto, *De Justitia et Jure*, IV.iv. I, fol. 107r–108r. Also quoted in Hamilton, *Political Thought*, 31.
[115] Terrevermeille, *Three Tractates*, (ed.) Giesey, 1.1.13–14; 1.1.24. Cf. Giesey, 'The Juristic Basis of Dynastic Right', 3–47.
[116] Hotman, *Francogallia*, 254.

feudal analogy in its broadest sense to argue that the king only had an administrative power over the patrimony.[117] This would suggest that Rossaeus was working towards a theory of monarchy which made the people *dominus* and the king vassal, as we saw in the *Vindiciae*. However, he did not pursue that analogy. Instead, Rossaeus seemed more to be using it as a shorthand for his argument about the royal patrimony, as a contribution to a theory which gives the community power but is not wholly dependent on a feudal analogy to do so. In fact, it would seem that the natural law theories of Soto and Vitoria were more instrumental in governing Rossaeus' political theory than these feudal analogies.

The particular problem Rossaeus sought to address was the notion that a king was born into a condition of lordship (he 'never dies'), and that the people have no agency.[118] Blackwood also targeted the question of succession as key to determining the king's relationship to the domain. Blackwood held that the succession was governed by primogeniture and that when a king inherited, he did so with an infinite fullness of power including the right to change and abrogate existing laws.[119] Blackwood argued that the royal heirs were not heirs to the kings they would succeed, but to the kingdom itself. This reinforced the fullness of power attributed to the monarchy, because it did not bind the king to any of the laws of his predecessors.[120] However, it also reinforced the relationship between patrimony and primogeniture, which was to become one of the real testing points of League political theory in the 1590s.

Rossaeus attempted to dismiss Blackwood's argument as absurd – arguing that, on his understanding, any stupid or insane son of a king could damage the well-being of the commonwealth.[121] He went on to argue that such a commonwealth would be a deformed one, recalling the idea of the natural political community as a perfectly formed body. Blackwood, he claimed, had not described a commonwealth (*'res publica'*), but private ownership (*'res privata'*), it was not a free consociation of men (*'liberam hominum consociationem'*) but slavery.[122] The limited power of the king is therefore a key aspect of this freedom. However, Rossaeus does not let matters lie there, his statement on the liberty of the commonwealth is reiterated in his seventh chapter, but with a particular emphasis on the

---

[117] *De Justa Reipublicae Christianae Authoritate*, fol. 55v.   [118] Ibid., 1.5. fol. 13v.
[119] Blackwood, *Pro Regibus Apologia*, 71–4, 96, 115.
[120] 'George Buchanan and the anti-monarchomachs', 14–15.
[121] *De Justa Reipublicae Christianae Authoritate*, fol. 13v–14r.
[122] Ibid., fol. 15v: *'hoc modo sceleratissime non rempublicam, sed privatam, non liberam hominum consociationem, sed servilem mancipiorum'*.

destructive nature of Calvinist faith with regards to that liberty. Rossaeus'
argument about the nature of the French succession is thereby embedded
in the broader question of the Catholicity of the French commonwealth.

Finally, Rossaeus took the issue of ownership further with regards to the
question of tax. Overly heavy taxation was, as we saw in Chapter 1, one of
the most frequent complaints of the League, and indeed many
Frenchman, against Henri III, who was seen to have abused his position
in this regard. He argued that the parliaments of France, England and
Spain did not pay tribute to their kings because they were ordered to, but
because they were requested to (*non imperantur sed impetrantur*) –
a subtle and meaningful distinction. Continuing from this, he argued
that nor were they obliged by a law of ownership (*iure dominii*), but gave
freely of their own will.[123] Once again, he employed historical examples
to support this theory. Describing the English parliament under Henry
III from Holinshed's *Chronicles*, he refers in particular to moments where
they refused to accede to his requests for money, often accusing him of
breaching faith and imposing unnecessary burdens on his people. André
Thevet's *Cosmographie Universelle* covers a similar point for Spain. By far
the longest exposition on this subject is on France, using Belleforest's
Chroniques et Annales de France, which is notable for its historical analysis
of the power of the estates over the monarch in France. In keeping with
the *politique*-Leaguer position outlined in Chapter 2, Rossaeus argued
that Blackwood's argument was 'pseudopolitical' and a usurpation of the
very name of *'politique'* to argue that the French king was owner and lord
in his kingdom.[124]

In *De Justa Reipublicae Christianae Authoritate*, Rossaeus was not simply
reiterating the relationship between *sacerdotium* and *regnum* as it had been
discussed at length in the medieval period, but was engaging with the work
of contemporary theologians in re-evaluating these ideas in the light of
confessional division. Rather than splicing medieval theology with
Huguenot 'radicalism', Rossaeus undertook a much more subtle operation
in his treatise, building his argument upon a complex network of source
material. In Huguenot treatises such as the *Vindiciae,* the civil and the

---

[123] Ibid.: '*Unde & quae in Parlamentis, vel generalibus Comitiis Galliae, Angliae, Hispaniae, pecuniae regi tribuuntur aliquando, non imperantur sed impetrantur, nec auferuntur tanquam iure dominii debitae, sed condonantur voluntate Ordinum libere . . .*'

[124] *De Justa Reipublicae Christianae Authoritate*, fol. 57r: '*Quae omnia manifesto convincunt regem regalis patrimonii & aeraii esse procuratorem, dispensatorem, oeconomum, non dominum, non possessorem, non proprietarium; falsissimumque esse quod ab istis pseudopoliticis & politicorum nomine indignis usurpatur, omnia quae sunt in regno, regum esse proprietate & dominio.*'

spiritual realms are implicitly conceived as two different societies; in League thought they are explicitly conceived as one body, or one community, as J. N. Figgis once put it, with 'two separate departments'.[125] This treatise offers more than a justification of legitimate tyrannicide; it sought to provide a blueprint for the French commonwealth in a period when 'the state' had yet to emerge as an abstract idea.

[125] Figgis, *From Gerson to Grotius*, 202.

CHAPTER 7

Jean Bodin and the League

In March 1589, the League overtook the town of Laon where Jean Bodin was *procureur du roi*. Bodin's relations with the League hitherto had not been cordial: he was suspected by leading Leaguers of being a Huguenot in May 1587, when his appointment as *procureur* was opposed. They tried to follow up the challenge with an official search of his dwellings but were prevented by the intervention of several priests and local dignities. He was apparently nearly killed in the violence in Paris in 1588, the so-called day of the barricades and in January 1590 the League did manage to authorise a search of his house, setting some of his books on fire on his doorstep. After Henri of Navarre abjured Protestantism, Bodin left Laon to join his side in April 1594.[1]

The evidence suggests that Bodin's subsequent membership of the League was the result of coercion, and indeed this was the view of many contemporaries.[2] Seen from the intellectual perspective of what is conventionally understood, in Bodin's political thought, as his 'absolutism', it would further seem that this affiliation of Bodin's to the League could not have come from any genuine commitment to the movement.[3] Such a view is compounded by the fact that, in 1576, Bodin had openly condemned the formation of leagues in a monarchy. When he defined a commonwealth as a union of households under sovereign power in the *République,* he established that a league with independent claims to sovereignty called the very existence of the commonwealth into question.[4] Bodin had argued that whilst certain leagues between equals who recognised a common sovereign

---

[1] Lloyd, *Jean Bodin*, 195; Richart, *Mémoires sur la Ligue*.

[2] See Richart, *Mémoires sur la Ligue*. Bodin's relation to the League is discussed further in Lawrence Rose, 'The Politique and the Prophet'.

[3] Franklin, *Jean Bodin and the Rise of Absolutist Theory*. Bodin's 'absolutism' is carefully considered in Salmon, 'The Legacy of Jean Bodin'.

[4] Bodin, *République*, I.ii, 8: '*Mesnage est un droit gouvernement de plusieurs sugets, sous l'obeissance d'un chef de famille, et de ce qui luy est propre.*'

power could exist as commonwealths unto themselves, the simple fact of being an association such as an estate or a diet did not automatically confer any sovereign power.[5] This position was in keeping with his broader perspective on the indivisibility of sovereign power in commonwealths.

The implications of this message for an anti-League argument was taken up by contemporaries. In the *Readvis & abjuration d'un gentilhomme de la Ligue* (1577), written as though by a former Leaguer who, having renounced the League of 1576, decided to publish his reasons for doing so, a Bodinian case against leagues was made:

> A League in a political constitution is a solemn contract, sworn between equals, and not subjects to the power of another, in order to conserve and preserve their liberty ... From which definition there are two necessary conclusions: one that Subjects cannot contract a League in a monarchical constitution without renouncing the protection of the Prince, and, as a consequence, shaking off the subjection that they owe to the sovereignty. The other is that the King, in signing a League with his Subjects, divests himself of the sovereign power which he has over them, and receives them and their society in peace.[6]

The author's reference to the king who signs up to a league with his subjects is to the fact that Henri III had declared himself 'head' of the League in December of 1576, in an attempt to bring it back under his control. But importantly, for this author, that action signified a relinquishment of Henri's own sovereignty. The author's definition of a league as a contract between people who are 'not subject to another's power' looks to be a deliberate echo of the argument Bodin had made in his *République*. The author of the *Readvis & Abjuration* used Bodin's arguments to argue that the *Sainte Union* could not legitimately be considered as representative of the French commonwealth in the way it claimed, because its very existence challenged the sovereign authority of Henri III and Henri IV.[7]

---

[5] Ibid., I.vii, 72–87.

[6] *Readvis & abjuration d'un Gentil-homme de la Ligue*, 4: 'Que (Ligue) en état politique, est un contrat solomnel, juré entre personnes égales, & non sujettes à la puissance d'autrui, pour conserver & maintenir leur liberté, tant offensivement que défensivement envers & contre tous. De laquelle définition procédent deux conclusions nécessaires, l'une que les Sujets ne peuvent contracter une Ligue en l'Etat monarchique, sans renoncer à la protection du Prince, & par conséquent, sécouer l'obéissance & sujéction qu'ils doivent à la souveraineté: l'autre que le Roi signant une Ligue avec ses Sujets, se dépouille de la puissance souveraine qu'il a sur eux, & les reçoit en paix & société d'icelle.'

[7] Even those who became committed Leaguers in the 1580s had doubts about the validity of forming a League in the 1570s. See Epinac, *Harengue*, 38 where he expressed the desire for: ' ... *une loy generale du consentement des Estats, & qui aura mesme authorité que la Salique; par laquelle sera défendu tres*

Pierre de Belloy used a similar method to attack the League in his *Apologie Catholique,* where he argued that the League 'leagued against nature' in challenging the French succession and that they were illegitimately attacking their monarchy by claiming any power for themselves. By 'leaguing against nature', Belloy demonstrated his disagreement with the fundamental principle of Leaguer thought that a political community founded in nature could, on the principles of rationality, act to defend itself. Contrary to this, in *De l'autorité du roy* (1587), Belloy argued that *la police* was a gift from God, that the king was the 'organ' and 'mouth' of *la police,* and that it remained silent unless he spoke.[8] Kings had no temporal superiors, and received their power directly from God. Belloy claimed that the people had transferred their power to the king, in such a manner that they 'tied their own hands, so they can have no redress so long as any male of royal blood remains'.

Two points are significant here. First, that the people were the original possessors of power, an argument crucial to the Leaguers, but one that could always be manipulated to prove that they had irrevocably transferred that power on the basis of *lex regia.* The second is that they 'tied their own hands'. Here Belloy was subverting a more conventional application of this analogy in canonist dictum that the pope 'never tied his own hands', interestingly noted in passing by Bodin at 1.8 in the *République.* In contrast to the fullness of power implied in having unbound hands, the people in Belloy's political community had entirely sacrificed theirs. A political community, conceived in this way, could not be 'self-sufficient' or act to preserve its own being once it had so thoroughly alienated its own power. For Belloy, there could be no separation from the union with the king. He tried to reinforce this point to such an extent that it was not only sovereignty that the king received from God, but government as well, drawing on Bodin's ideas to do so.

Bodin's application of Roman imperial law to royal sovereign power in the *République* was, therefore, immediately influential on contemporaries in France, and quickly put to use in the polemics of the League years in anti-League writings.[9] This might plausibly be used to reinforce the point

---

expressement à toutes sortes & manieres de gens, de dresser aucunes pars, associations, ou ligues, de traiter des affaires du Royaume avec les estrangers, les solliciter de venir en France, ou faire levée de gens, soyent estrangers, soyent François, sans le consentement & exprès commandement de vostre Maiesté. Et que toutes personnes qui directement ou indirectement auron contrevenu a ladicte ordonnance, soyent tenus pour rebelles, ennemis du pays, & perturbateurs de l'estat'.

[8] Belloy, *Apologie Catholique,* fol. 21v; 31r. Cf. *De l'autorité du roy,* fol. 17r–v where he describes kings as 'patrons' of *la police.*

[9] On which subject, see Giesey, 'Medieval Jurisprudence in Bodin's Concept of Sovereignty' in Denzer, *Jean Bodin,* 167–86.

that Bodin could only ever be considered a Leaguer in a very superficial sense. Nevertheless, as has been astutely observed by John Salmon, the proximity of Bodin's arguments to those 'anarchic' principles he was apparently endeavouring to defeat in the *République* renders the intellectual situation complex.[10] Changing circumstances and the growing unpopularity of Henri III, as well as Bodin's own justification of his membership of the League, reinforces this complexity.[11] In his private correspondence, Bodin explicitly rejected the notion that he had been forced into taking the League oath.[12] He wrote that he had followed the principle *salus populi suprema lex esto*, further adding, somewhat conveniently, that 'rebellion' should not be considered rebellion when it is universal.[13]

It may well be the case that Bodin was coerced into signing the oath of allegiance to the League, and it certainly cannot be said that Bodin was transformed into an '*archi-Ligueur*' overnight. But there may also be truth in the self-justificatory statements in his letters. Ideologically, Bodin may have found affinity with some principles of the League, even if he disapproved of its methods and the fanaticism of the Paris *Seize*, as others, like Guillaume Du Vair did.[14] Historians need not, therefore, see in his affiliation to the League a conversion, from *politique* to Leaguer.[15] Instead, as suggested in Chapter 2, we can see Bodin in terms of a *politique*-Leaguer and in doing so, explore the intellectual connections between Bodin's work and the ideas of the Leaguers in some depth. Whilst Bodin's perspective on the League has been very thoroughly considered from the point of view of his Old-Testament prophetic persona, there remains room to explore his political thought, and the uses it was put to, in the context of the League years.[16]

---

[10] Salmon, 'Bodin and the Monarchomachs' in his *Renaissance and Revolt*, 119–20.
[11] Bodin, Lettre de Monsieur Bodin.   [12] Moreau-Reibel, 'Bodin et la Ligue', 422–40.
[13] Ibid., 426–7: '*Ce qui m'a fait promptement diligenter l'éxecution, mettant aprez plusieurs raisons, ceste loi souveraine Salus populi, suprema lex esto pour leur oster la crainte qu'ils avoient des supplices accoutumez contre les rebelles. Je leur ay fait entendre qu'une rébellion universelle ne se doit appeler rébellion. L'union de tant de citez et de peuples que j'ay remarqué ne pouvant être chastiée; veu principalement que tout premièrement tous les parlemens de ce Royaume qui sont les fortes barrières de la France sont uniz; de mesme le vostre duquel j'ay remonstré autant qu'il m'a este possible la grandeur, authorité, scavoir et expérience, s'est bandé pour la conservation de la Religion et de l'Estat de ce Royaume; Et qu'à ceste occasion il ne faloit pas disputer aprez vous de la puissance de la Prince, ny du serment aprez la résolution de la Sorbonne authorisée par le Pape et Saint Consistoire des Cardinaux, que j'avais en main*'.
[14] The comparison is usefully drawn by Lawrence Rose, 'The Politique and the Prophet', 787. Cf. Tarrête, 'Un gallican sous la Ligue'; Radouant, *Guillaume Du Vair*.
[15] As suggested by Lawrence Rose, 'The Politique and the Prophet', 783.
[16] See Lawrence Rose, 'The Politique and the Prophet'.

When Bodin claimed to be acting on behalf of the well-being of the commonwealth in supporting the League, it is possible that Bodin was employing the famous quotation from Cicero's *De Legibus* term in the dual sense of *salus*, and perhaps also returning to the principles of his *Methodus*:

> For all the [reasons] that the laws and the commonwealth are discussed, there is none more important, nor that merits more diligent attention, than to make a prince understand that he came to this earth to honour God in true worship. In the final analysis, it is the only point on which the well-being of the commonwealth and all its laws depends.[17]

Bodin had removed the salvific implications of this use of the term *salus* by the time he wrote the *République*, but it is possible that it was a return to this definition of *salus* that brought him round to the *Sainte Union*.[18] Whilst historians should certainly be sceptical about Bodin's relationship to the League, his own explanation of his actions renders them, at the very least, more comprehensible.

Another unexplored route to understanding Bodin's membership of the League is to be found, however, in considering his views on the restraining power of natural and divine law on sovereign power. Bodin's concept of sovereignty rested on the idea that a sovereign could not be restrained by any laws or temporal authorities:

> Because there is nothing greater on earth after God, than sovereign princes, and they are established by him as his lieutenants, to govern other men, it is necessary to preserve their status, in order to respect and revere their majesty in complete obedience, to feel and speak of them honourably: because he who scorns his sovereign Prince, scorns God, of whom he is the image on earth.[19]

This description of sovereign power has led scholars to understand Bodin to mean that a king ruled like a god on earth, free from all restraints and that his subjects were bound to obedience.[20] However, in Bodin's famous discussion in the *République*, (at 1.8 in all the editions subsequent to the

---

[17] Bodin, Methodus, ed. *Miglietti*, VI, 604: '*Nam omnium quae de legibus et Republica disputantur, nihil maius est, aut maiore studio dignum, quam ut Princeps intelligat se ad verum Dei cultum in hanc lucem venisse. In eo solo versatur Reipublicae ac legum omnium suprema salus*'.

[18] Bodin, De Republica, 4.3, 426 [the quotation from Cicero is not included in the first, 1576 edition].

[19] Bodin, République, 1.11, 190: '*Puis qu'il n'y a rien plus grand en terre apres Dieu, que les Princes souverains, et qu'ils sont establis de luy comme ses lieutenants, pour commander aux autre hommes, il est besoin de prendre garde à leur qualité, afin de respecter, et révérer leur majesté en toute obéissance, sentir et parler d'eux en tout honneur: car qui mesprise son Prince souverain, il meprise Dieu, duquel il est l'image en terre*'.

[20] Couzinet, 'La Logique Divine' in Foisneau, Politique, Droit, et Théologie, 47–70; Courtine, Nature et empire de la loi, 33–4.

1576 edition), where he wrote that monarchs were free from the laws, he
was explicit that they were still bound to natural and divine law.[21] The only
time at which the Estates, or an individual magistrate, could refuse to obey
a monarch's commands was if he transgressed natural or divine law. The
Leaguers considered Henri III to have done this by tolerating heresy and
assassinating the Guise brothers, and had taken action accordingly: the
coercive force of natural and divine law can be seen to have been made
manifest in their actions, largely working through the institution of the
Estates General, but also bringing the power of the clergy and papacy to
bear.

The role of natural and divine law in Bodin's thought bears further
investigation. Underpinning Bodin's political philosophy is a 'metaphysics
of order', which fuses Platonic ideals with medieval scholastic principles.[22]
In Book VI, this order is expressed mathematically, where the balance
between the Estates and monarchy, and therefore between all the members
of the political community in their correct position in the political hierarchy, is shown to imitate the hierarchy of nature in which inferior is
subordinated to superior.[23] Bodin drew heavily here on classical wisdom,
particularly that of Plato, when he described the commonwealth as
a reflection of the nature of man, comparable to Plato's city-soul analogy
in the *Republic*.[24] The disparate parts of man's soul are united by the
intellect (*logos*), Bodin argued, embodied in the prince. Like a good musi-
cian, the prince orders and unifies the people in a commonwealth, so that
they operate in harmony, their passions controlled by prudence. The
prince therefore existed above the people, as the highest point in this
civil order, and, in reflecting the image of God, dispensed a divine justice:
'Because if justice is the end of law, the law the work of the prince, the
prince the image of God, it follows that the law of the prince is modelled on
the law of God'.[25]

Writing in scholastic terms, Bodin considered the divine to be the 'first
mover'.[26] His analysis of change came from a fusion of Aristotelian
categories of causality in the *Physics* with a predominantly Scotian concept
of voluntarism. Bodin considered Aristotle to have 'enslaved' God by

[21] Bodin, *République*, I.ix, 129–30.
[22] Greenleaf, 'Bodin and the Idea of Order' in Denzer, *Jean Bodin*, 23–38.
[23] Bodin, *République*, VI.vi, 756.   [24] Plato, *Republic*, 435a–436a
[25] Bodin, *République*, I.ix, 154: '*Car si le justice est la fin de la loy, la loy oeuvre du Prince, le Prince est image de Dieu, il faut par mesme suite de raison que la loy du Prince soit faicte au modelle de la loy de Dieu.*'
[26] Ibid. I.i.5–6. In reference to Aristotle, *Physics*, 6.

arguing that divine action was a product of necessity. Duns Scotus provided him with a rejection of that Aristotelian notion, for he had claimed that if the first cause was necessary action, then its products would be infinite. The earth, however, was not infinite and therefore the argument from necessity was false because it would impose restraints on God.[27] Bodin's political thought functioned on this eschatological scale of divine action, and the restraints placed on kings – under God – in the *République* similarly functioned in these terms. Bodin's concept of sovereignty depended on the transferral of terms of analysis usually applied in theological contexts to the sphere of politics and to the figure of the king.[28] This dovetails with his application of Roman imperial power to the king, and describes – in the fullest possible terms – the nature of Bodin's 'absolutism'. Bodin sought to give the sovereign godly powers of creativity and action.[29] Simultaneously, he restrained his sovereign-god with divine and natural law, the latter providing the glue of his entire scholarly apparatus by preserving the order of the commonwealth.[30]

Bodin's concept of natural causality is underpinned by his eschatology; he defined 'natural' as 'celestial', and argues for the proximity of these two spheres: 'for there is no-one of sound judgement, who does not acknowledge the marvellous effects of the celestial bodies on all of nature, in which the power of God is admirably demonstrated'.[31] For Bodin, this prevented kings from disrupting the very order to which they owed their power; his concept of sovereignty is dependent on natural and divine law. The latter regulates both the paternal relationship between a father and his family, and the royal relationship to the commonwealth in a comparable manner: this is the essence of Bodin's concept of order in the commonwealth, built on a principle of harmonious proportions.

In his scholastic approach to the concept of order and unity in the commonwealth, Bodin was very much in keeping with contemporary intellectual traditions. He did not separate the cosmic and political orders – or the

---

[27] Isnardi-Parente, 'Le voluntarisme de Jean Bodin' in Denzer, *Jean Bodin*, 39–52. Isnardi Parente draws primarily from the *Methodus*, the *Daimonomanie* and the *UNT* to demonstrate the relative impact of Scotus and Maimonidus on Bodin, but it is clear these ideas influence the *Six Livres* as well. Cf. Couzinet, 'La Logique Divine', 50–1.

[28] Courtine, *Nature et empire de la loi*, 38. Cf. older formulations of this idea in scholarship: Gierke, *Political Theories of the Medieval Age*; Ullmann, *Principles of Government*.

[29] Couzinet, 'La logique divine'; Courtine, *Nature et empire de la loi*; Renoux-Zagamé, *De Droit de Dieu*.

[30] Cf. Giesey's astute observations to this effect in 'Medieval Jurisprudence' and Ann Blair's more recent discussion of the role of nature in Bodin's thought: *The Theater of Nature*, esp. 124.

[31] Bodin, *République*, IV.ii 430: '*Or il n'y a personne de sain jugement, qui ne confesse les merveilleux effects des corps celestes en toute la nature, ou la puissance de Dieu se monstre admirable . . .* '

natural and celestial spheres as he called them – but used their proximity to reinforce his 'harmonious' concept of absolute sovereignty and government.[32] This relationship between natural and divine law forges the connection to League political thought, which drew heavily on the same intellectual resources to argue that Henri III and Henri IV had broken both laws, and destroyed the order of the French commonwealth.

Historians may never satisfactorily get to the bottom of Bodin's membership of the *Sainte Union*. Likewise, his own religious beliefs have remained a conundrum for scholars. However, if Bodin had worked on the principle of *salus populi*, and the governing notion of the *bien commun* determined by unity of faith and under the rule of a Catholic monarch, then his membership of the League was most likely driven by a genuine conviction that unity of religion was the only way out of the chaos of the religious wars. For him, it would then have been about the concept of order more than anything else: if, by breaking the divine law in committing heresy, a king could thereby be demonstrated to have attacked the foundations of his own sovereignty, and the order of the commonwealth, then the argument to take up arms against him is consistent with central aspects of Bodin's argument. This emphasis on order as the key to the *bien commun*, conceived in reference to the divine order, combined with the obvious and intense pressures to join the movement in Laon or face imprisonment or execution, renders his membership of the movement less curious.

Jean Bodin and René Choppin

Bodin's relationship to the League has been compared here to that of Guillaume Du Vair, but his friendship with the lawyer, and fellow Angevin, René Choppin, who would become an ardent supporter of the League in the 1580s, is even more pertinent. Both moved in legal circles which included as many lawyers who condemned the League as would join it, including Étienne Pasquier, Simon Marion, Antoine Loisel and, notably, Barnabé Brisson who became the first president of the League *parlement* in 1589 (only to be executed in 1591). Certainly, however, Choppin's commitment to the League was far less ambiguous than that of Bodin, and drew more fire from the Huguenots, notably in the *Anti-Choppinus*. It is significant, nevertheless, that Bodin drew on Choppin's ideas, and used them to underpin his own views on sovereign power.

---

[32] I'm making a distinction here from Couzinet's analysis, which argues that the two are separate.

Choppin's *De Domanio Franciae* was, as discussed in earlier chapters, widely influential in legal circles. It was also plundered by the author of the *Vindiciae* for its resources on the question of the inalienability of the kingdom.[33] This question dominated political thought in the work of French jurists in the sixteenth century, and so the influence of Choppin on this point was by no means the preserve of resistance theorists (nor had Choppin intended the book to be read in that way in the 1570s).[34] In 1566, a long-standing French constitutional principle was authoritatively restated when the chancellor Michel de l'Hôpital established the Edict of Moulins. Here the French domain was defined as the domain of the crown – bound, consecrated and incorporated into the royal crown – a point which had also been authoritatively confirmed by Charles Du Moulin. The king, in this context, was commonly conceived of as the 'spouse' of the crown, the domain the dowry, an idea usually attributed to the medieval Dominican Ptolemy of Lucca. The crown, therefore, had a reality of its own, and could be considered the incarnation of France: the body politic in its entirety. The king could not alienate something which did not belong to him, but to the whole. Choppin's treatment of this question in *De Domanio Franciae* was, therefore, seen as an authoritative defence of a long-standing principle in the French constitution that needed protecting and restating.

Jean Bodin incorporated Choppin's arguments on this point into his *République* in 1576, in defence of this principle which he had himself defended at the meeting of the Estates General in that year.[35] In the second chapter of his sixth book, he cited the Edict of Moulins at regular intervals to demonstrate the inalienability of the kingdom, using Choppin's *De Domanio Franciae* in support.[36] Choppin had usefully reiterated here the established point that the French king was the 'spouse' of the kingdom and the public domain was a dowry.[37] This was why, he argued, kings are not called 'seigneurs' or 'owners', but guardians and conservators of the state. This was, he argued, at root a custom that had developed over the centuries as something *'utile'* that annexed to the crown all those attributes which were honourable for the conservation of the kingdom and the dignity of the royal majesty. All the lands and possessions of the king were incorporated with the crown, and so were not possessed by

[33] I discuss the nature of this borrowing in Nicholls, 'Ideas on Royal Power'.

[34] Choppin, *De Sacra Politia*, Praefatio 18, n.p., on the necessity of writing in Latin, to prevent books such as his being wrongly interpreted.

[35] Bodin, *Recueil*, 347–8.   [36] Bodin, *République*, VI.2, 620, 623.

[37] Cf. *Vindiciae*, ed. Garnett, 114, n.309.

him as an individual, but only insofar as he held the highest office in the land. Likewise, the rights of sovereignty and rules of fidelity (these were basically feudal) were all bound to the domain and could not be alienated or sold.

For Bodin, this was one of the unusual and distinctive areas wherein ancient customs took precedence over the king's legislative power and any change to them required the consent of the Estates General. Bodin's important definition of the commonwealth protected private property and did not allow princes to impose taxation on their people or take their goods without permission; it was also designed to confirm the juridical (customary law) principle that the public domain was inalienable.[38] This, Bodin demonstrated, was the case in France, Spain, Poland and England (he cites national edicts, ordinances and charters in each case rather than Roman law). In the French case, Bodin gave examples of several occasions where the Paris *parlement* was in the position of judging cases where kings had allotted their lands to the use of either the nobility or religious communities. He cited the Edict of Moulins of 1566 which, he argued, provided evidence to support the idea that the ancient customs of the French kingdom conformed both to modern edicts but also to the ordinances of other peoples (he cites Poland in this case), and so to the *ius gentium*. Wise princes, Bodin argues, always recognized that the domain belonged to the commonwealth and so the permission of the *parlement* should always be obtained before alienating any part of it.

Bodin observed that, unlike a man with his wife's dowry, the ruler of a realm could not abuse the 'dowry' of the public domain in any way he liked.[39] This particular authority to preserve and protect the realm therefore lay with the Estates, as the repository of customary law. The true sovereignty of the prince was encapsulated, he argued, in the moment when the Estates General assembled and presented requests to the prince with no power to command or any deliberative voice.[40] Interestingly, Bodin's was rather a different view to that of Choppin; Bodin supporting the rights of the Estates General as well as those of the Paris *parlement* to defend the kingdom, and Choppin preferring to uphold those of the *parlement* to guard and preserve the domain in place of the Estates. Choppin also significantly suggested that kings could not alienate the

---

[38] Cf. Skinner's discussion in *Foundations*, II, 295–6; Lemaire, *Les lois fondamentales*, 126.

[39] Bodin, *République*, VI.2, 619.

[40] Ibid.: '*Et en cela se cognoist la grandeur et majesté d'un vray Prince souverain, quand les estats de tout le peuple sont assemblez, presentans requeste et supplications à leur Prince en toute humilité, sans avoir aucune puissance de rien commander, ni decerner, ni voix deliberative.*'

towns of their kingdom, and that, if they did, the oath of obedience taken by subjects at the coronation would no longer be enforceable.[41] Bodin, writing after the Huguenots had made a case for resistance on exactly this basis, was more circumspect and cautious in limiting the power of the monarch in such a way. He acknowledged that there were ideals by which a king *should* conduct himself, but that simultaneously there were no mechanisms for preventing him exercising his will so long as it was in accordance with justice and natural reason.[42]

Neither Bodin nor Choppin were interested in thinking seriously about resisting tyrannical power in the 1570s. Both were focused instead on the preservation of order and the fundamental laws. However, their works were put to use by resistance theorists, and intellectually they can be considered *politique*-Leaguers. Clearly, Choppin's friendship with Bodin, and their shared intellectual interests, suggest that Bodin's own membership of the League may not have been so at odds with his political thought as might appear at first glance. The affiliation of these two lawyers to the League can, therefore, be seen in light of the principled positions they laid out in the 1570s and 1580s, when both of them spoke out at various points against Henri III when he was seen to be going beyond the limits of his power.

The Reception of Bodin's Ideas in the 1580s

Much like Choppin's *De Domanio Franciae*, Bodin's *République* was put to varied use subsequent to its first publication. As discussed previously, Bodin's ideas on sovereign power were harnessed to make the case against the League. However, Leaguers also found resources in the *République* that they could make use of, often in complex and interesting ways.

The *Articles de la Saincte Ligue* described the French monarch as God's 'lieutenant', and argued for the complete submission to a Catholic monarch's authority.[43] The writers in the League presented the idea, perfectly consistent with theories of absolute royal power, that when natural and divine laws were overruled, obedience to a monarch is no longer guaranteed:

> The second article of this union is to render full obedience and fidelity to our sovereign prince ... Therein lies the essence of our confederation, which we confirm and sign in our blood with such a firm and constant will that all the tricks and subtleties they perform ... cannot distract us from the fidelity

---

[41] Choppin, *De Domanio Franciae*, II.i.3.   [42] Ibid.   [43] *Articles*, fol. 17r.

owed to God and the King, but truthfully if a heretic King (which God does
not permit) wants to govern us, we will leave this alliance and confederation
because we do not owe obedience to one who has betrayed his own God and
is a traitor to his Faith.[44]

The author shows here that if the king's status as king is defined by his
individual relationship with God and the Catholic faith, then corruption
of this relationship necessarily impacts on that status. Crucially, the argument that the League was a confederation allowed the author to submit to
the reader the idea that it could separate from the 'confederation' of the
king.[45]

Certain League writers found a useful resource in Bodin's work to
reinforce this line of argument. This is particularly the case in *De la
puissance des roys*, which took a magpie approach to Bodin's *République*,
picking and choosing the parts that suited his case. The author began his
work by taking issue with a common argument of both Machiavelli and
Bodin: that political communities originated in 'force and violence'.[46]
Bodin had argued that 'natural reason' takes us to this conclusion; he
will have known that in claiming this he was going against the idea that the
origins of political community were located in a natural and rational desire
for fellowship. The author of *De la puissance des roys* takes an interesting
angle in his response to this idea. He argued that man 'first assembled in
a body, as much for mutually exercising the works of love, brotherhood,
justice and virtue as for preventing incursions and violence which may be
set against them'.[47] He did not exclude force and violence from the agenda

---

[44] Ibid.: '*Le second article de ceste union est de render toute obeissance & fidélité à nostre souverain
prince . . . C'est là le sel de nostre confédération, laquelle nous confirmerons & signerons de nostre sang
avec une si ferme & constante volonté que toutes les artifices & subtilitez fussent elles . . . ne pourront nous
distraire de la fidélité deüe à Dieu & au Roy, mais à la vérité si un Roy hereticque (ce que Dieu ne
permette) nous vouloit commander nous sortirions de ceste alliance & confédération car nous ne devons
obéissance à celuy qui est traitre à son Dieu & proditeur de sa Religion.*'

[45] This federal argument ran counter to Bodin's views on federations in the *République* where he
argued that federations could exist perfectly legitimately, unless they were subject to another's
absolute sovereign power.

[46] *De la puissance des roys*, 8: '*De l'origine des Republiques l'opinion à mon avis la plus véritable est, qu'elles
ont eu commencement non seulement de la force & violence, comme quelques Politiques nouveaux ont
estimé, mais encore de l'amour & dilection, qui est naturelle en la race des hommes, pour s'entretenir &
s'entraymer les uns les autres.*' The author's references are to the first chapter of Machiavell's
Discourses, probably *Discourses on Livy*, trans. Bondanella, I.2, 24; 1.3, 28; and to Bodin,
République, I.vi, 50. The author is explicitly echoing Bodin's words here: '*La raison et lumière
naturelle nous conduit à cela; de croire que la force et violence à donné source et origine aux Republiques.*'

[47] *De la puissance des roys*, 8–9: '*Et ainsi nous devons estimer que les homes se sont premièrement assemblez
en un corps, tant pour y exercer mutuellement les œuvres d'amour, de fraternité, de justice & de vertu, que
pour empescher les incursions & violences qui leur pourroient estre dressées.*'

entirely, and by doing so, his work did not fully reject this Machiavellian-Bodinian thesis (as he presented it), but modified it.

The author established, in keeping with convention, that monarchy was the 'best' constitution, in accordance both with the divine 'will' and natural 'instinct' (reason). Looking for a royalist model, the author engaged again with Bodin and, in particular, his concept of seigneurial monarchy outlined in the *République*.[48] Bodin had defined this as the rule of a prince who had been made lord (*seigneur*) of the possessions and people he ruled as a result of war. He compared this kind of rule to that of the head of a family (the father), over his slaves. The author of *De la puissance des roys* took particular exception to Bodin's argument that this form of kingship was the first of its kind.[49] The choice to focus on Bodin's definition of seigneurial power is striking; had the author used his description of 'royal' monarchy as the best form of that constitution it might have been less problematic, because there Bodin argued monarchs explicitly preserved the natural liberty and property of their subjects.[50] The author fixated on seigneurial monarchy only because Bodin took it to be the 'first' example of monarchical power, but was disingenuous in doing so. His aim was to provide an opening for a doctrine of royal election. He used Herodotus, for example, describing the Medes choosing their first king Deioces because of his reputation for dispensing justice.

Thus far, it would appear as if the author was simply using Bodin as a caricature of a Machiavellian opponent in his conception of monarchy. However, turning to examine the nature of the author's paternalistic vision of royal rule demonstrates a more profound Bodinian influence. The author of *De la puissance des roys* presented his case for a domestic model of monarchy as a *contrasting* narrative to Bodin's analogy of the power of fathers over slaves.[51] On his account, the heads of families were the first to rule 'as kings', governing the people related to them in 'love and fear of God, in complete freedom to do well'.[52] The author was manipulating Bodin's ideas here: the paternal model of power was a fundamental component of Bodin's theory of sovereign power. Furthermore, it was explicitly differentiated from rule over slaves. The author isolated one particular reference of Bodin's to the paternal power and took it out of context in

---

[48] Bodin, *République*, II.ii, 232–8.
[49] *De la puissance des roys*, 10–12; Bodin, *République*, II.ii, 234–8.
[50] Bodin, *République*, II.iii, 238–45.   [51] Ibid., I.iv, 21–33.
[52] *De la puissance des roys*, 11: '*D'ou nécessairement il faut dire ce qui est très-veritable, que les premiers chefs de famille estoient comme Roys, qui gouveroient le peuple descendu d'eux, en la crainte & amour de Dieu, & en toute liberté de bienfaire.*'

order to construct a polemical argument against Navarre's succession: if the author could show that Navarre, through his attack on *l'état*, was usurping the position of monarchy understood in its most ancient sense as a paternal role characterised by justice, then his readers could be convinced of Navarre's unsuitability. Ironically, his argument could have been derived from Bodin's *République*, even as he explicitly rejected aspects of Bodin's definitions of monarchy.

A sceptical reading here would be that a paternalistic concept of sovereign power is by no means exclusively 'Bodinian', and the author could therefore have taken his argument from a plethora of medieval resources. This would be a very fair observation, and could be further supported by the fact that the author doesn't engage with Bodin's definition of *république* as a collection of households, for the reason that it would undermine a principle of elective monarchy built on corporation theory. However, the author makes it very clear to his reader that he *did*, in fact, accept one of Bodin's central principles. The author described royal power as 'absolute' and claimed himself to be in agreement with 'all the *politiques*' on this point, thought he looks to have had Bodin specifically in mind:

> And yet when I speak of the Prince in this way, I understand him as the one who has absolute and sovereign power, because I am in agreement with all the *Politiques*, that all kinds of Kingdoms, in which the King does not command absolutely, are not properly Royal: he is properly King who recognises no human power greater than his own.[53]

Consistent with the *République*, the author argued that kings who commanded absolutely were also free from the laws: 'The Prince is the law, because his good life should serve as lord and example to all his subjects: he is greater than the law. He is released from the law because he gives the law, and he who gives is greater than that which he gives'.[54] The author was determined to demonstrate that membership of the League need not

[53] Ibid., 18: '*Or quand je parle ainsi du Prince, j'entend de celuy qui a la puissance absolue & souveraine, car je suis d'accord avec tous les Politiques, que toutes espèces de Royaumes, ausquels le Roy ne commande point absoluement, ne sont proprement Royautez; celuy est proprement Roy qui ne recognoist puissance humaine plus grande que la sienne.*'

[54] *De la puissance des roys*, 18–19: '*De tel Prince on a accoustumé de dire, qu'il est deslié de la loy: que les lois regardent seulement ceux qui sont égaux de race & pouvoir, mais entre le peuple & le Roy il n'y a point d'egalité: qu'au prince ne peut estre imposée loy, estant luimesme la loy; qu'en tout Royaume souverain la coustume est, que tout se dispose selon la volonté & plaisir du Roy, mais tels dires doivent estre entendus sainement. Le Prince est la loy, parce que sa bonne vie doit servir de patron & d'exemple à tous ses subjects; il est plus grand que la loy, il est deslié de la loy, par ce qu'il donne la loy, & que celuy qui donne est plus grand que ce qu'il donne.*'

conflict with these essential principles; judging by Bodin's own subsequent membership, he might have been right.

Warming up to his theme, the author's next move was – quite naturally – to take up that exception in Bodin's account to the argument that sovereign power is above the laws: the only scenario in which a magistrate or the Estates General could legitimately refuse to obey their monarch was if he flouted natural and divine law. *De la puissance des roys* made exactly the same case, arguing that no ruler could be released from divine and natural law. The author argued that *all* laws were natural in their foundations, a point which – as suggested previously – was similarly the glue to Bodin's thesis (notwithstanding his attempts to find some clarity in those laws that were part natural, part civil – such as the *ius gentium*).[55] But arguments from natural law alone were not sufficient to make the case for resistance, as Bodin knew, and so the author added a proviso to this statement not included in the Bodinian account. The author partially defined natural and divine law as commanding the monarch to have no other end and point of his government than the utility of his people: a king was bound to rule with prudence and justice.[56] What was so disquieting for Leaguers in the Bodinian account – and note here that Bodin located the origins of government in force and violence – was that no such restrictions applied. A Bodinian sovereign was not bound by any agreements to act for the well-being of his subjects, for if that were the case then he would not be truly sovereign: 'the commonwealth can be well governed and still afflicted with poverty and abandoned friendships, besieged by enemies and overrun with many other calamities'.[57]

In *De la puissance des roys*, a king's sphere of potential illegitimate action was widened substantially, and so he could very easily be deposed. This could be the case because the people, or the *république* on the author's

---

[55] Ibid., 20–1: Cicero's definition of all laws as coming originally from nature in his *De Legibus*, I.x.28, is the author's source for his argument here.

[56] Ibid., 19: '*mais cela est entendu de la loy civile, non de la divine & naturelle, de laquelle le Prince n'est pas deslié, laquelle luy commandant n'avoir autre fin & but de son administration que l'utilité de son peuple, si les lois mesmes ordonnées par luy regardent le bien d'iceluy, il doit vivre selon icelles, & ne les changer & rompre témérairement. Aussi est il astreinct aux lois qui concernent l'estat du Royaume, & l'establissement d'iceluy, d'autant qu'elles sont unies & annexées à la couronne, & par ainsi il n'y peut aucunement déroger. Et quant à ce qu'on allegue de la volonté & plaisir du Roy, il les faut prendre mesurez à la loy & à la raison, ainsi que disoit un Sage, que nous ne devons pas désirer que tout suive nostre volonté, mais plutoist que nostre volonté soit régie de la Prudence, & de la Justice. Parquoy nous prendrons la volonté du Roy comme nous prenons la coustume, laquelle nous disons surmonter la loy, pourveu qu'elle soit juste & équitable'.*

[57] Bodin, *République*, I.i.3: '*Car la Republique peut estre bien gouvernee, et sera neanmoins affligee de povreté, delaissee des amis, assiegee des ennemies, et comblee de plusieurs calamitéz.*'

definition, were the source of monarchical power. Monarchs were chosen
by the people, united as a body, to rule for their benefit. The people *elected*
their kings in order to maintain their own liberties, to be governed justly
and honestly and be defended from violence.[58] This is the real difference
between Bodin's account and that of the author: in the former, there was
a consensus between the people and their sovereign, but no contract or
election. The people – in their households – could still be considered the
authors of sovereign power, but they were not its guardians. On the
Leaguer account, the transfer of power from community to king was
conditional. The author was cautionary though, remarking that 'to give
the licence to the people to take up arms in all cases of injustice committed
by the prince is to attack the monarchical state and give substance to
rebellions', thus faintly echoing Bodin's concern that under such conditions a prince's position would constantly be threatened by conspiracy and
pretexts for rebellion.[59]

The deliberate, explicit engagement by the author of *De la puissance des
roys* with Bodin's *République* demonstrates a desire to remain consistent
with French royalist theory, whilst modifying that account to include the
possibility of legitimate resistance on the part of the political community.
The author exploited the notion that sovereign power was located originally in the commonwealth to make this case. In doing so, he made use of
a familiar scholastic framework: power, the author argued, originated from
God, who gave it to people so that they could create kings.[60] The same
manoeuvre takes place in the *République*: power travels from God to people
to monarch, and Bodin was explicit that the French monarchy could not
compromise the 'natural liberty of the people'.[61] Bodin's sources were
predominantly Roman-legal, but the same story could be told from
a scholastic basis that would allow for a more comprehensive understanding of the content of divine and natural law in a theological sense than
appears in Bodin's work. In this way, the author could claim that

---

[58] *De la puissance des roys*, 14: '. . . *le peuple n'a pas esleus le Roy, pour estre foulé par luy, tyrannisé &
massacré, mais au contraire pour estre maintenu en ses franchises & libertez, gouverné iustement &
droictement, & défendu des incursions & violences*'.

[59] Ibid., 16–17: '*Donc il est necessaire pour bien establir l'estat Monarchique, de prescrire des cas ausquels le
peuple pourra resister au Prince, non tous ceux la lesquels quelques unes mettent pour discerner le Prince
du Tyran, mais lors que le Prince s'efforce de renverser les fondemens du Royaume, & d'opprimer
entierement la liberté ancienne & coustumiere du peuple. Car à la vérité de donner licence au peuple
de prendre les armes en tout cas iniuste commis par le prince, c'est abbatre l'estat Monarchique, & donner
matière aux rebellions.*' Cf. Bodin, *République*, II.v, 253–63.

[60] *De la puissance des roys*, 22–3. The reference for this is Deuteronomy 18.

[61] Bodin, *République*, II.iii, 238–9. Cf. Boucher's *Sermons* 262 where he reiterates this point.

a monarch's power was absolute but could still be reclaimed by the community.

There were other League writers who took greater liberties with Bodin's arguments than the author of *De la puissance des roys*. The author of the pamphlet *l'Arpocratie*, for example, took the natural–divine law case to extremes in order to defend Jacques Clément's assassination of Henri III. God, the author argued, had certainly inspired Clément, and the author supported this with Old Testament examples: David killed Goliath, so the French could kill Henri. But it was also on the basis of nature that a tyrant may legitimately be killed. Here he quoted John of Salisbury's *Policraticus* alongside Bodin's *Republique* in support.[62] Boucher took a similar approach to Bodin's text, ruthlessly harnessing Bodin's analysis of the Valerian and Solonian laws on tyranny to the concept of legitimate tyrannicide, thus employing a similarly undeveloped Bodinian shorthand to *l'Arpocratie*, which looks to be in noticeable contrast to the engagement of the author of *De la puissance des roys*.[63]

Other League authors were more circumspect than Boucher and the author of *l'Arpocratie* in appropriating Bodin's ideas, notably the pseudonymous 'Rossaeus'. In Rossaeus' expansive discussions, Bodin features as providing an authority on the history of the French kingdom more than an authority on absolute sovereign power. He is found quoted, for example, in the company of François de Belleforest and Philippe de Commines in Rossaeus' discussion on forms of government (1.3), and the nature of 'ruling and being ruled' (*imperandi et parendi*).[64] At this point, Rossaeus was drawing on the customs of the kings of Poland and Denmark to make a point about the relationship between royal and baronial power. His conclusion was that the powers of the kings of England and France have never had an 'infinite' authority since the tenth century, but one circumscribed by fixed boundaries or limitations.[65] Rossaeus' reference to Bodin here is to 1.9, where Bodin analysed the question of whether or not

---

[62] *l'Arpocratie*, 100; John of Salisbury, *Policraticus*, Nederman, ed., 206–12; Bodin, *République*, II.v, 253–63.

[63] Boucher, *De Justa Abdicatione*, fol. 171v. He quoted this same reference to similar effect in his defence of Chastel's attempted assassination of Henri IV: *Apologie pour Jehan Chastel*, 86. Cf. Bodin, *République*, II.v, 253–63. Bodin, using Plutarch's *Life of Publicola* as his source, argued for a compromise between the two laws: that if a ruler was suspected of tyranny, the Solonian law applied (whereby due process of law ought to be followed), and if a ruler outrightly declared himself to be a tyrant, then the Valerian law (whereby he could be killed) applied.

[64] Rossaeus, *De Justa Reipublicae Christianae Authoritate*, I.ii, fol. 7v.

[65] Very strikingly, the author attributes this development to Hugh Capet's reign, and so directly contradicts Hotman's *Francogallia*, which – as Garnett has recently demonstrated – located the original decline of the ancient constitution to Hugh Capet's accession and his transferal of the

a tributary or feudal prince could be considered 'sovereign'. Bodin's answer was emphatically in the negative.[66] Not unlike the author of *De la puissance des roys*, Rossaeus conveniently overlooks this elephant in the room in order to claim Bodin's scholarship – which in this particular section relates to the status and customs of Burgundy in particular – for his own purpose.

Rossaeus' second reference to Bodin is to his analysis of coronation oaths at 1.8 in the *République*, reinforcing his earlier reference to 1.9, where the kings of France assured the *regnicoles* that if they violated their sacred oaths, no one would be obliged to obey them.[67] This quoting of the coronation oath was bread and butter in resistance theory, but it was certainly unusual to cite Bodin as an authority on this particular aspect of the oath.[68] It would seem as though Rossaeus was seeking to capitalise on Bodin's point about the sovereign being bound to the principles of his own power, for at this point in 1.8 Bodin goes on to discuss the Salic law as a law concerning 'the state of the kingdom', and from which no king could derogate. Likewise, as discussed previously, Bodin goes on to describe the relationship of the king to customary law, wherein kings were not in the habit of changing these without consulting the Estates or particular bailiwicks.

This mining of Bodin's *République* in League texts demonstrates the points at which distinct analyses of royal power overlap and integrate, even as they pull in opposite directions. This was particularly in the case of Rossaeus' *De Justa Reipublicae Christianae Authoritate* and *De la puissance des roys*, texts which demonstrates that Bodin's *République* was not read by contemporaries solely for its now-famous definition of sovereignty, but as a repository of resources on the history of commonwealths in Europe and relationships between sovereign power and governmental authority.

---

nobles 'dignities' to the power of the king rather than the public council. Garnett, 'Scholastic Thought', 798.

[66] Bodin, *De Republica*, 112–13.

[67] *De Justa Reipublicae Christianae Authoritate*, fol. 30r. Rossaeus' reference here is to 2.9 in Bodin's text, which doesn't exist. The quotation from the coronation oath is certainly to 1.8.

[68] On the French history underpinning of some of these claims, see Du Haillan, *l'Histoire de France*, 19, 123–4. On coronation oaths in this literature, see Giesey, *If Not, Not*; Prodi, *Il sacramento del potere*; Jackson, *Vive le Roi!* and his 'Elective Kingship'; Condren, *Argument and Authority*, 233–89.

CHAPTER 8

Amor Patriae

This book has so far framed its analysis through the concept of common-wealth, or *respublica*, and yet in many ways the political thought of the League deliberately, explicitly transcends the boundaries of the temporal sphere. It is, therefore, fruitful to consider ways in which their concept of the commonwealth, bound by religion, was embedded within the universal community of the church. Here, the concept of the *patrie*, or *patria*, played a dynamic role in the Leaguers' analysis of legitimate resistance.

As the early maps of France by Orence Finé and Jean Jolivet demonstrate, France was conceived in the sixteenth century as a concrete, territorial space, as well as an idea.[1] Culturally, linguistically and geographically, an increasing awareness and consideration of French national identity can be identified.[2] Projects for linguistic unification, launched in the shape of anti-Italian polemic, were further symptomatic of this movement. Henri Estienne's *Deux dialogues du nouveau langage françois italianisé* (1578) expressed the anti-Italian sentiment which had been doing much in this epoch to lend solidity to conceptions of French identity. Joachim du Bellay's *Deffence et illustration de la langue française* (1549) used the language of *pays, patrie* and *nation* to describe France as the object of patriotic loyalty and love, indicative of the symbiotic relationship between the vernacular and heightened national consciousness.[3]

Yet by the 1580s all this coherence had disappeared.[4] The Pléiade poets and their circle produced lyrical descriptions of the French landscape in which they perceived of a France that had been corrupted, destroyed or

---

[1] Jolivet's original map was included in Bouguereau's first 'atlas' of France, dedicated to Navarre: *Le Theatre Francois*.
[2] Developments influentially explored in Braudel, *l'identité de la France* and Nora, *Les lieux de mémoire*. From a literary perspective, see Hampton, *Literature and Nation*.
[3] For a closer consideration of the linguistic developments in this period, see Castor and Cave, *Neo-Latin and the Vernacular*.
[4] Mackenzie, *The Poetry of Place*, 5.

lost, of which Joachim Du Bellay's *Les Regrets* (1588) is a fine example. Bellay's famous poem was written whilst he was miserably homesick in Italy, but that sense of loss also correlates with opinions voiced in pamphlets, treatises and histories: that France was 'lost', by corruption or invaded with sickness; the many tropes used to describe the effect of the civil wars. These kinds of lyrical reflections on French space found their way into the polemics of the Catholic League. In *De la puissance des roys*, the author explicitly appealed to the works of Du Bellay and Ronsard and their emotive responses to French Calvinism as destructive of the church and the very fabric of France. The poets of the Pléiade had successfully created an idea of France, bound to the landscape, which had sufficiently captured the imagination of their fellow Frenchmen to play an important role in the polemics of the religious wars.

However, whilst landscape and geographical space were becoming increasingly part of the intellectual culture of the period, questions of political well-being were almost exclusively discussed in terms of the organic metaphor of the body politic. There is, therefore, a division between the developing idea of France as a territory within clearly defined boundaries, and France as a political community, ruled by a king. Domain was a concept relating to jurisdiction; it did not concern maps, territories or economies, so much as it concerned the expansion of the king's authority as a form of protection.[5] It also, crucially, concerned the issue of inalienability: René Choppin's *De Domanio Franciae* was hugely influential precisely because it sought to clarify the laws of the domain. Choppin drew on the customs of the *patria*, and the wisdom of the ancient courts of France, to make the case that the king could never alienate the French domain.[6]

Recent scholarship has considered the apparent problem that territory is the fundamental material of sovereignty, a point which medieval theorists of imperial power such as, to take one example, Marsilius of Padua, were well aware, but in the classic 'theories of the state', of which Bodin's *République* is one, the spatial dimension is overlooked in favour of relations of power.[7] It has become conventional to argue that only in the seventeenth century and beyond does such a notion of a sovereign, territorial state develop, largely as a consequence of reason-of-state theory, and any

[5] Wood, 'Regnum Francie': 136–41.
[6] Choppin, *De Domanio Franciae*, proemium, n.p: '*Mihi autem novum scribendi argumentum sumpsi, non ex auditorio Aemilii Papiniani depromptum, sed quod e vetusta fori, nostrorumque hominum observatione, quasi μογαγραφοι, primus scriptis publicarem: Gallis fortasse non ingrate futurum.*'
[7] Senellart, 'L'espace de la souveraineté'.

such concept is not fully integrated into political theory until the modern era. Contract-based political theory necessarily 'de-territorialises' sovereignty, by engendering a disjunction between the people and the land.[8]

Such analyses of the foundations of a modern, territorial concept of the state rely on a framework in which they were established after the peace of Westphalia (1648), and expressed most effectively in Thomas Hobbes' *Leviathan* (1651).[9] This approach precludes a consideration of the relationship between the temporal and spiritual spheres or – to use the current term – 'spaces', precisely because religious sentiment, particularly Catholicism, was portrayed so effectively in the sixteenth century as antithetical to nationhood. Crucially, in the context of political thought, it has been recently suggested that this is a flawed approach, and that 'the boundaries of political space were fundamentally contested' in the Early Modern era, 'not only at a practical but at a theoretical level' on the basis of natural law conceptions of political community.[10] Using this expanded framework for thinking about the conception of space in political thought in this era, this chapter considers religious conceptions of civic loyalty, or *amor patriae*.

The question of whether or not there is a nascent 'nationalism' in the polemics of the League years has been thoroughly considered in scholarship, but it is clear that the concept of the *patrie* or *patria* needs further thought.[11] Hitherto, it has been primarily discussed, very effectively, within a Protestant framework, but this chapter proposes instead to consider the implications of the language of *patrie* in the Catholic context, specifically for the concept of the Christian commonwealth.[12] In the first instance, the analysis offered here confirms the point that the Leaguers don't have anything approaching a 'modern' concept of the state. However, further to this, and more significantly, using the concept of *patrie* to explore League political thought demonstrates the very essence of their conception of political community, in which religious and civic obligations were fused, and which transcends, but does not exclude, the concept of *l'état*.

The Idea of *la Patrie*

Conventionally, the Leaguers have been seen as anti-national, hostile to any temporal loyalties or bonds that might distract from spiritual ones.

---

[8] Ibid.   [9] Brett, *Changes of State*, 3.   [10] Ibid.
[11] See, in particular, Yardeni, *La Conscience Nationale*.
[12] Friedeberg: 'In Defense of Patria'; 'The Office of the Patriot'.

However, as this chapter seeks to demonstrate, the opposite is in fact the case. Members of the League did not see their Catholicism and their French identity as, in any way, mutually exclusive. As Jean Boucher put it, to be French and to be a priest were not two contrary things.[13] Defending the position of the latter could, therefore, be construed as a way of defending the former.

Defence of the *patrie* was, therefore, engrained in the political thought of the Leaguers: Dorléans argued in his speech to the Paris *parlement* in 1593 that being a 'true' Frenchman required a precise understanding of love of country according to the ecclesiastical hierarchy in which love of the *patrie* is situated within the greater homage owed to God. To side with Henri de Navarre and choose a king 'nourished' by Calvinism was disloyal to the *patrie*.[14] Dorléans described the Huguenots as having deserted the church, betrayed their God, their king and their *patrie*.[15] In Lyon, Claude Rubis praised his fellow councillors as 'true fathers' of the *patrie* in rooting out the 'plague' of heresy which had infected it.[16] In early 1589, when Paris was under League control, the *parlement* issued an *Arrest* proclaiming any enemies of the *Sainte Union* to be simultaneously public enemies of the *patrie*.[17]

Defence of the *patrie* also, importantly, legitimated civil resistance: in *De la puissance des roys*, the author clearly stated that the subjects of the king could arm themselves against their ruler when the salvation of the *patrie* was at stake, in the same way that children could rebel against their father in the interests of their own salvation.[18] The League case was, therefore, built on a traditional, paternalistic framework of justifying resistance insofar as it related both to the 'common good', conceived of in civic terms, and to a good that transcended civil life: obedience to divine, and eternal, law. On this understanding, obedience to the principles governing the well-being of France, the *patrie*, became synonymous with obedience to Catholicism in League texts. The very bond of the commonwealth depended on expelling the Huguenots.

The Leaguers were thoroughly in keeping with medieval tradition when they drew on this concept of *patrie*.[19] In the high middle ages, the term *patria* was conventionally associated with the heavenly city: Pierre Abélard, for example, appealed to the idea of heavenly Jerusalem as the true *patria* in contrast to the earthly Babylon where Christians lived in a long exile. Jean

---

[13] Boucher, *Sermons*, 370–1.   [14] Dorléans, *Plaidoyé*, 50–2.   [15] Dorléans, *Advertissement*, 40.
[16] Rubis, *Discours sur la contagion de peste*, 10.   [17] *Arrest de la Cour de Parlement*.
[18] *De la puissance des roys*, 15.   [19] Kantorowicz, 'Pro patria mori'.

Gerson, addressing Charles VI, advised him that his true *patrie* was in heaven, not on earth.[20] The concept of the *patrie/patria* in League debates was in keeping with modes of political Augustinianism: theologians and lawyers in this era disregarded Augustine's own clear rejection of the Ciceronian definition of *respublica* in *City of God*, and fused their theological concept of *patria* with the classical, predominantly Ciceronian, language of duty to, and love of, the *respublica* and *patria* understood in both civil and spiritual terms.[21] Civic loyalty was therefore a significant component of this concept of *patria,* insofar as it was cohesive with the order of divine and eternal law.

However, there is evidence of a rupture with the intellectual traditions of the past. Traditionally, in a Catholic monarchy, the concepts of kingdom (*regnum*) and a subject's native land (*patria*) were coherent; the territorial sphere of jurisdiction bound up with loyalties and obligations to a spiritual end and the ecclesiastical jurisdiction of the church.[22] Yet, in the religious wars, these concepts of kingdom and *patria* had become separated from one another. The League notion of the *patrie/patria* was distinct, therefore, from the medieval concept of jurisdiction which cohered with territory.[23] It was not so much concerned with questions of locality and territory, as the idea of being 'native by faith'.

The slippage between the particularity of the French case and the universalising framework of Christian theology rendered the crisis an eschatological as well as a constitutional one.[24] Precisely because we are not dealing, in this period, with a consistently and clearly defined notion of the nation as both territorially bound and sovereign, there is intellectual interest in considering the concept of *patrie/patria*, in the League polemic as an idea that could encompass the particular and universalising instincts of contemporaries.[25] Whether located in Paris, as the *communis patria*, or in France as a new Jerusalem, the concept of commonwealth – the common good and the collective salvation of the people – is identified

---

[20] Quoted in Beaune, *Naissance de la nation*, 324, n.100–1.
[21] Augustine, *City of God*, II.21. Cf. Arquillière, *l'augustinisme politique*; Viroli, *For Love of Country*, 18–40.
[22] Krynen, *l'empire du roi*.
[23] The implications of this are discussed in Brett, *Changes of State*, 170.
[24] On the 'collective anxiety' wrought by this eschatological crisis, see Crouzet, 'Représentation du temps'.
[25] See Dupont-Ferrier, 'Le sens des mots "patria" et "patrie"'; Friedeberg, 'In Defense of Patria'. David Bell has also written on the importance of the concept of *patrie* in sixteenth century France for shaping the idea of the nation in future centuries. Bell, *The Cult of the Nation*. And see particularly Brett, *Changes of State*; Benton, *A Search for Sovereignty*; Senellart, 'L'espace de la souveraineté' for analyses of these ideas beyond France.

through the language of *patrie/patria* in these polemics. This is particularly the case when Leaguers sought to embed the French commonwealth within the cosmopolitan religious framework of Christendom as a whole and draw out both the international and universal nature of the French crisis. The attempt to apply an ancient, ecclesiastical framework to the temporal institution of the church, within a civil context, is the essence of thinking about the nature of the Christian commonwealth in these Catholic debates.

Natives by Religion

On 31 December 1584, Phillip II of Spain concluded the proceeds of the Treaty of Joinville, through his representatives, which was signed by the princes of the League. It was intended as a Catholic alliance against heresy, directed in part against Elizabeth I's rule in England, and more immediately against Navarre's succession. In the Treaty, the Cardinal de Bourbon was declared next in line to the throne, and Philip promised to provide financial support to the League. Even though there was serious reluctance on the part of the Leaguer nobility to put themselves in the hands of Spanish power, and enthusiasm for the connections only came wholeheartedly from the clerical Leaguers, the League would from this moment on be firmly associated with hostile, foreign power and the threat of imperial takeover in the eyes of its opponents.[26] The reliance of the League on Spanish power thus became its biggest weakness.

The Leaguers were portrayed as 'denaturalised' Frenchmen, allying themselves with the 'ancient and mortal' enemies of France.[27] In 1585, a group of Catholics described the League as causing a 'universal conflagration of *la patrie*', by opposing the French laws of succession and thereby threatening the kingdom with a state of eternal damnation.[28] Duplessis Mornay described the Leaguers as '*les premiers Espaignols François*': the first Spanish Frenchmen. In opposition to the idea – central to the *Sainte Union* – that a spiritual bond united the Catholic commonwealth, Mornay argued that the French *patrie* was a body united by a civil bond

---

[26] Moreuil, *Résistance et collaboration sous Henri IV*, and Baumgartner, *Radical Reactionaries*, 231–3, both take the line that the Spanish affiliations of the League have been exaggerated. Lozinsky takes particular issue with Jenson's *Diplomacy and Dogmatism* and his interpretation of the League through the activities of diplomats and the nobility: Lozinsky, 'La "Ligue" et la diplomatie espagnole'.

[27] *Satyre Ménippée*, ed. Martin, 115, 149. The authors also referred to the Leaguers as 'François Espagnols' at 62.

[28] 'Protestation des Catholiques qui n'ont point voulu signer la Ligue', in Goulart, *Mémoires*, 1, 106.

that transcended religious differences.[29] He sought to destroy the connection the Leaguers drew between Catholicism and the well-being of the French commonwealth, and he did so by connecting that argument to a wider concern with the decidedly unpatriotic affiliations of the League with Spain and the papacy.[30]

Opponents of the League often based their arguments on the principle that the two nations of France and Spain were fundamentally incompatible. Writers showed that Catholicism was not a sufficient reason to make a treaty with Spain. As one anonymous author wrote: 'consider the inequality of these two nationals: the Frenchman is liberal, faithful, brave, magnanimous, courteous and a lover of simplicity; the Spaniard is haughty, miserly, cruel, jealous, suspicious, rude, a great braggart and entirely incompatible [with the French]'.[31] In the anti-Spanish polemic, Spain is frequently described as tyrannous, 'wolf-like' and manipulative, aiming to reduce France to the status of one of its colonies under the guise of piety. The problem of Spain was deepened for the League by its close connection to the movement's association with papal power: the threat of double tyranny made the League look as though it was deeply anti-French. An anonymous pamphlet of 1590, *Les lauriers de roy,* took the line that Spain should not be allowed to rule France, locating the source of the problem not in the League itself, but in the papal excommunication of Navarre. It thereby reoriented the discussion around the question of obedience. Regardless of the fact of excommunication, the author argued, Leaguers owed their obedience to the rightful successor to the throne. To place a Spaniard in charge would be a corruption of the ancient foundations of the French monarchy, which determined that the French monarch has always been French by birth.[32]

Not only was the League under threat from without, it also faced deep divisions within the movement after Henri's assassination in August 1589. The murder of the king initially brought more Catholic royalists into the League as the potential threat of a heretic monarchy now became a reality. There was a brief illusion of unity, when the favoured candidate for the throne, the Cardinal de Bourbon, held in captivity by Henri IV and

---

[29] Mornay, 'Remonstrance à la France sur la protestation des chefs de la ligue, faicte l'an 1585', in *Mémoires et Correspondance de Duplessis-Mornay,* 3, 49.

[30] Yardeni, 'Antagonismes nationaux'; Pallier, *Recherches sur l'Imprimerie à Paris,* 86, 174–8.

[31] *Le manifeste de la France,* 24, also quoted in Yardeni, 'Antagonismes nationaux', 278, n.4: '*Considérez l'inégalité de ces deux naturels: le François est libéral, fidèle, brave, magnamine, courtois et amateur de simplicité: l'Espagnol est superbe, avare, cruel, envieux, soupçonneux, insolent, grand vanteur et par tout incompatible.*'

[32] *Les lauriers de roy.*

suffering from increasing ill-health, was declared Charles X. Charles was celebrated as a new Melchisedech – a priest-king who would bring unity to France – by old and new adherents to the League, including Jean Bodin, and thus the movement sought to rally its members behind Charles.[33] He was declared king in an *arrêt* by the League *parlement* of Paris in November, 1589, swiftly followed by declarations to the same effect in the *parlements* of Rouen, Dijon, Toulouse and Aix. Portraits of the new king were circulated, coins minted and pamphlets and poems produced in an attempt to persuade the population that there really was a new, legitimate, Catholic king on the throne – despite the absence of a coronation.[34] The Sorbonne confirmed the status of Bourbon as king early in 1590, and the Paris *parlement* issued another *arrêt* in March.[35] These desperate attempts to sustain the illusion of a successful coup were not convincing, however. Phillip, in particular, saw an opportunity to place one of his own on the French throne, and so he made a series of proposals through his men on the ground, Bernardino de Mendoza and – from January 1591 – Don Diego de Ibarra, which members of the Sixteen found increasingly tempting, particularly after the death of the Cardinal in May of 1590.[36]

In late 1589, the Sixteen proposed the acceptance of Philip II's idea to set himself up as 'protector' of France, which would have allowed him to bring an army into the country, raise taxes there and give orders to French forces in exchange for various enticements – including the offer of Franche Comté in exchange for the marriage of a prince of the blood to the Infanta, free commerce in the Spanish Americas, and six million livres.[37] There was, however strong opposition to Philip's self-serving suggestions from Mayenne, Epinac, Jeannin, Villeroy and Brisson, and it was these divisions which severely weakened the League.

As the *Seize* grew in strength and consolidated its position in Paris over a weakened Mayenne, Palma Cayet and L'Estoile reported that its leaders – Boucher and Génébrard among them – sent letters to the pope, Gregory XIV, and Philip in 1591, putting themselves under the former's protection

---

[33] L'Estoile, M-J, V, 13. L'Estoile mentions that a famous lawyer in the *parlement* dedicated his 'De Sacra Politica [*sic*]' to Charles as king of France. This is probably René Choppin's *De Sacra Politia*, though I have as yet been unable to trace a copy with the dedicatory epistle. It may well be that these were destroyed on Choppin's rehabilitation in the eyes of Henri IV in 1594. On Bodin's support for Charles, see Bodin, *Lettre de Monsieur Bodin*. On the significance of Melchisedech, see Rossaeus, *De Justa Reipublicae Christianae Authoritate*, fol. 485r and cf. Trinquet, 'L'allégorie politique'.

[34] L'Estoile, M-J, V, 13; L'Estoile, *Les Belles Figures*; Trinquet, 'L'allégorie politique', 646. Cf. Baumgartner, *Radical Reactionaries*, 161–3.

[35] *Archives Curieuses de l'histoire de France*, 13, 225–6.   [36] Jenson, *Diplomacy and Dogmatism*.

[37] Wilkinson, *A History of the League*, 100.

and effectively offering the latter the kingdom.[38] Correspondingly, opposition to Spanish interference within the League grew. In 1593, L'Estoile
recorded Guillaume Rose interrupting Parma's speech to the Estates
proposing the Spanish Infanta, Isabella, as Henri III's heir with
a prolonged invective against the Spanish and their greedy imperial
ambitions.[39] Increasingly, to the royalists in the League, Henri's conversion
looked to be the only solution to the increasing fragmentation of the
movement designed to prevent his succession.

The Spanish problem in the League is illuminated by an exchange of the
early 1590s between the French Catholic lawyer and supporter of Navarre,
Antoine Arnauld, and Claude Rubis. Arnaud's *l'Anti Espagnol* and Rubis'
Response à l'Anti Espagnol take us to the heart of the matter. Arnaud was one
of the more eloquent opponents of the League, a fact demonstrated in his
two emotive and pointed 'Philippics to France' in which he mourns – styling
himself as a French Demosthenes – for his damaged and war-torn country
and attacks the tyrannical motivations of Phillip II.[40] In *l'Anti Espagnol,*
Arnaud directed his eloquence to the problem of Spanish association particularly, and here he drew on the theme of liberty. The work opened with an
invective against those Frenchmen who had declared themselves Spanish
and, the author claims, agreed to sell the kingdom to Spain, thus making the
French people slaves to 'the greatest tyrant on earth', Philip II.[41]

The accusation of tyranny flung at the Spanish was a common one.
What is interesting about Arnaud's treatment is that he tried to present the
League's alliance with Spain as an attack on Catholicism. He managed this
by arguing that when Catholicism was first established in France, it was
exclusively responsible for severing France from bondage under Roman
rule – that is, from any bondage to a foreign ruler.[42] In making this
argument he drew a direct and strong connection between French
Catholicism and French liberty.

Arnaud's tactics were a deliberate attempt to reappropriate the notion of
liberty back from the Leaguers. Characteristic of much of the League

---

[38] Descimon, Barnavi, *La Sainte Ligue*, 187.
[39] L'Estoile, *Mémoires-Journaux*, 6, 291, also quoted in Baumgartner, *Radical Reactionaries*, 192–3.
[40] Arnaud, *La premiere philipique*; *La seconde philipique*.
[41] [Attrib. A. Arnauld], *l'Anti Espagnol*, 1–6.
[42] It is striking that Arnaud attributes this liberation to Catholicism. We can contrast this, for example, to the account in Hotman's *Francogallia* where he attributes the French acquisition of freedom from Rome to the courage and strength of their own ancestors: 'We cannot offer sufficiently high praise for the worth of our ancestors because they were the first in the world to begin to remove from their necks the yoke of so powerful a tyrant, and to claim for themselves release from their servitude under so monstrous an oppressor'. Hotman, *Francogallia*, ed. Giesey and Salmon, 178–9.

discourse was an association between liberty and the absence of heretical rule. For example, in his *Second avertissement,* also published in 1590, Dorléans had defined Christian (Catholic) liberty as freedom from the rule of a heretic.[43] In his *Sermons,* Boucher argued that Navarre was imposing tyranny on the laws of Christian liberty by consorting with heretics in Germany and England.[44] He reiterated the point in another sermon, arguing that whilst the ancient pagan kings were kings of slaves, Christian kings of Christian peoples were kings of free people.[45] The connection between liberty and Christianity was strongly drawn, and indeed contributed to the assassination of Henri III. The author of *l'Anti Espagnol* used that potent connection deliberately, it seems. By arguing that introducing Spanish rule to France was akin to enslaving the French people, he succeeded in portraying the League as opposed to both French liberty and, by extension, the Catholics who defended that liberty.

A second tactic adopted by Arnaud was to question how the Leaguers proposed to split sovereign power in the manner they were suggesting. Under the proposal, which came from the Sixteen, that Philip II be appointed the 'protector' of France, the author of *l'Anti Espagnol* imagined in horror the inevitable severance between constitutional affairs and matters of faith which would take place if the king of France, who had previously had no other protector than God, would be under the 'protection' of Philip II:

> But let us imagine that what we have said were to be true, and that we would have a Protector of our Catholic faith, and still a King who was not strong enough to protect our Religion and who needed a protector: which of these two, I ask you, would take us to war and command our armies? Who would make governments, offices, benefices? And if they had a problem, a debate in their administration separating Religion on one side, and the state on the other, if one wanted to set upon the other, who would make them agree? Oh these beautiful Chimeras! Can the world have two Suns? Can one state have two sovereigns?[46]

Bodin's views on the indivisibility of sovereign power in the *République* look to be supported in Arnaud's discussion here, but even if Arnaud did

---

[43] Dorléans, *Premier et second advertissement des catholiques anglois,* fol. 3v, 126v.
[44] Boucher, *Sermons,* 156.   [45] Ibid., 262.
[46] [Arnauld], *l'Anti Espagnol,* 10–11: '*Mais figurons nous que ce qu'on nous disoit, fust vray, & que nous eussions un Protecteur de nostre foy catholique, & encores un Roy qui ne fust assez fort pour conserver nostre Religion & qui eut besoin d'un protecteur: lequel des deux, je vous supplie, commanderoit à la guerre & aux armées? Qui donneroit les gouvernemens, les offices, les benefices? Que s'il leur survenoit quelque debat en leurs administrations separées de la Religion à part, & de l'Estat à part, si l'un voulout entreprendre sur l'autre, qui les accorderoit? O les belles Chimeres! Le monde peut-il avoir deux Soleils? Un mesme Estat peut-il avoir deux souverains?*'

not intend to produce a particularly 'Bodinian' argument, it was still an effective response to the Spanish connections in the Sixteen. The League argument depended on a fusion of religious and civic ideals to make a case against Henri IV; Arnaud presents this as a chimera. The implications of Phillip's protectorate are also drawn out importantly here, and revealed to be a play for power in France that the Sixteen had naively misunderstood. Finally, the suggestion that the Sixteen were defending the notion of dual sovereignty is shown, ironically, to contradict an idea that we have seen in this book to be a centrepiece of League political thought: the notion of the *Roi Tres Chrétien*, built on the stability of *one* king, *one* faith, *one* law, not two.

Finally, Arnaud clinched his argument by accusing the Leaguers of acting contrary to nature in choosing a Spanish ruler. He argued that the introduction of Philip II as 'protector' of the Catholic faith in France was a usurpation of the position of France's legitimate king who has been given to them by God, nature and the laws of the kingdom.[47] He demonstrated that a king's 'natural' status was strongly attached to the fact of his being French. In order to be the natural king of France, you had to be born in France. The king was, in this sense *'le mignon de nature'*, the 'darling' of nature.[48] He was also – and perhaps here Arnaud was again channelling Bodin – France's 'natural father': 'he is our true father, our legitimate and natural father, and we are all his children'.[49] By describing this paternal relationship as natural and legitimate, the author implied that the League was introducing something unnatural and illegitimate. Once again, the author was playing with the established terms of the polemic by redescribing and redefining language familiar from the League literature. The author of *l'Anti Espagnol* showed that through the Spanish alliance, the League threatened the very core of French civic duty. It would be impossible, in Arnaud's eyes, to have a Spanish king and still claim to be a 'natural' and 'free' Frenchman.

In his *Response à l'Anti Espagnol*, Claude Rubis defended the League by accusing Navarre and his supporters of trying to divorce the people from their attachment to Catholicism, and thus threaten the salvation of the *patrie* as a whole.[50] Rubis argued that by their actions, no Catholic could

---

[47] Ibid., 31.
[48] In the polemic, the term *'mignon'* is familiar as a negative; Henri III's treatment of his mignons was a famous factor in alienating his subjects. The author is perhaps being a little sly with this use of the term mignon here.
[49] [Arnauld], *l'Anti Espagnol*, 78: 'c'est nostre vray pere, nostre pere naturel & legitime, nous sommes tous ses enfans'.
[50] Ibid., 9.

argue that the Leaguers were not true, good, 'natural' Frenchmen who
would recognise no other than a French king.[51] Rubis conceived of being
French in Catholic terms; the *patrie* could only be rescued by preventing
Navarre from inheriting the throne. It would be fatal for France, Rubis
argued, if Navarre were to rule, and at the end of the work he argues that
the Estates should declare Navarre and his followers officially as enemies of
the *patrie*.[52]

Loyalty to France is a central motif of Rubis' works, but there still
remained the delicate task of negotiating the Sixteen's relationship with
Philip II. Rubis here presented a line that seems more in tune with that of
Mayenne's supporters than the Sixteen, wherein Phillip's role is simply to
ensure Charles X's position on the throne in the first instance.[53] But Rubis
did go so far as to suggest that not having a French monarch would not
necessarily be a betrayal of his French duty. He justified his case for Spanish
intervention on the basis that the Catholic faith needed to be defended
above all other priorities, and not on the basis that the League wanted
a Spanish king of France.[54] Catholicity therefore takes priority over place of
birth and – less explicitly – dynastic succession. Rubis takes the opportunity then to accuse the author of *l'Anti Espagnol* of atheism, for defending
heretics and the promoting the destruction of the French state, which,
importantly, he treats as one and the same crime.[55]

Finally, and most significantly for the consideration of the role of *la
patrie* in these debates, Rubis demonstrated explicitly the Augustinianism
underpinning his argument. He transplanted the notion of citizenship out
of its civic context into the community of the faithful, using Augustine's
City of God as his prop. It was on this basis that Rubis constructs his
strongest defence of the League's association with Spain:

> For in that which concerns our faith, religion and consciences, all true
> Christians and Catholics ... are Citizens of the same city: which is the
> City of God described by Saint Augustine in that beautiful and learned
> treatise entitled the City of God. So much so that all citizens are of the same
> mother which is the holy Catholic, Apostolic, Roman Church ... We are
> bound to join all together for the defence of our City, Mother, and common

[51] Ibid., 21: '*Et n'y a homme de bien, vray Catholique, zelé à sa religion, & au bien de ce Royaume, qui puisse remarquer en nos deportemens chose par laquelle il puisse iuger que nous ayons volonté d'estre autres que bons, vrais, & naturels François, ny recognoistre pour nos Roy autre qu'un Prince François.*'
[52] Ibid., 21–2, 59, 62.
[53] At the end of the work, Rubis declares his support for the Cardinal of Bourbon's claim to the throne. Bourbon died in prison in March 1590.
[54] Dorléans also made this argument in his *Apologie*, 28–31.
[55] Rubis, *Response*, 4–8. Note the slippage between 'state' and '*patrie*'.

nourishment. And if for this result which is not at all a temporal question, but only that of the honour of God and the conservation of our religion, we join our arms with those of the King of Spain, or other Catholic princes, no true Christian and Catholic can with truth say that we are introducing a foreigner into France more than in that which concerns the faith and religion. No-one should be censored as a foreigner, because in this regard all true Catholics are children of the same mother and Citizens of the same city.[56]

The argument that no Catholic could ever be considered a foreigner to a Catholic community is at the heart of the League concept of *la patrie*, which sought to encompass national and supranational elements. Rubis placed the Catholic conscience centrally in his notion of patriotism, in order to show that the alliance with France did not compromise the country, but supported it by preserving its Catholic character. Rubis' idea of the *patrie* was strongly French, yet extended beyond the limits of the nation in embracing the universal Catholic community.

Rubis' concept of the *patrie* demonstrates the way in which Leaguers rationalised the Spanish support for their cause, but it was also consistent with broader trends in French Catholic thought. As Jean Boucher had argued in his sermons, there were no foreigners in the house of God.[57] Montaigne, in his essay 'of Vanity' (written in the late 1580s), for example, argued that Rome could be taken as an object of love that united all Christians and so transcended particular, national difference:

> this very Rome that we behold deserves our love, allied for so long and by so many claims to our crown: the only common and universal city. The sovereign magistrate who commands there is acknowledged equally else-where. It is the metropolitan city of all Christian nations; the Spaniard and the Frenchman, every man is at home there. To be one of the princes of that state one need only be of Christendom.[58]

---

[56] Ibid., 24–6: '*Car en ce qui concerne nostre foy et religion, & nos consciences, tous vrais Chrestiens & Catholiques ... sont Citoyens d'une mesme cité: qui est la Cité de Dieu, descripte par Sainct Augustin en ce beau & docte traicté qu'il à intitulé De Civitate Dei. Tellement qu'estant tous citoyens d'une mesme mere qui est la saincte Eglise Catholique, Apostolique, Romaine ... nous joindre tous ensemble pour la defence de nostre Cité, Mere, & nourriture commune. Et si pour cest effect où il n'est question de rien de temporel, mais seulement de l'honneur de Dieu, & de la conservation de nostre religion, nous joignons nos armes avec celles du Roy d'Espagne, ou autres Princes Catholiques, nul vray Chrestien & Catholique peut avec verité dire que nous introduisons l'estranger en France plus qu'en ce qui concerne la foy et la religion, nul ne doibt estre censé estranger, puis que pour ce regard tous vrais Catholiques sont tous enfans d'une mere & Citoyens d'une mesme Cité.*' NB. The maternalism of the Catholic church complementing the paternalism of Catholic monarchy.

[57] Boucher, *Sermons*, 403.

[58] Montaigne, *Essais*, III.9, 1043–44. For more on Montaigne and the League, see Supple, 'Montaigne and the French Catholic League'.

Christendom, it seems, held its appeal into the late sixteenth century, even as the concept of Europe was beginning to supplant it.

Examining the concept of homeland, or nation, in these polemics brings out the extent to which the Leaguers sought to portray their movement as loyal to the traditions, laws and customs of France, without compromising their bond with the church. On the polemical level, the concept of *patrie/patria* clearly functioned very importantly for opponents of the League who sought to destroy these connections. However, it is also clear that this concept of the *patrie* was also operating at a theoretical level for League lawyers and theologians. Accepting this point has corresponding implications for the interpretation of League texts at a polemical level. For example, when the *'manant'* in the *Dialogue d'entre le maheustre et le manant* argued that he would rather be a Spanish Catholic with the possibility of salvation than a French heretic with an endangered soul, he was not being unpatriotic, but was explicitly expressing love for his country, France, 'of which I am a native for my Religion' (*je suis natif pour ma Religion*). For the Leaguers, the soul of the commonwealth could not be nourished if the body was not ruled by a Catholic head.[59]

English Exiles and the Catholic League

A feeling of dislocation from a homeland was very familiar to the exiled English Catholic community in France. And whilst this particular experience of exile has received much recent attention, little has been done to address this question of how far there was an intellectual exchange between French and English Catholics in the League years.[60] Alienated geographically as well as in conscience from their native country, these Jesuit exiles shared an intellectual connection with the Leaguers, a point demonstrated clearly in their writings.

When Louis Dorléans posed as a Catholic Englishman in writing his *Advertissement des catholiques anglois aux françois catholiques* (1586) it is quite possible that he was exploiting this connection to a League advantage.[61] He advises his French readers to listen to the advice of the

---

[59] See Dorléans, *Responce des vrays catholiques françois*, for an extended example of the employment of this serviceable analogy.

[60] Recently, see Gibbons, *English Catholic Exiles*; Bowden, Kelly, eds., *The English Convents in Exile*; Highley, *Catholics Writing the Nation*; Janssen, *The Dutch Revolt*. For a classic study, see Bossy, *The English Catholic Community*, 7,13, which makes a strong case for the 'Englishness' of this community. Cf. Salmon's *The French Religious Wars* which mentions the League and Douai briefly, 19–20, 34–6.

[61] Dorléans, *Advertissement des catholiques anglois*.

English who have 'tasted each day the fruits of subjection' to a heretic ruler and encourages them to act, not just for the whole of Europe, but for the preservation of Christianity itself. 'France and England', he wrote, 'are two close kingdoms, only divided by a sea crossing, as are two neighbours by a stream which splits the middle of their street'.[62] Catholicism, he argued, has allowed these kingdoms to flourish for as long as they have, and was the only remedy to their respective troubles. So long as the English Jesuits still believed that they could convert their homeland back to Catholicism, it seems there was much in common between these groups, and contemporaries recognised this common cause that would restore Christendom to its former, united state.

William Allen, later Cardinal, established the English seminary at Douai in the Spanish Low Countries in 1568, as part of the university Philip II had founded there in 1562, to 'conserve and maintain the Catholic faith'.[63] Allen, working in the theology faculty of the university, designed the seminary with Pius V's approval to attract 'intelligent and devoted' Catholics to serve the cause of England's conversion.[64] The seminary was forced to move to Reims in 1578, placing itself under the protection of the house of Guise, and finally settled in Rouen in 1584. Three of Allen's disciples who had connections with the League – Robert Persons, William Gifford and William Rainolds – spent time in the seminary.[65] Persons, Allen and Gifford all benefited directly from patronage by the Guise family which thus constituted a direct link to the League.[66] In common with the Guises, Rainolds, Gifford and Persons also shared a close relationship with Philip II's ambassador Mendoza. In his confession in 1584, the Scottish Jesuit William Creighton, head of the Scottish college at Douai, indicated that the Guises had planned to join the exiles and the Spanish in the invasion of England.[67]

Gifford and Rainolds have both been linked to the *De Justa Reipublicae Christianae Authoritate*; Rainolds has been proposed as one possible author

---

[62] Ibid., 4: '*La France & l'Angleterre sont deux Royaumes proches, & seulement divisez d'un trajet de mer, comme sont deux voisins, d'un ruisseau qui tranche le milieu de leur rue.*'

[63] Cardon, *La Fondation de l'université de Douai*, ii.   [64] Allen, *An Apologie*, fol. 16v–17r.

[65] The best source of information on the Douai college is still Knox, *The First and Second Diaries of the English College*. On William Gifford, see Haudecoeur, *William Gifford*; Williams, 'Gifford, William', *Oxford Dictionary of National Biography*. On William Rainolds, see Blom, 'Rainolds, William (1544?–1594)', *Dictionary of National Biography*. See also Guilday, *The English Catholic Refugees*.

[66] For evidence of the Guise connection with Douai, see Knox, *The Letters and Memorials of William Cardinal Allen*, 12, 47.

[67] Ibid., 433.

and Gifford edited the 1590 edition. Haudecoeur also writes that there was a friendship between Gifford and Rainolds, and certainly there were similarities in background and experience. After a university education at Oxford, Rainolds arrived at Douai in 1577, and was ordained as a priest in 1580. Allen appointed him professor of Hebrew and scripture, and he also helped with the translation of the Douai-Rheims Bible. He died in Antwerp in 1592.

After an Oxford education, Gifford left England for Louvain where he studied under Robert Bellarmine. In 1577, Allen invited him to Douai to teach theology and it is recorded that he lectured on the first part of Aquinas' *Summa Theologiae*. Gifford edited the 1592 edition of the *De Justa Reipublicae Christianae Authoritate*, probably responsible for removing the tenth chapter on tyrannicide. He also completed Rainolds' *Calvino-Turcismus* (1597), a work comparing Calvin to Mohammed.[68] Gifford's patronage by the Guise family from 1583, which resulted in him writing *Un Traité en faveur de la Ligue* on their behalf, also establishes a direct link between Gifford and the League independently of Rainolds.[69] It is therefore entirely possible that Gifford could have collaborated with a French author of *De Justa Reipublicae Christianae Authoritate*. After William Allen's death, Gifford's career was marked by his dispute with the Jesuits and notably a distancing between himself and Robert Persons. Their quarrel supposedly centred on Persons' Spanish contacts and the latter's reluctance to countenance James' succession to the English throne, further indication of how divisive this subject was amongst Catholics.[70]

Douai was designed as a centre for English exiles focussed on the reconversion of England to Catholicism. As such, it became the centre of controversy. Its League connections only contributed to this controversy, and the intellectual implications of these connections are worth some consideration, particularly within the framework of thinking about the *patrie* as a source of duty and obligation. William Allen's *A True, Sincere and Modest Defense of English Catholics,* first published in English in 1584 (possibly in Rheims), was swiftly translated into Latin for a European readership, and provides a useful opening for this analysis.[71] Allen died in 1594, and there is no testimony of any direct connections with the Catholic League beyond the Guise patronage. However, Allen's work is nevertheless evidence that he was confronting similar issues considered

[68] Cf. Matthew Sutcliffe's reply, *De Turco-Papismo*.   [69] This work is not extant.
[70] Haudecoeur, *Gifford*, 18–20; Williams, 'Gifford', *Dictionary of National Biography*.
[71] Cecil, Allen, *The Execution of Justice*, ed. Kingdon, xxii.

earlier in the context of the League, and it is very likely that he was seen as being connected to the movement by contemporaries.[72] In his *Defense*, Allen redescribes the purposes, function and identity of the Catholic community in the face of the disjunction caused by heresy. His solutions are not precisely the same as those of the League, but they provide helpful background for considering the work of Robert Persons, where direct connections to the League are much stronger.

The *Defense* was written as a response to William Cecil's *Execution of Justice* (1583), and more broadly to events in England in the 1570s and 1580s. In 1581, the English parliament issued a penal statute, declaring the conversion of any of Elizabeth's Protestant subjects to Catholicism to be a treasonous offence. That association between Catholicism and treason was an important one for the *Defense*, resulting in an inevitable alienation between Elizabeth and many of her Catholic subjects. It also raised the question of national loyalty and to what, precisely, English Catholics should be loyal and obedient. This question of treason separates the English experience slightly from the French. Members of the Catholic League were accused of disloyalty, and subverting French monarchical institutions, but rarely so clearly accused of treason in the legal sense. The League situation at this time was difficult, but not desperate. Only in 1594 did members of the League who refused to support Henri IV's sovereignty face the choice between exile and death.[73] Despite this difference, the English and French experience on this matter found common ground in the sense of alienation from the country, or *patrie,* in conscience, when faced with the reality of rule by an excommunicate.

The accusation of treason, along with Allen's exiled status, gave the *Defense* a sharp polemical edge. In the work, Allen described England as 'our lost country'. He argued that declaring Elizabeth head of the church destroyed the balance of church and civil life. It meant that anyone not under her dominion would be a 'foreigner also in respect to the church'. In other words, being 'foreign' to her rule equated with being 'foreign' to the institution of the church with her at its head. Allen redefines the idea of being 'native' by introducing the notion that it was possible to find one's 'nation' in the church – surely a source of comfort to the English exiles. In his *Apologie and True Declaration of the Institution and Endevours of the Two English Colleges* he clarified the alternative for Catholics in exile, arguing that it was 'natural' for them to seek refuge with the pope, 'to him, that

[72] Zwierlein, *Political Thought of the League,* 174–5.
[73] See Descimon and Ruiz Ibáñez, *Les Ligueurs de l'Exil.*

counteth no Christian nor domestical of faith, a stranger to him, whose citie and Seate is the native of al true belevers'.[74] Allen proposed Rome, the papal seat, as the alternative source of identity for those exiles who refused to accept Elizabeth's new status and had chosen, on the basis of conscience, to flee England.

The idea of Rome as a universal city and source of Christian, Catholic identity was pervasive in Catholic imagination in this period. As discussed above, this derived from interpretations of *patria* in the Middle Ages, and we also find figures like Montaigne thinking about Rome in exactly these terms. It was entirely possible for a Catholic to describe the pope as 'sovereign magistrate' in charge of a 'state' of which all Christian princes were part. However, describing Rome as the native city of all true believers could also be a highly polemical statement, which is clearly brought out if we compare his claims to those of Claude Rubis. Rubis' argument, that all Catholics were members of the city of God, expressed the same sense of belonging to a community defined by faith rather than place of birth. He identified that as a kind of native affiliation; no Catholic could ever be considered a 'foreigner' in a Catholic country.

However, whilst there is a similarity to Allen's argument in the claim for a universal Catholic community, there is also an important difference. Rubis ambivalently argued for the notion of a transcendental community as a haven for those divorced from their civil nation; Allen provocatively located the Catholic source of national identity geographically, and institutionally, in Rome. There is, therefore, a difference in emphasis to be noted, which can partly be explained by the currents of Gallican liberty in League thought that prescribed a certain distance from the Roman institution.

Allen was seeking to erode Elizabeth's fullness of sovereignty over her Catholic subjects, with a particular view to opposing William Cecil. Cecil had made a distinction in his *Execution of Justice* between defending Catholicism, which he deemed not to be a treasonous crime, and defending the pope, which he did deem treasonous. Seen in this light – English Catholic martyrs as 'martyrs for the pope' – made them 'traitors against their sovereign and queen in adhering to him, being the notable and only hostile enemy in all actions of war against Her Majesty, her kingdoms, and people'.[75] Seeking haven and citizenship in Rome was a deliberate provocation on Allen's part

---

[74] Allen, 'A Modest Defense of English Catholics' in *The Execution of Justice*, 68–9, 100; *Apologie*, fol. 16v–17r.
[75] Cecil, 'The Execution of Justice in England' in *The Execution of Justice*, 14–15.

against Cecil, a challenge to the accusation that doing so would be treasonous. But it is noticeable that the English did not argue the case for the 'Englishness' of Catholicity, in the way League writers did for France. Allen did not present the argument that England had to have a Catholic ruler in the same, historically grounded (i.e. Gallican) way, and did not deny that heretics were still English. Allen was much more at ease with the idea that Rome could be a haven, and an alternative source of identity and sovereignty, than the Leaguers.

Allen's attack on Elizabeth's sovereignty, in claiming this alternative source of national identity in Rome, is explained further by his under-standing of how the civil and spiritual spheres related to each other. Above all, for Allen, this was a question of conscience, and it is this thread which connects to the work of the League most strongly. The notion of a universal Catholic conscience was a unifying factor for all Catholics everywhere, and made submitting to heretic rule intolerable for many. In explaining how the two spheres related, Allen argued explicitly that the civil was subordinated to the spiritual:

> Where the laws of Christ are received and the bodies politic and mystical, the Church and civil state, the magistrate ecclesiastical and temporal, concur in their kinds together (though ever of distinct regiments, natures and ends), there is such a concurrence and subalternation betwixt both that the inferior of the two (which is the civil state) must needs (in matters pertaining any way either directly or indirectly to the honour of God and benefit of the soul) be subject to the spiritual and take direction from the same.[76]

It is worth emphasizing the fact that Allen accepted that the clergy were under the dominion of a monarch in the sense that they were legally required to obey his or her civil laws.[77] Allen negotiated the uncertain borders between temporal and spiritual relations in order to show that support for the papacy did not necessarily undermine obedience to the monarch, but in fact (ordinarily) reinforced that obedience. This was a feature of that facet of Gallican thought which aligned with the League.

A continuing problem with defining the boundaries between temporal and spiritual power is a feature of Allen's work, in attempting to identify the points at which the jurisdictions of these two realms are clearly distinct, whilst maintaining that they coexist; a major theme of Catholic discourse in this period. One of Allen's central points is that the correct order of the two spheres had been subverted by the declaration that Elizabeth was head

---

[76] Allen, 'Defense', 154–5.   [77] Ibid., 113–14.

of the church. Temporal matters had been given pre-eminence and spiritual life had become, he argued, 'but an accessory'. However, in a Catholic civil commonwealth such as England, the civil ought to be clearly subordinated to the spiritual. Allen argued that it is for the benefit of such a society that it maintains that order: 'the temporal power consisteth most safely, and endureth longest, when it hath good correspondence and subordination to the spiritual'.[78]

Allen's understanding of temporal–spiritual relations explains why he described the oath of supremacy acknowledging Elizabeth as head of the church as 'the torment of all English consciences', usurping the correct political and ecclesiastical order. The oath demanded that every person 'must swear that in conscience he taketh and believeth her so to be, and that no priest or other born out of the realm can have or ought to have any manner of power in spiritual matters over her subjects'. Making 'a king and a prince all one, no difference betwixt the state of the Church and a temporal commonwealth, giving no less right to heathen princes to be governors of the Church in causes spiritual than to a Christian king' has made English Catholics 'foreigners' to the church.[79]

On this basis of conscience, Allen argued that it could not possibly be considered treason for Catholics to resist in such circumstances: 'By all which you see that to resist the magistrate, defend themselves in cases of conscience, and to fight against the superior for religion, is a clear and ruled case and no treasonable opinion at all against the prince'. Catholics, he argued, agree with the Protestants on this, but differed in the manner of executing the resistance 'as far as reason and conscience differ from fury and frenzy'.[80] The connection between reason and conscience is strongly drawn here, a theme we also see expressed in the work of Robert Persons which in many ways builds on Allen's idea of Catholic community sketched out in his Defence.

Robert Persons' *Conference* in the League Context

French League connections are clearer and stronger in Persons' work. Indeed, English contemporaries disparaged the negative influence of the

---

[78] Ibid., 154–5.   [79] Allen, *Defence*, 67–8, 150.

[80] Ibid., 138–9, 143. Kingdon argues that Allen borrowed his 'resistance theory' from Protestant writers such as Beza. However, it is clear from Allen's use of Aquinas, and his emphasis on the papal power of deposition, that this is not straightforwardly the case, even though Allen acknowledges similarities between the two. It is crucial that he claims the 'method' is different. See Kingdon, 'William Allen's use of Protestant Political Argument', in Carter, *From the Renaissance to the Counter-Reformation*.

League on the Jesuit, comparing his work to that of Dorléans, 'Rossaeus' and Boucher.[81] Persons had received patronage from the Guise family, and had been based at Douai with Rainolds and Gifford.[82] League connections are further reinforced by the fact that Persons' *Epistle of the Persecution of Catholickes in England* (Rouen, 1582), was translated into French by the League preacher, Matthieu de Launoy, in 1586.[83] Finally, the influence of the text of 'Rossaeus' on Persons' *Conference* is plain, and has contributed to the argument that *De Justa Reipublicae Christianae Authoritate* was written by Rainolds.

In his *Conference*, it is clear that Persons found direct parallels between the French and English Catholic situations; parallels he sought to exploit. Persons' use of particular French historical examples as models for the English succession served to redefine the ways in which English Catholics perceived their monarchy, with specific reference to France.[84] The question of whether Henri III could be legitimately deposed, or of whether or not Navarre should succeed to the throne, were pressing for the universal Catholic community. The English Catholics shared French concerns about the Catholicity of their crowns, and what happened in France could have set a precedent for what happened in England. In addressing the English situation, Persons therefore found a wealth of arguments in the League polemic to help him construct his case. The problem of non-Catholic dominion, and the possibility of Spanish rule, brought the two sides together.

Notably, Persons reiterated the League case against Henri de Navarre, making the point that a monarchy that is destructive to the commonwealth *and* 'hurtful to all christendom', is illegitimate.[85] The claims of Lorraine and the Spanish Infanta were closer in blood, he argued.[86] This indicates a shift in the intellectual position of English Catholic exiles by 1594. In 1585, Allen was unwilling to make any kind of claim to that effect, deliberately avoiding an engagement with the argument that the English monarch had to be Catholic. However, it appears that at the time of writing the *Conference* (published in 1594, the year of Allen's death), Persons was still

[81] Sutcliffe, *A New Challenge Made*; Hayward, *An Answer to the First Part of a Certain Conference*; Morton, *Exact Discoverie of Romish Doctrine.*
[82] Salmon records Persons as claiming that Gifford was the author of the Rossaeus text in his *French Religious Wars*, 75, n.27.
[83] Persons, *Epistre de la persecution.*
[84] Du Haillan, Belleforest and Du Tillet are his most cited French historical sources, which were all also important sources for Rossaeus.
[85] Persons, *Conference*, I.76. Cf. I., 164–5. His references are stock: Belleforest; Du Haillan.
[86] Ibid., I., 32.

holding out for the conversion of James.[87] Everything was in still question,
therefore, regarding the English succession. Persons' work ought to be read
in that context of uncertainty, despite the fact that he did end up supporting the Infanta's claim. Reading the *Conference* as the first step towards the
development of a Catholic policy on the succession, rather than
a straightforward piece of 'resistance theory', creates space for the analysis
of the work in concert with the French concern about succession.[88] This
was obviously a significant intellectual context for Persons, and it makes its
way into the *Conference* in various explicit ways.[89]

As Rossaeus had, Persons' *Conference* identifies the work of Pierre de
Belloy as its central target. Significantly, the first reference in Part I of the
Conference is to Belloy's *Pro Regibus Apologia*, and Persons' argument
regarding succession law is framed explicitly against this work of Belloy's,
along with his *Apologia Catholica*.[90] Persons is dismissive of an argument
that permitted any madmen to rule the country as king, and framed
Belloy's piece as against the dictates of conscience and reason. Despite
his dismissal, Persons nevertheless returns to Belloy's arguments in
a prolonged and direct engagement which suggests that the Frenchman's
case might have been a little stronger than he initially suggested. A classic
rhetorical technique, this targeting of Belloy importantly emphasises
Persons' League connections. If there was one figure in the entire French
Catholic population that Leaguers universally despised, it was Navarre's
irritating little lawyer.

In his opening argument on the question of succession, Persons establishes two important points that demonstrate his indebtedness to the
Thomist intellectual framework that underpinned Jesuit, and Dominican,
political thought in this era. First, that there must be a higher authority than
the prince who decides on these matters; second, that the source of authority
was the commonwealth (*respublica*) itself. The commonwealth, and its
government by magistrates, was the product of nature: a species of *ius*

---

[87] Houliston, *Catholic Resistance.*   [88] Ibid., 75–6, 83–6.
[89] For a consideration of the broader continental context of the *Conference*, see Tutino, 'The Political
Thought of Robert Persons's *Conference*'. For a treatment of Persons in an exclusively English
context, see Carrafiello, *Robert Parsons*. On the troublesome issue of defining Jesuit political thought
more broadly, see Höpfl, *Jesuit Political Thought*; Annabel Brett, 'Harro Hopfl, Jesuit Political
Thought'.
[90] Persons, *Conference*, I, 2; I, 123–40. Belloy's *Apologia Catholica* was translated into English in 1585/6,
and published again in London 1590, as *A Catholicke Apologie*. Aspects of the English reception of
Belloy's work are considered in Salmon, *French Wars of Religion*, 34–6. The Belloy-Persons
connection has recently been analysed by Innes 'Robert Persons's *Conference* and the Salic Law
debate'.

gentium.[91] But the particular form of a constitution came from neither God or nature, but came down to the choice of individual commonwealths to decide on a form that suited the nature and condition of their people.[92] Arguments about the succession that were based solely on bloodlines, or 'propinquity in blood', could, therefore, be rendered null and void on the basis of Persons' framework for thinking about the laws of a commonwealth as designed to fit the particular nature of the people.[93] Persons' strongly Aristotelian point underpinned his claim that succession laws vary from country to country: 'every particuler countrey and commonwealth hath prescribed these condicions to it selfe and hath authority to do the same'.[94] Persons' *Conference* could thereby argue that the 'conscience' of the commonwealth prevented the possibility of having an irreligious ruler.[95] This position was by no means unique to Persons. The argument that the commonwealth was the source of its own authority (not the pope, or the monarch), and that conditions varied from country to country was an established part of Dominican and Jesuit discourse, as can be seen – for example – in the work of Francisco de Vitoria, Luis de Molina and Francisco Suárez.[96]

Significantly, in arguing that 'the highest and chiefest end of every commonwealth, is ... the service of God, and religion, and consequently that the principal care and charge of a prince and magistrate even by nature itselfe, is, to look thereunto', Persons drew on an authoritative League theologian: Gilbert Génébrard.[97] From this influential Hebraist, Persons draws analysis of passages of Genesis, Deuteronomy and Paralipomenon, and the suggestion that kings in antiquity were also priests. Jews, Gentiles and 'heathens' recognised the fundamental, theocratic point that Persons sought to make: 'the cheefest, and highest ende that God and nature appointed to every commonwealth, was not so much the temporal felicity of the body, as the supernatural and everlasting of the soul'.[98]

Building on Persons' theocratic argument, Belloy's *Regibus Apologia* and the *Apologia Catholica* are taken to represent the destruction of 'all reason, conscience and commonwealth', by bringing the people of France to 'absolute tyranny' that no people in the world could tolerate (not even, he argues, 'the Turke himselfe').[99] At the core of this anti-tyrannical stance

---

[91] Persons, *Conference*, I, 2–8   [92] Ibid., I, 9.
[93] Ibid., I, 32; I, 120. This is an argument that draws on Aristotle's elision of the citizen body with the commonwealth in *Politics* III.
[94] Ibid., I, 1–2.   [95] Ibid., I, 212.   [96] Brett, *Changes of State*, particularly chapter seven, 169–94.
[97] Persons, *Conference*, I, 207. Génébrard, *Chronologia Hebraeorum*.
[98] Persons, *Conference*, I, 204.   [99] Ibid., I, 36.

lay the Ciceronian notion that the commonwealth belonged to the people, and so it was particularly Belloy's claim that the king was owner of all the property of the commonwealth that grated with Persons.[100] He listed other pernicious tenets of Belloy's argument as follows: first, that the power of kings came directly from God; second, that the laws of succession were fixed and immune to challenge; third, that the king 'never dies'; fourth, that a prince is law unto himself, and subject to no temporal laws; fifth, that madness in an heir had no effect on the succession.[101] In opposition to Belloy, Persons went on to build an argument supportive of the merits of primogeniture succession, suspicious of elective monarchy, but thoroughly grounded on the notion that the well-being of the commonwealth lay at the heart of any political theory. On this basis, Persons was quick to suggest that kings could be lawfully deposed and deprived of their right to rule on the basis that they did not meet the requirements of the laws and conditions under which they were made king.[102] He was as quick, however, through the character of the civil lawyer, to distance himself from those who contended, on the one hand, for too much rebellion, and those on the other – like Belloy – who flattered princes excessively.[103] Like many of the best scholars in the League, Persons demonstrated a level of caution in associating himself or his claims with rebellion: he designed his argument to fit within a strongly royalist framework.

Instead of emphasising the right to resist as the purpose of his *Conference*, Persons explicitly emphasised the necessity of having a Catholic ruler. He thereby shifted the emphasis of his argument onto good government, arguing that it was far better to consider whether a government is just, peaceful, secure, wealthy, that it protects the innocent and punishes the guilty, rather than care whether the governor is a foreigner or not. The character of the common lawyer demonstrates that 'besides lack of conscience and religion, it was in like manner against all human wisdom and policy, to favor a pretender of a different religion'.[104] Here, the comparison to the French situation is explicitly drawn.[105] Persons praised the French for acting 'justly and religiously'

---

[100] NB. Although Belloy is often compared to Bodin, this claim is distinct to Bodin's definition of commonwealth in the *République*.

[101] Persons, *Conference*, I, 123–5.   [102] Ibid., I, 32; I, 72.

[103] Ibid,. I, 35. In his *Treatise tending to Mitigation*, responding to Morton's *Exact Discoverie*, Persons draws an explicit connection between the seditious ideas he distanced himself from here, and the writings of notorious Calvinists. Salmon notes that in this text, he astutely aligned his views with those of William Barclay, suggesting Barclay had only been wrong to align Boucher with the Calvinist authors: Salmon, *The French Wars of Religion*, 70.

[104] Persons, *Conference*, II, 238.   [105] Ibid., I, 212.

against Navarre, as England would likely have to do when it came to deciding on the succession. Here he provocatively predicted the likelihood of a Spanish queen of England. Strikingly, Persons made it both a 'matter of conscience' and also 'reason of state ... and worldly policie' that 'it cannot be be but great folly and oversight for a man of what religion soeever he be, to promote to a kingdom in which himselfe must live, one of a contrary religion to himselfe'. In such a case, the only option is for that person to 'dissemble deeply and against his own conscience' or choose exile: 'To avoyd this everlasting perdition, he must break withal the temporal commodityes of this life, and leave the benefits which his countrey and realme might yield him'.[106] Reason and conscience, therefore, provide Persons' with his framework for thinking about the English succession.

For Persons, like the Leaguers, the greatest obstacle to his argument was presented by the succession laws. Here, therefore, he found a useful resource in the League polemic and particularly in the work of Rossaeus. Following his model, Persons responded to Belloy's legal challenge with historical precedent as his weapon. He drew a parallel between French political custom and English, with the hope of showing that Belloy's argument was as little relevant for France as for England. The coronation ceremonies in both countries provided Persons with his material.[107] Even though he had argued that the customs of political life varied from country to country, and that England had peculiarly English political characteristics, this did not prevent him from comparing the French and English systems in order to give himself polemical advantage over Belloy. Persons argued that France directly influenced the way in which England handled its monarchical system:

> Seeing it is so goodly a kingdome, and so neere to Ingland, not only in situation, but also in Lawes manners and customes, and as the race of Inglish kings have come from them in divers manner, so may it be also supposed that the principal ceremonies and circumstances of this action of coronation, hath bine received in like manner from them.[108]

He argued that in France, the ceremony required consent of the subjects to their monarch's rule. The Archbishop of Canterbury therefore performed the same function as the Archbishop of Rheims, in presiding over this ceremony.[109] Persons later compared it to a marriage which can be broken, a point which Dorléans also made, but which was also standard fare in

---

[106] Ibid., I, 217–8.   [107] Ibid., I, 114–17.   [108] Ibid., I, 100   [109] Ibid., I, 114–17.

resistance theory.[110] Persons was torn between trying to make an argument which would fit the specifically English situation he was concerned with, and still cohere with his argument that the monarch had to be a Catholic. In the arguments of the French League, he had a rich store of material which could both provide national and supranational arguments for the Catholicity of monarchy: 'I for my part, do feele myself much of the French opinion ... that so the ship be wel and happely guyded, I esteeme it not much important of what race or nation the pilote be'.[111]

It is safe to say that familiarity with the League polemic informed Persons' *Conference*. Works such as Charles de Bourbon's *Declaration des Causes*, the *Articles de la Sainte Ligue* and Dorléans' *Apologie* demonstrate places in the League polemic where the coronation ceremony is used to argue, often specifically against Belloy, about the nature of the obligations between ruler and ruled. In the final chapter of *De Justa Reipublicae Christianae Authoritate,* the author made the coronation ceremony the centrepiece of its justification for Henri III's deposition and assassination. At the ceremony, the Archbishop of Rheims anointed the king, thus confirming his coronation in the eyes of God, the Roman church and the people. The bonds of obligation between subject and king were established when the king took his oath to defend the Catholic faith and protect his subjects. Rossaeus had explicitly argued that Belloy had destroyed that holy bond. By claiming that monarchs received their power solely from God (note Persons' problem with this point, discussed previously), Belloy had deliberately undermined the power of the commonwealth.[112]

In his treatment of the English coronation ceremony, Persons accepted a controversial claim that those English institutions were, at bottom, French. However, he moved beyond this argument to put forward the idea that, in fact, these institutions are even older than historians have claimed the ancient customs of France were:

> And yet have I bin the larger in this matter of France, for that I do not thinke it to be improbable which this author and others do note, to wit, that most nations round about have taken ther particular formes of anoynting and crowning their kings, from this ancient custom of France, though the substance thereof, I meane of ther sacring and anoynting, be deduced from examples of far more antiquity, to wit, from they very first kings among the people of Israel, who God caused to be anoynted by his priests

[110] Dorléans, *Le Banquet*, 60.   [111] Persons, *Conference*, I, 178.
[112] Note Persons' reiteration of this argument: *Conference*, I, 123–4.

and prophets, in token of his election, and as a singular priviledge of honor and preheminence unto them.[113]

Not only did the English coronation ceremony and the ideas underpinning their concept of monarchical obligation and obedience come from France, but the sacred aspect of the ceremony was directly inherited from Israel. In this respect too, then, Persons would appear still to be working on the basis of Leaguer texts. The League writers argued that precisely because of this ancient Hebrew connection, the French monarchy was sanctified but also destined. The Hebrew model acknowledged its ultimate source as the divine, destined as the people of God, but within that it allowed room for human creativity. Significantly, the ancient Hebrews made no necessary connection between land and commonwealth: their political community was bound by faith, not territory. Crucially, as Persons had evidently noted, the Hebrew model further gave a specific role to the priesthood in anointing kings.

This chapter began with a consideration of the language of the *patrie/patria* in the League polemics, and the ways in which their distinct concept of loyalty to the French commonwealth met the challenges of disloyalty they so regularly faced. What we have seen, is that League writers like Rubis, but also Dorléans and various other anonymous contributors, were deeply conventional in some respects, in their employment of this concept. Insofar as the appeal to the *patrie/patria* was a case of reorienting the discussion towards a traditional, Augustinian concept of loyalty, in which the natural order was firmly subordinate to the supernatural order, the Leaguers were saying nothing their medieval forefathers would not have recognised to be true. The difference being, primarily, one of context, in which the Leaguers were bringing this medieval material to bear on a case where they had to argue that kings of France could only be Catholic, and not Protestant. They simply stretched that Augustinian material to argue that the particular nationality of a ruler was less important than his faith.

However, where things start to look distinct from the medieval tradition is – as discussed earlier – the point at which the *patrie/patria* can be seen to be distinct from the territory of the kingdom (*regnum*), but nevertheless still to encompass the notion of Christian commonwealth (*respublica*). This would seem to offer another route to solving the question of the relationship between the two 'ends' for man, in the Thomist–Aristotelian

---

[113] Persons, *Conference*, I, III.

framework, in which piety towards the *patrie/patria* fuses the civic goal of
the common good with the spiritual goal of collective salvation. That was
the goal of Rossaeus. Furthermore, the comparison to the English case, and
to Persons in particular, demonstrates the extent to which the League
analysis of the succession crisis was cohesive with the broader concerns of
Catholic lawyers and theologians in the context of a Christendom that had
lost all cohesion.[114]

Expanding this analysis of the League polemic beyond the borders of
France further demonstrates the significance of definitions of the commonwealth that are not tied to territory. Here we have seen the importance
of the model of the Hebrew commonwealth in the Catholic context, not as
a model of republicanism, but as a model of theocratic kingship wherein
nationality is defined through following God's law. There are further
significant connections here, most notably to the Jesuit and Dominican
analysis of the porosity of commonwealths in this period. In this context,
interest in the temporality of politics (i.e. its territory and borders), is
subordinate to interest in the liminality of the political sphere.[115] In some
ways, it could be argued that this is a reiteration of a long-disputed
relationship between the temporal and spiritual spheres from the purported Donation of Constantine, but what we see in the Early Modern
era, arguably, is a new understanding of political space, within which the
definition of Christian commonwealths is at stake.

---

[114] The intervention of Cardinal Bellarmine is further testimony to the international scale of these
debates, discussed in Zwierlein, *Political Thought of the League*. It is an area of research that could be
opened up further, which I hope to pursue in the future.
[115] As demonstrated by Brett, *Changes of State*.

Conclusion

When Henri IV issued the Edict of Nantes in 1598, he required that his subjects extinguish the memory of the recent wars, having already ordered the libelous and radical texts of those years to be publicly burnt.[1] But this command of *oubliance*, an existing tradition in the edicts of pacification issued from 1562 onwards, was not so easily obeyed.[2] The deliberate conservation of the documents and imagery of these troubled years, often at great personal risk, served to remind contemporaries of the entrenched nature of the confessional division. The desire of individuals like Pierre de L'Estoile, Pierre Pithou and Simon Goulart to preserve these records testifies to a profound commitment to particular memories of the wars of religion, and a notable sense of duty to expose the 'abuses, impostures, vanities and furies of this great monster of the League'.[3] Others wrote of the 'chimeras' of League political thought, and depicted the League as a monster, often a hydra, that would be the death of France.[4]

Some took the idea of *oubliance* literally, and sought to efface the League from the historical record entirely: archives were destroyed, and families obliterated their connection with the movement over subsequent generations.[5] Those that chose to write about the League, particularly Palma Cayet in his *Chronologie Novenaire*, committed the movement to the flames, aiming to reveal it in all its devilish follies, and to strip away its façade of piety.[6] Out of the chaos of the League years, Paris was seen to

---

[1] See the first article of the Édit de Nantes: http://elec.enc.sorbonne.fr/editsdepacification/edi t_12#art_12_01; L'Estoile, M-J, vi, 201; Arch Nat Xıa 8641; Arch Nat Xıa 1730, 30 Mar. 1594.

[2] Although see Loisel, *Amnestie*, for one important example of a demonstration of support for the notion of *oubliance* and amnesty.

[3] L'Estoile, M-J, III, 177–80.

[4] Savoie, *Les chimeres monarchiques de la Ligue*; BN, Cbt des Estampes, M 88285–7.

[5] Benedict, 'Shaping the Memory of the French Wars of Religion, 123.

[6] See also Bonderoy, *Histoire des singeries de la Ligue*; Matthieu, *Histoire des derniers troubles de France*.

have been 'restored to her senses', and Henri IV emerged as the saviour of France, having at last restored peace to this troubled kingdom.[7]

Oubliance of a kind, therefore, did succeed in effacing anything other than an entirely selective, partisan record of the years of the League, in which the movement was thoroughly demonised and associated with Spanish tyranny.[8] And as the League disbanded, its members choosing exile or reconciliation with the king, there was no immediate attempt amongst them to salvage its reputation for posterity in the face of Catholic and Huguenot censure. There is certainly no public body of accounts to rival the overwhelming Protestant and Catholic condemnation of the League that became so authoritative in the seventeenth century. Contemporaries simply did not record the history of the movement, with the exception of the *l'Histoire de la ligue*, a journal which circulated in manuscript form and has only survived in fragments, probably authored by Pierre Rozée.[9] The former Leaguer magistrate of Lyon, Claude Rubis, chronicled the history of his town during the wars, in which he praised the swiftness with which it demonstrated its loyalty to the king on his abjuration, but conveniently overlooked his own role in the League as an arch defender of Spanish intervention.[10]

The absence of League chronicles is easily explained. For those who chose exile, mostly in the Low Countries, producing a memoir of the League could not be seen as a requirement when, after all, the war for the 'true' religion continued.[11] Amongst these exiles, a vibrant *catholicisme ligueur* was expressed in the turn towards Spain, hoping for an alliance between the two countries in a crusade against the 'heresies' of the North, and the perceived Ottoman threat from the East.[12]

For those who sought amnesty from Henri IV, writing a defensive account of the League years would have been impolitic and unnecessary.

---

[7] Abadia, *Henri IV et la reconstruction du royaume*, 119; Greengrass, *France in the Age of Henri IV*, 82–8; de Waele, *Réconcilier les Français* , 191–216, 241–66.

[8] The pro-Spanish element of the League was certainly exaggerated, as many scholars now agree. See Baumgartner, *Radical Reactionaries*, 232–3.

[9] For an incomplete version of the manuscript, see Valois, ed., *Une histoire inédite de la Ligue*. For a discussion of the text itself, and a consideration of authorship, see Valois, *Histoire de la Ligue*, 1–39; Descimon, *Qui Étaient Les Seize?*, 214; Greengrass, with Penzi and Critchlow, 'Unfinished Business' in Diefendorf, *Social Relations*, 212–36.

[10] Rubis, *Histoire véritable de la ville de Lyon*.

[11] On the aftermath of the League, and particularly the examination of the formation of an exiled 'community', see Descimon, Ruiz Ibáñez, *Les Ligueurs de l'Exil*, 187–254. For their dictionary of exiled Leaguers, see 261–75. See also, Forrestal and Nelson (eds.), *Politics and Religion in Early Bourbon France*.

[12] Descimon, Ruiz Ibáñez, *Les Ligueurs de l'Exil*, 7–49.

Instead, former Leaguers wrote panegyrics addressed to Henri IV, and continued to pursue their professional interests.[13] To all intents and purposes, the League appeared to have dissolved, a fact confirmed by the swift volte-face on the part of Leaguers lucky to have escaped with their lives after 1594. And yet, despite this, there is evidence to suggest that the League by no means disappeared entirely. In the minds of many Parisians in the early seventeenth century, the League remained on the cusp of being resurrected. In 1615, a Protestant pamphlet was produced, protesting against the Spanish alliance proposed by Marie de Medici and the tyranny of Concino Concini's ministry, entitled '*La Ligue ressuscité*', which raised the spectre of a re-formation of the League.[14] If the League could be said to have 'died' by 1598, its ghost promised to continue to stir up trouble in the difficult years to 1629.[15] There was, therefore, no need to consign to the past a movement that was in some sense still living.

There are further proofs of the continuing liveliness of the spirit of the League in seventeenth-century France. The engagement of many former Leaguers in the political life of seventeenth-century France is indicative of the extent to which the ideas that had been put forward in the League years were repurposed in the reign of Henri IV and the regency of Marie de Medici.[16] Partly, the Nicodemism of the Parisian Leaguers who remained after Henri's abjuration allowed for the survival of a '*catholicisme ligueur*' which developed alongside a '*catholicisme royal*' and shaped the future of Catholic reform.[17] Amongst them, it took shape in the position of the *dévots* and their debates with the *libertins*.[18] An important example is that of the jurist and former Leaguer Michel de Marillac, who rejected Cardinal

---

[13] For example, see René Choppin, *Panegyricus*; Dorléans, *Remerciment au Roy*.

[14] It was met with a Catholic response: Maingoua, *La Ligue renversée*.

[15] See Holt, *The French Wars of Religion*, 178–94.

[16] Here I take the opposite view to Baumgartner, that 'it is apparent that Leaguer political thought had very little impact on French theory in the seventeenth century except in a negative fashion, promoting the promulgation of absolutist theory'. Instead, the Gallican ideas at the heart of theories of legitimate absolute power regarding the connection between church and state require some closer examination, and it is clear that once we expand our analysis of League thought beyond the framework of popular sovereignty, tyrannicide and 'absolutism', there is much to be said of the influence of League ideas in the seventeenth century. Baumgartner, *Radical Reactionaries*, 241. Cf. Holt, *The French Wars of Religion*, 221, which makes a similar point. Baumgartner, however, was absolutely right to indicate the importance of the reception of Leaguer texts and ideas in England, the best study of which remains Salmon, *The French Religious Wars in English Political Thought*.

[17] Descimon, Ruiz Ibáñez, *Les Ligueurs de l'Exil*, 21–2; Elizabeth Tingle, 'The Origins of Counter Reform Piety in Nantes', in Forrestal and Nelson (eds.), *Politics and Religion in Early Bourbon France*, 203–20.

[18] A point importantly brought to light by Richet, *De la Réforme à la Révolution*.

Richelieu's version of *raison d'état* as he and others like him continued the Leaguer battle for 'true', heavenly, reasoning to triumph over false.

Amidst these *dévots* and their children, the distinction between the Leaguers and the *archi-ligueurs* became particularly significant: '*la bonne Ligue*', the League of devout, Catholic, aristocratic supporters of Mayenne as opposed to the zealous, ambition-driven, populist clergy of the *Paris Seize*, was seen to have protected France from foreign rule, and by bringing about Henri IV's decision to abjure Protestantism, could even be seen as the instrument of peace.[19] In this view, the devout Catholicism of the Mayennistes was emphasised, in order to bring about a rehabilitation of those aspects of the League which could be determined to be truly 'holy', and in which members played the role of 'good Frenchmen', conceived in Gallican terms. This is evident in the unpublished history of Nicolas Lefèvre de Lezeau (1581–1680), son of a former Leaguer, also known for his biography of Marillac.[20] Lefèvre shouldn't necessarily be seen as reinventing League history here; his account was entirely consistent with the presentation of the League by its Mayenniste members discussed in this study.[21] It is evident, therefore, that this particularly Mayenniste aspect of the League survived well into the seventeenth century, in a Nicodemite fashion.

In the years after the League, there was also a continuing emphasis on the need for internal spiritual renewal, corresponding to the impetus of the Catholic Reformation. The work of the *dévots*, like Marillac, within France, was furthered by the founding of religious orders that became a source of asylum for former Leaguers. The *Oratoire de France*, established by Pierre Bérulle (1575–1629), in 1611 became a known sanctuary for Leaguers and their descendants: Claude Ameline (1635–1706), Sébastien Rainssant (1627–1707), and notably Daniel Hotman (1558–1634), the prodigal son of François Hotman, and nephew to the Leaguers Charles and Antoine, were all members.[22] Along with his cousin, Barbe Acarie (1566–1618), Bérulle also

---

[19] Maimbourg was heartily dismissive of the latter presentation of events: *Histoire de la Ligue*, 3v–4r.

[20] Nicolas Lefèvre de Lezeau, 'Memoires sur la vie de Messire Michel de Marillac, Chevalier, Garde des Sceaux de France', BNF NAF 82–3; 'De la religion catholique en France, 1560 à 1604', in *Archives curieuses*, 14, 1_91 (published from an eighteenth-century manuscript). Barbara Diefendorf estimates that Lefèvre wrote this history somewhere between 1655 and 1665 in her 'Reconciliation and Remembering'. Lefèvre's perspective has also been evaluated more recently by Fabrice Micallef, 'Comment la bonne ligue sauva la monarchie'.

[21] In this, I differ from Diefendorf who argues that Lezeau's piece demonstrates a 'reshaping' and 'reconstruction' of the memory of the League.

[22] The notion of a close association of the League with the Oratory was taken up again in the later seventeenth century: Batterel, *Mémoires domestique*; Joseph Bicaïs, *Notice de l'Oratoire de France ou recherches sur les membres de cette congrégation*, Bibliothèque Méjanes, Aix-en-Provence, ms. 331, t.I.

helped found the order of Discalced Carmelites. Barbe Acarie was married to Pierre Acarie, a devoted member of the *Seize* (subsequently exiled), and her particular emphasis on individual reform through spiritual mysticism was indicative of the significance of a pervasive French mysticism that long outlived the League.[23] Acarie looked back on the League years as a 'golden age', and actively sought to continue what she saw as her Catholic duty to reject Protestant heresy, demonstrating an important connection between League spirituality and Catholic renewal.[24]

The notion of legitimate tyrannicide, so closely associated with the League movement, also remained very much alive after Henri IV took control of the capital. Jean Chastel's attempt on the king's life was taken up by Boucher as further evidence of the legitimacy of assassinating tyrants. Boucher's *Apologie pour Jehan Chastel* was republished in 1610 when Ravaillac succeeded in murdering the king, and translated into Latin in 1611, thus contributing to the ongoing debate about tyrannicide.

The blame for Henri's death fell on the shoulders of the Jesuits, but it seems that the influence of the same ideas taken up by the Leaguers in their analysis of legitimate tyrannicide was strongly felt.[25] The work of the Portugese Jesuit, Manuel de Sâ, for example, proffered a casuistic analysis of the doctrine of tyrannicide, and was published in France in 1601 and 1609.[26] Juan de Mariana, whose *De Rege et Regis Institutione* (1599) was condemned by the *parlement* of Paris in 1610, is often associated with Leaguer ideas.[27] Finally, Bellarmine, who had made his voice heard in the League years, presented an ambiguous reading of resistance to tyranny that could be seen as supportive of the same doctrine in his *Controversiae*, circulating in manuscript form from 1581.

That the idea of legitimate tyrannicide had many supporters is well known, but in the French case it is wise to pause before associating these ideas exclusively with the League, or indeed the Huguenot writers of the 1570s. As this present study has sought to demonstrate, the sources of these arguments are not peculiar to the League, and as other scholars have also suggested, scholastic sources and particularly Dominican casuistry lay at

Cited in Rodier, 'Fils de ligueurs et 'enfants de la guerre' in Daubresse, Haan, *La Ligue et ses frontiers*, 195. Cf. Richet, *De la Réforme à la Révolution*, 83–94.
[23] Diefendorf, *From Penitence to Charity*; Descimon, Ruiz Ibáñez, *Les Ligueurs de l'Exil*, 27–8; Ramsay, *Liturgy, Politics and Salvation*; Ramsay, 'From Ontology to Religious Experience' in Donnelly, Maher, *Confraternities and Catholic Reform*, 135–53; Rodier, 'Fils de ligueurs', 192.
[24] Diefendorf, 'An Age of Gold?', in Wolfe, *Changing Identities*, 169–90.
[25] On the imputation of blame on the Jesuits, see Mousnier, *L'assassinat d'Henri IV*, 36–9.
[26] Manuel de Sâ, *Les Aphorismes*; *Aphorismi confessariorum*.
[27] Mousnier, *L'assassinat d'Henri IV*, 85–7.

the heart of such analyses of tyranny.[28] The blame for Henri's assassination was laid primarily at the door of the Jesuits in the early seventeenth century, a fact which indicates that – as this study has proposed – there was more to the League than the doctrine of tyrannicide.

The longevity of the League in intellectual terms is further demonstrated by the fact that former Leaguers continued to pursue central themes in their works, which had been encompassed by, but extended beyond, the movement. Gilbert Génébrard, who submitted to Henri's authority, was nevertheless banished by his local *parlement* for publishing his *De Sacrarum Electionum* in 1593, which argued against the king's authority to elect bishops. René Choppin, on the other hand, had planned to leave France with a group of exiles. His wife, Marie Baron, had also become an '*archiligueur*', and it was said that she was so devoted to the cause that Henri's abjuration drove her insane; a madness which killed her. Choppin only escaped punishment by death because Jacques-Auguste de Thou pleaded with the king on his behalf, and he was permitted to stay in Paris. In gratitude, Choppin wrote a gushing panegyric to the king.[29] Choppin then returned to his writing, and after his *De Civilibus Parisiorum moribus* (1596), he produced a text on canon law, the *Monasticon* of 1601. When he died, in 1606, every lawyer in the *parlement* attended his funeral, testimony to the fact that such professional bonds were hard to break.

The exiles similarly continued to write. After his books had been publicly burnt, and whilst in exile in the Low Countries, Louis Dorléans turned to academic study, producing an edition of the works of Tacitus (heavily influenced by Justus Lipsius, with whom he was in correspondence), and writing a curious treatise on absolute royal power after Henri IV's death, dedicated to Marie de Medici, and entitled *La plante humaine*.[30] This analysis of the close connection between monarchy and human nature was written in response to Louis Turquet de Mayerne's *La Monarchie aristo démocratique* (1611), a natural-law discourse on the advantage of a mixed constitution, which further defended the merits of commercial activity. Dorléans' response indicated his deep attachment to the conventions of French monarchy, conceived as a protective guardianship over the French people, and his rejection of the particular political science offered by Turquet. In effect, the treatise is a long panegyric to Henri IV,

---

[28] Gabriel, 'Réalisme politique et rationalité', 141–59.
[29] Choppin, *Panegyricus*. Cf. Jean-Papire Masson's biography, appended to *Les Oeuvres de Me René Choppin*.
[30] Dorléans, *Novae cogitations in libros annalium c. cornelii taciti qui extant*; Dorléans, *La plante humaine*.

and also made some suggestive observations on the relationship between kings and clergy which indicate consistency with Dorléans' Leaguer writings. It also demonstrates continuity with the anti-republicanism Dorléans had expressed in his engagement with Huguenot texts, an anti-Calvinist position which thrived in seventeenth-century France.[31]

Also writing from exile, Jean Boucher continued to hound Protestants in his texts: he published his *Mystère d'infidelité* in 1600, in which he compared them to witches. He also continued to embrace academic controversy, offering his views on Edmond Richer (1559–1631) and the conciliar ideas he put forward in his *Libellus de ecclesiastica et politica potestate* (1611), condemned in Paris in 1612 and placed on the papal index in 1613.[32] Richer had been a member of the League, and swore loyalty to Henri IV after 1593, from which point he became a central figure in the Gallican controversies of the Sorbonne through his relentless defence of what has been called a 'paradoxical' fusion of royalism with conciliar doctrine in its most provocative form.[33] Notably, in the face of this controversy, Richer found few protectors, but amongst them were the former Leaguer Claude Leprestre, a councillor in the League *parlement*. The ecclesiology of some former Leaguers led them to an anti-Tridentine position in these disputes of the early seventeenth century, which fundamentally challenged papal power.[34] This fits with the argument made here, that the 'ultramontanism' of the League was, for the large part, a polemical exaggeration. Instead, it is clear that the conciliar ideas at the heart of their conceptions of Gallican liberty remain deeply significant in the seventeenth century.[35]

Boucher's unfailing energy led him deeper into international Counter-Reformation arguments on papal power, which were, as is well documented, spearheaded by Bellarmine.[36] Boucher engaged in the Casaubon controversy over his *Epistola ad Frontonem*, which had been largely directed against Bellarmine's doctrine of 'indirect' papal power. However, it was

---

[31] Herman, 'The Huguenot Republic'.

[32] Boucher, *Avis sur l'appel interjeté par Me Émond Richer*.

[33] See his collected works of Gerson, Almain and Mair published during the Venetian Interdict crisis: *Opera*, ed. Richer. Cf. Cottret, 'Edmond Richer'; Sutto, 'Une controverse ecclésiologique'.

[34] A point observed by Descimon, Ruiz Ibáñez, *Les Ligueurs de l'Exil*, 20.

[35] Bergin, *The Politics of Religion in Early Modern France*, importantly traces the connections between the wars of religion and the developments in Gallican thought in the seventeenth century. Oakley has pursued the significance of conciliarism, through a 'constitutionalist' framework, into the nineteenth century: *The Conciliarist Tradition*. As suggested in Chapter 5, there is scope to reconsider this trajectory from the angles suggested by Arabeyre and Tallon in, *Les Clercs et Les Princes*, 253–70; 285–96.

[36] Franceschi, *La Crise Théologico-Politique*. On Bellarmine specifically, see Tutino, *Cardinal Bellarmine and the Christian Commonwealth*.

Casaubon's treatment of Caesar Baronius' *Annales Ecclesiastici* (1588) in this work which angered Boucher and, indeed, many others, including de Thou.[37] Here, too, the spectre of one of Boucher's most formidable and vituperative opponents had been resurrected by Casaubon, who was an admirer of William Barclay's *De Potestate Papae* (posthumously published in 1609).[38]

Boucher, therefore, remained absolutely consistent to the views he had expressed in the League years in the shifting intellectual climate of the early seventeenth century. Further evidence of this is found in his last published work, on absolute royal power. His *Couronne Mystique* (1623–4) dedicated to Isabella of Spain, in the course of which he attacked both Protestants and Ottoman Muslims, to reiterate many of the views on pious, just kingship that he had put forward elsewhere.[39] Dying at around the grand age of 95, Boucher's last will and testament expressed his fervent Catholicism, his loyalty to royal power, and a condemnation of France's part in the Thirty Years War, which he viewed as a disgrace, and the very opposite of the 'holy war' undertaken during the League years.[40]

The political thought of the League has been treated, in this study, as part of a matrix of ideas regarding political authority in the Wars of Religion. The hitherto under-studied works of important figures including Génébrard, Choppin, Dorléans, 'Rossaeus' and, on the other side, Belloy, have been brought to light and analysed with a view to the wider implications of their ideas for French political thought in this era. The upholding of divine law and eradication of heresy in service to the Roman Catholic Church; a promise to conserve the true status of the 'Very Christian Kings'; and an aim to reinstate the provinces and the Estates of France to their ancient rights, pre-eminences, franchises and liberties were the key features which bound the movement, otherwise highly intellectually diverse, together.[41] The Leaguers saw themselves as crusaders, fighting a holy war in defence of the 'true' religion, and whilst the category of 'resistance theory' can be useful for defining their political thought up to a point, this study has emphasised the limitations that this category imposes on the ideas of the League.

---

[37] Boucher, *Conviction des fautes principalles.*
[38] Touched on in Franceschi, *La Crise Théologico-Politique*, 388. On Barclay and Boucher, see Nicholls, 'Catholic Resistance Theory'.
[39] Boucher, *Couronne mystique.*
[40] Boucher's will is discussed in Descimon, Ruiz Ibáñez, *Les Ligueurs de l'Exil*, 255–60.
[41] Palma Cayet, *Chronologie novenaire*, fol. 1r–4r.

Moving the framework for thinking about League political thought beyond that of the Calvinist resistance theory of the Huguenots, has demonstrated the greater significance of the relationship between natural and divine law in the relevant sources, without excluding the obvious influence of texts like the *Francogallia* and the *Vindiciae* from the analysis. Within this expanded framework, the expressly anti-republican position of thinkers like Louis Dorléans helps to explain and clarify the nature of the intellectual relationship of the Leaguers to the Calvinist 'resistance theory' of the 1570s, and views on the roles of the Estates General and Paris *parlement* in defining, and acting on, tyranny in the body politic. At the most abstract, academic level of League political thought, it is also clear that the reinvigorated scholasticism of the Salamancan school was making its intellectual mark on French thought in this era. This scholasticism thrived in the Sorbonne, even in the face of changing intellectual method-ologies, and there is scope for further research into the survival of Aristotelianism in the seventeenth century.[42]

This book has deliberately sought to move the analysis of political thought in this era beyond the structure of 'absolutism' and 'constitutionalism', without seeking to diminish the importance of the legal frameworks under-pinning such analyses. It has done so in order to connect the juridical analysis of the French constitution to the wider intellectual context which includes a whole range of sources: Augustinian, stoic, scholastic, Aristotelian, Thomist, humanist etc. The outcome of this has been to demonstrate the intersection between Leaguer ideas and those of the major thinkers of the era including Guillaume du Vair, Michel de Montaigne, Étienne Pasquier and Jean Bodin. In this way, the League can now be seen as positioned at the centre of intellectual debate on the purpose and nature of politics, in relationship to the church, and not the periphery.

The fate of the Leaguers after Henri's abjuration, and their work, demonstrates a significant contribution to the expanding spheres of religious and political thinking that developed as the Catholic, or Counter, Reformation gained momentum in France and internation-ally. Gallican debates continued to rage fiercely, and the corporatist approach of the Leaguers to the idea of political community was sus-tained into the seventeenth century, with figures like Jacques-Bénigne

---

[42] Here I have in mind particularly the ongoing tensions between humanism and scholasticism in the face of the 'New Philosophy' of the Cartesians, and the *querelle des anciens et des modernes*. On scholastic thought in France through to the eighteenth century, see the work of Jacob Schmutz, in particular his "From Theology to Philosophy', and 'Le Petit Scotisme du Grand Siècle'.

Bossuet defending the Catholic community in the face of dangerous
'Protestant' individualism.[43] These ongoing confessional tensions came
to the fore in the 1680s in the lead-up to the revocation of the Edict of
Nantes, which could itself be seen as a product of a long-surviving
catholicisme ligueur.[44]

Considering Leaguer ideas in an international context has also demonstrated the important connections to the English exiled community, and
the work of Robert Persons in particular, which suggests a much more
meaningful, international context for Leaguer ideas than has hitherto been
proposed. Here the idea of the *patrie*, or *patria*, is arguably more significant
than that of the state: encompassing the idea of a universal, Christian
community within which individual, political communities were embedded. The very porous nature of this concept of community is key to the
political-theological thinking of this era, supportive of the notion that the
state was not yet conceived of as a territorially bound juridical unit, and
that such boundaries as there were between sacred and secular concepts of
communities were entirely permeable.[45]

---

[43] Bossuet, *Histoire*, 15, 179. Cited in Kearns, *Ideas in Seventeenth-Century France*, 119. Cf. Zuber,
'Cléricature intellectuelle'; Bergin, *The Politics of Religion*.
[44] Cf. Bossuet, *Defensio declarationis conventus cleri Gallicani*.   [45] Brett, *Changes of State*.

Bibliography

Manuscript Sources

Arch Nat Xɪa 8641.
Arch Nat Xɪa 1730, 30 mars 1594.
Archives Municipales, Dijon, B 457.
BnF Cbt des Estampes, M 88285–88287.
BnF NAF 82–83.
BnF MS Dupuy 428.
Summa legationis Guysianicae ad Pontificem Max. deprehensa nuper inter chartas Davidis Parisiensis Advocati, Darmstadt, Hessisches Staatsarchiv, A.IV, konv.50, Fast.3.
Jean Gerson, *De ecclesiastica potestate et de origine iuris et legum tractatus* ([Paris: ca. 1473–4]). Bod-inc G-124.

Unpublished Theses

Claussen, Emma. 'A Study of Uses of the Term Politique During the French Wars of Religion, c. 1562–98', Unpublished DPhil diss., University of Oxford, 2016.
Gagne, Lyne. 'La Pensée politique d'un juriste du XVIᵉ siècle: Pierre de Belloy', Unpublished MA thesis, Sherbrooke University, 1985.
Gould, R. C. 'The Life and Political Writings of Louis Dorléans, Publicist of the French Catholic League', Unpublished PhD thesis, Bryn Mawr College, March 1975.
Marabuto, M. *Les Theories Politiques des Monarchomaques Française*. Unpublished PhD thesis, Bibliothèque Cujas, 1967.
Martin, S. *Pierre de Beloy: Un paradigme du 'politique' à l'époque de la Ligue.* Unpublished PhD thesis, Paris IV Sorbonne, 2007.
John, Philip Owen. 'Publishing in Paris 1570–1590: A Bibliometric Analysis', Unpublished PhD Dissertation, University of St Andrews, 2011.

Printed Primary Sources

1 Anonymous Publications

Ad Quaestionem an pro Rege orandum in Canone missae facultatis Parisiensis responsum. Cui adiectae sunt cum licentia superioris duae collectae pro principibus Catholicis et victoria contra hostes obtinenda (Paris, 1589).

Advertissement aux Catholiques sur la bulle de nostre Sainct Pere touchant l'excommunication de Henry de Valois: avec plusieurs exemples des punitions estranges & merveilleux iugements de Dieu sur les excommuniez (Paris, 1589).

Advertissement sur la reception & publication du Concile de Trente (n.p., 1583).

Advis aux Catholiques francois sur l'importance de ce qui traicté aujourd'huy, sur l'irresolution de quelques scrupuleux: ensemble & principalement sur les ruze des Politiques, Atheistes, forgeurs de nouvelles & aultres ennemys de Dieu (Paris, 1589).

Advis d'un François à la noblesse catholique de France, sur la remonstrance d'un ligueur, auquel le devoir des catholiques à la mémoire du seu Roy et envers le Roy à présent régnant, ensemble la conjuration de la Ligue contre l'Estat, ses traitez et alliances avec l'Espagnol sont déclarez (Tours, 1590).

Advis & resolutions de la faculté de Theologie de Paris, pour la conservaion de la Foy Catholique. Assemblee au College de Sorbone, le 7. de ce présent moys de Janvier, 1589. Traduit fidèlement en François, pour le soulagement de ceux qui n'entendent la langue Latine (n.p., 1589).

Articles de la Saincte Union des Catholiques Francois (n.p., 1588).

Conference Chrestienne de quatre theologiens, & trois fameux advocates, sur le faict de la Ligue, & levee des armes: faite depuis quelque temps en France, au nom de monseigneur le Reverendiss. & illustriss. Prince, Charles, cardinal de Bourbon: contenant response, au libelle intitulé, Le Salutaire, publié par ceux de ladite Ligue: le tout addressé audit Seigneur Cardinal, par le secrétaire qui à resuite en escrit la susdite conférence (n.p., 1586).

Conspiration faicte en Picardie, sous fausses & meschantes calomnies, contre l'edict de pacification (n.p., 1576).

Coppie d'une lettres escripte par un Catholique à un Politique sur l'arrest prononcé en la Synagogue de Tours le cinquiesme d'aoust dernier (Lyon, 1591).

Les Cruautez Execrables commises par les heretiques, contre les Catholiques de la ville de Nyort en Poictou (n.p., 1589).

Declaration des causes qui ont mû Monseigneur le Cardinal de Bourbon, & les Pairs, Princes, Seigneurs, Villes & Communautes Catholiques de ce Royaume de France, de s'opposer à ceux qui par tous moyens s'efforcent de subvertir la Religion Catholique & l'Etat (n.p., 1585).

Declaration des justes causes qui ont contrainct le Roy de Navarre et ceux de la religion à prendre les armes. Aussi avons bien voulu inserrer cy dedans de mot a mot la ligue des papistes (Montpellier, 1577).

De la puissance des roys, et droict de succession aux royaumes, contre l'usurpation du tiltre qualité de roy de France, faicte par le roy de Navarre (Paris, 1589).

Description du Politique de nostre temps (Paris, 1588).

Discours sur les estats de France (Paris, 1587).

Discours de ce qui s'est faict et passé en la ville d'Orleans, par Monsieur le Chevalier d'Aumalle, & les habitans d'icelle, contre les gouverneurs de la Citadelle, & autres qui estoient à l'entour de ladicte ville (n.p., 1589).

Double d'une letter envoiée à un certain personnage contenante le discours de ce qui se passa au cabinet du roy de Navarre en sa présence, lors que M. le duc d'Epernon fut vers luy l'an 1584 (Frankfurt, 1585).

Erklärung der Ursachen, welche den card. Von Bourbon, die Pares, Fürsten, Prelaten, Herren, Stett und catholischen Gemeinden des Königreichs Franckreich bewegt, sich gefaßt zumachen, wider die, so sich understehn die Religion unnd den Staht umbzustoßen (Augsburg, 1585).

Extraict des registres des Estats tenus à Blois en 1576, sur la réception du Concile de Trente au Royaume de France (Paris, 1594).

Le Guidon des Catholiques sur l'Edict de Roy, nouvellement publié en sa cour de Parlement (Paris, 1587).

Histoire contenant les plus memorables faits et advenus en l'an 1587. Tant en l'armee commandee par Monsieur le Duc de Guyse, qu'en celle des Huguenots, conduite par le Duc de Bouillon ... Le tout envoyé par un Gentil-homme François à la Royne d'Angleterre (Paris, 1588).

Histoire au vray de meurtre et assassinat proditoirement commis au cabinet d'un Roy perfide & barbare, en la personne de Monsieur le Duc de Guise, Protecteur & Deffenseur de l'Eglise Catholique & du Royaume de France: Ensemble du massacre aussi perpetré en la personne du Cardinal, son frère, sacré & dedié à Dieu: Où sont balancez les services de ses Predecesseurs & les siens, avec une tant inhumaine cruauté & ingrate rémunération. Pour estre le tout veu & diligemment consideré par gents de bien (n.p., 1589).

Une histoire inédite de la Ligue, oeuvre d'un contemporain anonyme (1574–1593), ed. C. Valois (Mâcon, 1908).

Iurisconsultus Catholicus de theologorum assertione: ad quondam parochum & tres excommunicatorum patronos (n.p., 1590).

Justification des actions des catholiques unis contre les calomniateurs (Paris, 1589).

Le Labyrinthe de la Ligue et les Moyens de s'en retirer (n.p., 1590).

Les Lauriers du Roy, contre les foudres pratiquez par l'Espagnol (Caen, 1590).

Lettre d'un gentil-homme francois, a dame Jacquette Clement, Princesse boiteuse de la ligue (n.p., 1590).

Lettres d'unyon pour estre envoyes par toute la Chrestienté. Touchant le meurtre & assassinat commis envres les personnes de monsieur le Duc de Guyse, & monsieur le Cardinal de Guyse son frère, & autres Princes & Seigneurs Catholiques, lesquels ont evité la cruaté commise en la ville de Blois (n.p., 1589).

Lettre missive aux Parisians d'un Gentilhomme servituer du Roy (n.p., 1591).

Les cruautez execrables commises par les Heretiques, contre les Catholiques de la ville de Nyort en Poictou (Paris, 1589).

Le Manifeste de la France aux Parisiens et à tout le peuple François (n.p., 1589).

Les Meurs, Humeurs et Comportements de Henry de Valois representez au vray depuis sa Naissance. Quels ont este ses Parrains, & leur Religion, ensemble celles de ses Precepteurs, & en quoy ils l'ont instruit iusques à présent. Avec les instructions & mémoires des points fort notables, concernants la Religion & estat du Royaume (Paris, 1589).

La nullite de la pretendue innocence & iustification des massacres, de Henry de Valois. Par le contraire de son artificelle declaration, envoyes par les villes de France, pour estre publiee (n.p., 1589).

Les raisons pour lesquelles Henry de Bourbon soy disant Roy de Navarre ne peult et ne doit estre recue approuve Roy de France (n.p., 1591).

Le Reveille Matin des François, et de leurs voisins (Edinburgh [Strasburg], 1574).

Procedure faicte contre Jean Chastel Escholier estudiant au College des Jesuites, pour le parricide par luy attenté sur la personne du Roy Tres-Chrestien Henry IIII. Roy de France & de Navarre. Et Arrests donnez contre le parricide & contre les Jesuites (Paris, 1595).

Proposition de Messieurs les Princes, Prelats, Officiers de la Couronne, Seigneurs, Gentils-hommes & autres Catholiques estans du party du Roy de Navarre: avec la Response de Monseigneur le Duc de Mayenne Lieutenant général de l'Estat Royal & Couronne de France, Messieurs les Princes, Prelats, Seigneurs & Deputez des Provinces, assemblez à Paris (Paris, 1593).

Protestation de l'ordre du clergé, aux États de Blois, contre l'aliénation des biens ecclésiastiques, datée du 22 février 1577 (n.p., n.d.).

Protestation des liguez faicte en l'assemblee de Mildebourg 16 déc 1584 (n.p., 1585).

Remonstrance faicte au Roy et a la Royne Mere par Messieurs les Cardinaux, de Bourbon, de Guyse, assistez de M.de Guyse, & autres Pairs de France, sur les plaintes, & doleances des Troubles de Se Royaume (Paris, 1587).

Remonstrance au peuple francoys sur la diversité des vices qui regnent en ce temps, avec le remède d'iceux (n.p., 1587).

Remonstrance aux trois estats sur la publication & reception du Sainct Concile de Trente en France (Lyon, 1589).

Response a l'examen d'un heretique, sur le discours de la loy salique, faussement pretendu contre la maison de France, et la branche de Bourbon (n.p., 1587).

Response a un ligueur masque du nom de catholique anglois. Par un vray Catholique bon François (Geneva, 1587).

Response a un livre de Belloy plein de faulsetez et calomnies, deguisé souz cet excellent, & beau titre de l'authorité du Roy (Paris, 1588).

Réponse aux Calomnies proposées contre les Catholiques (n.p., 1588).

Le Serment de la Saincte Union pour la conservation de la religion Catholique, & de l'Estat (n.p., 1588).

Le Tocsain, contre les massacreurs et auteurs de confusion en France (Rheims, 1577).

Traicte du Concile. En ce traite est demonstré qu'un Concile st très nécessaire & utile en ce temps (n.p., 1590).

La vie et condition des Politiques & Atheistes de ce temps. Avec un advertissement pour ce garder d'eux & de n'admettre indiffrement tous ceux qui s'offrirent au party de la saincte union (Paris, 1589).

2 Authored Primary Sources

Aimoin de Fleury. *Aimoinimona Monachi, qui antea annonii nomine editus est, Historiae Francorum Lib.V. Ex Veterib. Exemplaribus multos emendatiores. Cum indice copiosissimo, qui etiam locorum communium ac eiptomes vicem supplet* (Paris, 1567).

Allen, W. *Ad Persecutores Anglos Pro Catholicis Domi Forisque persecutionem sufferentibus; contra falsum, seditiosum, & contumeliosum Libellum, inscripturm; Iustitia Britannica. Veram sincera, & modesta Responsio* ... (Douai, 1584).

An Apologie and True Declaration of the Institution and Endevours of the Two English Colleges (Henault, 1581).

Almain, J. *Libellus de auctoritate ecclesiae* (Paris, 1512).

Acutissimi doctoris theologi magistri Jacobi Almain, ... Clarissima & admodum utilis expositio circa decisiones quaestionum M. Guillermi Ockam, super potestate summi pontifices (Paris, 1537).

Aquinas, T. *Summa Theologica ... Cum commentariis T. de Vio, Cardinalis Cajetani* (Padua, 1698).

Opusculum de Regimine Principum (nova editio, emendata), ed. F. Seguin (Avignon, 1853).

Summa Theologiae, 61 vols., ed. Blackfriars (London: Eyre & Spottiswoode, 1964–80).

Aquinas, T., Cajetan, C. *Angelici doctoris Sancti T. Aquinatis Summa Theologica. In quinque tomos distributa. Cum commentariis T. de Vio, Cardinalis Cajetani, et elucidationibus literalibus* (Padua, 1698).

Aristotle. *Politics*, trans. H. Sinclair (London: Penguin, repr. 1992).

Arnaud, A. *l'Anti Espagnol* (n.p., 1590).

La premiere philipique, à la France (n.p., 1592).

La seconde philipique, à la France (n.p., 1592).

d'Aubigné, A. *Histoire Universelle* (Maillé, 1616–20).

Tragiques (Maillé, 1616).

Augustine. *City of God*, trans. J. O'Meara (London: Penguin, repr. 1984).

Barclay, W. *De Regno et Regali Potestate adversus Buchanum, Brutum, Boucherium, & reliquos Monarchomachos, Libri Sex* (Paris, 1600).

De Potestate Papae: an & quatenus in Reges & Principes seculares ius & imperium habeat. Liber posthumous (London, 1609).

The Kingdom and the Regal Power, trans. George A. Moore (Chevy Chase, Md., Country Dollar Press [1954]).

Baricave, J. *La Défence de la monarchie françoise et autres monarchies contre les détestables et exécrables maximes d'état d'Estienne Junius Brutus et de Louis de Mayerne Turquet et leurs adhérans* (Toulouse, 1614).

Batterel, L. *Mémoires domestique pour servir à l'histoire de l'Oratoire* (Paris, 1903).

Bauduin, F. *Ad leges de famosis libellis et de calumniatoribus, commentarius* (Paris, 1562).

Commentarius de jurisprudentia muciana (Basle, 1558).

Delibatio africanæ historiæ ecclesiasticæ, sive Optati Milevitani libri VII. ad Parmenianum de schismate donatistarum. Victoris Uticensis libri III. de persecutione vandalica in Africa. Cum annotationibus ex Fr. Balduini j. c. commentariis rerum ecclesiasticarum (Paris, 1569).

Beauxamis, T. *Remonstrance au peuple françois, qu'il n'est permis à aucun subjet, sous pretexte que ce soit, se rebeller ne prendre les armes contre son Prince et Roy* (Paris, 1575).

Belleforest, F. de. *Des Grandes Annales et Histoires Generale de France, des la venue des Francs en Gaule, iusques au regne du Roy Tres-Chrestien Henry III* (Paris, 1579).

Belloy, P de. *Apologia Catholica ad famosos et seditiosos libellos coniuratrum qui, ab Alencon: regii fratris unici obitu, ad turbandam puelicam Regni Francici tranquillitatem, & Suevertendam regiae maiestatis dignitatem insurrexerunt, conscripta, & bono publico edita* (Paris, 1584).

A Catholicke Apologie against the libels, declarations, advices, and consultatios made, written, and published by those of the League, perturbers of the quiet Estate of the Realme of France. Who are risen since the decease of the late Monsieur, the Kings onely brother (London, 1585).

Apologie Catholique contre les libelles declarations, advis et consultations faictes, escrotes & publiees par les Liguez perturbateurs du repos du Royaume de France; qui se sont esleuz depuis les deces de seu Monseigneur, frère unique du Roy (n.p., 1585).

Examen du discours publié par ceux de la Ligue contre la Maison royalle de France (n.p., 1587).

Mémoires et recueil de l'origine, alliances, & succession de la royale famille de Bourbon, branche de la Maison de France . Ensemble, de l'histoire, gestes, & services plus mémorables, faictz par les Princes d'icelle, aux Rois, & Couronne de France (n.p., 1587).

Replicque faicte à la responce que ceux de la Ligue ont publiée contre l'examen qui avoit esté dressé sur leur précédent discours touchant la loy salique de France (n.p., 1587).

De l'authorité du Roy (n.p., 1587).

Panégyric et remonstrance pour les sénéchal, juge mage et criminel de Tolose contre les notaires et secretaries du roi de ladite ville (n.p., 1582).

Declaration du droit de legitime succession sur le royaume de Portugal (n.p., 1582).

Variorum juris civilis libri quatuor, item disputationes aliquot . . . de succes. ab intestat., de jur. pignor. vel marq., de compensat (n.p., 1583).

Moyens d'abus, enterprises et nullitez du rescrit et bulle du Pape Sixte V du nom, en date du mois de septembre 1585 . . . Contre Henri de Bourbon roy de Navarre, premier prince du sang* (n.p., 1586).

Recueil des édits de pacification des troubles esmeus au royaume de France pour le fait de religion (Paris, 1600).

Édict et déclaration du Roy Henry Quatriesme de France, et 3 de Navarre, sur l'union et incorporation de son ancien patrimoine mouvant de la Couronne de France au domaine d'icelle; avec l'arrest de la Court de Parlement de Tolose, sur la vériffication, publication et registre dudit édict, ensemble l'interprétation des causes d'iceluy, par Mr Maistre Pierre de Beloy (Toulouse, 1608).

Ordonnance de Messieurs les commissaires députez pour la recherche des francs-fiefs et nouveaux acquests au ressort du Parlement de Tolose, sur l'exemption requise par le sieur visconte de Tureine, en l'estendue dudit visconté, avec les conclusions sur ce princes par Monsieur Maistre Pierre de Belloy, conseiller et advocat général de Sa Majesté audit Parlement de Tolose (Toulouse, 1609).

Bellarmine, R. *Disputationes Roberti Bellarmini Politiani, Societatis Iesu, De Controversiis Christianae Fidei, Adversus huius temporis Haereticos, Tribus Tomis comprehensa. Ad S.D.N. Sixtum V. Pont. Max.* 3 vols. (Ingolstadt: Sartorius, 1590).

    Responsio ad Praecipua Capita Apologia. Quae falso Catholica inscribitur, pro successione Henrici Navarreni, in Francorum Regnum (n.p., 1591).

Benoist, R. *Ad Assertionem, seu famosum libellum, contra Clericos, praefertim Episcopos, qui participaverunt in divinis scienter & sponte, cum Henrico Valesio Rege, post Cardinalicidium responsio* (n.p., 1590).

    Exhortation Christienne aux fideles et esleue de Dieu, de batailler par tous moyens possibles pour le Grand Seigneur contre l'Antichrist (Paris, 1587).

Bernard, A., ed., *Procès-verbaux des États généraux de 1593* (Paris, 1842).

Blackwood, A. *Adversus Georgii Buchanani Dialogum, De Iure Regni Apud Scotos, Pro Regibus Apologia, qua regii nominis amplitudo, & imperii maiestas ab haereticorum famosis liellis, & perduellium iniuria vindicatur* (Paris, 1588).

Blaiseau, C. *Coppie du sermon prononcé en l'église cathédrale de Troyes, au retour de la procession générale, le dimanche trentiesme jour d'aoust mil cinq cens quatre vingts et sept* (Troyes, 1587).

Blythe, J. M., ed., *On the Government of Rulers: De Regimine Principum. Ptolomy of Lucca with Portions Attributed to Thomas Aquinas* (Pennsylvania: University of Pennsylvania Press, 1997).

[Breton, F. le.] *Remonstrance aux trois estats sur la publication & reception du Sainct Concile de Trente en France* (n.p., n.d.).

Brisson, B., ed., *Code du roy Henry III. Roy de France et de Pologne* (Paris, 1587).

Bodin, Jean. *Les Six Livres de la République* (Paris, 1576).

    De Republica Libri Sex (Lyon/Paris, 1586).

    Les Six Livres de la République/De republica libri sex: Livre premier/Liber I, ed. M. Turchetti, texte établi par Nicholas de Araujo, préface de Quentin Skinner (Paris: Classiques Garnier, 2013).

    Methodus de facilem historiarum cognitionem (1563), ed. and trans. S. Miglietti (Pisa: Scuola Normale Superiore Pisa, 2013).

    Lettre de Monsieur Bodin (Troyes, 1590).

    Recueil de tout ce qui s'est negotié en la compagnie du tiers estat de France (Paris, 1577).

Bonderoy, Jean de la Taille de [Jean de la Taille], *Histoire des singeries de la Ligue, contenant les folles propositions & frivoles actions usitees en faveur de l'authorité d'icelle, en la ville de Paris, depuis l'an 1590 jusques au 22 du mois de mars 1594* (n.p., 1596).

Bossuet, Jacques-Bénigne. *Defensio declarationis conventus cleri Gallicani an.1682 de ecclesiastica potestate*, 2 vols. (Mainz, 1745).

Histoire des variations des églises protestantes, *Œuvres complètes de Bossuet*, ed. F. Lachat, 31 vols. (Paris, 1863).

Botero, G. *Raison et Gouvernement d'Estat, en dix livre* (Paris, 1599).

Boucher, J. *Apologie pour Jehan Chastel, parisien, exécuté à mort, et pour les pères & escholliers, de la Société de Jésus, bannis du Royaume de France. Contre l'arrest de Parlement, donné contre eux à Paris, le 29. décembre, 1594. Divisée en cinq parties* (Paris, 1595)

Iesuita sicarius, hoc est Apologia pro Iohanne Castello, a Francisco de Verone (Lyon, 1611).

Sermons de la simulée conversion et nullite de la pretendue absolution de Henry de Bourbon, Prince de Bearn, a S. Denys en France, le Dimanche 25. juillet, 1593 (Paris, 1594).

De Justa Henrici Tertii Abdicatione e Francorum Regno (Paris, 1589).

Lettre Missive de L'Evesque du Mans. Avec la response d'icelle, faicte au mois de Septembre dernier passé, par un Docteur en Theologie de la faculté de Paris: en laquelle est respondu à ces deux doutes: A scavoir si on peut suivre en seureté de conscience la party du Roy de Navarre, & le recognoistre pour Roy . A scavoir si l'acte de Frere Iacques Clement Iacobin d'oit estre approuvé en conscience, & s'il est louable, ou non (Paris, 1589).

[Attrib.] *Response des docteurs de la faculte de Paris sur la question scavoir sil falloit prier pour le Roy au Canon de la Messe. A laquelle sont adioustes avec licence du superieur deux oraisons colliges pour la conservation des Princes Catholiques & pour obtenir victoire encontre les ennemys* (Paris, 1589).

Avis sur l'appel interjeté par Me Émond Richer, docteur et ci-devant syndic de la Faculté de théologie à Paris, de la censure de son livre intitulé: 'De ecclesiastica et politica potestate' (n.p., 1612).

Couronne mystique, ou Armes de piété contre toute sorte d'impiété, hérésie, athéisme, schisme, magie et mahométisme, par un signe ou hiéroglyphe mystérieux fait en forme de couronne (Tournay, 1623–4).

Conviction des fautes principalles tant contre la Religion chrestienne que contre la majesté du Roy tres chrestien trouvées en l'Épistre par laquelle le Sr Casaubon a desdié au Sereniss. Roy de la Grande Bretagne ses seize travaux contre les 'Annalles' du Rme cardinal Baronius, par Pompée de Ribémont, seigneur d'Espiney (Châlons, 1614).

Bouguereau, M. *Le Theatre Francois, où sont comprises les chartes generales et particulieres de la France* (Tours, 1593).

Buchanan, George. *A Dialogue on the Law of Kingship among the Scots*, eds. R. A. Mason, Martin S. Smith (Aldershot: Ashgate, 2004).

Opera Omnium, ed. Thomas Ruddiman. 2 vols. (Edinburgh, 1714–15).

Rerum Scoticarum Historia auctore Georgio Buchanano Scoto (Edinburgh, 1582).

Budé, G. *Annotationes . . . in Quatuor et Viginti Pandectarum Libros* (Venice, 1534)

Cappel, Guillaume. *Le Prince de Nicolas Machiavelle . . .; traduit d'italien en françois par Guillaume Cappel* (Paris, 1553).

Cajetan, T. de V. *Auctoritas papae et concilii sive ecclesiae comparata* (Rome, 1511).

Apologia de comparate auctoritate papae et concilii (Venice, 1514).

Castellion, S. *Conseil à la France Désolée* (n.p., 1562).

Cayet, P. *Chronologie novennaire, histoire des guerres de Henri IV de 1589 à 1598* (Paris, 1606).

Caumont, Jean de. *De l'union des Catholiques avec Dieu entre eux mesmes* (Paris, 1587).

Advertissement des advertissemens au peuple tres Chrestien (n.p., 1587).

Cecil, William, Allen, William. *The Execution of Justice in England by William Cecil and a True, Sincere, and Modest Defense of English Catholics by William Allen*, ed. R. M. Kingdon (New York: Cornell University Press, 1965).

Chasseneuz, B. de. *Commentaria . . . in consuetudines ducatus burgundiae* (n.p., 1517)

Choppin, R. *De Sacra Politia* (Paris, 1589).

De Domanio Franciae (Paris, 1574).

De Legibus Andium municipalibus (Paris, 1584).

De Civilibus Parisiorum moribus (Paris, 1596).

De Privilegiis Rusticorum (Paris, 1575).

Panegyricus (Paris, 1594).

Les Oeuvres de Me René Choppin: divisées en cinq tomes (Paris, 1663).

Clary, Francois de. *Philippiques contre les bulles, et autres pratiques de la faction d'Espagne* (Tours, 1592).

Corpus Iuris Canonici, ed. A. Friegberg, 2 vols. (Graz: Akademische Druck-u. Verlagsanstalt, 1959).

Cromé, F. *Dialogue d'entre le Maheustre et le Manant contenant leurs raisons de leur debats et questions en ses présens troubles au Royaume de France*, ed. P. M. Ascoli (Geneva: Droz, 1977).

Cunerus, P. *De Christiani Principis Officio* (Cologne, 1580).

The Digest of Justinian, eds. P. Kreuger, T. Mommsen, A. Watson. 4 vols. (Philadelphia: University of Pennsylvania Press, 1985)

Delamare, N. *Traité de la Police*, 4 vols. (Paris, 1705–38)

de Thou, J.-A. *Historiarum sui temporis . . .*, 3 vols. ([lieux divers] 1620).

Histoire universelle . . . traduite sur l'édition latine de Londres, 16 vols. (London, 1734)

Des Ursins, J-J, *Les écrits politiques de Jean Juvenal des Ursins*, 3 vols., ed. P. S. Lewis (Paris: Klincksieck 1978–92).

D'Oremet, J. *Responce contenant la Refutation et Solution des plus remarquable erreurs, & principales obiections des pretendu reformez, ver l'Eglise Catholique . . . .* (Paris, 1598).

Dorléans, L. *Advertissement des catholiques anglois aux françois catholiques de danger où ils sont de perdre leur religion et d'expérimenter, comme en Angleterre, la cruaté des ministres s'ils reçoivent à la couronne un roy qui soit héretique* (n.p., 1586).

Apologie ou defence des Catholiques unis les uns avec les autres, contre les impostures des Catholiques associez a ceux de le pretendue Religion (n.p., 1586).

Le Banquet et Apres Dinee du Conte d'Arete, ou il se traicte de la dissimulation du Roy de Navarre, & des moeurs de ses partisans (Paris, 1594).

Novae cogitations in libros annalium c. cornelii taciti qui extant. Ad Christianiss. Regem Francorum & Navarrorum Ludivocum XIII. Auctore Ludovico Dorleans Parisiensi. Quibus addita sunt reliqua eiusdem Taciti opera. Cum indicibus copiosissimis (Paris, 1622).

Plaidoyé des Gens du Roy Faict en Parlement en plaine audience, toutes les chambres assemblees le 22 Jour de Decembre Mil.V.C. Quatre Vingt Douze. Sur la Cassation d'un Pretendu Arrest Donné au Pretendu Parlement de Chalons le 18 Jour de Novembre auduct an (Paris, 1593).

La plante humaine. Sur le trespas du roy Henry le Grand. Où il se traicte du rapport des hommes avec les plantes qui vivent & meurent de mesme façon: et où se réfute ce qu'a escrit Turquet contre la Régence de la Royne & le Parlement, en son livre de la Monarchie aristodémocratique. A la Royne mère du roy Louys XIII (Paris, 1612).

Premier et second advertissement des catholiques anglois aux françois catholiques (Paris, 1590).

Remerciment au Roy (Paris, 1605).

[Attrib.] *Remonstrance aux Catholiques de tout les estats de France pour entre en l'association de la Ligue* (n.p., 1586).

Replique pour le catholique anglois contre le catholique anglois contre le catholique associé des Huguenots (n.p., 1588).

[Attrib.] *La Foy et Religion des Politiques de ce temps, contenant la refutation de leur heresies*, 2nd ed. (Paris, 1588).

Du Moulin, C. *Conseil sur le Faict du Concile de Trente, par messier Charles du Moulin, Docteur es droicts, professeur des sainctes letters, Iurisconsulte de France & Germanie, Conseiller, & Maistre des Requestes de l'Hotel de la Royne de Navarre* (Lyon, 1564).

Caroli Molinaei Franciae et Germaniae Celeberrimi Jurisconsulti, et in supremo parisiorum senatu antiqui advocati, omnia quae extant opera … Editio novissima quinque tomis distributa, auctior & emendatior. Horum seriem pagina sequens indicabit. Tomus Quintus (Paris, 1681).

Commentaire sur l'edit du roi Henri second contre les petites dates et abus de la cour de Romme (Lyon, 1554).

Du Bellay, Joachim. *Deffence et illustration de la langue française* (Paris, 1549).

Les Regrets et autres œuvres poetiques (Paris, 1590)

Du Vair, Guillaume du. *De la constance* (Paris, 1594).

De l'éloquence françoise, ed. René Radouant (Paris, 1907).

Dupuy, P. *Histoire du Différend d'entre le Pape Boniface VIII et Philippe le Bel, Roy de France* (Paris, 1655).

Dyson, R., ed., *Aquinas: Political Writings* (Cambridge: Cambridge University Press, 2002).

Édict du Roy sur la pacification des troubles de ce royaume (Troyes, 1576).

Epinac, P. d'. *Response de par Messieurs de Guyse à un advertissement* (n.p., 1585).

Advertissement de la part de Monseigneur le Reverendiss. Archevesque, Comte de Lyon, Primat des Gaules, au Clergé de son diocèse: Touchant la réduction des defuoyez & heretiques à la saincte Eglise Catholique

Apostolique Romaine. Avec la Confession de la foy, faicte par ordonance du S. Concile de Trente (Lyon, 1585).

Harengue prononcée devant le Roy, feant en ses Estatz généraux à Bloys, Par Reverened père en Dieu, Messire Pierre d'Epinac, Primat des Gaules, au nom de l'Estat Ecclesiastique de France (Lyon, 1577).

L'Estoile, P. de. *Mémoires-Journaux*, eds. G. Brunet et al., 12 vols. (Paris, 1875–96).

Les belles Figures et Drolleries de la Ligue avec les peintures Placcars et Affiches iniurieuses et diffamatoires contre la memoire et honneur du feu Roy que les Oisons de la Ligue apeloient Henri de Valois, imprimées, criées, preschées et vendues publiquement à Paris par tous les endroits et quarrefours de la Ville l'an 1589. Desquelles la garde (qui autrement n'est bonne que pour le feu) tesmoingnera à la Postérité la meschanceté, Vanité, Folie, et Imposture de ceste ligue infernale, et de combien nous sommes obligés à nostre bon Roi qui nous a délivrés de la Serviture et Tirannie de ce Monstre (n.d., n.p.)

Les Belles figures et drolleries de la Ligue, ed. G. Schrenck (Geneva: Droz, 2016).

Estienne, Henri. *Deux dialogues du nouveau langage françois italianisé* (Geneva, 1578).

Ferrault, J. *Tractatus, jura seu privilegia aliqua regni Franciae continens* (Paris, 1514).

Feuardent, F., *Sepmaine première des dialogues* (Paris, 1585).

Alphonsi a Castro, ... Opera omnia duobus tomis comprehensa ... Accessit Appendix ad libros contra haereses in tres libros distributa, quibus quadraginta ab eodem authore vel praetermissae vel ab ejus obitu natae et deprehensae refelluntur, authore F. Francisco Feuardentio (Paris, 1578).

Fregeville, J. *The Reformed Politicke. That is, an apologie for the generall cause of Reformation, written against the sclaunders of the Pope and the League. With most profitable advises for the appeasing of schisme, by abolishing superstition, and preserving the state of the Clergie. Whereto is adioyned a discourse upon the death of the Duke of Guise, prosecuting the argument of the book. Dedicated to the king by John Fregeville of Gaul* (London, 1589).

Fumo, B. *Summa Casuum Conscientiae aurea armilla nuncupata* (Venice, 1578).

Gay, J. *Histoire des Scismes et Heresies des Albigeois conforme à celle du présent: par laquelle appert que plusieurs grands princes, et seigneurs sont tombez en extrêmes désolations et ruynes, pour avoir favorisé aux hérétiques* (Paris, 1561).

Génébrard, G. *Chronologia Hebraeorum* (Paris, 1572).

De Clericis, Praesertim Episcopis, qui participarunt in divinis scienter et sponte cum Henrico Valesio post Cardinalicidium (Paris, 1589).

Excommunication des Ecclesiastiques, principalement des evesques, Abbez et Docteurs, qui ont asissté au divin service, sciemment & volontairement avec Henry de Valois, âpres le massacre du Cardinal de Guyse (Paris, 1589).

Histoire de Fl. Josephe (Paris, 1578).

Librorum Giberti Genebrardi Benedictini Theologi Parisiensis, Divinarum Hebraicarumque literarum professoris Regii Catalogus (Paris, 1591).

De Sacrorum Electionum Iure et Necessitate. Ad Ecclesiae Gallicanae redintegrationem (Paris, 1593).

Traicté de la liturgie, ou S.Messe; selon l'usage et forme des Apostres, & de leur disciple Sainct Denys, Apostre des François (Paris, 1592).

Gentillet, Innocent. *Discours sur les moyens de bien gouverner et maintenir en bonne paix un royaume ou autre principauté contre Nicolas Machiavel* (n.p., 1576).
Anti-Machiavel, Edition de 1576 avec commentaires et notes par C. Edward Rathé (Geneva: Droz, 1968).

Gerson, Jean. *Harangue faicte devant le roy Charles sixiesme et tout le conseil . . . faite par Maistre Jean Gerson de par l'Université de Paris* (Paris, 1588).
Oeuvres Complètes, ed. P. Glorieux, 10 vols. (Paris: Desclée et Cie, 1963–73).
Opera, ed. E. Richer, 4 vols. (Paris, 1606).
Opera Omnia, ed. L. E. du Pin, 5 vols. (Antwerp, 1706).

Giron, M. *Au Roy sur le sacre de sa Majesté: avec l'espistre synodale des prelates de l'Eglise de France assemblez en la ville d'Orléans: ensemble l'ordre du sacre de Henry IV, tres chrestien Roy de France et de Navarre* (Paris, 1594).

Goulart, S. *Mémoires de l'estat de France sous Charles neufiesme. Contenans les choses plus notable, faites & publiees tant par les Catholiques que par ceux de la Religion, depuis le troisieme edit de pacification fait au mois d'Aoust 1570, iusques au regne de Henry troisiesme* (Geneva, 1578).

Goulart, S. *Mémoires de la Ligue. Contenant les évenements les plus remarquables depuis 1576, jusqu'à la paix accordée entre le Roi de France et le Roi d'Espagne en 1598*, 6 vols. (Amsterdam, 1758).

Gousté, G. *Traicté de la puissance et authorité des Roys. Et par qui doyvent estre commandez les Diettes ou Conciles solonnels de l'Église* (n.p., 1561).

Grassaile, C. de. *Regalium Franciae libri duo* (Paris, 1538).

Guymier, C. *Caroli septimi Pragmatica sanctio a Cosma Guymier glossata* (Lyon, 1488).

Haillan, G. du. *De l'Estat et Succez des Affaires de France* (Paris, 1609).
De l'estat et succez des affaires de France (Paris, 1571).

Hayward, J. *An Answer to the First Part of a Certain Conference* (London, 1603).

l'Hôpital, M. de. *Oeuvres complètes de Michel de l'Hôpital*, ed. Pierre Duféy, 5 vols. (Paris, 1824–6).

Hotman, Antoine. [Attrib.] *Advertissement sur les lettres octroyés à M. le Cardinal de Bourbon* (n.p., 1588).
Lettres Patentes du Roy, Declaratives des Droicts, Privileges & Prerogatives de Monseigneur le Cardinal de Bourbon. Publiées en la cour de Parlement, le vingt-sixiesme jour d'Aoust, l'an 1588 (Paris, 1588).
[Attrib.] *Sur la déclaration du Roy pour les droits de prérogative du Monseigneur le Cardinal de Bourbon* (Paris, 1588).
Traicté des Libertez de l'Eglise Gallicane. Laquelle composition monster la pure & sincere intelligence de cez libertez [selon la ligue] (Paris, 1608).
[Attrib.] *Sur la declaration du Roy pour les droits de prerogative de Monsieur le Cardinal de Bourbon* (Paris, 1588).
[Attrib.] *Advertissement sur les letters octroyess a M. le Cardinal de Bourbon* (n.p., 1588).

Hotman, François. *Brutum fulmen Papae Sixti V. aduersus Henricum Sereniss. Regem Nauarrae & illustrissimum Henricum Borbonium, Principem Condaeum . . .* (Rome, 1585).

The Brutish Thunderbolt: Or Rather Feeble Fier-Flash of Pope Sixtus the Fift (London, 1586).

Disputatio de controversia successionis regiae inter partuum et fratris praemortui filium (n.p., 1585).

Francogallia (Frankfurt, 1586).

Francogallia. Latin text R. E. Giesey, trans. J. H. M Salmon (Cambridge: Cambridge University Press, 1972).

Francogallia Editio tertia locupletior (Cologne, 1576).

De Jure successionis regiae in regno Francorum (n.p., 1588).

Ad Tractatum Matthaei Zampini I.C. (n.p., 1589).

Hotman, F., Hotman, J. *Hotomanorum et clarorum virorum ad eos epistolae* (Amsterdam, 1700).

Ivo of Chartres, *Iuonis episcopi Carnotensis epistolæ. Eiusdem chronicon de regibus Francorum* (Paris, 1585).

Knox, T. F. *The First and Second Diaries of the English College, Douay, and an Appendix of Unpublished Documents, edited by fathers of the congregation of the London Oratory, with an Historical Introduction by Thomas Francis Knox, D. D., priest of the same congregation* (London, 1878).

The Letters and Memorials of William Cardinal Allen (1532–1594) (London, 1882).

Le Caron, Louis. *De la tranquillité de l'esprit* (Paris, 1588).

De l'obeissance deue au Prince. Pour faire cesser les armes, et restablir la Paix en ce Royaume. Au Roy (Caen, 1590).

La Claire, ou de la prudence de droit (Paris, 1554).

Pandectes ou Digestes du droict françois (Paris, 1587).

La Philosophie (Paris, 1555).

Le Roy, Louis. *De l'excellence du gouvernement royale* (Paris, 1575).

De l'origine, antiquité, progrès, excellence et utilité de l'art politique (Lyon, 1568).

Les Politiques d'Aristote (Paris, 1599).

Des troubles et differens advenans entre les hommes par la diversité des religions. Ensemble du commencement, progrez, & excellence de la chrestienne (Lyon, 1566).

Lipsius, J. *De Constantia. Libri duo qui alloquium præcipue continent in publicis malis* (Antwerp, 1584).

Loisel, A. *Amnestie ou De l'oubliance des maux faicts et receus pendant les troubles et a l'occasion d'iceux* (Paris, 1595).

Lorraine, C. de. *Plaintes et Doleances du Prince de Joinville fils de tres-haut, & trespuissant, feu Henry de Lorraine, Duc de Guyse. Envoyes aux villes Catholiques de France* (n.p., 1589).

Declaration faicte par Monseigneur le Duc de Mayenne Lieutenant general de l'Estat & Couronne de France, pour la Reunion de tous les Catholiques de ce Royaume (Paris, 1593).

Maillard, A. de. *Apologie de Maistre André Maillart Conseiller du Roy & maistre des Requestes ordinaires de sa Maiesté* (n.p., 1588).

Advertissement au roy de Navarre de se réunir avec le Roy et à la foy catholique (n. p., 1585)

Machiavelli, N. *Discourses on Livy*, ed. and trans. J. Conaway Bondanell, P. Bondanella (Oxford: Oxford University Press, repr. 2003).

The Prince (London: Penguin, 1999).

Maimbourg, L. *The History of the League*, trans. John Dryden (London, 1684).

Maingoua, J. *La Ligue renversée, ou réponse à 'La Ligue ressuscitée'* (n.p., 1615/1616).

Mariana, Juan de. *De Rege et Regis Institutione* (n.p., 1605).

Marsilius of Padua, *The Defender of the Peace*, ed. and trans. A. Brett (Cambridge: Cambridge University Press, 2005).

Masson, P. *Responsio ad maledicta Hotomani cognomento Matagonis* (Paris, 1575).

Matherel, A. *Ad Franc. Hotomani Franco-Galliam Antonii Matherellii . . . responsio* (Paris, 1575).

Matthieu, Pierre. *Histoire des derniers troubles de France sous les règnes de Henry III . . ., et Henry IV . . . contenant ce qui s'est passé depuis les premiers mouvements de la Ligue jusques à la closture des Estats de Blois, le seizième de janvier 1589* (Lyon, 1597).

Ménage, G. *Vitae Petri Aerodii* (Paris, 1675).

Meulen, Jan van der [Molanus]. *De Fide Haereticis Servanda* (Cologne, 1584).

Montalboddo, F. de. *Paesi novamente ritrovati* (Milan, 1507).

Montgaillard, B. *Response de Dom Bernard, doyen de l'oratoire de S. Bernard des Feuillantins les Paris, à un lettre à luy escrite & envoyee par Henry de Valois* (Paris, 1589).

Montaigne, Michel de. *The Complete Works*, trans. D.M. Frame (London: Everyman, 2003).

Montaigne, Les Essais. Édition de 1595, eds. J. Balsamo et al. (Paris: Gallimard, 2007).

Mornay, P. Duplessis *Mémoires et Correspondance de Duplessis-Mornay: pour servir à l'histoire de la réformation et des guerres civiles et religieuses en France, sous les règnes de Charles IX, de Henri III, de Henri IV et de Louis XIII, depuis l'an 1571 jusqu'en 1623*, eds. Fontenelle de Vaudoré et al., 12 vols. (Paris, 1824–5).

[Attrib.], *Lettre d'un gentilhomme Catholique François, contenant brève response aux calomnies d'un certain prétendu Anglois* (n.p, 1586).

Morton, T. *Exact Discoverie of Romish Doctrine in the Case of Conspiracie and Rebellion* (London, 1605).

Noue, François de la. *Discours Politiques et militaires du seigneur de La Noue* (Basle, 1586).

Owen, D. *Herod & Pilate reconciled: or, the concord of Papist and Puritan (against cripture, fathers, councels and other orthodoxall writers) for the coercion, deposition, and killing of kings* (Cambridge, 1610).

Optatus, *De schismate Donatistarum* (Paris, 1563).

Pasquier, E. *Ecrits Politiques*, ed. D. Thickett (Geneva: Droz, 1966)

Lettres historiques pour les années 1556–1594, ed. D. Thickett (Geneva: Droz, 1966)

Des Recherches de la France Livre premier. Plus, un pourparler du Prince (Paris, 1560).

Recherches de la France, 3 vols., eds. M-M Fragonard, F. Roudaut (Paris: Honoré Champion, 1996)

Persons, R. *A Conference on the next succession to the crowne of Ingland, divided into two partes* (n.p., 1594).

A Briefe Apologie, or Defence of the Catholike Ecclesiastical Hiererarchie, & subordination in England, erected, these later yeares by our holy Father Pope Clement the eyght; and impugned by certayne libels printed & published of late both in Latyn & English; by some unquiet persons under the name of Priests of the Seminaries. Written and set forth for the true information and stay of all good Catholikes, by Priests united in due subordination to the Right Reverend Archpriest, and other their Superiors (n.p., 1601).

Epistre de la persecution meue en Angleterre contre l'Eglise chrestienne, catholic et apostolique, et fidelles membres d'icelle, trans. Matthieu de Launoy (Paris, 1586)

The Judgement of a Catholicke Englishman, living in banishment for his religion: written to his private friend in England. Concerning a late Booke, set forth, and entituled, Triplici nodo, triplex cuneus, or An Apologie for the Oath of Allegiance. Against two breves of Pope Paulus V to the Catholickes of England; & a Letter of Cardinall Bellarmine to M. George Blackwell Arch-priest. Wherein the said oath is shewed to be unlawfull unto a Catholicke Conscience; for so much as it conteyneth sundry clauses repugnant to his Religion (n.p., 1608)

Treatise Tending to Mitigation towards Catholicke Subjectes in England (Saint-Omer, 1607).

Pithou, P. *Les Libertez de l'Eglise Gallicane* (Paris, 1594).

Porthaise, Jean. *Chrestienne Declaration de L'Eglise, et de L'Eucharistie, en forme de response, a livre nommé la cheute & ruine de l'Eglise Romaine* (n.p., 1567).

Cinq Sermons du R.P.F.I. Porthaise de l'ordre St Francois, Theologal de l'Eglise de Poictiers, par luy prononcez en icelle. Esquels traicté tant de la simulee conversion du Roy de Navarre, que de droict de l'absolution Ecclesiastique, & d'autres matieres propres a ce temps, declarez en la quatriesme page (Paris, 1594).

Rossaeus, G. '*De Justa Reipublicae Christianae in Reges Impios et Haereticos authoritate: Iustissimaque Catholicorum ad Henricum Navarraeum & quemcunque haereticum a regno Galliae repellendum confoederatione* (Paris, 1590).

De Justa Reipublicae Christianae in Reges Impios et Haereticos authoritate: Iustissimaque Catholicorum ad Henricum Navarraeum & quemcunque haereticum a regno Galliae repellendum confoederatione (Antwerp, 1592).

Rubis, C. *Discours sur la contagion de peste qui a este ceste present annee en la ville de Lyon. Contenant les causes d'icelle, l'ordre, moyen & police tenue pour en purger, nettoyer & delivrer la ville* (Lyon, 1577).

Response à l'Anti Espagnol (Lyon, 1590).

Sâ, Manuel de. *Les Aphorismes des confesseurs* (Paris, 1601).

Saconay, Gabriel de. *Aphorismi confessariorum* (Paris, 1609).

De la Providence de Dieu sur les Roys de France Tres Chrestiens, par laquelle sa saincte religion catholique ne defaudra en leur royaume. Et comme les Gotz Ariens, et les Albigeois, en ont esté par icelle dechassés (Lyon, 1568).

Salisbury, John of. *Policraticus*, trans. and ed. C. J. Nederman (Cambridge: Cambridge University Press, 1990)

Satyre Menippee de la vertu du Catholicon d'Espagne et de la tenue des Etats de Paris, ed. M. Martin (Paris: Honoré Champion, 2007).

Savoie, Charles-Emmanuel de. *Les chimeres monarchiques de la Ligue: instructions données en 1593 par le duc de Nemours au baron de Tenissé* (n.p., 1595).

Seyssel, C. *La grant monarchie de France composee par missire Claude de Seyssel lois(?) evesque de Marseille et a present Archevesque de Thurin adressant au roy treschrestien francoys premier de ce nom* (Paris, 1519).

The Monarchy of France, trans. J. H. Hexter, ed. D. R. Kelley (Yale: Yale University Press, 1981).

Sheldon, R. *Certain general reasons, proving the lawfulness of the oath of allegiance . . . whereunto is added, the treatise of that learned man, M. William Barclay, concerning the temporall power of the Pope. And with these is joined the sermon of M. Theophilus Higgons, preached at Pauls Crosse the third of March last, because it containeth something of like argument* (London, 1611).

Silvestro, M. *Summa Summarum* (Antwerp, 1581).

Sorbin, A. *Histoire de la ligue saincte, faicte il y a CCCLXXX. ans, a la conduite de Simon de Mont-fort, contre les heretiques Albigeois tenans les pays de Bearn, Languedoc, Gascongne, & quelque partie de Guienne & Dauphiné* (Paris, 1585).

Le Vrai réveil-matin pour la deffense de la majesté de Charles IX (n.p., 1574).

Le vray resveil-matin des calvinistes et publicains françois, où est amplement discouru de l'autorité des Princes et du devoir des sujets envers iceux (Paris, 1575; 1576).

Soto, Domingo de. *De Justitia et Jure* (Lyon, 1569).

Saint-Julien, P. de. *Discours par lequel il appareistra que le royaume de France est electif et non hereditaire* (Lyon, 1591).

De l'origine des bourgognons, et antiquité des estats de Bourgogne (Paris, 1581).

Stephanus, H. *Princeps Monitrix Musa, sive de Principatu bene instituendo & administrando* (Basle, 1590)

Sutcliffe, M. *A New Challenge Made to N.D* (London, 1600).

De Turco-Papismo (London, 1599).

Tillet, Jean du. *Sommaire de l'Histoire de la Guerre faicte contre les Heretiques Albigeois, extraicte du Tresor des Chartres du Roy par seu Jehan du Tillet* (Paris, 1590).

Toledo, Francisco de. *Summa Casuum Conscientiae sive de Instructione Sacerdotum.* Lyon, 1599.

Summa Casuum Conscientiae sive De Instructione Sacerdotum (Cologne, 1601).

In Summam Theologiae S. Th. Aquinatis Enarratio, ex autobiographo in Bibl. Coll. Rom., 2 vols., ed. José Paria (Rome, 1869).

Viguier, N. *Traicté de l'estat et origine des anciens François* (Troyes, 1582).

Vindiciae, Contra Tyrannos, trans. and ed. G. Garnett (Cambridge: Cambridge University Press, 1997).

Vitoria, Francisco de. *Political Writings,* ed. and trans. A. Pagden, J. Lawrence (Cambridge: Cambridge University Press, 1991).

Relectiones Theologicae in Duos Tomos Divisae (Lyon, 1557).

Winzet, N. *Velitatio in Georgium Buchananum circa dialogum, quem scripsit de iure regni apud Scotos* (Ingolstadt, 1582).

Zampini, M. *Ad Calumnias et Imposturam a Pseudo-Parliamentis, Cathalaunensi, & Turonensi, ac Carnotensi, Conventiculo, ad Catholicae Religionis perniciem, Populique deceptionem, impie confictas in GREGORIUM xiiii. Illiusque monitionis literas, ad Clerum, Principes, Nobiles, & Populos Franciae. Responsio Matthaei Zampini* (Lyon, 1591).

De la succession du droict et prerogative de premier Prince du sang de France, déférée par la loy du Royaume, à Monseigneur Charles Cardinal de Bourbon, par le mort de Monseigneur François de Valois Duc d'Anjou (Lyon, 1589).

Des Etats de France, et de leur puissance (Paris, 1588).

De Origine, et atavis Hugonis Capeti, Illorumque cum Carolo Magno, Clodoveo, atque antiquis Francorum Regibus, Agnatione, & Gente (Paris, 1581).

De Statibus Franciae, illorumque potestate, epitome (Paris, 1578).

Secondary Sources

Abadia, L. *Henri IV et la reconstruction du royaume* (Pau: Centre départemental de documentation pédagogique, 1989).

Association Henri IV 1989, *Henri IV, le roi et la reconstruction du royaume. Volumes des actes du colloque Pau-Nérac* (Pau: J & D Éditions, 1990).

Allen, J. W. *A History of Political Thought in the Sixteenth Century* (London: Methuen and Co., 1960.)

Amalou, T. *Le Lys et la Mitre; Loyalisme monarchique et pouvoir épiscopal pendant les guerres de Religion (1580–1610)* (Paris: Éditions du Comité des travaux historiques et scientifiques, 2007).

Une Concorde Urbaine. Senlis au temps des réformes (vers 1520–vers 1580) (Limoges: Pulim, 2007).

'Entre réforme du royaume et enjeux dynastiques. Le Magistère intellectuel et moral de l'Université de Paris au sein de la Ligue (1576–1594)', *Cahiers de Recherches Médiévales*, 15, 2008.

Les universités dans la ville XVIe-XVIIIe siècle (Rennes: Presses Universitaires de Rennes, 2013).

'Une Sorbonne régicide? autorité, zèle et doctrine de la faculté de théologie de Paris pendant la ligue (1588–1593)', in Julia, D. et al., eds., *Les universités en Europe (1450–1814)* (Paris: Presses de l'université Paris-Sorbonne, 2013).

'Deux frères ennemis, deux sensibilités catholiques: les prédications de René Benoist et de Gilbert Génébrard à Paris pendant la Ligue (1591–1592)', in. J. Bouvignies, F. Gabriel, M.Penzi, eds., *La période des Guerres de Religion: historiographie et histoire des idées politiques* (Lyon: École normale supérieure éditions, forthcoming).

Anglo, S. *Machiavelli – The First Century: Studies in Enthusiasm, Hostility and Irrelevance* (Oxford: Oxford University Press, 2005).

Anquetil, L-P. *L'Esprit de la Ligue* (Paris, 1770).

Archives de Bretagne. *Recueil d'actes, de chroniques, et de documents historiques rares ou inédits. Publié par la Société des Bibliophiles Bretons et de l'histoire de Bretagne. Tome xi, Documents sur la Ligue en Bretagne. Correspondqnce du Duc de Mercoeur et des Ligeurs Bretons avec l'Espagne* (Nantes, 1899).

Armstrong, E. *The French Wars of Religion: Their Political Aspects* (Oxford: Blackwell, 1904).

Armstrong, M. C. *The Politics of Piety: Franciscan Preachers during the Wars of Religion, 1560–1600* (Rochester, NY: University of Rochester Press, 2004).

Arquillière, Henri-Xavier. *l'augustinisme politique: Essai sure la formation des théories politiques du Moyen Âge* (Paris: J. Vrin, 1955).

Arabeyre, P., Basdevant-Gaudemet, B., eds., *Les Clercs et les Princes* (Paris: l'École Nationale des Chartes, 2013).

Ascoli, P. 'A Radical Pamphlet of Late Sixteenth Century France: Le Dialogue de'Entre Le Maheustre et le Manent', *Sixteenth Century Journal*, 5, 2 (Oct. 1974): 3–22.

'French Provincial Cities and the Catholic League', *Occasional Papers of the American Society for Reformation Research*, I (1977): 15–40.

Baird Smith, D. 'William Barclay', *Scottish Historical Review*, 11 (1913–14): 136–63.

Le Bachelet, Xavier-Marie. *Bellarmin avant son Cardinalat* (Paris: Gabriel Beauchesne, 1911).

Bakos, A., ed., *Politics, Ideology and the Law in Early Modern Europe: Essays in Honor of J. H. M. Salmon* (Rochester, NY: University of Rochester Press, 1994).

Baranova, T. D. *À Coups de Libelles. Une culture politique au temps des guerres de religion (1562–1598)* (Geneva: Droz, 2012).

Barbier-Mueller, Jean Paul. 'Pour une chronologie des premières éditions de la Satyre Ménippée (1593–1594)', *Bibliothèque d'Humanisme et Renaissance*, 67, 2 (2005): 373–93.

Barnavi, E. 'Centralisation ou fédéralisme? Les relations entre Paris et les villes à l'époque de la Ligue (1585–1594)', *Revue Historique*, 259 (1978): 335–44.

'La Ligue Parisienne (1585–1594): Ancetre des parties totalitaires modernes?' *French Historical Studies* (1979): 29–57.

Le parti de Dieu, Étude sociale et politique des chefs de la Ligue parisienne, 1585–1594 (Louvain: Nauwelaerts, 1980).

Barnavi, E., Descimon, R. *La Sainte Ligue, le juge et le potence* (Paris: Hachette, 1985).

Barnes, A. 'The Wars of Religion and the Origins of Reformed Confraternities of Penitents: A Theoretical Approach', *Archives de Sciences Sociales des Religions*, 63 (1987), 117–36.

'Religious Anxiety and Devotional Change in Sixteenth-Century French Penitential Confraternities', *Sixteenth Century Journal*, 19 (1988): 389–405.

Battista, Anna Maria, 'Direzioni di ricerca per una storia di Machiavelli in Francia', in *Atti del convegno internazionale su il pensiero politico di Machiavelli e la sua fortuna nel mondo* (Florence: Istituto nazionale di studi sul Rinascimento, 1972), 37–66

Baumgartner, F. J. *Radical Reactionaries: The Political Thought of the French Catholic League* (Geneva: Droz, 1976).

Beame, Edmond M. 'The Use and Abuse of Machiavelli: The Sixteenth-Century French Adaptation', *Journal of the History of Ideas*, 43, 1 (1982): 33–54.

'The *Politiques* and the Historians' *Journal of the History of Ideas*, 54, 3 (1993): 355–79.

Beaune, C. 'Saint Clovis: histoire, religion et sentiment national en France à la fin du Moyen Âge', in B. Guénée, ed., *Le Métier d'historien au Moyen Âge* (Paris: Publications de la Sorbonne, 1977), 139–56.

Naissance de la Nation France (Paris: Gallimard, 1985).

'Clovis dans les grandes chroniques de France', in Michel Rouche, ed., *Clovis: Histoire & Mémoire. le Baptême de Clovis, son Écho à Travers l'Histoire*, 2 vols. (Paris: Presses de l'université de Paris-Sorbonne, 1997), 191–212.

Becker, A. 'Jean Bodin on Oeconomics and Politics', *History of European Ideas*, (2014): 135–54.

Bell, D. A. 'Unmasking a King: The Political Uses of Popular Literature under the French Catholic League, 1588–9', *Sixteenth Century Journal*, 20, 3 (Autumn 1989): 371–86.

The Cult of the Nation in France: Inventing Nationalism, 1680–1800 (Cambridge MA: Harvard University Press, 2003).

Benedict, P. *Rouen during the Wars of Religion* (Cambridge: Cambridge University Press, 1981).

Benedict, P., Daussy, H., Léchot, P-O., eds., *L'Identité huguenote. Faire mémoire et écrire l'histoire (XVIe-XXIe siècle)* (Geneva: Droz, 2014).

Benton, L. *A Search for Sovereignty: Law and Geography in European Empires, 1400–1900* (Cambridge: Cambridge University Press, 2009).

Bergin, J. *The Making of the French Episcopate, 1589–1661* (New Haven; London: Yale University Press, 1996).

Church, Society and Religious Change in France, 1580–1730 (New Haven; London: Yale University Press, 2009).

The Politics of Religion in Early Modern France (Yale: Yale University Press, 2014).

Bernstein, H. *Between Crown and Community: Politics and Culture in Sixteenth Century Poitiers* (Ithaca: Cornell University Press, 2004).

Berthold, J, Fragonard, M-M., eds., *La Mémoire des Guerres de Religion. La concurrence des genres historiques (xvie- xviiie siècles)* (Geneva: Droz, 2007).

Birely, R. *The Counter-Reformation Prince: Anti-Machiavellianism or Catholic Statecraft in Early Modern Europe* (London/Chapel Hill: University of North Carolina Press, 1990).

Blair, A. *The Theater of Nature: Jean Bodin and Renaissance Science* (Princeton: Princeton University Press, 1997).

Blum, A. *l'Estampe satirique en France pendant les Guerres de Religion* (Paris: M. Giard et E. Brière, 1916).

Bock, G., Skinner, Q., Viroli, M., eds. *Machiavelli and Republicanism* (Cambridge: Cambridge University Press, 1990).

Bontems, C., Raybaud, L-P., Brancourt, J-P. *Le Prince dans le France des XVIᵉ et XVIIᵉ siècles* (Paris: Presses universitaire de France, 1965).

Bossy, J. *The English Catholic Community 1570–1850* (London: Darton, Longman and Todd, 1975).

Boüard, M. de. 'Sixte Quint, Henri IV et la Ligue: la légation du cardinal Caetani en France 1589–1590', *Revue des questions historiques*, 60 (1932), 59–140.

Boucher, J. 'Culture des notables et mentalité populaire dans la propaganda qui entraîna la chute de Henri III', in J. Nicolas, ed., *Mouvements populaires et conscience sociale, XVIe-XIXe siècles* (Paris: Maloine, 1985).

Société et mentalités autour de Henri III (Paris: Classiques Garnier, 2006).

Boulet-Sautel, M. 'Police et administration en France à la fin de l'ancien régime. Observations terminologiques', in W. Paravicini, K. F. Werner, eds., *Histoire comparée de l'administration (IVe-XVIIIe siècles). Actes du XIVe colloque historique franco-allemand (Tours, 27 mars- 1er avril 1977)* (Munich: Artemis Verlag, 1980).

Bourke, R., Skinner, Q., eds. *Popular Sovereignty in Historical Perspective* (Cambridge: Cambridge University Press, 2016).

Boutcher, W. *The School of Montaigne*, 2 vols. (Oxford: Oxford University Press, 2017).

Bouvignies, I. 'Monarchomaquie: tyrannicide ou droit de résistance ?', in Nicolas Piquet, Ghislain Waterlot, eds., *Tolérance et réforme, éléments pour une généalogie du concept de résistance* (Paris: Montréal, 1999), 105–38.

Bouwsma, W. 'Gallicanism and the Nature of Christendom', in A. Molho, J. A. Tedeschi, eds., *Renaissance Studies in Honor of Hans Baron* (Florence: G.C. Sansoni, 1971), 809–30.

'The Two Faces of Humanism: Stoicism and Augustinianism in Renaissance thought', in H. A. Oberman, T. A. Brady, eds., *Itinerarium Italicum: The profile of the Italian Renaissance in the Mirror of Its European Transformation* (Leiden: Brill, 1975), 3–60.

Bowden, C. Kelly, J. E., eds. *The English Convents in Exile, 1600–1800. Communities, Culture and Identity* (London: Routledge, 2013).

Braudel, B. *l'Identité de la France*, 2 vols. (Paris: Flammarion, 1986).

Brett, A. *Liberty, Right and Nature: Individual Rights in Later Scholastic Thought* (Cambridge: Cambridge University Press, 1997).

'Individual & Community in the "Second Scholastic": Subjective Rights in Domingo de Soto & Francisco Suarez', in C. Blackwell, S. Kusukawa, eds., *Philosophy in the Sixteenth and Seventeenth Centuries: Conversations with Aristotle* (Aldershot: Ashgate, 1999), 146–68.

'Authority, Reason and the Self-Definition of Theologians in the Spanish "Second Scholastic"', in G. H. Tucker, ed., *Forms of the 'Medieval' in the 'Renaissance'* (Charlottesville: Rockwood, 2000), 63–90.

'What Is Intellectual History Now?', in D. Cannadine, ed., *What Is History Now?* (Basingstoke: Palgrave, 2002), 113–31.

'Scholastic Political Thought and the Modern Concept of the State', in A. Brett, J. Tully, eds., *Rethinking the Foundations of Modern Political Thought* (Cambridge: Cambridge University Press, 2006), 130–48

'Harro Höpfl, Jesuit Political Thought: The Society of Jesus and the State, c. 1540–1630, Ideas in Context 70', in *History of Political Thought*, 28, 1 (2007): 183–5.

Changes of State. Nature and the Limits of the City in Early Modern Natural Law (Princeton: Princeton University Press, 2011).

'Later Scholastic Philosophy of Law', in F. Miller, C-A Biondi, eds., *A History of the Philosophy of Law from the Ancient Greeks to the Scholastics*, 2nd ed., (Dordrecht: Springer 2015), 335–76.

Brett, A., Tully, J., eds. *Rethinking the Foundations of Modern Political Thought* (Cambridge: Cambridge University Press, 2006).

Brosse, O. de La. *Latran V et Trente* (Paris: Éditions de l'Orante, 1975).

Brunet, S. "'Confréries ligueuses, confréries dangereuses": Fraternités de combat dans le Sud-Ouest de la France durant les guerres de Religion', in M. Venard and J. Dominique, eds., *Sacralités, culture et devotion: Bouquet offert à Marie-Hélène Froesché-Chopard* (Marseilles: La Thune, 2005): 129–70.

'De l'Espagnol dedans le ventre!' Les catholiques du Sud-Ouest de la France face à la Réforme (vers 1540–1589) (Paris: Honoré Champion, 2007).

ed., *La Sainte Union des catholiques de France et la fin des guerres de Religion (1585–1629)* (Paris: Classiques Garnier, 2016).

Burns, J. H., ed., *The Cambridge History of Medieval Political Thought, c. 350–c. 1450* (Cambridge: Cambridge University Press, 1988).

The Cambridge History of Political Thought 1450–1700 (Cambridge: Cambridge University Press, 1991).

'Scholasticism: Survival and Revival', in *The Cambridge History of Political Thought 1450–1700* (Cambridge: Cambridge University Press, 1991), 132–58.

'George Buchanan and the Anti-Monarchomachs', in N.T. Phillipson, Q. Skinner, eds., *Political Discourse in Early Modern Britain* (Cambridge: Cambridge University Press, 1993), 3–22.

The True Law of Kingship: Concepts of Monarchy in Early Modern Scotland (Oxford: Oxford University Press, 1996).

Conciliarism and Papalism, with T. M. Izbicki, ed. (Cambridge: Cambridge University Press, 1997).

Cameron, K. *A Maligned or Malignant King?: Aspects of the Satirical Iconography of Henry III* (Exeter: University of Exeter Press, 1976).

ed., *From Valois to Bourbon. Dynasty, State and Society in Early Modern France* (Exeter: University of Exeter Press, 1989).

Cameron, K., Greengrass, M., Roberts, P., eds. *The Adventure of Religious Pluralism in Early Modern France, Papers from the Exeter Conference, April 1999* (Oxford-Berne: Peter Lang, 2000).

Canning, J. *Ideas of Power in the Late Middle Ages, 1296–1417* (Cambridge: Cambridge University Press, 2011).

Cardascia, Guillaume., 'Machiavel et Jean Bodin.' *Bibliothèque d'Humanisme et Renaissance* 3 (1943): 129–67.

Cardon, G. *La Fondation de l'université de Douai* (Paris, 1892).

Caroll, S. 'The Guise Affinity and Popular Protest during the Wars of Religion', *French History* (1995), 9 (20): 125–52.

Carrafiello, M. L. *Robert Parsons and English Catholicism, 1580–1610* (London: Associated University Presses, 1998).

Castor, Grahame, Cave, Terence. *Neo-Latin and the Vernacular in Renaissance France* (Oxford: Clarendon Press, 1984).

Cardon, G. *La fondation de l'université de Douai, Thèse présentée à la faculté des lettres de Paris* (Paris, 1892).

Carpi, O. *Une République Imaginaire: Amiens pendant les troubles de religion (1559–1597)* (Paris: Éditions Belin, 2005).

Carter, C. H., ed., *From the Renaissance to the Counter-Reformation, Essays in Honour of Garrett Mattingly* (London: Jonathan Cape, 1966).

Chanteur, J. 'La loi naturelle et la souveraineté chez Jean Bodin', in *Théologie et Droit dans lq science politique de l'état moderne. Actes de la table ronde organisée par l'école française de Rome avec le concours du CNRS* (Rome: École Française de Rome, 1991), 283–94.

Chartier, R. *The Cultural Uses of Print in Early Modern France*, trans. L. G. Cochrane (Princeton: Princeton University Press, 1987).

Chérel, Albert. *La Pensée de Machiavel en France* (Paris: l'Artisan du Livre, 1935).

Christin, O. *La paix de religion. L'autonomisation de la raison politique au xvie siècle* (Paris: Seuil, 1997).

Church, W. F. *Constitutional Thought in Sixteenth-Century France* (Cambridge, MA: Harvard University Press, 1941).

Clancy, T. H. *Papist Pamphleteers. The Allen-Persons Party and the Political Thought of the Counter-Reformation in England, 1572–1615* (Chicago: Loyola University Press, 1964).

Claussen, E. 'Vilain et deshonneste': Anti-*Politique* Polemic at the End of the Wars of Religion, *Early Modern French Studies*, 39:2 (2017): 157–68.

    Politics and Politiques in Sixteenth-Century France: A Conceptual History (Cambridge: Cambridge University Press, forthcoming).

Clancy, T. H. *Papist Pamphleteers. The Allen-Persons Party and the Political Thought of the Counter-Reformation in England, 1572–1615* (Chicago: Loyola University Press, 1964).

Collins, J. B. *The State in Early Modern France* (Cambridge: Cambridge University Press, 1995).

    'La guerre de la ligue et le bien public', in J.-F. Labourdette, ed., *Le Traité de Vervins* (Paris: Presses de l'Université de Paris-Sorbonne, 2000), 81–96.

    The State in Early Modern France, 2nd ed. (Cambridge: Cambridge University Press, 2009).

La monarchie republicaine: État et société dans la France moderne (Paris: Odile Jacob, 2016).

'Jacques Clément et Jean Chastel, assassins de la "Respublicque françoise"', in I. Pébay-Clottes et al., eds., *Régicides en France et en Europe (xvie-xixe siècles)* (Geneva: 2017), 95–112.

Collot, C. *l'école doctrinale de droit public de Pont à Mousson* (Paris: Librairie générale de droit et de jurisprudence, 1965).

'La réponse de Pierre Grégoire professeur et doyen en l'université de Pont-à-Mousson au conseil donné par Dumoulin sur la dissuasion de la réception du concile de Trente en France', in *L'université de Pont à Mousson et les problèmes de son temps. Actes du colloque organisé par l'Institut de recherche régionale en sciences sociales, humaines et économiques de l'Université de Nancy II* (Nancy 16–19 October 1972) (Nancy: Université de Nancy, 1974), 101–20.

Condren, C. *Argument and Authority in Early Modern England. The Presupposition of Oaths and Offices* (Cambridge: Cambridge University Press, 2006).

La Conscience Européene au XVe et au XVIe siècle. Actes du Colloque international organize à l'Ecole Normale Supérieure de Jeunes Filles (30 septembre- 3 octobre 1980) avec l'aide de C.N.R.S (Paris: l'Imprimerie Chirat, 1982).

Cosandey, F., Descimon, R., eds. *l'Absolutisme en France: Histoire et historiographie* (Paris: Presses universitaires de France, 2002).

Cottret, M. 'Edmond Richer (1539–1631). Le politique et le sacré', in H. Méchoulan, ed., *l'État baroque 1610–1652* (Paris: J. Vrin, 1985), 159–77.

'La justification catholique du tyrannicide', *Parlement[s], Revue d'histoire politique*, 6, 3 (2010): 107–17.

Courtine, J. F. *Nature et empire de la loi: études suaréziennes* (Paris: Presses universitaires de France, 1999).

Couzinet, M. D. *Bibliographie des Ecrivains Francais. Jean Bodin* (Paris: Memini, 2001).

Histoire et Méthode à la Renaissance. Une lecture de la Methodus de Jean Bodin (Paris: J. Vrin, 1996).

Crimando, T. I., 'Two French Views of the Council of Trent', *The Sixteenth Century Journal*, 19, 2 (1988), 169–86.

Crouzet, D. 'La représentation du temps à l'époque de la Ligue', *Revue Historique*, T.270, 2 (1983): 297–388.

Les guerriers de Dieu: la violence au temps des troubles de religion, vers 1525-vers 1610 (Seyssel: Champs Vallon, 1990).

Daubresse, S. *Le parlement de Paris, ou, La voix de la raison (1559–1589)* (Geneva: Droz, 2005).

Daubresse, S., Haan, B., eds. *La Ligue et ses frontières: Engagements catholiques à distance du radicalisme à la fin des guerres de Religion* (Rennes: Presses universitaires de Rennes, 2015).

Daubresse, S., Morgat-Bonnet, M., eds. *Le Parlement en Exil ou Histoire Politique et Judiciare des Translations du Parlement de Paris (xve-xviiie siècle)* (Paris: Champion, 2007).

Daussy, H. *Les Huguenots et Le Roi. Le combat politique de Philippe Duplessis-Mornay (1572–1600)* (Geneva: Droz, 2002).

Denzer, H., ed., *Jean Bodin: Proceedings of the International Conference on Bodin in Munich* (Munich: C. H. Beck, 1973).

Descimon, R. 'La Ligue à Paris (1585–1594): une révision', *Annales. Économies, Sociétés, Civilisations*, 37, 1 (1982): 72–111.

'La Ligue: des divergences fondamentales', *Annales. Economies, Sociétés, Civilisations*, 37, 1 (1982): 122–28.

Qui étaient les Seize ? Mythes et réalités de la Ligue parisienne, 1585–1594 (Paris: Klincksieck, 1983).

Descimon, R., Ibanez J. J. R. *Les Ligueurs de l'Exil; le refuge Catholique Français après 1594* (Seyssel: Champ Vallon, 2005).

Diefendorf, B. 'Simon Vigor: A Radical Preacher in Sixteenth Century Paris'. *Sixteenth Century Journal*, 18, 3 (1987): 399–410.

'An Age of Gold? Parisian Women, the Holy League, and the Roots of Catholic Renewal', in M. Wolfe (ed.), *Changing Identities in Early Modern France* (Durham NC: Duke University Press, 1996), 169–90.

'Reconciliation and Remembering: A Dévot Writes the History of the Holy League', *Cahiers d'Histoire*, XVI, 2 (1997): 69–79.

From Penitence to Charity. Pious Women and the Catholic Reformation in Paris (Oxford: Oxford University Press, 2004).

ed. *Social Relations, Politics and Power in Early Modern France. Robert Descimon and the Historian's Craft* (Kirksville MI: Truman State University Press, 2016).

Donnelly, J. P., Maher, M. W., eds., *Confraternities and Catholic Reform in Italy, France and Spain* (Kirksville: Thomas Jefferson University Press, 1999).

Doyle, J. P. 'Francisco Suarez on the Law of Nations', in M. W. Janis, C. Evans, eds., *Religion and International Law* (The Hague: Martinus Nijhoff, 1999), 103–20.

Doucet, R. *Les bibliothèques parisiennes au XVIe siècle* (Paris: Picard, 1956).

Drouot, H. *Mayenne et La Bourgogne 1587–1596, Contribution a l'histoire des provinces Françaises pendant la Ligue*, 2 vols. (Dijon, 1937).

La Première Ligue en Bourgogne et les débuts de Mayenne (Dijon, 1937).

Dubois, C-G. *Celtes et Gaulois au XVIe Siècle. Le développement littéraire d'un mythe nationaliste, avec l'édition critique d'un traité inédit de Guillaume Postel. D ce qui est premier pour reformer le monde* (Paris: J. Vrin, 1972).

Dubois, E. *Guillaume Barclay jurisconsulte écossais, professeur à Pont-à-Mousson et à Angers, 1546–1608* (Nancy/Paris, 1872).

Dunbabin, J. 'Aristotle's Politics: Reception and Interpretation', in N. Kretzmann, A. Kenny, J. Pinborg, eds., *The Cambridge History of Later Medieval Philosophy* (Cambridge: Cambridge University Press, 1988), 723–37.

Dupont-Ferrier, G. 'Le sens des mots 'patria' et 'patrie' en France au moyen age et jusqu'au debut du xviiie siecle', *Revue historique*, 188–9 (1940): 89–104.

Egio, José Luis. 'Pierre de Belloy, Philippe Duplessis Mornay, Innocent Gentillet. Attribution et contenu de la Conference Chrestienne (1586)', *Bibliothèque d'Humanisme et Renaissance*, 75, 1 (2013): 67–88.

Estier, D. '1589–1594: la maîtrise de l'opinion à Lyon pendant la Ligue, ou le secret nécessaire', *Rives méditerranéenees*, 17 (2004): 63–83.

Faussemagne, J. *L'Apanage ducal de Bourgogne dans ses rapports avec la monarchie française* (1363–1477) (Lyon, 1937).

Favier, J. *Philippe le Bel* (Paris: Fayard, 1978).

Figgis, J. N. *Political Thought from Gerson to Grotius*. 2nd ed. (Cambridge: Cambridge University Press, 1916).

'On Some Political Theories of the Early Jesuits'. *Transactions of the Royal Historical Society*, 11 (1897), 89–112.

The Divine Right of Kings (Cambridge: Cambridge University Press, 1914).

Filhol, R. 'The Codification of Customary Law in France in the Fifteenth and Sixteenth Centuries', in H. J. Cohn, ed., *Government in Reformation Europe, 1520–1560* (London: Macmillan, 1971), 265–83.

Foisneau, L., ed., *Politique, Droit et Théologie chez Bodin, Grotius et Hobbes* (Paris: Éditions Kimé, 1997).

Forrestal, A., Nelson, E., eds., *Politics and Religion in Early Bourbon France* (Basingstoke: Palgrave Macmillan, 2009).

Fontana, B. *Montaigne's Politics. Authority and Governance in the Essais* (Princeton: Princeton University Press, 2008).

Franceschi, S. H. de. 'Ambiguités Historiographiques du Théologico-Politique. Genèse et Fortune d'un Concept', *Revue Historique*, cccix/3 (2007): 653–85.

La Crise Théologico-Politique du Premier Âge Baroque. Antiromanisme doctrinal, pouvoir pastoral et raison du prince: le Saint Siège face au prisme français (1606–1627) (Rome: École Française de Rome, 2009).

Franklin, J. H. *Jean Bodin and the Rise of Absolutist Theory* (Cambridge: Cambridge University Press, 1973).

Jean Bodin and the Sixteenth-Century Revolution in the Methodology of Law and History (New York: Columbia University Press, 1963).

Frémy, E. *Essai sur les Diplomates du temps de la Ligue, d'après des documents nouveaux et inédits* (Paris, 1873).

Friedeberg, R. V. 'In Defense of Patria: Resisting Magistrates and the Duties of Patriots in the Empire from the 1530s to the 1640s', *Sixteenth Century Journal*, 32, 2 (Summer, 2001): 357–82.

'The Office of the Patriot: the Problems of Passions and Love of Fatherland in Protestant Thought, Melancthon to Althusius, 1520s-1620s', *Studies in Medieval and Renaissance History*, 3, III (2006): 241–73.

Frisch, A. *Forgetting Differences: Tragedy, Historiography and the French Wars of Religion* (Edinburgh: Edinburgh University Press, 2016).

Fumaroli, M. *L'Age de l'éloquence: rhétorique et 'res literaria', de la Renaissance au seuil de l'époque classique* (Geneva: Droz, 1980).

Gabriel, F. 'Réalisme politique et rationalité: Juan de Mariana entre royauté et respublica', in Anne Molinié, Alexandra Merle, Araceli Guillaume-Alonso, eds., *Les jésuites en Espagne et en Amérique, Jeux et enjeux du pouvoir (XVI e - XVII e siècle)*, (Paris: Presses de l'Université Paris-Sorbonne, 2007), 141–59.

Garnett, G. *Marsilius of Padua and the 'Truth of history'* (Oxford: Oxford University Press, 2006).

'Law in the Vindiciae, Contra Tyrannos: A Vindication', *The Historical Journal*, 49 (2006), 877–91.

'Scholastic Thought in Humanist Guise. Francois Hotman's Ancient Constitution', in P. Linehan, J. L. Nelson, M. Costambeys, eds., *The Medieval World* (London: Routledge, 2018), 789–810.

Gambino, L. *Il De republica di Pierre Grégoire: ordine politico e monarchia nella Francia di fine Cinquecento* (Milan: Giuffré, 1978).

Génestal, R. *Les origines de l'appel comme d'abus* (Paris: Presses universitaires de France, 1950).

Gibbons, C. M. *The Experience of Exile and English Catholics: Paris in the 1580s* (Woodbridge: Boydell, 2011).

Gierke, Otto V. *Political Theories of the Medieval Age*, trans. F. W. Maitland (Cambridge: Cambridge University Press, repr. 1987).

Giesey, R. 'The French Estates and the Corpus Mysticum Regni', *Album Helen Maud Cam*, 1 (1960): 153–71.

'The Juristic Basis of Dynastic Right to the French Throne', *Transactions of the American Philosophical Society*, 51 (1961): 3–47.

Le rôle méconnu de la loi salique. La succession royale XIV⁻ᵉ XVIᵉ siècles (Paris: Les Belles Lettres, 2007).

'Medieval Jurisprudence in Bodin's Concept of Sovereignty', in H. Denzer, ed., *Jean Bodin* (Munich: C. H. Beck, 1973), 167–86.

'The monarchomach triumvirs: Hotman, Beza and Mornay', *Bibliothèque d'humanisme et Renaissance*, 32 (1970): 41–56

The Royal Funeral Ceremony in Renaissance France (Geneva: Droz, 1960).

If Not, Not: The Oath of the Aragonese and the Legendary Laws of Sobrarbe (Princeton: Princeton University Press, 1968).

Goff, H. le. *La Ligue en Bretagne. Guerre civile et conflit international (1588–1598)* (Rennes: Presses universitaires de Rennes, 2010).

Goldie, M. 'The Ancient Constitution and the Languages of Political Thought', *The Historical Journal*, 62, 1 (2019): 3–34.

Gould, K. *Catholic Activism in South-West France, 1540–1570* (Aldershot: Ashgate, 2006).

Grafton, A., Blair, A. eds., *The Transmission of Culture in Early Modern Europe* (Philadelphia: University of Pennsylvania Press, 1990).

Greengrass M. *Governing Passions: Peace & Reform in the French Kingdom 1576–1585* (Oxford: Oxford University Press, 2007).

France in the Age of Henri IV, 2nd ed. (London: Longman, 1995).

A Day in the Life of the Third Estate: Blois, 16th December 1576', in A. Bakos, ed., *Politics, Ideology and the Law in Early Modern Europe. Essays in Honour of J.H.M. Salmon* (New York: Univeristy of Rochester Press, 1994), 73–90.

'The *Sainte Union* in the Provinces: The Case of Toulouse', *The Sixteenth Century Journal*, 14, 4 (1983): 469–96.

'Europe's "Wars of Religion" and Their Legacies', in John Wolffe, ed., *Protestant-Catholic Conflict from the Reformation to the Twenty-first Century. The Dynamics of Religious Difference* (Basingstoke: Palgrave Macmillan, 2013).

Greenleaf, W. H. 'Bodin and the Idea of Order', in Denzer, *Jean Bodin*, 23–38.

Guilday, P. *The English Catholic Refugees on the Continent 1558–1795. Vol. 1, the English Colleges and Convents in the Catholic Low Countries 1558–1795* (London: Longmans, Green and Co, 1914).

Hamilton, B. *Political Thought in Sixteenth-Century Spain. A Study of the Political Ideas of Vitoria, De Soto, Suarez, and Molina* (Oxford: Oxford University Press, 1963),

Hamilton, T. *Pierre de L'Estoile and His World in the Wars of Religion, 1546–1611* (Oxford: Oxford University Press, 2017).

Hampton, T. *Literature and Nation in the Sixteenth Century: Inventing Renaissance France* (Ithaca: Cornell University Press, 2001).

Hayden, H. *The Counter-Renaissance* (New York: Charles Scribner's Sons, 1950).

Hanley, S. *The Lit de Justice of the Kings of France: Constitutional Ideology in Legend, Ritual, and Discourse* (Princeton: Princeton University Press, 1983).

'The French Constitution Revised: Representative Assemblies and Resistance Right in the Sixteenth Century', in M. P. Holt, ed., *Societies and Institutions in Early Modern France* (Athens, GA: University of Georgia Press, 1991), 36–50.

Harding, R. 'Revolution and Reform in the Holy League: Angers, Rennes, Nantes', *The Journal of Modern History*, 53, 3 (1982): 379–416.

The Anatomy of a Power Elite: The Provincial Governors of Early Modern France (New Haven: Yale University Press, 1978).

Haudecoeur, M. l'Abbé. *William Gifford, dit Gabriel de Sainte: maire de l'ordre de Saint-Benoit, 87ᵉ Archevêque de Reims* (Reims, 1898).

Hauser, H. *Les Sources de l'Histoire de France. XVIe siècle (1494–1610)*, 4 vols. (Paris: A. Picard, 1906–15).

Heller, H. 'A Reply to Mack P. Holt', *French Historical Studies*, 19 (1996): 853–61.

Herman, A. 'The Huguenot Republic and Antirepublicanism in Seventeenth-Century France', *Journal of the History of Ideas*, 53, 2 (1992): 249–69.

Highley, C. *Catholics Writing the Nation in Early Modern Britain and Ireland* (Oxford: Oxford University Press, 2008).

Holt, M. P. *The French Wars of Religion, 1562–1629*, 2nd ed. (Cambridge: Cambridge University Press, 2005).

'Putting Religion Back into the Wars of Religio', *French Historical Studies*, 18 (1993): 524–51.

Höpfl, H. *Jesuit Political Thought, the Society of Jesus and the State, c. 1540–1630* (Cambridge: Cambridge University Press, 2004).

Höpfl, H. Thompson, M. P. 'The History of Contract as a Motif in Political Thought', *The American Historical Review*, 84, (1979): 919–44.

Houliston, V. *Catholic Resistance in Elizabethan England: Robert Persons's Jesuit Polemic, 1580–1610* (Aldershot: Ashgate, 2007).

Huchard, C. *D'encre et de sang: Simon Goulart et la Saint-Barthélemy* (Paris: Classiques Garnier, 2006).

Hyver, C. *Le doyen Pierre Gregoire de Toulouse et l'organisation de faculté de droit de Pont à Mousson* (Pont à Mousson, 1874).

Innes, M. J. M. 'Robert Persons's Conference and the Salic Law debate in France, 1584–1594', *History of European Ideas*, 45, 3 (2019): 421–35.

Isnardi-Parente, M. 'Le voluntarisme de Jean Bodin', in Denzer, *Jean Bodin*, 39–52.

Jackson, R. A. 'Elective Kingship and Consensus Populi in France', *Journal of Modern History*, 44, 2 (June 1972): 155–71.

  Vive le Roi! A History of the French Coronation from Charles V to Charles X (Chapel Hill: University of North Carolina Press, 1984)

Janssen, G. H. *The Dutch Revolt and Catholic Exile in Reformation Europe* (Cambridge: Cambridge University Press, 2014)

Jenson, D. *Diplomacy and Dogmatism: Bernard de Mendoza and the Catholic League* (Cambridge, MA: Harvard University Press, 1964)

Jones, C., ed., *John of Paris, Beyond Royal and Papal Power* (Turnhout: Brepols, 2015).

Jouanna, A. *La France du XVIe siècle: 1485–1598* (Paris: Presses universitaires de France, 1996).

  Le Pouvoir Absolu: Naissance de l'imaginaire politique de la royauté (Paris: Gallimard, 2013).

  Le Devoir de Révolte: La noblesse française et la gestation de l'État moderne (1559–1661) (Paris: Fayard, 1989).

Kantorowicz, E. H. 'Pro patria mori, in medieval political thought', *American Historical Review*, 56 (1951), 472–92.

  The King's Two Bodies: A study in Medieval Political Theology (Princeton: Princeton University Press, 1957).

Kearns, J. E. *Ideas in Seventeenth-Century France* (Manchester: Manchester University Press, 1979).

Kelley, D. R. 'Fides Historiae: Charles Dumoulin and the Gallican View of History', *Traditio*, 22 (1966): 347–402.

  'Jean du Tillet, Archivist and Antiquary', in *The Journal of Modern History*, 38, 4 (1966): 337–54.

  'Murd'rous Machiavel in France: A Post Mortem'. *Political Science Quarterly*, 85, 4 (1970): 545–59.

  Francois Hotman: A Revolutionary's Ordeal (Princeton: Princeton University Press, 1973).

  The Beginning of Ideology: Consciousness and Society in the French Reformation (Cambridge: Cambridge University Press, 1981).

  'Second Nature: The Idea of Custom in European Law, Society and Culture', in Grafton, A., Blair, A., eds., *The Transmission of Culture in Early Modern Europe* (Philadelphia: University of Pennsylvania Press, 1990): 131–72.

Kempshall, Matthew S. *The Common Good in Late Medieval Political Thought* (Oxford: Oxford University Press, 1999).

Kenz, David El. 'La propaganda et le problème de sa réception, d'après les Mémoires-Journaux de Pierre de L'Estoile', *Cahiers d'histoire. Revue d'histoire critique*, 90–91 (2003): 19–32.

Kern, F. *Kingship and Law in the Middle Ages*, trans. S. B. Chrimes (Oxford: Basil Blackwell, 1948).

Kingdon, R. M. 'Some French Reactions to the Council of Trent', *Church History*, 33 (1964): 149–56.

Myths about the St Bartholomew's Day Massacres, 1572–1576 (Cambridge: Cambridge University Press, 1988).

Knecht, R. J. 'Review Article: Absolutism in Early Modern France', *European History Quarterly*, 27, 2 (1997): 251–6

Konnert, M. *Civic Agendas and Religions Passion: Châlons-sur-Marne during the French Wars of Religion, 1560–1594* (Kirksville, MO: Sixteenth Century Journal Publishers, 1997).

Kuijpers, E., Pollmann, J. S., Müller, J. M., Steen, J. A. Van Der, eds., *Memory before Modernity: Practices of Memory in Early Modern Europe* (Leidan: Brill, 2013).

Kretzmann, N., Kenny, A., Pinborg, J., eds., *The Cambridge History of Later Medieval Philosophy* (Cambridge: Cambridge University Press, 1988).

Krynen, J. *L'empire du roi. Idéés et croyances politiques en France. XIIIe-XVe siècle* (Paris: Éditions Gallimard, 1993).

Labitte, C. *De la démocratie chez les prédicateurs de la ligue* (Paris, 1866).

Lange, T. 'Gallicanisme et Réforme: le constitutionnalisme de Cosme Guymier (1486), *Revue de l'Histoire des Religions*, 226 (2009): 303–10.

'Constitutional Thought and Consitutional Practice in Early Sixteenth-Century France: Revisiting the Legacy of Ernst Kantorowicz', *The Sixteenth Century Journal*, 42, 4 (2011): 1003–26.

The First French Reformation (Cambridge: Cambridge University Press, 2014).

Lee, D. *Popular Sovereignty in Early Modern Constitutional Thought* (Oxford: Oxford University Press, 2016).

Lecler, J. 'Aux origines de la Ligue. Premier Projets et Premiers Essais', *Études. Revue Catholique d'Intérêt Géneral*, 227 (1936): 188–208.

Leclercq, Jean. *Jean de Paris et l'ecclésiologie du XIIIe siecle* (Paris: J. Vrin, 1942).

Leguai, A. *Les Ducs de Bourbon pendant la crise monarchique du XVe siecle: Contribution a l'etude des apanages* (Paris: Les Belles Lettres, 1962).

Lelong, J. *Bibliothèque Historique de la France contenant le catalogue de tous les ouvrages tant imprimez que manuscrits qui traitent de l'histoire de ce roïaume ou qui y ont rapport, avec des notes critiques et historiques* (Paris, 1768).

Lemaire, A. *Les lois fondamentales de la monarchie Français, d'après les théoriciens de l'ancien régime* (Paris: Fontemoing, 1907).

Lenient, C. *La Satire en France, ou la Littérature Militante au XVIᵉ siècle*, 2 vols. (Paris, 1886).

Leyte, G. *Domaine et domainalité publique dans la France Mediévale (XII-XVe siècles)* (Strasbourg: Presses Universitaires de Strasbourg, 1996).

Lloyd, H. A. *The State, France and the Sixteenth Century* (London, G. Allen and Unwin, 1983).

'The Political Thought of Adam Blackwood', *The Historical Journal* 43, 4 (2000): 915–35.

Jean Bodin, 'This Pre-eminent Man of France': An Intellectual Biography (Oxford: Oxford University Press, 2017).

Lozinsky, A. A. 'La « Ligue » et la diplomatie espagnole', *Annales. Économies, Sociétés, Civilisations*, 23, 1 (1968): 173–7.

Mackenzie, L. *The Poetry of Place: Lyric, Landscape, and Ideology in Renaissance France* (Toronto: Toronto University Press, 2011).

Marcilloux, P., ed., *Laon, 1594: Henri IV, la Ligue et la Ville. Actes du Colloque organisé par la Societé historique de Haute-Picardie (19–20 Novembre 1994)* (Laon: Archives départementales de l'Aisne, 1996).

Markus, R. A. *Saeculum. History and Society in the Theology of St. Augustine* (Cambridge: Cambridge University Press, 1970, repr. 2007)

Mariejol, H. *La reforme, la Ligue, l'edit de Nantes 1559–1598* (Paris: Tallandier, 1983).

Martin, H-J. 'Ce qu'on lisait à Paris au XVIe siècle', in *Bibliothèque d'Humanisme et Renaissance* (1959): 222–30.

Livre, pouvoirs et société à Paris au xviie siècle (1581–1701) (Geneva: Droz, 1969).

Martin, M. 'Rumeur, propagande et désinformation à Paris durant le règne de Henri IV'. Quelques réflexions préliminaires à partir des Mémoires-journaux de L'Estoile', *Albineana, Cahiers d'Aubigné*, 23 1 (2011): 267–83.

Martin, V. *Le Gallicanisme et la Réforme Catholique. Essai historique sur l'introduction en France des décrets des Concile de Trente (1563–1615)* (Paris: A. Picard, 1919).

Le Gallicanisme Politique et le Clergé de France (Paris: A. Picard, 1929).

Mattingly, G. 'William Allen and Catholic Propaganda in England', *Travaux d'humanisme et Renaissance*, 28 (1957): 325–39.

McCuaig, W. 'Paris/Jerusalem in Pierre de l'Estoile, the Satyre Ménippée, and Louis Dorléans', *Bibliothèque d'Humanisme et Renaissance*, 64 (2002), 295–315.

McLaren, A. 'Rethinking Republicanism: Vindiciae, Contra Tyrannos in Context', *The Historical Journal*, 49 (2006): 23–52.

McIlwain, C. H. *Constitutionalism and the Changing World* (Cambridge: Cambridge University Press, 1939).

Mellet, P.-A., ed., *Et de sa bouche sortait un glaive: les Monarchomaques au xvie siècle* (Geneva: Droz, 2006).

Les traités monarchomaques: confusion des temps, résistance armée et monarchie parfaite, 1560–1600 (Geneva: Droz, 2007).

Mémoires de l'Académie Impériale de Sciences, inscriptions et belles lettres de Toulouse (Toulouse, 1855).

Mesnard, P. *L'Essor de la Philosophie Politique au XVIe siècle*, 2nd ed. (Paris: J. Vrin, 1951).

Migne, J-P. *Patrologia Latina*, 217 vols. (Paris, 1844–55).

Moreau-Reibel, J. *Jean Bodin et le droit public comparé dans ses rapports avec la philosophie de l'histoire* (Paris: J. Vrin, 1933).

'Bodin et la Ligue, d'après les letters inédites', *Bibliothèque d'Humanise et Renaissance*, 2 (1935), 422–40.

Morel, H. *l'Idée Gallicane au temps des Guerres de Religion*, repr. (Aix-en-Provence: Presses universitaires d'Aix-Marseille, 2003).

Martimort, A. G. *Le Gallicanisme de Bossuet* (Paris: Cerf, 1953).

McIlwain, C. M. *Constitutionalism and the Changing World* (Cambridge: Cambridge University Press, 1939).

Mousnier, R. *Les hiérarchies sociales de 1450 à nos jours* (Paris: Presses universitaires de France, 1960).

L'assassinat d'Henri IV, 14 mai 1610 (Paris: Gallimard, 1964).

Murray, R. *The Political Consequences of the Reformation: Studies In Sixteenth Century Political Thought* (London: E. Benn, 1926).

Nadeau, C. 'Les constitutionnalistes Français face au problème de la constitution mixte: Claude de Seyssel et Jean Bodin', in Marie Gaille-Nikodimov, ed., *Le Gouvernement Mixte. De l'idéal politique au monstre constitutionnel en Europe xiiie-xviie siècle* (Saint-Étienne: Publications de l'Université de Sainte-Étienne, 2005), 95–116.

Napoli, P. '"Police": la conceptualisation d'un modèle juridico-Politique sous l'ancien régime', *Droits. Revue Française de théorie juridique*, 20 (1994): 183–96.

Nederman, C. J. 'Conciliarism and Constitutionalism: Jean Gerson and Medieval Political Thought', *History of European Ideas*, 12, 2, (1990): 189–209.

'Constitutionalism – Medieval and Modern: Against Neo-Figgisite Orthodoxy (Again)', *History of Political Thought*, 17, 2 (1996): 179–94.

Nelson, E. *The Hebrew Republic: Jewish Sources and the Transformation of European Political Thought* (Cambridge, MA: Harvard University Press, 2010).

Nelson, E. *The Jesuits and the Monarchy, Catholic Reform and Political Authority in France (1590–1615)* (Aldershot: Ashgate, 2005).

Neuman, K. 'Political Hebraism and the Early Modern "Respublica Hebraeorum": on defining the field', *Hebraic Political Studies*, I, 1 (Fall 2005): 57–70.

Nicholls, S. 'Gallican liberties and the Catholic League', *History of European Ideas Special Issue, 'Thinking about Intellectual History'*, 40, 7 (2014): 940–64.

'*De Justa Reipublicae Christianae in Reges Impios et Haereticos Authoritate* (1590): questions of authority and heretic kings in the political thought of the Catholic League'. *Bibliothèque d'Humanisme et Renaissance*, LXXVII, 1 (2015): 81–101.

'Pierre Grégoire', in Luc Foisneau (dir.), *Dictionnaire des philosophes français du XVIIe siècle: acteurs et réseaux du savoir en France entre 1601 et 1700* (Paris: Classiques Garnier, 2015).

'Catholic Resistance Theory: William Barclay versus Jean Boucher' in *Resistance Theory in Intellectual History and Political Thought, History of European Ideas*, 44, 4 (2018): 404–18.

'Sovereignty and Government in Jean Bodin's *Six Livres de la République*, 1576', *Journal of the History of Ideas*, 80, I (2019): 47–66.

'Ideas on Royal Power in the French Wars of Religion: The Influence of René Choppin's De Domanio Franciae (1574), *French History*, 34, 2 (2020): 141–60.

'Parlementarisme et communautés politiques: le moment Ligueur', in I. Brancourt (ed.), *Au cœur de l'état: parlement(s) et cours souveraines sous l'ancien regime* (Paris: Classiques Garnier, 2020).

Nora, P. *Les lieux de mémoire*, 3 vols. (Paris: Gallimard, 1984–92).

Oakley, F. 'Nederman, Gerson, Conciliar Theory and Constitutionalism: *Sed Contra*', *History of Political Thought*, 16, 1 (1995): 1–19.

 The Conciliarist Tradition: Constitutionalism in the Catholic Church, 1300–1870 (Oxford: Oxford University Press, 2003).

O'Brien, J. 'Mais de quel roi parlez-vous, et de quel prince? Sovereign Power, Freedom and La Boétie's Servitude volontaire in the 1580s', *Early Modern French Studies* (forthcoming, 2021).

Oestreich, G. *Neostoicism and the Early Modern State* (Cambridge: Cambridge University Press, 1982).

Pagden, A., ed., *The Languages of Political Theory in Early Modern Europe* (Cambridge: Cambridge University Press, 1987).

Pallier, D. *Recherches sur l'Imprimerie à Paris pendant la Ligue (1585–1594)* (Geneva: Droz, 1976).

Papin, P. 'Duplicité et traîtrise: l'image des 'politiques' durant la Ligue', *Revue d'histoire moderne et contemporaine*, 38 (1991): 3–21.

Parsons, J. *The Church in the Republic: Gallicanism and Political Ideology in Renaissance France* (Washington: Catholic University of America Press, 2004).

Patterson, J. *Representing Avarice in Late Renaissance France* (Oxford: Oxford University Press, 2015)

Penzi, M. 'Tours contre Rome au début du règne d'Henri IV', *Revue de l'histoire des religions*, 226 (2009): 329–47.

Pettegree, A., Nelles, P., Conner, P., eds. *The Sixteenth-Century French Religious Book* (Aldershot: Ashgate, 2001).

Pettegree, A., Walsby, M., eds., *Netherlandish Books: Books Published in the Low Countries and Dutch Books Printed Abroad Before 1601* (Leidan: Brill, 2011).

Pettegree, A. 'Centre and Periphery in the European Book World', *Transactions of the Royal Historical Society*, 18 (2008): 109–13.

Petey-Girard, B., Tarrête, A., eds. *Guillaume du Vair: parlementaire et écrivain (1556–1621): colloque d'Aix-en-Provence, 4–6 octobre 2001* (Droz: Geneva, 2005).

Pocock, J. *Politics, Language and Time. Essays on Political Thought and History* (Chicago: University of Chicago Press, 1989).

 The Ancient Constitution and the Feudal Law, repr. (Cambridge: Cambridge University Press, 2004).

Poncet, O. *La France et le pouvoir pontifical, 1595–1661: l'esprit des institutions* (Rome: École française de Rome, 2011).

Potter, J. M. 'The Development and Significance of the Salic Law of the French', *The English Historical Review*, 52, 206 (1937): 235–53.

Powis, J. 'Gallican Liberties and the Politics of Later Sixteenth-Century France' in *The Historical Journal*, 26, 3 (1983): 515–30.

Prat, P. J. M. *Maldonat et l'université de Paris au xvie siècle* (Paris, 1856).

Prodi, P. *Il sacramento del potere: il giuramento politico nella storia costituzionale dell'Occidente* (Bologna: Mulino, 1992).

Poupé, E. *La Ligue en Provence et les Pontevès-Bargème, correspondance relative à la prise d'armes carciste de 1578–1579* (Aix: B. Niel, 1904).

Racault, L. 'The Polemical Use of the Albigensian Crusade during the French Wars of Religion, *French History*, 13 (1999): 261–79.

Hatred in Print: Catholic Propaganda and Protestant Identity during the French Wars of Religion (Aldershot: Ashgate, 2002).

'Nicolas Chesneau, Catholic Printer in Paris during the French Wars of Religion', *The Historical Journal*, 52, 1 (2009): 23–41.

'Reason of State, Religious Passions and the French Wars of Religion', *The Historical Journal*, 52, 4 (2009): 1075–83.

'The Sacrifice of the Mass and the Redefinition of Catholic Orthodoxy during the French Wars of Religion', *French History*, 24, 1 (2010): 20–39.

''La boutique de malédiction': Jean Boucher et l'hypocrisie', *Œuvres et Critiques*, 38, 2 (2014): 83–94.

Radouant, R. *Guillaume Du Vair, l'homme et l'orateur, jusqu'a la fin des troubles de la Ligue (1556–1596)* (Paris: Société française d'imprimerie et de librairie, 1908).

Renoux Zagamé, M. F. *Du Droit de Dieu au Droit de l'Homme* (Paris: Presses universitaires de France, 2003).

Reure, O. C. *La Presse Politique a Lyon pendant la Ligue (24 fevrier 1589 – 7 fevrier 1594)* (Paris, 1898).

Richard, P. *La papauté et la Ligue française. Pierre d'Épinac, Archevêque de Lyon (1573–1599)* (Paris, 1901).

Richart, A., *Mémoires sur la Ligue dans le Laonnais* (Laon, 1869).

Richet, D. *De la Réforme à la Révolution* (Paris: Aubier, 1991).

Rigaudière, Albert. 'Les ordonnances de police en France à la fin du Moyen Age', in Michael Stolleis, ed., *Policey im Europa der Frühen Neuzeit* (Frankfurt am Main: Vittorio Klostermann, 1996), 97–161.

Penser et construire l'état dans la France du Moyen Âge (XIIIe–XVe siècle) (Paris: Comité pour l'histoire économique et financière de la France, 2003).

Rivière, J. *Le problème de l'église et de l'état au temps de Philippe le Bel* (Paris: H. Champion, 1926).

Robinet, J. B. *Dictionnaire universel des sciences morale, économique, politique et diplomatique*, 30 vols. (London, 1777–83).

Roelker, N. L. *One King, One Faith: The Parlement of Paris and the Religious Reformations of the Sixteenth Century* (California: University of California Press, 1996).

Rose, P. L. 'The Politique and the Prophet: Bodin and the Catholic League 1589-1594', *The Historical Journal*, 21, 4 (1978): 783–808.

Bodin and the Great God of Nature: the Moral and Religious Universe of a Judaiser (Geneva: Droz, 1980).

Russell Major, J. *Representative Government in Early Modern France* (New Haven: Yale University Press, 1980).

Ryan, M. 'Corporation theory', in H. Lagerlune, ed., *Encyclopaedia of Medieval Philosophy*, 2 vols. (New York: Dordrecht, 2010), I, 236–40.

'Political Thought', in D. Johnston, ed., *The Cambridge Companion to Roman Law* (Cambridge: Cambridge University Press, 2015), 423–51.

Salmon, J. H. M. *The French Religious Wars in English Political Thought* (Oxford: Oxford University Press, 1959).

'French Satire in the Late Sixteenth Century', in *The Sixteenth Century Journal*, V, 3 (1975): 57–88.

Society in Crisis. France in the Sixteenth Century (London: Methuen and co., 1979).

Renaissance and Revolt: Essays in the Intellectual and Social History of Early Modern France (Cambridge: Cambridge University Press, 1987).

'Appendix: A Note on the Dialogue d'entre le Maheustre et le Manant', in *Renaissance and Revolt*, 264–6.

'Bodin and the Monarchomachs' in *Renaissance and Revolt*, 119–35.

'Cicero and Tacitus in Sixteenth-Century France', in *Renaissance and Revolt*, 27–53.

'The Paris Sixteen, 1584–1594': The Social Analysis of a Revolutionary Movement' in *Renaissance and Revolt*, 235–66.

'Clovis and Constantine. The Uses of History in Sixteenth-Century Gallicanism', *The Journal of Ecclesiastical History* (1990): 584–605.

'Catholic Resistance Theory, Ultramontanism, and the Royalist Response, 1580–1620', in J. H. Burns, ed., *The Cambridge History of Medieval Political Thought 1450–1700* (Cambridge: Cambridge University Press, 1991), 219–53.

'The Legacy of Jean Bodin: Absolutism, Populism or Constitutionalism?', *History of Political Thought*, XCII (1996): 500–22.

'France', in H. A., Lloyd, G.,Burgess, S., Hodson, eds., *European Political Thought 1450–1700: Religion, Law and Philosophy* (New Haven: Yale University Press, 2007), 458–97.

Saulnier, E. *Le Rôle politique du Cardinal de Bourbon (Charles X), 1523–1590* (Paris, 1912).

Sauzet, R., ed., *Henri III et son temps. Ouvrage publié avec le concours du Centre National de la Recherche Scientifique* (Paris: J. Vrin, 1992).

Sawyer, J. K. *Printed Poison: Pamphlet Propaganda, Faction Politics, and the Public Sphere in Early Seventeenth Century France* (Berkeley: University of California Press, 1990).

Schmutz, J. 'Le Petit Scotisme du Grand Siècle. Etude Doctrinale et Documentaire sur la Philosophie au Grand Couvent des Cordeliers de Paris, 1517–1789', in P. Porro, J. Schmutz, eds., *The legacy of John Duns Scotus* (Turnhout: Brepols, 2008).

'From Theology to Philosophy: The Changing Status of the Summa Theologiae, 1500–2000', in J. Hause, ed., *Aquinas's Summa theologiae: A Critical Guide* (Cambridge: Cambridge University Press, 2018): 221–41.

Senellart, M. *Les arts de gouverner: Du regimen medieval au concept de gouvernement* (Paris: Seuil, 1995).

'Machiavel à l'épreuve de la "gouvernamentalité"', in G. Sfez, M. Senellart, eds., *L'enjeu Machiavel* (Paris: Presses universitaires de France, 2001), 211–30.

'La technisation de la Politique au début des Temps Modernes', in C. Collot-Thélène, P. Portier, eds., *La Métamorphose du Prince: Politique et culture dans l'espace occidental* (Rennes: Presses universitaires de Rennes, 2014), 43–52.

Shennan, J. H. *The Parlement of Paris*, rev. ed. (Stroud: Sutton, 1998).

Skinner, Q. *The Foundations of Modern Political Thought*, 2 vols. (Cambridge: Cambridge University Press, 1978).

Machiavelli (Oxford: Oxford University Press, 1981).

Visions of Politics, Volume 2, Renaissance Virtues (Cambridge: Cambridge University Press, 2002).

Smet, I. de. *Menippean Satire and the Republic of Letters 1581–165* (Geneva: Droz, 1996).

'Philosophy for Princes: Aristotle's Politics and Its Readers during the French Wars of Religion', *Journal of the Warburg and Courtauld Institutes*, 76 (2013): 23–47.

Stefanovska, M., Paschoud, A., eds. *Littérature et politique: Factions et dissidences de la Ligue à la Fronde* (Paris: Classiques Garnier, 2015).

Supple, J. J. 'Montaigne and the French Catholic League', in Desan, P., ed, *Montaigne Studies*, IV, 1–2 (1992): 111–26.

Sutto, C. 'Une controverse ecclésiologique au début du XVIIe siècle: le Libellus de ecclesiastica et politica potestate d'Edmond Richer (1611)', in *Homo Religiosus, autour de Jean Delumeau* (Paris: Fayard, 1997).

Tallon, A. *La France et le Concile de Trente (1518–1563)* (Rome: École Française de Rome, 1997).

'Gallicanism and Religious Pluralism in France in the Sixteenth Century', in Cameron, K., Greengrass, M., eds., *The Adventure of Religious Pluralism in Early Modern France: Papers from the Exeter Conference April 1999* (Oxford: Oxford University Press, 2000), 15–30.

Conscience nationale et sentiment religieux en France au xvi⁽ᵉ⁾ siècle. Essai sur la vision gallicane du monde (Paris: Presses universitaires de France, 2002).

Le Concile de Trente (Paris: Cerf, 2007).

Tarrête, Alexandre. 'Un gallican sous la Ligue: Guillaume Du Vair (1556–1621)', *Revue de l'histoire des religions*, 3, 2009, 497–516.

Thireau, J-L. *Charles Du Moulin* (Geneva: Droz, 1980).

Thompson, M. P. 'The History of Fundamental Law in Political Thought from the French Wars of Religion to the American Revolution', *The American Historical Review*, 91, 5 (1986): 1103–28.

Tierney, B. *Foundations of the Conciliar Theory: The Contribution of the Medieval Canonists from Gratian to the Great Schism* (Cambridge: Cambridge University Press, 1955).

'Aristotle, Aquinas and the Ideal Constitution', *Patristic, Medieval and Renaissance Studies*, 4 (1979): 1–11.

Tizon-Germe, A-C. 'Juridiction spirituelle et action pastorale des légats et nonces en France pendant la Ligue (1589–1594)', *Archivum Historiae Pontificiae*, 30 (1992): 159–230

'La Répresentation Pontificale en France au début du règne d'Henri IV (1589–1594): cadre politique, moyens humains et financiers', *Bibliothèque de l'École de Chartres*, 151 (1993), 37–85.

Trinquet, R. 'L'allégorie politique dans la peinture française au temps de la ligue: l'Abraham et Melchisédech d'Antoine Caron', *Bibliothèque d'Humanisme et Renaissance*, 28, 3 (1966), 638–67.

Turchetti, M. 'Une question mal posée: l'origine et l'identité des *Politiques* au temps des guerres de Religion', in T. Wanegfellen, ed., *De Michel de l'Hospital à l'Edit de Nantes: Politique et religion face aux églises* (Clermont Ferrand: Presses Universitaires Blaise-Pascal, 2002), 357–90.

Tyrannie et Tyrannicide de l'Antiquité à nos jours (Paris: Classiques Garnier, 2006).

Tutino, S. *Empire of Souls: Cardinal Bellarmine and the Christian Commonwealth* (New York: Oxford University Press, 2010).

'The Political Thought of Robert Persons's Conference in Continental Context'; in *The Historical Journal*, 52, 1 (2009): 43–62.

Ullmann, W. 'The Development of the Medieval Idea of Sovereignty', *The English Historical Review*, 64, 250 (1949): 1–33;

The growth of Papal Government in the Middle Ages: A Study in the Ideological Relation of Clerical to Lay Power (London: Methuen, 1955).

Principles of Government and Politics in the Middle Ages (London: Methuen, 1966).

'This Realm of England Is an Empire', *The Journal of Ecclesiastical History*, 30, 2 (1979): 175–203.

Vicaire, M.-H. 'Les albigeois ancêtres des protestants: assimilations catholiques', *Cahiers de Fanjeaux*, 14 (1979): 23–46.

Viennot, E. 'Des femmes d'État' au XVIe siècle: Les princesses de la Ligue et l'écriture de l'histoire', in D. Hasse-Dubosc, E. Viennot, eds., *Femmes et pouvoirs sur l'ancien regime* (Paris: Editions Rivages, 1991): 77–97

Viroli, M. *From Politics to Reason of State: The Acquisition and Transformation of the Language of Politics, 1250–1600* (Cambridge: Cambridge University Press, 1992).

For Love of Country: An Essay on Patriotism and Nationalism (Oxford: Oxford University Press, 1997).

De Waele, M. 'De Paris à Tours: La crise d'identité des magistrats Parisiens de 1589 à 1594', *Revue Historique*, 300, 3 (607) (1998): 549–77.

Réconcilier les Français: la fin des troubles de religion (1589–1598) (Paris: Hermann Éditeurs, 2010).

Walsby, W. 'Printer Mobility in Sixteenth-Century France', in B. Rial Costas, ed., *Print Culture and Peripheries in Early Modern Europe* (Leidan: Brill, 2013).

Wanagffelen, T. ed., *Ni Rome, Ni Genève . Des fidèles entre deux chaires en France au XVIe siècle* (Paris: Classiques Garnier, 1997).

Une difficulté fidélité. Catholiques malgré le concile en France XVIe –XVIIe siècles (Paris: Presses universitaires de France, 1999).

De Michel de l'Hospital à l'Édit de Nantes. Politique et religion face aux Églises (Clermont Ferrand: Presses Universitaires Blaise-Pascal, 2002).

Weill, G. *Les Théories sur le Pouvoir Royal en France pendant les Guerres de Religion* (Paris, 1892).

Wells, C. *Law and Citizenship in Early Modern France* (Baltimore: Johns Hopkins University Press, 1995).

Wilks, M. J. *The Problem of Sovereignty in the Later Middle Ages* (Cambridge: Cambridge University Press, 1963).

Wilkinson, M. 'A Provincial Assembly during the League', *Transactions of the Royal Historical Society*, 9, (1915): 65–76.

History of the League, or Sainte Union, 1576–1595 (Glasgow: Jackson, Wylie and Co., 1929).

Wolfe, M. *The Conversion of Henri IV: Politics, Power and Religious Belief in Early Modern France* (Cambridge, MA: Harvard University Press, 1993).

Wood, Charles T. 'Regnum Francie: A Problem in Capetian Administrative Usage' *Traditio*, 23 (1967): 136–41.

Philip the Fair and Boniface VIII: State vs. Papacy (Huntington, NY: Holt, Rinehart and Winston, 1976).

Yardeni, M. *La Conscience Nationale en France pendant les guerres de religion*, (1559–1598) (Paris: Béatrice-Nauwelaerts 1971).

'Le Christianisme de Clovis aux XVIe et XVIIe', in O. Guyotjeannin, ed., *Clovis chez les Historiens* (Geneva: Droz, 1996), 153–72.

'Antagonismes nationaux et propagandes durant les Guerres de Religion' in *Revue d'historique moderne et contemporaine*, 13, 4 (1996): 273–84.

Enquêtes sur l'identité de la 'nation France'. De la Renaissance aux Lumières (Seyssel: Champ Vallon, 2004).

Zuber, R. 'Cléricature intellectuelle et cléricature érudite: le cas des érudits gallicans (1580–1620)', *Travaux de linguistique et de littérature*, XXI, 2 (1983): 123–34.

Zwierlein, C. *The Political Thought of the French League and Rome (1585–1589)* (Geneva: Droz, 2016).

Online sources

http://elec.enc.sorbonne.fr/editsdepacification/edit_07

Blom J., Blom, F. 'Rainolds, William (1544?–1594)', Oxford *Dictionary of National Biography*, www.oxforddnb.com/view/article/230300.

Dauchy, S. 'French Law and Its Expansion in the Early Modern Period', in H. Pihlajamäki, M. D. Dubber, M. Godfrey, eds., *The Oxford Handbook of European Legal History* (Oxford: Oxford handbooks online, 2018), DOI: 10.1093/oxfordhb/9780198785521.013.32.

Micallef, F. 'Comment la bonne ligue sauva la monarchie. 1593 selon Nicolas Lefèvre de Lezeau', *Les Dossiers du Grihl*, 2011, *Nicolas Lefèvre de Lezeau et l'écriture*, http://journals.openedition.org/dossiersgrihl/4708.

Mellet, P.-A., Foa, J. 'Une "politique de l'oubliance"? Mémoire et oubli pendant les guerres de Religion (1550–1600)', *Astérion*, 15, 2016, http://journals.openedition.org/asterion/2829.

Penzi, M. 'Loys Dorléans and the 'Catholiques Anglois': A Common Catholic History Between Violence, Martyrdom and Human and Cultural Networks', *Culture & History Digital Journal*, 6, 1, 2017, http://dx.doi.org/10.3989/chdj.2017.004.

Senellart, M. 'L'espace de la souveraineté', *Transeo*, 2010, https://halshs.archives-ouvertes.fr/halshs-00494316.

Terrevermeille, J. de. *Three Tractates*, ed., R. E. Giesey, http://www.regiesey.com/terrevermeille/terrevermeille_home.htm.

Williams, W. E. 'Gifford, William (1557/8–1629)', *Oxford Dictionary of National Biography*, http://www.oxforddnb.com/view/article/10668.

Index

Milton Keynes UK
Ingram Content Group UK Ltd.
UKHW021209030624
443304UK00020B/135